The Decline in Marriage Among African Americans

Causes, Consequences, and Policy Implications

The Decline in Marriage Among African Americans

Causes, Consequences, and Policy Implications

M. Belinda Tucker
and
Claudia Mitchell-Kernan

RUSSELL SAGE FOUNDATION
New York

The Russell Sage Foundation

Library of Congress Cataloging-in-Publication Data

The decline in marriage among African Americans : causes,
    consequences, and policy implications / M. Belinda Tucker and
    Claudia Mitchell-Kernan, editors.
        p.   cm.
    Includes bibliographical references and index.
    ISBN 0-87154-887-9
    ISBN 0-87154-886-0 (pbk)
    1. Afro-Americans—Marriage.   2. Afro-American families.
I. Tucker, M. Belinda.   II. Mitchell-Kernan, Claudia.
E185.86.D43   1995
306.81′08996073—dc20   94–39624
                                                                    CIP

To our families:

Keith Kernan
Claudia L. Kernan
Ryan J. Kernan
Russell L. Stockard
Desmond Mosi Tucker Stockard
Daren Blake Tucker Stockard

Our parents:

Margaret Chandler
Robert B. Tucker
Claudia Whiting Mitchell Tatum
Joseph Mitchell

Our friend and colleague:

A. Wade Smith

CONTENTS

SECTION THREE

CONSEQUENCES AND CORRELATES
OF AFRICAN AMERICAN MARITAL DECLINE

SECTION FOUR

PUBLIC POLICY AND AFRICAN AMERICAN FAMILY FORMATION

CONTRIBUTORS

Phillip J. Bowman is an associate professor in the School of Education and Social Policy at Northwestern University. He chairs the Graduate Program in Counseling Psychology and is on the faculty of the Human Development and Social Policy Program.

Lynn C. Burbridge is deputy director of the Center for Research on Women at Wellesley College.

Sheldon Danziger is professor of social work and public policy and a faculty associate in Population Studies at the University of Michigan. He also directs the Research and Training Program on Poverty, the Underclass, and Public Policy.

William A. Darity, Jr., is the Cary C. Boshamer Professor of Economics at the University of North Carolina at Chapel Hill. He is also the director of the Minority Undergraduate Research Program.

Elizabeth Douvan is professor of psychology and the Catherine Neaffie Kellogg Professor of Psychology and Women's Studies at the University of Michigan. She is also a research scientist in the Survey Research Center of the Institute for Social Research.

Mark A. Fossett is associate professor of sociology at Texas A&M University.

Shirley J. Hatchett is associate professor of sociology at the University of Illinois at Urbana-Champaign and is a faculty affiliate of the Afro-American Studies and Research Program.

David M. Heer is professor of sociology at the University of Southern California. He is also the associate director of the Population Research Laboratory.

James S. Jackson is the director of the Program for Research on Black Americans and a research scientist in the Research Center for Group Dynamics at the Institute for Social Research, University of Michigan. He is also professor of psychology and chairs the Social Psychology Program.

K. Jill Kiecolt is associate professor of sociology at the Virginia Polytechnic Institute and State University.

Marilyn Krogh is a doctoral candidate in the sociology department at the University of Chicago.

Claudia Mitchell-Kernan is professor of anthropology and of psychiatry and biobehavioral sciences at the University of California-Los Angeles. She is also the vice chancellor for Academic Affairs and dean of the Graduate Division.

Hector F. Myers is professor of psychology at the University of California-Los Angeles. He is also the director of the Biobehavioral Research Center, department of psychiatry, at the Charles R. Drew University of Medicine and Science.

Samuel L. Myers, Jr., is the Roy Wilkins Professor of Human Relations and Social Justice at the Hubert H. Humphrey Institute of Public Affairs, University of Minnesota. He directs the Roy Wilkins Center, a research, teaching, and community outreach arm of the Humphrey Institute.

Melvin L. Oliver is professor of sociology at the University of California-Los Angeles. He is also director of the Center for the Study of Urban Poverty and a faculty associate of the Center for Afro-American Studies.

Robert J. Sampson is professor of sociology at the University of Chicago. He is also a research fellow of the American Bar Foundation.

Robert Schoen is a professor in the Department of Population Dynamics at Johns Hopkins University.

A. Wade Smith died on April 3, Easter Sunday, 1994, before he could see the final fruits of his labors in connection with this book. At the time of his death, he was professor of sociology and chaired the department of sociology at Arizona State University.

Brenda Stevenson is associate professor of history at the University of California-Los Angeles. Currently, she is also a postdoctoral fellow in the department of history at the University of California-Berkeley.

Mark Testa is an associate professor in the School of Social Service Administration of the University of Chicago. He also is research and policy director for the Illinois Department of Children and Family Services.

M. Belinda Tucker is associate professor of psychiatry and biobehavioral sciences at the University of California-Los Angeles. She is also a faculty associate of the Center for Afro-American Studies.

Joseph Veroff is professor of psychology and a research scientist at the Survey Research Center at the University of Michigan.

ACKNOWLEDGMENTS

THIS BOOK is the culmination of many efforts, including those marshaled to produce the 1989 conference that initiated this journey. We are most grateful to the agencies that funded the conference and supported the preparation of this manuscript. First and foremost, we thank the Russell Sage Foundation for both financial and moral support. Lisa Nachtigall and Charlotte Shelby were meticulous in their reviews and enormously encouraging throughout. We thank the William and Flora Hewlett Foundation for conference funding and appreciate the support and guidance of Dr. Faith Mitchell. Conference activities were also funded through the UCLA Afro-American Studies Program in Interdisciplinary Research, established by a grant from the Ford Foundation to the authors. Finally, a Research Scientist Development Award (grant no. K01 MH 0068) to the first author supported both conference and manuscript development activities.

The conference itself drew upon the considerable skills, graces, and tolerances of the staff of the UCLA Center for Afro-American Studies. In particular, we thank Jan Chapple and Donna Armstrong who, with wit and humor, performed minor miracles and produced a meeting that was memorable for its absence of problems. We also thank Ross Steiner for his photographic skills and all-around helpfulness; and Sandra Sealy and Steve Tymon for able assistance wherever needs arose.

A number of people also made significant contributions to the preparation of the manuscript: Chérie Francis provided exceptional editorial service; and Ellen Lodge and Angela James researched the many statistical references that seemed to require endless updating.

Although we have worked as a team for over fifteen years, we each wish to acknowledge those areas where our lives diverge and those separate sets of influences and sources of support.

My husband Russell L. Stockard, Jr., and children Desmond and Daren gave immensely of their time, providing understanding and endless support. No matter how long I'd been at the office, I could always count on greetings and hugs and kisses and whale drawings. As he is a fellow academic and devoted to language as an art, Russell's critique of ideas and editorial advice were on target throughout the process.

Every one of my academic accomplishments, including this book, derives primarily from the commitment to learning displayed and fostered by those in my family who believed in me and supported all my efforts: my mother Margaret Louise Jones Tucker Chandler; my father Robert Benjamin Tucker; my grandmothers Mary Jones and Catherine Tucker Harrison; and my wonderful and wise great-grandmother Irene Byrd Carter.

M. Belinda Tucker

My husband Keith Kernan has been a source of intellectual and personal support for almost thirty years and my children Claudia and Ryan have been sources of joy in my life. Most recently, as their own academic and scholarly interests have developed, I find that their ideas, excellent observational skills, and critical faculties are an increasing influence on my own thinking. It has been rewarding to share so many common interests with them. There is never an occasion where I should fail to acknowledge the strong influence of my late mother Claudia Whiting Mitchell Tatum on my personal and intellectual development.

Claudia Mitchell-Kernan

INTRODUCTION

B Y THE MID-1980s, it had become apparent that patterns of family formation in the United States had undergone quite dramatic changes. During
the previous two decades, the divorce rate had nearly tripled, the percentage of children living in single-parent homes had doubled, being married by
one's early twenties was no longer normative for women, and the proportion
of families being headed by women alone increased by over 50 percent. Some
predicted that marriage would become less likely for American women in general. The family formation changes that took place between 1960 and 1980
were the most substantial of this century and they have continued into the
1990s, albeit at a somewhat slower pace.

These changes have been pervasive throughout American society, but in
certain respects they have been displayed more sharply in the African American
population. Although shifts in black divorce rates and shifts in the proportion
of children in single-parent households paralleled general population trends,
changes in marital timing and prevalence have been far more dramatic among
blacks. Fifty years ago, African American women and men were far more likely
to have married by age twenty to twenty-four than the general American population—with nearly 60 percent of black women and 40 percent of black men
having wed by that age. Today, one-quarter of black women and less than one
of eight black men have married by their early twenties. In a reversal of the
previous trend, blacks now marry considerably later than do Americans in general. The proportion of black women and men who ever marry has also declined
significantly—particularly over the past twenty years (although black marital
prevalence peaked in 1970). Simultaneously—due in large part to these interrelated patterns of later marriage, high rates of divorce, and increased singlehood—the percentage of African American women maintaining families
alone has increased dramatically since 1970, and more than half of all black
children now reside in single-parent homes.

The recent changes represent a significant shift in the basic structure of the
African American community and family life, which would seemingly have
serious implications for community functioning and individual well-being.

Black children being raised by mothers alone are three times more likely to be impoverished than those raised by two parents (Sweet and Bumpass, 1987). There are other less measurable potential effects. For example, concerns about the societal consequence of having large numbers of young males unattached to the traditional socializing structures have been raised (Rossi, 1984). Young men not committed to the responsibilities of being husbands or fathers and not engaged in other formative pursuits (such as college or meaningful work) may choose to affiliate with alternative, less societally appealing social forms, such as gangs. The increasing alienation of economically disadvantaged young African American men from the stabilizing influence of family has broad societal implications, not the least of which is the welfare of future generations who may be deprived of paternal input.

In the summer of 1989 we convened a meeting to discuss the recent and rapid marital decline among African Americans—to empirically examine the likely causes, correlates, and potential impact of such change on both communities and individuals, and to discuss the policy implications. Scholars conducting research on this issue were relatively few at the time and spread among a number of disciplines. As a consequence, there had been little opporunity for scholarly exchange. The research conference was designed to provide a vehicle for the presentation of ideas, for discussion, and for debate by bringing together leading researchers on African American marital decline and related subjects. This book derives from that effort. Most of its chapters were first delivered at the meeting as working papers.

The variety of perspectives included in this book reflects an unusual disciplinary range among the authors—anthropology, demography, economics, criminal justice, history, social psychology, and urban sociology. Some chapters also reflect the disciplinary perspectives of others who did not present at the conference but who contributed significantly to the discussions, including law, clinical psychology, psychiatry, and social welfare.

Several conceptual perspectives receive unusual attention in this book because they have dominated scholarly discussions of this subject. Issues of "mate availability" (including sex ratio) and whether and how limited marital options may affect both social psychological adaptation and the broader community structure are explored in a number of chapters. The speculations offered by Maria Guttentag and Paul Secord (1983) concerning the effects on societies of sex ratio imbalance have served as a springboard for a good deal of research and debate on this topic. Relatedly, several chapters explore the issue of increasing unemployment and underemployment among African American men and its consequences for family structure and family maintenance. A particular focal point of this latter work is William Julius Wilson's (1987) theory that marital decline and particularly the increase in female-headed families among African Americans are functions of the declining availability of men with stable employment.

We do not approach this subject dispassionately, for we believe that the African American family has been the primary survival mechanism through centuries of oppression. Furthermore, we do not hold the view that either the nuclear family or marriage is the only vehicle permitting the development of healthy communities and individuals. Yet we do view the dramatic decline in African American marriage with some alarm. The work presented herein is an attempt to achieve an objective understanding of the issues involved in such change. As discussed in Chapter 1, changes in the manner in which families are formed and maintained is a global phenomenon that reflects, in part, a changing world view about the status of women and fundamental shifts in the economic structures of many societies. Clearly, many marriages have benefited neither women and children nor men. Societies worldwide are struggling to redefine both marriage and family—some progressively, and others regressively, in our view. Our hope is that this volume will contribute substantively to such discussions in our own society, at a time when the matter has become grist for a rather vitriolic national debate.

Chapter Précis

This volume is divided into four sections: Sociological and Historical Context; Sociological Antecedents of African American Marital Patterns; Consequences and Correlates of African American Marital Decline; and Public Policy and African American Family Formation. The two chapters in Section One and the last chapter in Section Four are more conceptual than empirical in orientation. However, the remaining chapters present the results of original, often controversial, research. Since this is still a rather new area of investigation and a key aim of this volume is to advance future work, we have included a critical response for each empirical article. The critiques evaluate the contributions of the studies and identify new questions raised by these works. In essence, then, the commentaries provide a guide for further research development on the question of African American family formation. In this volume, rather than attempt to espouse a particular perspective, we have elected to present a range of viewpoints and research strategies. In this way, the reader will obtain a broad view of the issues and controversies that currently characterize this very passionate debate. Summaries of each of the chapters follow.

Two chapters form Section One. In Chapter 1 (Tucker and Mitchell-Kernan), we present the statistical background that stimulated the aforementioned conference and which forms the demographic context for this volume. Trends in the United States over the last fifty years (1940–1990) in family formation and household organization are presented and analyzed. Statistics are presented for both the national population and for blacks, Hispanics, and whites. We also present and discuss the major theoretical formulations offered to explain the recent trends in family formation.

In Chapter 2, Brenda Stevenson, of UCLA's Department of History, discusses the historical context of African American family formation. She critically analyzes prevailing historical treatments of black family structure and reconceptualizes the link between the conditions of slavery and late twentieth century African American marital behavior. From Stevenson's neorevisionist perspective, she argues that the slavery experience created and fostered critical differences between African American and white families that have persisted and led to current racial differences in family formation behavior. Plantation records are used to explore the nature of family formation and maintenance during slavery.

We believe that an historical frame for this book is critical—that current trends must be examined within the context of previous patterns and previous influences. Stevenson's paper is part of an emerging body of empirical historical work (e.g., Morgan et al., 1993; Ruggles, 1994) that contradicts a scholarly trend that followed publication of Daniel Patrick Moynihan's (1967) controversial "Report" on African American families (discussed in greater depth in Chapter 1). A number of historical treatments in the late 1960s and the 1970s showed remarkable similarity in African American and white family structure in the nineteenth and early twentieth centuries, despite the harsh effects of slavery. However, these new writers assert that there have always been fundamental differences in the way that persons of African descent and persons of European descent arranged households in this society and that the impact of slavery and oppression on black family forms was substantial. We would argue, then, that the historical evidence demonstrates that situational factors have been disruptive of African American family life since the time that Africans first arrived here as slaves. This unique history may make black families even more vulnerable to new situational challenges, such as higher male mortality and economic decline, and may therefore help account for the very recent more dramatic changes in family formation. That is, the absence of economic and ecological support for stable family life among African Americans, over a period of several hundred years, may have exacerbated the fragility of family forms.

Section Two is focused on the sociological antecedents of the new trends in marital behavior. We have elected to highlight sociological processes, as opposed to other kinds of phenomena (e.g., psychological) due to the prominence of such factors in current explanatory theorizing. Chapter 3, by University of Chicago sociologists Mark Testa and Marilyn Krogh, presents data from the very significant program of research mounted in inner-city Chicago by William Julius Wilson to examine the social and economic context of family formation. Testa and Krogh examine the relationship between employment and marriage among young men faced with out-of-wedlock pregnancy. They have employed as an interpretive framework Wilson's (1987) theory relating the decline in African American marriage to the decline in employment opportunities for minority males—particularly those in the inner cities. In an innovative approach in this area, they use event-history models to test and compare five distinct models of that relationship. Sheldon Danziger, of the University of Michigan's School of Social Welfare and the Institute for Public Policy Planning, provides the commentary on this research.

In Chapter 4, sociologist Robert Schoen, of Johns Hopkins University, argues that the underlying "propensity" to marry varies among ethnic groups and explains in part the recent divergence of black and white marriage patterns. In particular, he proposes that black women would be less likely to enter marriage since they do not benefit to the same degree as white women do from "traditional" marital exchanges in which women receive economic gains from marriage. Using 1980 census data from the state of Wisconsin, he explores this notion by analyzing intra- and interracial marriages among blacks and non-blacks. He also tests the still-debated theories forwarded by Davis (1941) and Merton (1941) regarding interracial marriages as exchanges of race and socio-economic status. The commentary is by David M. Heer from the University of Southern California's Department of Sociology.

In Chapter 5, sociologists K. Jill Kiecolt, of Virginia Polytechnic Institute and State University, and Mark A. Fossett, of Texas A & M University, have investigated the relationship between mate availability and marital outcomes among African Americans at both individual and aggregate levels. Using interview responses from the National Survey of Black Americans (linked with census indicators of sex ratio) and structural indicators from Louisiana cities and parishes, Kiecolt and Fossett have undertaken a unique test of the sex ratio hypotheses forwarded by Guttentag and Secord (1983) and others. Sociologist A. Wade Smith of Arizona State University comments on this study.

Three chapters form Section Three, which examines correlates and consequences of marital decline—including marital disruption. These studies were conducted by sociologists, psychologists, and an anthropologist and are focused on macro and micro (individual-level) processes. Our own work is presented first. In Chapter 6, we examine the attitudinal, as well as structural, correlates of current marital behavior and expectations among blacks, Latinos, and whites. Focusing in particular on individual perceptions of the macro processes believed to influence marital decline (i.e., mate availability, economic constraints), we explore the distinctive relationships among perceived structural conditions, attitudinal patterns, and marital behavior and expectation in different ethnic groups. Social psychologist James S. Jackson of the University of Michigan critiques that chapter.

Chapter 7 was prepared by sociologist Shirley Hatchett, of the University of Illinois at Urbana, and social psychologists Joseph Veroff and Elizabeth Douvan, of the University of Michigan. They present data from their longitudinal study of marital experience, which followed nearly 400 recently married black and white couples over a three-year period. In this chapter, they conduct a very elaborate examination of aspects of the initial period of marriage that are related to marital success and instability, focusing in particular on psychological and economic factors. UCLA clinical psychologist Hector F. Myers provides the commentary for this study.

Chapter 8, the last in this section, is authored by University of Chicago sociologist Robert J. Sampson. Starting with Wilson's (1987) theory of the influence of male employment on family structure, Sampson examines compromised male availability in a community as a function of unemployment and low sex ratios, and how the consequent changes in family structure are related to community crime levels. He offers and tests the hypothesis that persistent high crime rates stem largely from structural linkages among unemployment, economic deprivation, and family disruption. This study also tests Wilson's notion that the impact of male joblessness on family structure is more extreme in black than in white populations. Sampson explores these issues through analysis of census data and FBI offender rates from the 171 cities in the United States with populations greater than 100,000 in 1980. Comments on this highly provocative study are provided by UCLA sociologist Melvin L. Oliver.

Section Four includes two chapters specifically focused on public policy. The first, by economists William Darity, Jr., of the University of North Carolina, and Samuel Myers, Jr., of the University of Minnesota, considers the impact on family structure of a depleting supply of marriageable black men due to both increasing mortality and institutionalization. Consideration of this issue by economists is quite rare and, in the first part of their chapter, Darity and Myers discuss in some detail the linkage between black male marginality and the development of an underclass. Focusing on the years 1976 and 1985—perhaps the most critical expanse of time in changing marriage patterns among blacks—the authors employ the Census Bureau's Current Population Surveys (CPS) and other data sources to compare various indicators of male availability as predictors of female family headship among blacks and whites. They also directly test the competing notions of sex ratio and welfare payments as contributors to marital decline. The second part of the chapter is devoted to the consideration of policy options, based on projections of female headship probabilities for the year 2000 as a function of changes in sex ratios, welfare incomes, and other factors. The critique of this chapter is written by social psychologist Phillip J. Bowman of Northwestern University.

In Chapter 10, economist Lynn C. Burbridge of Wellesley College examines the policy implications of black marital decline. She explores how underlying values define the interpretation of the "problem" and what role government should play in addressing the issue. Burbridge presents and critiques a number of policy instruments that can be used to address the problems associated with changing marital behavior. Focusing in particular on governmental support for families and children and the relative absence of programs for men, she offers new directions to address contemporary and future concerns.

In Chapter 11, the concluding chapter of the book, we summarize and synthesize the findings reported in the research papers. We also discuss the implications of the presentations—the studies as well as the commentaries—for future research and social policy. We place these findings in global perspective and propose a research agenda, linked to policy, that is more appreciative of the various levels of analysis required to understand the complex issue of family formation behavior.

Two final comments. Notably absent from this volume is an empirical examination of the impact of marital decline on children. This omission is not a consequence of our belief that this is an unimportant question—quite the contrary! This question forms the centerpiece of many discussions of this issue and is currently the subject of so much heated debate that the presentation of a single study on children's effects seems terribly insufficient. We are simply unable to adequately address this topic within the empirical framework used for this book. We hope that a similar volume focused solely on the impact on children of new family formation trends is soon prepared.

Also, when we first proposed this conference, we had to rely on 1980 census data to examine trends. As described in greater detail in the first chapter, the 1990 data show that, in certain respects, African American changes have slowed or reversed slightly, while family formation trends in the general population continue unabated. Since marital decline is now more dramatically characteristic of American society in general, it has become more alarming to certain elements of the population at large. Recent scholarly reactions to this trend have begun to appear in the national lay press (e.g., Barbara Dafoe Whitehead's article in the *Atlantic* entitled "Dan Quayle Was Right," 1993). The emphasis is on the impact of marital decline on children and may be setting the stage for a major public policy campaign. When we began this work, it was within the context of a political environment that emphasized minimizing government involvement in social policy and human welfare. The political winds have now changed somewhat. It will be interesting to note the foci of future efforts directed toward the family and whether they approximate the areas identified by the authors of this volume as critical factors in African American marital decline.

REFERENCES

DAVIS, K. 1941. Intermarriage in caste societies. *American Anthropologist,* 43:376–395.

GUTTENTAG, M., AND SECORD, P. 1983. *Too many women: The sex ratio question.* Beverly Hills, CA: Sage Publications.

MERTON, R.K. 1941. Intermarriage and the social structure: Fact and theory. *Psychiatry,* 4:361–374.

MORGAN, S.P., MCDANIEL, A., MILLER, A.T., AND PRESTON, S.H. 1993. Racial differences in household structure at the turn of the century. *American Journal of Sociology,* 98:798–828.

MOYNIHAN, D.P. 1967. The Negro family: The case for national action. In L. Rainwater and W. L. Rainwater, eds., *The Moynihan report and the politics of controversy.* Cambridge, MA: MIT Press.

ROSSI, A.S. 1984. Gender and parenthood. *American Sociological Review,* 49:1–19.

RUGGLES, S. 1994. The origins of African American family structure. *American Sociological Review,* 59:136–151.

SWEET, J.A., AND BUMPASS, L.L. 1987. *American families and households.* New York: Russell Sage Foundation.

WHITEHEAD, B.D. 1993. Dan Quayle was right. *The Atlantic Monthly,* 271(4):47–84.

WILSON, W.J. 1987. *The truly disadvantaged.* Chicago: University of Chicago Press.

SECTION ONE

Sociological and Historical Context

1

TRENDS IN AFRICAN AMERICAN FAMILY FORMATION: A THEORETICAL AND STATISTICAL OVERVIEW

M. Belinda Tucker
and
Claudia Mitchell-Kernan

A FRICAN AMERICAN family formation patterns have been the subject of modern scholarship and debate for nearly one full century. Beginning with Du Bois's (1899, 1908) landmark studies of the black community in Philadelphia, social scientific inquiry has variously considered black families as adaptive, resilient, deviant, pathological, culturally distinctive, African retentive, and "just like yours." The particular form of the debate, and the direction of the research, have often been shaped by the politics of the moment—as evidenced by the reaction to Daniel Patrick Moynihan's (1967) now infamous "report" on the Negro family and the recent response to the "family values" theme of the 1992 presidential race (which many regarded as a thinly veiled attack on nonnuclear families).

We begin this chapter with a brief overview of the major thematic trends in research on African American family formation. Because a number of extensive reviews are available, we will not review the findings of the vast literature on the African American family (Billingsley, 1992; Hill, 1993; Taylor et al., 1991). Rather, our objective is to identify scholarly directions and the forces that appear to have shaped the research agenda over time. We will then examine the general and ethnic specific patterns of family formation and related indicators over the last fifty years in the United States, in order to detail the character and context of change among African Americans. Finally, the primary conceptual approaches that have been employed to interpret recent trends in black marriage will be considered.

A Century of Study:
Views of African American Family Formation

A long scholarly tradition has emphasized examination of the lives of persons of African descent in the United States. Community studies conducted over the first half of this century have been a particular strength (e.g., Du Bois, 1908; Davis et al., 1941; Drake and Cayton, 1945; Frazier, 1957) as these observers conveyed the complex texture of the black experience and the inter-connectedness of institutions, individuals, and societies. The psychology of African American life was also explored in landmark treatments (Clark and Clark, 1947; Rohrer and Edmonson, 1964; Kardiner and Ovesey, 1951) that left no doubt that the peculiar circumstances of blacks in America had left an indelible mark.

A central theme in these early studies, as well as in later research, has been the family, as both community institution and the predominant instrument of socialization. A particular focus has been patterns of family formation and ways in which African American families appear distinctive from those of the majority population, especially with regard to the lower prevalence of nuclear families and higher proportion of children born out of wedlock. In light of the recency with which the nuclear family emerged as the normative and dominant family form in the Western world, it is a bit paradoxical that family forms which depart from this model have so often been treated as deviant in the social scientific literature over the last half century. The incidence of families in which a husband-father is absent and which are headed by a female has been variously referred to as matriarchal, matrifocal, maternal, or matri-centered—terms which have been used to characterize African American families.

E. Franklin Frazier viewed the female-headed black family as both a symptom and source of family disorganization and a variety of other social ills and was quite blunt in his formulation of ills attendant to this type of family:

> The widespread disorganization of family life among Negroes has affected practically every phase of their community life and adjustment to the larger white world. Because of the absence of stability in family life, there is a lack of traditions. Life among a large portion of the urban Negro population is casual, precarious, and fragmentary. It lacks continuity and its roots do not go deeper than the contingencies of daily living. This affects the socialization of the Negro child. With a fourth to a third of Negro families in cities without a male head, many Negro children suffer the initial handicap of not having the discipline and authority of the father in the home. Negro mothers who have the responsibility for the support of the family are forced to neglect their children who pick up all forms of socially disapproved behavior in the disorganized areas in which these families are concentrated. (Frazier, 1957, pp. 636–637)

Although Frazier's views reflect the patriarchal conception of family roles characteristic of the period, his thoughts are not all that distinct from certain contemporary critiques of single-parent families. Recent revisionist assessments of the impact of single parentage on children also consider the loss of the father's involvement in childrearing problematic (e.g., Whitehead, 1993). Despite Frazier's harsh assessment of the impact of male absence on family life, unlike many contemporary critics, he believed that the root causes of such disorganization were racism, economic deprivation, ubanization, and other societal factors—rather than moral disintegration.

Irrespective of recent indictments of more general social trends in Western societies, much of the writing on African American family forms over the last quarter century challenged the pathological image of black families portrayed in earlier work. Since the mid-1960s, a number of scholars have devoted considerable attention to defending the African American family as a culturally rooted and adaptive family form. The single most important stimulus for this new direction of inquiry, which is manifest throughout the social sciences as well as in historical studies, was the publication of Daniel Patrick Moynihan's *The Negro Family: The Case for National Action*. Moynihan did not share the popular optimism of the time that conditions for blacks were improving (an optimism encouraged among some by the passage of the 1964 Civil Rights Act) and singled out as a special problem among black Americans those families that were without a husband-father and headed by a female. In his view, evidence was abundant that black communities were deteriorating and the situation of the black family was at the heart of the problem. Moynihan pointed out that one-quarter of all black families were "broken"; one-quarter were headed by women; and one-quarter of all black children were born out of wedlock. What seemed most alarming was the evidence that female-headed households were on the rise, increasing from 18 percent in 1950 to 25 percent of all black households in 1964.

Moynihan's monograph not only generated a heated controversy but spawned a substantial revisionist literature which continues to be influential in African American family studies. The late Herbert Gutman, in the introduction to *The Black Family in Slavery and Freedom* (1976), acknowledged Moynihan's influence in stimulating his own interest in historical studies of the African American family. Moynihan's title, *The Negro Family* (our emphasis), reflected the long-standing preoccupation with one type of lower-class black family. This focus provided the prevailing image of African American families and fueled the production of a report predicated on the characteristics of a single family type. Billingsley (1968) and Scanzoni (1971) demonstrated the limitations of such a perspective by documenting that a great range of family types characterized the African American population. Other work sought to challenge Moynihan's supposition (and Frazier's before him) that a family without a husband-father is by definition problematic. Such a perspective assumed that equivalence of structure denoted equivalence of function.

Indeed, the Moynihan report revived a decades-old debate that had been sparked by the differing perspectives of sociologist E. Franklin Frazier and anthropologist Melville Herskovits. While both men relied on historical arguments, the former saw the family form as emerging in the wake of a slavery-weakened institutionalized family, while the latter regarded it as a cultural retention of west African family organization. The west African "deep structure" of family forms among persons of African descent in the Western Hemisphere has been argued to be manifest in several organizational features observed among blacks in the United States, the Caribbean, and in South and Central America: a preference for blood kin ties over affinal ones (Sudarkasa, 1981); the great emphasis placed on children (Nobles, 1978); and, relatedly, the maternal role being accorded priority over the conjugal role (Bell, 1970).

A Politicized Research Agenda

Moynihan's book was indeed a turning point for both scholarly and political discussion of the African American family. Ten years after the publication of Moynihan's report, Walter Allen (1978) examined empirical approaches and the ideological underpinnings of scholarship on the black family. He found, not surprisingly, that much of the writing and research were focused on differences between the family structures of American blacks and whites and that this work was dominated by three ideological perspectives: cultural equivalence, cultural deviance, and cultural variance. [It is noteworthy that the classical community studies of Du Bois (1908), Drake and Cayton (1945), and Davis, Gardner, and Gardner (1941) had no such fixation with racial comparisons.] In sum, research from the *cultural equivalence* perspective de-emphasizes or undermines distinctions between black and white families. Included in this genre are studies that attribute racial differences to class factors. Allen argued that implicit in this view is the notion that white middle-class family organization and function constitute the norm that blacks must approximate to be viewed as legitimate. The *cultural deviance* perspective explicitly views the nuclear family with a male provider and head (which at that time was the most prevalent family form among white Americans) as normative. Black deviations from the nuclear family are judged to be dysfunctional or pathological. Allen cited Moynihan's work as exemplifying the cultural deviance ideology. The *cultural variation* argument views black distinctiveness not in negative terms, but as a positive outgrowth of distinctive sociocultural contexts. A particular focus of research espousing this view has been the adaptive quality of African American families. Walker (1988) conducted a similar review a decade later and found Allen's framework to be essentially applicable—an indication that, conceptually, at least, the primary thrust of African American family research had not changed all that much—with comparative work and explanations of racial differences still a dominant focus.

On the positive side, Moynihan's alarm did serve to stimulate a closer examination of black families, historically and contemporaneously. On the other hand, the research agenda of the next quarter century seemed to be largely dictated by a perceived need to respond to the Moynihan assertions. After all, Moynihan's report was specifically designed to influence public policy generally and federal priorities in particular. The intent of subsequent scholarship was therefore to correct misconceptions, to challenge biases, to offer alternative explanations for distinctive forms of family formation, and to more fully depict the variety of family forms found among African Americans. Certainly, from a tactical perspective, a directed research agenda of this nature was critically needed in order to thwart public initiatives based on what many believed to be a faulty interpretation of the African American "situation." Yet, a more expansive conception of inquiry may have led to earlier recognition of the dramatic change in African American family life that was afoot. Indeed, the invidious black-white comparisons that were often recast as "abnormal-normal" served to discourage global comparative work that might have helped us to understand the transformations in the context of societal change worldwide.

Most recently, Robert B. Hill (1993) led a team of scholars (including Andrew Billingsley, Eleanor Engram, and Carol Stack, among others) who once again examined research on black families. They found that the conventional treatment of black families in social scientific research included an investment in the "deficit model," a tendency still to "exclude the bulk of black families by focusing on only one subgroup," and a failure to acknowledge new research findings and programmatic insights. Moynihan's legacy has apparently endured. In a refreshing break from the past, however, the Hill group adopted what they termed a "holistic" perspective to focus specifically on the current "crises" facing black families. Acknowledging that they were simply complying with Du Bois's (1899, 1908) assertion that an understanding of the conditions of blacks in America required an assessment of the influence of history and culture along with social, economic, and political forces, they examined the impact of conditions in each of these areas, as well as psychological dynamics (e.g., discouragement, self-esteem) and public policy, on the well-being of African American families. They, in particular, emphasized the increasing diversity of experiences and life-styles among blacks in the United States. Although this study was not an analysis of research focused specifically on African American families, it reestablishes the legitimacy of the original empirical and conceptual paradigms for the study of black families, as framed by Du Bois (1908), Frazier (1957), Drake and Cayton (1945), and others. The reactive research agenda may have finally settled into the past.

In Search of New Conceptual Paradigms

Given the current heated political debate about "family values" and appropriate family forms, it is easy to see how the research agenda can be molded by political imperatives. Individual scholars are sensitive to the potential uses of their work and may conceptualize research with such concerns in mind. Nevertheless, it seems to us that the need to "defend" African American family forms has led to a narrow conceptualization of black family formation patterns and a failure to confront real problems. First, there is a notable absence of work focused on African American family formation in a global context. That is, the comparative dimension of black family researchers stands primarily in reference to white Americans (with a few comparisons with Caribbean and African populations). In fact, family formation is undergoing change in virtually all Western nations, and in most other countries and cultures as well (c.f. Clark, 1984; Eekelaar and Katz, 1980; Popenoe, 1988). While the underlying causes of these changes may differ substantially from one societal context to the next, we must consider the reality of a world that is increasingly linked through travel, communications, mass media, literature, and art. Very disparate societies are now interdependent and interinfluential. We may learn a great deal from a less provincial perspective.

A second problem is that only over the last half decade have researchers concentrated on the fact that African American family formation patterns have undergone recent, very rapid, change. The fact of these changes, their causes, and their consequences are now being considered by a fairly small group of sociologists and a few economists but have been virtually ignored by all other disciplines. A comprehensive multidisciplinary effort to understand a fundamental and dramatic societal shift is simply absent.

In the next section, we examine patterns of family formation and living arrangements among Americans in general, blacks, Latinos,[1] and whites from 1940 through 1990. We examine other ethnic groups, not for purposes of comparison, per se, but in order to provide a societal context for examination of African American patterns of family formation. That is, it has not always been clear in recent discussions of black families that change is pervasive in this regard throughout American society. For the most part, the Latino figures to be examined are limited to 1970 through 1990, and are presented for reference only, since interpretation of trends is limited to only a twenty-year period. Data on Asian American populations are simply too limited to be considered in this discussion. Our intent is to identify areas of both change and stability in the

---

[1] In general, we use the term *Latino* to describe Chicano populations and persons of Mexican and Latin American ancestry in the United States, with the following exceptions. When census data are being described, the Census Bureau's terminology for that particular census year will be employed: that is, *Hispanic* is used for the 1990 and 1980 census and related reports; *Spanish origin* is used for 1970 census and related reports.

United States as a whole, and for all three groups, and to pinpoint turning points for specific trends.

Statistical Trends: 1940–1990

Table 1.1 presents data from a variety of census reports at decennial points for the years 1940 through 1990 on marriage, divorce, household structure, household maintenance, women's labor force participation, and households with children in poverty. Obviously, this table does not provide the range of household characteristics available through census statistics, but it does illuminate the areas that we believe are key to an understanding of African American family change.

Marriage

Marital timing. The statistics clearly demonstrate that both women and men, as well as persons of all three focal ethnic groups, now marry later than was the case in any of the earlier decades. Since 1960, the percentage of women in the general population who married by age twenty to twenty-four has decreased by 46 percent. The corresponding figure for whites is 43 percent, but 64 percent among black women. The table also makes clear the oft-cited fact that the 1950s and early 1960s were distinctive in terms of marital patterns of this century—a period when marital prevalence was greatest and early marriage was normative among all groups (for discussion of this phenomenon see Cherlin, 1981). If 1940 is used as the comparison point, change is somewhat less substantial: 27.5 percent for the total population of women and 20.3 percent for white women. However, change among black women is still quite striking at 62.2 percent. The male figures are very similar. In the general and white populations, 1960 to 1990 change was 54.8 percent and 51.8 percent, respectively. The 1940 to 1990 change, though, was only 24.5 percent for the total population and 14.6 percent among white males. Change among black males was substantial for both periods: 70.1 percent since 1960 and 65.5 percent since 1940. Among both sexes, it is evident that blacks married earlier than whites in 1940, but that the pattern reversed itself among women in 1960 and among men, most clearly, in 1970.

Ever married. Again, the tendency to marry at least once has been quite variable over the last fifty years. It is notable, however, that the peak period of marriage differs for blacks and whites. Both black women and men were most likely to have been ever married in 1970, while the peak year for whites was 1960. In fact, over the last fifty years, the likelihood of ever getting married has actually *increased* in the total and white populations and remained essentially

TABLE 1.1

Family Formation Patterns and Living Arrangements, United States: 1940–1990

Variable/Ethnicity	1940	1950	1960	1970	1980	1990
Women married by age 20–24 (percent)						
Total	51.3	65.6	69.3	64.2	44.8	37.2
Black	59.6[a]	65.7[a]	61.9[a]	55.8	21.6	22.5
White	50.3	65.6	70.4	65.2	43.1	40.1
Hispanic	NA	NA	NA	NA	43.8	44.4
Men married by age 20–24 (percent)						
Total	27.4	39.9	45.8	45.3	31.2	20.7
Black	38.7[a]	43.9[a]	44.5[a]	40.1	15.3	13.3
White	26.1	39.4	46.3	46.4	27.9	22.3
Hispanic	NA	NA	NA	NA	29.9	26.5
Women ever married (percent)						
Total	70.8	79.9	81.0	77.0	77.1	77.2
Black	73.9[a]	79.2[a]	77.7[a]	82.6	65.9	63.1
White	72.3	80.0	81.4	78.7	78.8	79.4
Hispanic	NA	NA	NA	73.5	72.4	72.5
Men ever married (percent)						
Total	65.2	73.6	75.1	71.9	70.3	70.1
Black	64.5[a]	71.3[a]	69.5[a]	75.7	59.4	56.6
White	65.3	74.0	75.6	72.9	77.5	72.0
Hispanic	NA	NA	NA	67.8	65.7	63.1
Divorce rate per 1,000 married women						
Total	NA	NA	42.0	60.0	120.0	166.0
Black	NA	NA	78.0	104.0	258.0	358.0
White	NA	NA	38.0	56.0	110.0	153.0
Hispanic	NA	NA	NA	81.0	132.0	155.0
Women living alone (number)						
Total	NA	NA	NA	7,149	11,269	13,950
Black	NA	NA	NA	675	1,096	1,525
White	NA	NA	NA	6,425	9,800	12,161
Hispanic	NA	NA	NA	NA	591	442
Women living alone (percent)						
Total	NA	NA	NA	9.3	12.4	13.6
Black	NA	NA	NA	8.5	10.6	12.9
White	NA	NA	NA	9.4	12.4	14.0
Hispanic	NA	NA	NA	NA	12.5	6.0
Men living alone (number)						
Total	NA	NA	NA	3,965	7,075	9,049
Black	NA	NA	NA	518	910	1,084
White	NA	NA	NA	3,384	5,905	7,718
Hispanic	NA	NA	NA	NA	303	415

Sources: National Center for Health Statistics, 1990; U.S. Bureau of the Census, 1950, 1951a, 1951b, 1953, 1955, 1961, 1963a, 1963b, 1963c, 1964, 1966, 1971, 1973, 1975a, 1975b, 1980, 1982, 1984, 1990a, 1991b, 1991c, 1992a, 1992b.

[a] Based on "nonwhite" rather than black populations.
[b] Based on 1952 CPS data.
[c] Based on 1988 reported and inferred data.

Variable/Ethnicity	1940	1950	1960	1970	1980	1990
Men living alone (percent)						
Total	NA	NA	NA	5.6	8.5	10.1
Black	NA	NA	NA	7.5	10.8	12.4
White	NA	NA	NA	5.4	8.2	9.9
Hispanic	NA	NA	NA	NA	6.8	5.7
Adults living alone as percentage of all households						
Total	NA	11.9[b]	13.1	17.1	22.6	24.6
Black	NA	NA	NA	1.9	2.5	NA
White	NA	NA	NA	15.4	19.9	NA
Hispanic	NA	NA	NA	NA	.007	NA
Nonfamily households (percent)						
Total	9.9	10.8	15.0	18.8	26.3	29.2
Black	14.7[a]	NA	18.5[a]	22.0	28.0	28.8
White	NA	NA	14.7	18.4	26.2	29.4
Hispanic	NA	NA	NA	13.0	17.8	18.4
Families maintained by women alone (percent)						
Total	15.2	15.0	9.3	10.7	14.6	16.5
Black	22.6[a]	24.0[a]	27.0[a]	28.0	40.3	43.8
White	14.5	15.0	16.0	8.9	11.6	12.9
Hispanic	NA	NA	NA	15.3	20.1	23.1
Birthrates for unmarried women (age 15–44)						
Total	7.1	14.1	21.6	26.4	29.4	36.6[c]
Black	35.6[a]	71.2[a]	98.3[a]	95.5	82.9	88.9
White	3.6	6.1	9.2	13.9	17.6	26.6
Hispanic	NA	NA	NA	NA	NA	NA
Children in single-parent homes (percent)						
Total	NA	7.1	9.1	11.9	19.7	24.7
Black	NA	NA	21.9	31.8	45.8	54.8
White	NA	NA	8.4	8.7	15.1	19.2
Hispanic	NA	NA	NA	NA	21.1	30.0
Families with children under 18 years of age below poverty level (percent)						
Total	NA	NA	19.7	11.6	14.7	15.5
Black	NA	NA	66.6[a]	34.9	35.5	35.4
White	NA	NA	15.3	8.5	11.2	11.8
Hispanic	NA	NA	NA	24.5	27.2	29.8
Women in labor force (percent)						
Total	25.8	29.0	34.5	41.4	49.9	57.4
Black	37.6[a]	37.1[a]	41.7[a]	47.5	53.2	58.7
White	24.1	28.3	33.6	40.6	51.2	57.2
Hispanic	NA	NA	NA	38.1	47.4	53.5
Married couples with both wife and husband in labor force (percent)						
Total	29.6	23.8	30.5	39.2	52.0	49.5
Black	NA	31.8[a]	33.5[a]	50.7	58.9	53.0
White	NA	20.7	30.2	38.2	51.3	49.1
Hispanic	NA	NA	NA	34.9	51.3	45.9

stable since 1970, following a steep decline from 1960. Declines from peak periods are minimal for whites (2.5 percent among women, 4.8 percent among men), but higher among blacks (23.6 percent for women, 25.2 percent for men). Today, blacks as a group are less likely to marry than either whites or Hispanics. This was not the case fifty years ago. The fact that change is not more substantial among blacks, despite popular notions to the contrary, is due in part to the pervasiveness of marriage among older black women. Although 94 percent of black women born in the 1930s married eventually, some demographers have estimated that, based on recent trends, only 70 percent of black women born in the 1950s will marry (Rodgers and Thornton, 1985). Using even more recent data, Norton and Miller (U.S. Bureau of the Census, 1992b) estimate that fewer than three of four black women overall can expect to marry, compared to nine of ten white women.

Since blacks, Latinos, and whites evidence different age structures (with whites being oldest as a group and Latinos being youngest), it is useful to examine age cohort data whenever available. In a recent Census Bureau report that analyzed marriage patterns of women by age since 1975 (using data from the three most recent marriage history surveys—U.S. Bureau of the Census, 1992b), it is clear that some decline in marital prevalence is evident among both blacks and whites, aged thirty to thirty-nine (data on Latinas are not available for 1975). Among women aged forty to forty-four (a point at which the potential of ever marrying is reduced substantially), marital decline was minimal among whites (from 95.9 percent to 93.4 percent), but quite dramatic among blacks, declining from 95.1 percent to 82.1 percent (a nearly 14 percent decrease). Again, however, these data permit us to examine change only from the 1970s, a peak period of marriage for all groups.

Divorce.   Even if the chance of marrying has not changed as much for all groups as some believe, those marriages are less likely than ever to be maintained. Divorce has been an area of dramatic change for all groups. The 1990 overall divorce rate (the number of divorces per 1,000 married women) is nearly four times the 1960 rate. The factors of increase among whites and blacks since 1960 were very similar—4 and 4.6, respectively. Although 1960 figures are not available, divorce rates nearly doubled among Hispanics between 1970 and 1990. Still, black women divorce at a rate that is more than double that of either white or hispanic women.

Age cohort comparisons for divorce demonstrate significant change since 1975 among all groups for ages thirty to fifty-four (U.S. Bureau of the Census, 1992b). Even in the oldest cohort, fifty to fifty-four, the percent divorced after their first marriage increased among white women from 16.8 percent to 28.5 percent (a nearly 70 percent increase!). Among black women in the same age cohort, with a level that initially was almost twice that of whites, a 32 percent increase was evident, rising from 29.7 percent to 39.2 percent. The U.S. Bureau of the Census (1992b) estimate is that if recent trends continue, four of ten first marriages of the youngest cohort will end in divorce. The authors note that divorce rates in the United States are among the highest recorded in the world.

Living Arrangements

Living alone.   Simultaneous with changes in marriage patterns, living arrangements among Americans have also undergone transformation. Living alone is much more commonplace today than it was fifty years ago. Examining the available data since 1970, change in this area is evident among both women and men in all three ethnic groups. Notably, black women are slightly less likely to live alone than are white women—which may be a function of the greater longevity of white women, as well as the greater tendency of blacks to live in extended family situations. However, black men are somewhat more likely to live alone than either white or Hispanic men. Yet these differences are extremely small, indicating that, with the exception of Hispanics, the tendency to live alone in this society is quite similar across ethnic group and gender. The increase in the sheer volume of persons living alone is quite striking. As shown in Table 1.1, the total number of women living alone has nearly doubled just over the past twenty years, while the number of men living alone has increased by a factor of 2.3.

Nonfamily households.   The increase in the likelihood of living in households without other family members has been substantial and consistent across ethnic and gender groupings. The proportion of persons living in nonfamily households has doubled since 1960 and those proportions are nearly identical for blacks and whites. Nearly one-third of black and white households are nonfamily units. Although Hispanics are much less likely to live in such households, nearly one in five Hispanic households are made up of unrelated individuals.

Families maintained by women alone.   There is a perception afloat today that a much greater proportion of family units is being maintained by women alone. However, the statistics presented in Table 1.1 contradict this view for the United States population as a whole. The tendency of women to maintain families alone is essentially unchanged since 1940 and 1950. In fact, there has been a slight decrease in the proportion of white women heading families without men. These percentages have indeed fluctuated, with 1970 representing the point at which female headship was lowest among white women. But among both black and Hispanic families, change has been substantial. Black women are now twice as likely to maintain families alone as they were in 1940. Furthermore, the change has been a steady increase over that period of time, without the fluctuations observed among white women. Since 1970, the tendency of Hispanic women to maintain households alone has increased by 50 percent.

Children

Children born out of wedlock. Birthrates among unmarried women age fifteen to forty-four have steadily increased in the general population over the last fifty years. The 1988 out-of-wedlock birthrate (i.e., number of births per 1,000 unmarried women) represents a fivefold increase since 1940. The increase has been most dramatic among white women: the 1988 rate of birth among unmarried white women was seven times the 1940 rate. Out-of-wedlock births among black women have been consistently higher than those for whites. However, although the black rates have also increased, there has been a good deal more fluctuation in the black figures. Black rates peaked in 1960 and the black-white differential has decreased substantially. In 1940, black births among unmarried women were five times the white rate; by 1988, the differential had been halved.

Children in single-parent homes. The proportion of children who live with only one parent has grown quite dramatically among all ethnic groups. Overall, the extent of children living in single-parent homes has more than tripled since 1950. The ethnic breakdowns indicate that such living situations for children have been more prevalent among blacks than whites for all years for which data are available (i.e., since 1960). Still, the likelihood that children will live in one-parent homes is quite high—25 percent of all white children in 1990 and nearly one-third of all Hispanic children. The year 1990 has been a watershed year of sorts, with evidence that black children living in single-parent homes now make up the majority of all black children (54 percent).

Families with young children living below the poverty level. Although the changing living arrangements of children would suggest that their economic situation has severely declined, census poverty figures portray a somewhat different picture. The likelihood that families with children under the age of eighteen will be living below the poverty level has actually decreased since 1960 for all populations except Hispanics. The decrease has been greatest among black children, largely due to the fact that conditions were so severe in 1960, when two-thirds of all black families with young children were impoverished. Now one-third live in poverty, which is only slightly higher than the Hispanic proportion, yet triple the white proportion. Still, there are ominous trends in this area. After reaching new lows in 1970 in the level of poverty among families with children, impoverishment has steadily increased since that time among whites and Hispanics and, after increasing between 1970 and 1980, has remained essentially stable among blacks.

Family Employment

Women in the labor force.   One factor cited in marital delay, marital disruption, and nonmarriage has been the increased labor-force participation of women (e.g., Becker, 1981; Ross and Sawhill, 1975). However, mounting evidence suggests that although women's employment may delay marriage, working women are more likely than those who do not work to marry eventually (e.g., Cherlin, 1981; Goldscheider and Waite, 1991; Oppenheimer, 1988). It is clear that employment among all groups of women has increased steadily and substantially over the last fifty years. Now the majority of women in all ethnic groups work outside the home. This was not the case even in 1980.

Dual-worker married-couple families.   Married-couple families in which both female and male heads work have likewise increased and have nearly doubled in proportion since 1940. Black families have been and continue to be most likely to have dual workers, although the ethnic differential has declined. Since 1970, half of black families have had dual workers. Now close to half of all ethnic groups evidence this employment pattern.

Summary

These data make it clear that American patterns of family formation and maintenance have indeed undergone substantial change over the last fifty years in a number of important respects. Compared to 1940, American women and men marry later, are substantially more likely to divorce, and are far more likely to live alone or in homes without other family members.[2] It is clear that, with later marriage and more divorce, Americans are likely today to spend significantly more time outside of marital unions, even if marriage does occur at some point. And although women in the general population are no more likely to maintain families alone now than they did fifty years ago, the birthrates among unmarried women have increased dramatically. Because of this change and the increased rate of marital disruption, one in four American children now live in single-parent homes. [It is interesting to note that it was, apparently, the 25 percent threshold that stimulated Moynihan's aggressive attention to the African American family—i.e., a quarter of Negro births out of wedlock, a quarter of Negro families headed by women, a quarter of urban Negro marriages dissolved (Moynihan, 1967)]. In addition, most women in this society now work outside the home, and the employment of both wife and husband in a family is

---

[2] Sweet and Bumpass (1987) argue that reliance on census data actually understates the trend toward later marriage or nonmarriage, due to underestimation of female first marriage rates between the ages of twenty and twenty-four in 1969 by 11 percent and overestimation in 1979 by the same rate (p. 21).

now typical. This is the current societal context within which change in all sectors of American society must be considered.

It must be reemphasized that although we have described patterns of behavior for the major ethnic groups as a whole, these groups display different age structures. Examination of available age cohort data demonstrates both ethnic similarities and differences, but generally supports the overall data with respect to declining marital prevalence in American society at large. Indeed, the patterns of behavior displayed by a population as a whole are also significant indicators of societal demands, norms, and responses.

These society-wide changes also characterize African American patterns of family formation and maintenance. There are differences in degree of change and some countervailing trends. That is, change among blacks has been substantially greater than that observed in the general population in the areas of marital timing (i.e., greater delay) and in the likelihood that black women will maintain a family alone. The proportion of black women and men who ever marry has also declined by nearly 20 percent over the last fifty years, while the figures for the general population have remained steady. And that figure is even more striking among middle-age women. However, the rate of increase of out-of-wedlock births is substantially lower among African American women than the increase among women in general or whites. Still there are areas of special concern for African American families. The combined impact of greater marital delay, more nonmarriage, a very high divorce rate, and a continuing high rate of births out of wedlock (all interrelated phenomena) is observed most acutely through the living arrangements of children and the burden of family responsibilities borne by women. Although family impoverishment has not changed in recent decades, the majority of African American children are now living in single-parent homes. And, in more than four out of every ten black families a woman is maintaining that family without the support of another adult. It is toward these distinctive trends that relate very directly to the well-being of African American families and communities that this volume is addressed.

Understanding African American Marital Change

Given that African American family formation patterns have undergone such rapid change, with a greater degree of intensity in certain key respects than that observed in other sectors of this society, what accounts for these trends? The recent changes in family formation patterns in the United States in general, and the divergence of African American marital patterns in particular, have given rise to a renewed scholarly emphasis on the determinants of marital and childbearing behavior and family structure. This recent work can be distinguished from the black family work described at the outset of this chapter, for several reasons. First, the focus is the contemporary shift in African American family formation patterns, rather than the trends emerging from slavery and its aftermath. Second, the earliest thrust of this interpretive line was the impact on marriage of World War II-induced changes in birthrates in the society at large (described in greater detail below). Third, the primary emphasis has not been the defense of African American family forms, but rather the identification of forces that have altered long-standing traditions. The ideological paradigms identified by Allen (1978) to describe the earlier thrust of black family research—cultural equivalence, cultural deviance, and cultural variation—do not fully capture the foci of this new genre of work as a whole. Although individual researchers may indeed have a nuclear family ideal in mind when designing and interpreting their studies, the fact that the nuclear model does not currently describe the family formation pattern of any major sector of American society has diminished the likelihood that this ideal dictates the research agenda.

The predominant focus of this recent work has been macro-level economic and demographic constructs. Relatively little research has emphasized individual (micro) level analyses or the attitudinal dimensions of changing family formation patterns. A useful conceptual scheme for organizing the dominant theoretical formulations is found in the work of Dixon (1971). In attempting to understand cross-cultural differences in marriage behavior, she proposed three mediating factors between social structure and nuptiality: (1) the availability of mates; (2) the feasibility of marriage; and (3) the desirability of marriage. We briefly review the major work in this area using Dixon's analytical framework.

Mate availability. Demographers contend that a "marriage squeeze"— a decrease in the availability of marriage partners—among female members of the baby boom has led to delays in marriage and lower marriage rates, particularly for women (Glick, Heer, and Beresford, 1963; Rodgers and Thornton, 1985; Schoen, 1983). This shortage of partners is due to the gradual increase in birthrates following World War II, coupled with the tendency of women to marry slightly older men. Baby boom women were therefore seeking husbands from older but smaller cohorts. Although this marriage squeeze affected all races, it exacerbated the impact of the mortality-driven decline in African American sex ratios, evident since the 1920s (Cox, 1940; Jackson, 1971; McQueen, 1979; Staples, 1981a,b), and led, some think, to a broadening of mate selection standards among black women (Spanier and Glick, 1980).

Guttentag and Secord (1983) argued that imbalanced sex ratios throughout time have had major societal consequences, with male shortage leading to higher rates of singlehood, divorce, out-of-wedlock births, adultery, and transient relationships; less commitment among men to relationships; lower societal value on marriage and the family; and a rise in feminism. One impact of the marriage squeeze among white women, they suggested, is an increase in interracial marriage. They cited imbalanced sex ratios as a factor in black marital decline and an increasing out-of-wedlock birthrate. Epenshade (1985) noted, however, that some of the data presented by Guttentag and Secord appear to challenge their own thesis—for example, black sex ratios have declined since 1920, but marital decline has only been evident since the 1960s. Also, African American out-of-wedlock birthrates have declined since the 1960s. Nevertheless, there has been empirical support for some aspects of the Guttentag and Secord speculations from our own research and that of others (Jemmott, Ashby, and Lindenfeld, 1989; Secord and Ghee, 1986; South, 1986; South and Messner, 1988; Tucker, 1987). The inconsistencies noted by Epenshade may stem in part from the narrow focus on the demographic variable of sex ratio, rather than the range of issues related to an individual's potential for relationship formation (e.g., eligibility, sociocultural preferences).

Marital feasibility.   Sociologists and economists have been particularly concerned about the relationship between the economic condition of African American males and black family structure. They have argued that black marital feasibility has decreased because the increasing economic marginality of black males has made them less attractive as potential husbands, and less interested in becoming husbands, since they are constrained in their ability to perform the provider role in marriage (Darity and Myers, 1986/87; Wilson, 1987). There is empirical support for these arguments (e.g., Testa et al., 1989; Tucker and Taylor, 1989), although analyses by Mare and Winship (1991) suggest that socioeconomic factors cannot completely explain the drastic marital decline of the last thirty years. Other evidence suggests that the economic fortunes of younger American males of all races have declined (Easterlin, 1980; Lichter et al., 1991) and that therefore such concerns have affected overall marriage patterns.

Related to these arguments is a theory of marital timing proposed by Oppenheimer (1988) in which late marriage is seen as a function of an elongated search strategy fueled primarily by uncertainty regarding male economic prospects. With the dramatic decrease in young male economic viability generally (i.e., not blacks only) and the increased training period (e.g., college), there is no incentive to marry before more definitive information is available about the potential economic gains to be had through marriage. Although reminiscent in some ways of Becker's (1981) economic theories of marriage, Oppenheimer disputes Becker's claim that women's own improved economic prospects have served to undermine the institution of marriage [a view shared in part by Ross and Sawhill (1975), who saw the decreasing differential between black male and female income as a factor in marital decline and instability]. Importantly, however, both Becker and Oppenheimer also give primacy to male economic fortunes as a marital stimulant. They are therefore consistent on this one theme with Wilson (1987) and Darity and Myers (1986/87).

Desirability of marriage.   Information about whether marriage is any longer desirable can be obtained from two lines of work. Investigators have sought to determine whether cohabitation has become an acceptable substitute for marriage (and thereby accounts for the decline of marriage). Such formulations consider increased cohabitation as a cultural change, reflecting greater sexual freedom among adolescents and young adults, the greater availability of relatively effective contraception, increased financial independence of women, and changes in gender roles, among other factors. Tanfer (1987) used data from the 1983 National Survey of Unmarried Women, which includes never-married twenty- to twenty-nine-year-olds, to determine predictors of cohabitation prevalence. Cohabitation was most prevalent among white, Protestant, and lower- or lower-middle-class women, and twice as prevalent in the West as in the rest of the country. Few differences between cohabitators and noncohabitators on social-psychological attitudes emerged. Although this study did not include a personal income measure and (understandably) contained no indication of the financial wherewithal of actual and potential male partners, there is a clear economic component: cohabitating women were significantly more likely to be out of the labor force, and had significantly less education. Yet, black women were still less likely to cohabitate than white women, which Tanfer believed to be a function of the lack of available black male partners (Tanfer, 1987). Tanfer concluded that cohabitation was only an advanced state of courtship and did not constitute a marital substitute. Using the 1987–88 National Survey of Families and Households data, Bumpass et al. (1991) found that declines in both first marriage and remarriage rates have been offset in large part by increasing cohabitation, and that the cohabitation trend has been led by the least educated. It would seem then that the study of cohabitation in the United States has not resulted in definitive findings about whether Americans continue to desire marriage, although the available evidence does suggest that African Americans are not choosing cohabitation over marriage.

A few researchers have examined changing attitudes about marriage. In perhaps the most comprehensive assessment of changing attitudes toward family in the United States, Thorton (1989) reviewed results from a number of major data sets (including two national and one panel study). Examining responses to survey items from the late 1950s to mid-1980s, he found a substantial weakening over the period in the "normative imperative" to marry, to remain married, to have children, to be faithful to one's spouse, and to differentiate male and female roles. However, he found *no* significant shifts in the desire to marry eventually or the desire to remain single or childless. For example, more than 90 percent of respondents in the Study of American Families (a panel study of mothers and children) expected to marry, and there has been no decline in that proportion since 1960 (Thornton and Freedman, 1982). Our own survey of Southern Californians (which is discussed in detail in a later chapter) indicated that marriage was highly valued, and that when controlling for education, gender, and age, there were no differences in perceived importance of marriage on the basis of ethnicity. It is clear, however, that Americans in general, and African Americans in particular, have become increasingly more accepting of singlehood (e.g., Thornton and Freedman, 1982; Staples, 1981b), even if their personal preferences include eventual marriage. Thornton (1989) views such changes as a shift toward greater tolerance of a broader range of behaviors, rather than an endorsement of particular life-styles.

Integration and summary. Integrative research that examines and compares all of these various perspectives has simply not been conducted. A few recent studies have attempted to compare aspects of the demographic and economic arguments, with varied results: support for both availability and economic arguments (Bennett et al., 1989; Lichter et al., 1992), support for economic theories (Lichter et al., 1991), lack of support for economic theories (Mare and Winship, 1991), and lack of support for availability theories (Schoen and Kluegel, 1988). With the Census Bureau's Current Population Survey (CPS) data, Bennett et al. (1989) found that both demographic and economic factors accounted for the increasing divergence of black and white marriage patterns. In contrast, however, Mare and Winship's (1991) analysis of census microdata and CPS data showed little evidence that black or white marital entry was a function of labor market trends for either men or women, or schooling factors (thought by some to delay marriage). Although, when comparing census labor market areas, Lichter et al. (1991) found that spatial variations in marriage rates of both blacks and whites could be explained in part by differences in the local supply of economically "attractive" males (though these differences could not completely explain the black-white marriage differential). Significantly, Lichter et al. (1992) later demonstrated that women's marital timing was directly linked to the availability of men of similar age and race and to male economic circumstances.

It is notable that, to our knowledge, only two studies have found no support for either economic (Mare and Winship, 1991) or availability theories (Schoen and Kluegel, 1988), while all of the remaining investigations (including studies that do not explicitly compare perspectives) find some merit in one of these views. In fact, in one of the most comprehensive studies of the matter, Lichter et al. (1992) state that "racial differences in marriage are located more in structural marriage market opportunities than in the individual-level factors typically considered in previous research" (p. 797). They further note that their analyses demonstrate that "mate availability in local marriage markets is a significant factor contributing to delayed marriage—and perhaps nonmarriage—among black women" (p. 797). We conclude from all of this that there is significant value in pursuing these lines of investigation. This in no way should be construed to mean that these are the only potentially influential factors in changing family formation patterns in the United States in general or in accounting for diverging black marital trends. We recognize that a range of other factors is involved, including women's work-force participation, improved contraception, extended period of formal education, the declining gap between black female and male earnings, and changing conceptions of gender roles, among others (c.f. Cherlin, 1981; Ross and Sawhill, 1975; Blumstein and Schwartz, 1983)]. However, economic decline and high male mortality are targets for social change. To know their precise role in changing family structure could offer significant societal benefits. Because of the centrality of these phenomena and their targetability for social change, economic and demographic arguments are a particular focus of the empirical work presented in the chapters that follow.

Conclusion

This chapter has explored trends in African American family scholarship. This review suggested that the research agenda since the mid-1960s has been largely reactive, and consequently did not signal indications that dramatic changes in black family organization were under way. An examination of trends in United States family formation patterns demonstrated that fundamental society-wide change has occurred over the last half century (i.e., later marriage, more divorce, more singlehood, more births out of wedlock, more nonfamily living arrangements), but that in several significant respects, African American change has been more substantial than that observed in other ethnic groups in the United States. The large proportion of black families being maintained by women alone and the fact that most black children now live in single-parent households represent marked departures from earlier African American family patterns. The fact that black men and women are highly likely to live substantial periods of their lives as unmarried persons is also a significant change from just thirty years ago. Theory and research directed at understanding these very recent changes in family formation patterns, and greater decline of marriage among blacks, have implicated demographic and economic factors as causative. These arguments are explored in greater detail in later chapters.

Ultimately, we wish to understand the differential involvement of various factors in changing family formation patterns for different groups. That is, similar family formation trends can reflect different historical experiences. For example, we suggest, based on the research presented in this book and other recent studies, that changes in African American patterns of family formation are a function of a peculiar clustering of factors, including a history of oppressive experiences which fostered an adaptive fragility in family formation (see Brenda Stevenson's discussion of black family structure in colonial and antebellum Virginia), an ever-declining sex ratio (that became extremely critical by the 1960s in certain communities), the baby-boom-generated marriage squeeze, the declining economic viability of certain sectors of the black male population, increasing female employment, and society-wide value changes (in regard to gender roles and family formation). If we view marital change as a function of a conflux of situational constraints, then social policy must confront those constraints, rather than moralize.

REFERENCES

ALLEN, W. 1978. The search for applicable theories of black family life. *Journal of Marriage and the Family,* 40:111–129.

BECKER, G.S. 1981. *A treatise on the family.* Cambridge, MA: Harvard University Press.

BELL, R. 1970. Comparative attitudes about marital sex among Negro women in the United States, Great Britain, and Trinidad. *Journal of Comparative Family Studies,* 1:71–81.

BENNETT, N.G., BLOOM, D.E., AND CRAIG, P.H. 1989. The divergence of black and white marriage patterns. *American Journal of Sociology,* 95:692–722.

BILLINGSLEY, A. 1968. *Black families in white America.* Englewood Cliffs, NJ: Prentice-Hall.

BILLINGSLEY, A. 1992. *Climbing Jacob's ladder: The enduring legacy of African-American families.* New York: Simon & Schuster.

BLUMSTEIN, P., AND SCHWARTZ, P. 1983. *American couples.* New York: William Morrow.

BUMPASS, L.L., SWEET, J.A., AND CHERLIN, A.J. 1991. The role of cohabitation in declining rates of marriage. *Journal of Marriage and the Family,* 53:913–927.

CHERLIN, A.J. 1981. *Marriage, divorce, remarriage.* Cambridge, MA: Harvard University Press.

CLARK, K.B., AND CLARK, M.P. 1947. Racial identification and preference in children. In T.M. Newcomb and E.L. Hartley, eds., *Readings in social psychology,* pp. 551–560. New York: Henry Holt.

CLARK, M.H. 1984. Women-headed households and poverty: Insights from Kenya. *Signs: Journal of Women in Culture and Society,* 10:338–354.

COX, O.C. 1940. Sex ratio and marital status among Negroes. *American Sociological Review,* 5:937–947.

DARITY, W.A., JR., AND MYERS, S.L., JR. 1986/87. Public policy trends and the fate of the black family. *Humboldt Journal of Social Relations,* 14:134–164.

DAVIS, A., GARDNER, B.B., AND GARDNER, M.R. 1941. *Deep south.* Chicago: University of Chicago Press.

DIXON, R. 1971. Explaining cross-cultural variations in age of marriage and proportion never marrying. *Population Studies,* 25:215–233.

DRAKE, ST. CLAIR, AND CAYTON, J.R. 1945. *Black metropolis: A study of Negro life in a northern city.* New York: Harcourt, Brace.

DU BOIS, W.E.B. 1899. *The Philadelphia Negro: A social study.* Philadelphia: University of Pennsylvania.

DU BOIS, W.E.B. 1908. *The Negro American family.* Atlanta study No. 13. Atlanta: Atlanta University Publications.

EASTERLIN, R.A. 1980. *Birth and fortune: The impact of numbers on personal welfare.* New York: Basic Books.

EEKELAAR, J.M., AND KATZ, S.N. 1980. *Marriage and cohabitation in contemporary societies: Areas of legal, social, and ethnical change.* Toronto: Butterworths.

EPENSHADE, T.J. 1985. Marriage trends in America: Estimates, implications, and underlying causes. *Population and Development Review,* 11:193–245.

FRAZIER, E.F. 1957. *The Negro family in the United States.* Rev. ed., pp. 636–637. New York: Macmillan.

GLICK, P.C., HEER, D.M., AND BERESFORD, J.C. 1963. Family formation and family composition: Trends and prospects. In M.B. Sussman, ed., *Sourcebook in marriage and the family,* pp. 30–40. New York: Houghton Mifflin.

GOLDSCHEIDER, F.K., AND WAITE, L.J. 1991. *New families, no families? The transformation of the American home.* Berkeley: University of California Press.

GUTMAN, H. 1976. *The black family in slavery and freedom: 1750–1925.* New York: Pantheon.

GUTTENTAG, M., AND SECORD, P.F. 1983. *Too many women: The sex ratio question.* Beverly Hills: Sage Publications.

HILL, R.B. 1993. *Research on the African American family: A holistic perspective.* Westport, CT: Auburn House.

JACKSON, J.J. 1971. But where are all the men? *Black Scholar,* 3(4):34–41.

JEMMOTT, J.B., ASHBY, K.L., AND LINDENFELD, K. 1989. Romantic commitment and the perceived availability of opposite sex persons: On loving the one you're with. *Journal of Applied Social Psychology,* 19:1198–1211.

KARDINER, A., AND OVESEY, L. 1951. *The mark of oppression.* New York: Norton.

LICHTER, D.T., LeCLERE, F.B., AND McLAUGHLIN, D.K. 1991. Local marriage markets and the marital behavior of black and white women. *American Journal of Sociology,* 96:843–867.

LICHTER, D.T., McLAUGHLIN, D.K., KEPHART, G., AND LANDRY, D.J. 1992. Race and the retreat from marriage: A shortage of marriageable men? *American Sociological Review,* 57:781–799.

MARE, R.D., AND WINSHIP, C. 1991. Socioeconomic change and the decline of marriage for blacks and whites. In C. Jencks and P. Peterson, eds., *The urban underclass,* pp. 175–202. Washington, DC: The Brookings Institution.

McQUEEN, A.J. 1979. The adaptations of urban black families: Trends, problems and issues. In D. Reiss and H.A. Hoffman, eds., *The American family: Dying or developing,* pp. 79–101. New York: Plenum.

MOYNIHAN, D.P. 1967. The Negro family: The case for national action. In L. Rainwater and W.L. Rainwater, eds., *The Moynihan report and the politics of controversy.* Cambridge, MA: MIT Press.

NATIONAL CENTER FOR HEALTH STATISTICS. 1990. *Vital statistics of the United States, 1988,* Vol. I, *Natality.* DHHS Publication No. (PHS) 9-1100. Public Health Service. Washington, DC: U.S. Government Printing Office.

NOBLES, W. 1978. Africanity: Its role in black families. In R. Staples, ed., *The black family: Essays and studies,* pp. 19–26. Belmont, CA: Wadsworth.

OPPENHEIMER, V.K. 1988. A theory of marriage timing. *American Journal of Sociology,* 94:563–591.

POPENOE, D. 1988. *Disturbing the nest.* New York: Aldine de Gruyter.

RODGERS, W.L., AND THORNTON, A. 1985. Changing patterns of first marriage in the United States. *Demography.* 22:265–279.

ROHRER, J.H., AND EDMONSON, M.S., eds., 1964. *The eighth generation grows up: Cultures and personalities of New Orleans Negroes.* New York: Harper & Row.

ROSS, H.L., AND SAWHILL, I. 1975. *Time of transition: The growth of families headed by women.* Washington, DC: The Urban Institute.

SCANZONI, J. 1971. *The black family in modern society.* Boston: Allyn & Bacon.

SCHOEN, R. 1983. Measuring the tightness of the marriage squeeze. *Demography,* 20: 61–78.

SCHOEN, R., AND KLUEGEL, J.R. 1988. The widening gap in black and white marriage rates: The impact of population composition and differential marriage propensities. *American Sociological Review,* 53:895–907.

SECORD, P.F., AND GHEE, K. 1986. Implications of the black marriage market for marital conflict. *Journal of Family Issues,* 7:21–30.

SOUTH, S.J. 1986. Sex ratios, economic power, and women's roles: A theoretical extension and empirical test. *Journal of Marriage and the Family,* 50:19–31.

SOUTH, S.J., AND MESSNER, S.F. 1988. The sex ratio and women's involvement in crime: A cross-national analysis. *The Sociological Quarterly,* 28:171–188.

SPANIER, G.B., AND GLICK, P.C. 1980. Mate selection differentials between whites and blacks in the United States. *Social Forces,* 58:707–725.

STAPLES, R. 1981a. Race and marital status: An overview. In H.P. McAdoo, ed., *Black families,* pp. 173–175. Beverly Hills: Sage Publications.

STAPLES, R. 1981b. *The world of black singles.* Westport, CT: Greenwood Press.

SUDARKASA, N. 1981. Interpreting the African heritage in Afro-American family organization. In H.P. McAdoo, ed., *Black families.* Beverly Hills: Sage Publications.

SWEET, J.A., AND BUMPASS, L.L. 1987. *American families and households.* New York: Russell Sage Foundation.

TANFER, K. 1987. Patterns of premarital cohabitation among never-married women in the United States. *Journal of Marriage and the Family,* 49:483–497.

TAYLOR, R.J., CHATTERS, L.M., TUCKER, M.B., AND LEWIS, E. 1990. Developments in research on black families: A decade in review. *Journal of Marriage and the Family,* 52:993–1014.

TESTA, M., ASTONE, N.M., KROGH, M., AND NECKERMAN, K.M. 1989. Ethnic variation in employment and marriage among inner-city fathers. *Annals of the American Academy of Political and Social Science,* 501:79–91.

THORNTON, A. 1989. Changing attitudes toward family issues in the United States. *Journal of Marriage and the Family,* 51:873–893.

THORNTON, A.; AND FREEDMAN, D. 1982. Changing attitudes toward marriage and single life. *Family Planning Perspectives,* 14:297–303.

TUCKER, M.B. 1987. The black male shortage in Los Angeles. *Sociology and Social Research,* 71:221–227.

TUCKER, M.B., AND TAYLOR, R.J. 1989. Demographic correlates of relationship status among black Americans. *Journal of Marriage and the Family,* 51:655–665.

U.S. BUREAU OF THE CENSUS. 1950. *Statistical abstract of the United States.* 71st ed. Washington, DC: U.S. Government Printing Office.

U.S. BUREAU OF THE CENSUS. 1951a. American children: Economic characteristics of their families. *Current Population Reports,* series P-60, no. 8. Washington, DC: U.S. Government Printing Office.

U.S. BUREAU OF THE CENSUS. 1951b. *Statistical abstract of the United States.* 72nd ed. Washington, DC: U.S. Government Printing Office.

U.S. BUREAU OF THE CENSUS. 1953. *U.S. census of population: 1950*. Vol. II, *Characteristics of the population*, Part 1, United States summary. Washington, DC: U.S. Government Printing Office.

U.S. BUREAU OF THE CENSUS. 1955. *U.S. census of population: 1950*. Vol. IV, *Special reports*, Part 2, Chapter A, General characteristics of families. Washington, DC: U.S. Government Printing Office.

U.S. BUREAU OF THE CENSUS. 1961. Population characteristics: Households and families by type, 1961. *Current Population Reports*, series P-20, no. 109. Washington, DC: U.S. Government Printing Office.

U.S. BUREAU OF THE CENSUS. 1963a. *U.S. census of population: 1960*. Subject reports. Employment status and work experience. final report PC(2)-6A. Washington, DC: U.S. Government Printing Office.

U.S. BUREAU OF THE CENSUS. 1963b. *U.S. census of population: 1960*. Subject reports. Nonwhite population by race. final report PC(2)-1C. Washington, DC: U.S. Government Printing Office.

U.S. BUREAU OF THE CENSUS. 1963c. *U.S. census of population: 1960*. Subject reports. Persons by family characteristics. final report PC(2)-4B. Washington, DC: U.S. Government Printing Office.

U.S. BUREAU OF THE CENSUS. 1964. *U.S. census of population: 1960*. Vol. I, *Characteristics of the population*, Part 1, United States summary. Washington, DC: U.S. Government Printing Office.

U.S. BUREAU OF THE CENSUS. 1966. *U.S. census of population: 1960*. Subject reports. Marital status. final report PC(2)-4E. Washington, DC: U.S. Government Printing Office.

U.S. BUREAU OF THE CENSUS. 1971. Population characteristics: Marital status and family status, March 1970. *Current Population Reports*, series P-20, no. 212. Washington, DC: U.S. Government Printing Office.

U.S. BUREAU OF THE CENSUS. 1973. *U.S. census of population: 1970*. Subject reports. Persons by family characteristics. final report PC(2)-4B. Washington, DC: U.S. Government Printing Office.

U.S. BUREAU OF THE CENSUS. 1975a. *Historical statistics of the United States, colonial times to 1970*. Bicentennial ed., Part 1. Washington, DC: U.S. Government Printing Office.

U.S. BUREAU OF THE CENSUS. 1975b. *Historical statistics of the United States, colonial times to 1970*. Bicentennial ed., Part 2. Washington, DC: U.S. Government Printing Office.

U.S. BUREAU OF THE CENSUS. 1980. Marital status and living arrangements: March 1979. *Current Population Reports*, series P-20, no. 349. Washington, DC: U.S. Government Printing Office.

U.S. BUREAU OF THE CENSUS. 1982. *Statistical abstract of the United States: 1982–83*. 103rd ed. Washington, DC: U.S. Government Printing Office.

U.S. BUREAU OF THE CENSUS. 1984. *U.S. census of the population: 1980*. Vol. I, *Characteristics of the population*, Part 1, United States summary, Section A, Chapter D, Detailed population characteristics. Washington, DC: U.S. Government Printing Office.

U.S. BUREAU OF THE CENSUS. 1990a. Household and family characteristics: March 1990 and 1989. *Current Population Reports*, series P-20, no. 447. Washington, DC: U.S. Government Printing Office.

U.S. BUREAU OF THE CENSUS. 1990b. Money income and poverty status in the United States: 1989. *Current Population Reports,* series P-60, no. 168. Washington, DC: U.S. Government Printing Office.

U.S. BUREAU OF THE CENSUS. 1991a. The black population in the United States: March 1990 and 1989. *Current Population Reports,* series P-20, no. 448. Washington, DC: U.S. Government Printing Office.

U.S. BUREAU OF THE CENSUS. 1991b. Marital status and living arrangements: March 1990. *Current Population Reports,* series P-20, no. 450. Washington, DC: U.S. Government Printing Office.

U.S. BUREAU OF THE CENSUS. 1991c. *Statistical abstract of the United States: 1991.* 111th ed. Washington, DC: U.S. Government Printing Office.

U.S. BUREAU OF THE CENSUS. 1992a. Household and family characteristics: March 1991. *Current Population Reports,* series P-20, no. 458. Washington, DC: U.S. Government Printing Office.

U.S. BUREAU OF THE CENSUS. 1992b. Marriage, divorce and remarriage in the 1990's. *Current Population Reports,* series P-23, no. 180. Washington, DC: U.S. Government Printing Office.

WALKER, H.A. 1988. Black-white differences in marriage and family patterns. In S.M. Dornbusch and M.H. Strober, eds., *Feminism, children, and the new families,* pp. 87–112. New York: Guilford.

WHITEHEAD, B.D. 1993. Dan Quayle was right. *The Atlantic,* 271(4):47–84.

WILSON, W.J. 1987. *The truly disadvantaged.* Chicago: University of Chicago Press.

2 BLACK FAMILY STRUCTURE IN COLONIAL AND ANTEBELLUM VIRGINIA: AMENDING THE REVISIONIST PERSPECTIVE

Brenda E. Stevenson

B EGINNING MORE than twenty years ago, a number of prominent American historians sought to explain certain aspects of the black experience in the United States through a descriptive analysis of the development, survival, and function of the African American family.[1] Inspired by a sociopolitical movement that began to attain national prominence during the 1950s and that continued to capture public attention through the early 1970s, scholars were challenged to review this country's past for possible solutions to contemporary issues. Central to these issues were problems of racial injustice historically embedded in the notion that racial difference implied cultural inferiority or absence.

The conflicts of that era demanded not only a closer and revisionist look at the history of race relations in the nation but also a new perspective on the races themselves, their sociopolitical histories and cultural heritage. Fired by this initiative, revisionist scholars began to destroy unfounded and contradictory but popular images of blacks. They aimed their attention at powerful historical motifs found throughout scholarly, artistic, and literary texts that reduced black males to either submissive, dependent, emasculated shadows of men or violent, destructive beasts. As the woman's perspective found its place in historical

---

[1] Several important works on the black family are available. The most important book-length works that include descriptive analyses of the historic black family to emerge during this era include: Blassingame (1972), Breen and Innes (1980), Genovese (1974), Gutman (1976), Kulikoff (1986), Malone (1992), and White (1985).

27

and other academic literature, some scholars made a similar attempt to rectify denigrating depictions of black females, popularized as seductive wenches, traitorous mammies, and emasculating matriarchs.[2]

Centuries-old images and myths of blacks, many of which had become fundamental to the American social identity, were effectively challenged in intellectual and artistic circles. Revisionist scholars led the way, reexamining traditional sources of historical knowledge while unearthing and legitimizing other forms of information in their search for a "black" perspective on black historical identity and experiences. Their revolutionary work reflected a larger methodological and thematic shift occurring among historians internationally—the new "social history." Intellectuals began to view history from "the bottom up" in an affirmation of the historical importance and unabiding humanity of the "nonillustrious." In response to these social and intellectual challenges, scholars of the 1970s and 1980s were able to provide a wealth of information about the experiences of black Americans as laborers, revolutionaries, parents, religious beings, artists, philosophers, and creators of a culture and ethos that served them and the larger American society well.

In direct refutation of "traditional" history, scholarship, and social science findings that denied the existence or social importance of the preemancipation black family, revisionist scholars largely attributed the long-term survival of enslaved African Americans to the viability of the slave family as their principal sociocultural institution. Couching their discussions in the most available terms, many of these scholars were unable to resist the temptation to make implicit comparisons between the slave's marital and familial practices and those of European Americans. They inferred, through their choice of evaluative criteria, that if, and only if, they could document that the historical black family was similar in design, structure, function, and relations to that of whites, could they then effectively argue that it had positive impact on black life.

At issue in this critique, however, is not the revisionists' conclusions regarding the "worth" of the black family. These scholars have irrefutably documented, albeit conditionally, that black families were of immense importance and value to the African American individual and community. The purpose of this chapter is to scrutinize carefully the revisionist assumption that the historical black family, specifically the slave family, was similar to that of European Americans in intent or reality. Were, for example, the majority of slave families nuclear in structure? Were most slave marriages monogamous? Did most slave children grow up in households with two parents present? Were these domestic arrangements—monogamy, nuclearity, co-residential parenting—the over-

---

[2] See, for example, Blassingame's important discussion of the images of black males in southern literature and the southern white intellect and conscience (1972, pp. 132–216). Also see White's analysis of the "Jezebel" and "Mammy" images of black slave women (1985, esp. pp. 27–61) and White (1983).

whelming social and cultural ideals of slave men and women as they were for European Americans?

The basic premise asserted here is that the black family under slavery differed profoundly from that of European Americans structurally and in the ways in which family members functioned as contributors, administrators, and recipients of family resources. The slave family was not a static, imitative institution that necessarily favored one form of family organization over another. Rather, it was a diverse phenomenon, sometimes assuming several forms even among the slaves of one community. Moreover, this diversity cannot in itself be equated with a weak or flawed institution, although some variety certainly was part of the African American response to the difficulties of slave life. It also was a response to the slave's cultural difference. Far from having a negative impact, the diversity of slave marriage and family norms, as a measure of the slave family's enormous adaptive potential, allowed the slave and the slave family to survive.

Although this chapter focuses specifically on the colonial and antebellum slaves of Virginia, it has implications as well for the conditions and forms of black family life duplicated throughout the pre–Civil War South. This particular study draws on a number of sources of primary data for confirmation of its conclusions, but principally slave registers, farm books and manuals, slave narrative and autobiographical accounts, census records, and estate inventories. The first section surveys the historiography of the southern slave family principally centered on the major revisionist scholars of the 1970s and 1980s. The second section discusses the family structures, marriage styles, and familial ideals of colonial and antebellum Virginia slaves.

Old and New Revisionist Perspectives: An Overview

The prominent historian Kenneth Stampp reassured his readers in 1956:

> In Africa, the Negroes had been accustomed to a strictly regulated family and a rigidly enforced moral code. But in America the disintegration of their social organization removed the traditional sanctions which had encouraged them to respect their old customs. . . . Here, as at so many other points, the slaves had lost their native culture without being able to find a workable substitute and therefore lived in a kind of cultural chaos. (p. 340)

Stampp was only one of many pioneering scholars who, while contributing much to other aspects of the discussion of the African American experience, believed that southern blacks were unable to create a meaningful family institution because of the devastation of slavery. E. Franklin Frazier, W.E.B. Du Bois, Stanley Elkins, and others headed a list of forceful intellectuals who believed that the environment of the slave experience had been such as to exclude the development of black marriage and family norms. Revisionist historians defied this scholarship, successfully arguing that the slave was able to negotiate his or her bondage, maintain humanity, and construct a socially viable family. They were able to counter notions of black social disorganization and pathology not only by documenting slave family norms, but also by asserting that these norms were strikingly similar to those of European Americans.

Revisionist historians implied that white and black families were comparable in two important ways. First, they argued that the foundation of slave family life, like that of European Americans, was long-term, monogamous marriage. Second, they tried to demonstrate that most slaves, like whites, lived in nuclear families, that is, with parents and children present. It was not, however, just the familial structures of African Americans and European Americans that these scholars likened to one another. They also made analogous assertions about gender convention and roles within the context of domestic life.[3]

Even while labeling the slave family as uniquely "democratic" or "egalitarian," for example, revisionist historians maintained that slave men and women recognized and respected the slave man's patriarchal rights as husband and father. If the slave woman seemed to have an inordinate amount of influence on the slave family, they almost unanimously explained, it only was in the absence of her husband. The slave woman's principal domestic roles, the historians surmised, were caregiver to her children and loyal supporter of her husband.

Monogamous marriages, nuclear families in which children lived with both their parents, a wife's submission to her husband's leadership—the similarity of these "ideals" to those of the European American family is clear and deliberate in revisionist scholarship.

In *The Slave Community: Plantation Life in the Antebellum South,* Blassingame (1972) stated quite emphatically that "the Southern plantation was unique in the New World because it permitted the development of a monogamous slave family" (p. 77).[4] He argued that an equal male-female adult sex ratio among slaves that made marriage partners available, the desire of slaves

---

[3] Regarding the European American southern family of the past, see: Cashin (1990), Clinton (1982), Fox-Genovese (1988), Friedman (1985), Lebsock (1984), McMillen (1985), Morgan (1952), Scott (1970), Smith (1980), and Wyatt-Brown (1982, pp. 226–271).

For a descriptive analysis of the development of the "modern" family in the United States, see Degler (1980). He asserted four criteria for being categorized as the "modern American family," all of which recur in the recent literature of slavery scholars: the companionate marital relationship; woman's sphere centered in the home, whereas that of the male as "breadwinner," was outside at work; an increased interest in childrearing as a family function; and the development of a family limited in size to that of the mother, father, and children (pp. 8–9).

[4] Blassingame attributed this development primarily to a balanced adult sex ratio among antebellum slaves; the desire of the slaves themselves; and support of monogamy by many slaveholders who hoped to use close family relations to manipulate their slaves into obedience, to keep the slaves content, and to promote slave-quarter morality (1972, pp. 77–78, 80–81, 87–88).

to have monogamous marriages, and the religious sanction of slaveholders for slave monogamy were the key determinants of widespread monogamy among southern antebellum slaves.[5] Blassingame also explored slave family composition and relations, surveying a number of topics, including courtship rituals, marital problems, the impact of extended kin, and childbearing and -rearing. He especially was concerned with correcting the myth of the "absent" or "emasculated" slave husband and father. Although clearly sensitive to the problems of slave family and marriage, Blassingame viewed the antebellum slave family not just as a nuclear entity, but as a democratic institution "where men and women shared authority and responsibility." Yet, the "democracy" he described was one in which husbands and fathers worked hard to gain patriarchal status and authority; one in which the implied roles of the woman were dutiful mother and wife who provided food, attention, a comfortable home, and medical care. Thus, although circumstances of the slave's life might have prevented him or her from completely affecting the nuclear-core, patriarchal family of nineteenth century whites, one would surmise from Blassingame's discussion that this was the slave's ideal.[6]

His scholarly peers wholeheartedly agreed. Two years after the first edition of *The Slave Community* appeared, Eugene Genovese in *Roll, Jordan, Roll: The World the Slaves Made* (1974) was able to provide his audience with a more extensive and nuanced discussion of the slave family, but one with strikingly similar conclusions. Like Blassingame, Genovese considered the slave family to have been more "egalitarian" in nature than that of contemporary whites because he believed that slave women exercised greater household authority than white women. Yet Genovese still argued that the "impressive norms of family life" for slaves were those of monogamous marriages, nuclear families, and

---

[5] Blassingame particularly credited the impact of southern religious organizations on the survival of certain familial norms. He concluded that by the 1830s, for example, the "traditional African family the blacks remembered had been transformed," but "white churches reinforced in the quarters family patterns inherited from Africa." Yet, it is certain that the general impact of the "white church" on any part of slave life and culture is difficult to predict. Even if it was possible to do so, "white churches" undoubtedly only "reinforced" that which was culturally familiar to whites, and not that which was culturally different about blacks 1972/1979, pp. 149, 178–179).

[6] Although Blassingame noted on several occasions that the slaves encountered oppressive and abusive situations that deterred their performance in family groups in some "traditional" ways, he interpreted their family functions, relations, and structure in terms clearly defined by the model of the "modern" Western family. Discussing the function of the slave family with regard to the husband, for example, Blassingame noted that it was "in his family [that] he found companionship, love, sexual gratification, sympathetic understanding of his sufferings. . . ." The slave woman, on the other hand, could expect that her husband would be the "head of the family," provide some supplemental material support and loving attention. He chose to couch the means by which males and females received status within their families in traditional argument, ignoring other cultural influences that may have caused slaves to define their families and their experiences in them in other ways (1972/1979, pp. 78, 80, 88).

ideals of gender-differentiated domestic power that were more akin to than different from those of contemporary whites. According to Genovese, it was because of these similarities in white and black families and the "value" that slaves placed on a "two-parent, male-centered household" that freed slave families emerged in the postbellum South with a "remarkably stable base" (1974, pp. 451–452, 492).

In his extraordinary study, *The Black Family in Slavery and Freedom, 1750–1925* (1976), Herbert Gutman reinforced what by then were becoming increasingly popular beliefs among history scholars about the slave family. Although Blassingame and Genovese had outlined much of what Gutman said in his work, both the length of his book (664 pages) and its breadth (1750–1925) rendered it the most important work to emerge on slave family and marriage during this historiographical era.

From the beginning of the work, Gutman was clear about his intent. "This volume," he wrote in his introduction, "was stimulated by the bitter public and academic controversy surrounding Daniel P. Moynihan's *The Negro Family: The Case for National Action* (1965)." Moynihan, Gutman informed his audience, "had not created a fictive history" but had "reported what was then conventional academic wisdom" when he described the twentieth century black family as the root of the "tangle of pathology" characterizing African American life. Gutman's purpose was not to challenge the judgment that late twentieth century black life was socially pathological or that this pathology derived from a matriarchy. Rather, his principal goal was to demonstrate, through sound historical research, that the social problems of twentieth century blacks purportedly founded on "a fatherless matrifocal family" were not inherited from slave ancestors.[7]

Drawing on an array of primary source documents—most importantly detailed slave lists, the marriage records of freed slaves, and the testimony of former slaves—Gutman systematically made a case for southern slave family stability and basic "traditional" norms. African American slave marriages and families, he insisted, were distinct in some important ways, but "upon their emancipation most . . . ex-slave families had two parents, and most older couples lived together in long-lasting unions" (1976, p. 9). Monogamy, nuclear fami-

---

[7] Moynihan's (1965) analysis of his statistics of the mid-twentieth century black family had an immense impact on the generation of scholars of slavery that was emerging at that time. Gutman (1976) noted in his introduction, for example, that "the controversy between Moynihan and his critics sparked a preliminary study . . . which led to this book" (p. xvii). Moynihan's conclusions about the "pathology" of the black family, which derived in part from a matriarchal family unit and resulted in an emasculated and absent black husband and father, set the terms of description and analysis of the slave family that Blassingame (1972/1979), Genovese (1974), Gutman (1976), and others so ably addressed. These "terms," however, were part of an ethnocentric worldview that defined difference from the middle-class, Anglo-American norm as sociopathic. (See also Elkins, 1959; Frazier, 1939; Stampp, 1956.)

lies, and their stability clearly emerged in Gutman's study as the most important traits of slave families.[8]

Gutman's contentions are most clearly borne out in the post-emancipation documents he surveyed, especially the Union Army population census data from 1865 and 1866 and Freedmen's Bureau marriage registers. Yet, these records tell us much more about the social expectations of those recording these data and the immediate, and perhaps temporary, responses of slaves to their "freedom" than give conclusive evidence of slave marriage and familial ideals and realities. Providing some restraints to his own conclusions, for example, Genovese added the vital warning: "the postbellum record should not be projected backward" (1974, p. 501).

Although no other work of importance from the revisionist era focused specifically on antebellum southern slave marriage or family, other historians writing on related topics accepted what became termed the "Gutman thesis." Robert Fogel concluded as late as 1989, for example, that "most slaves in the United States . . . lived in 'nuclear' households consisting of two parents and children, sometimes with grandparents also present" (p. 150).[9] Even while emphasizing the "matrifocality" of slave families and the importance of the role of women in them, Jacqueline Jones in *Labor of Love, Labor of Sorrow: Black Women, Work, and the Family from Slavery to the Present* (1985) and Deborah White in *Ar'n't I a Woman?: Female Slaves in the Plantation South* (1985) unquestioningly accepted the dominance of the nuclear slave family and monogamous slave marriage as domestic structures. "The two parent, nuclear family," Jones wrote, "was the typical form of slave cohabitation regardless of the location, size, or economy of a plantation, the nature of its ownership, or the age of its slave community" (1985, p. 32). White followed suit in her exploration of female identity, labor, and power within the context of what she also termed the "egalitarian" slave family (1985, pp. 142–143, 149–160).

However, White must be credited with voicing some important "post-revisionist" views. She did establish the absolute importance of the slave woman in the slave family and, through her investigation of the colonial slave woman's experience, made important connections between an African cultural heritage and the domestic life of the antebellum slave. Indeed, most of the revisionists suggested some constraints on the Gutman thesis. Blassingame, for example, wrote vividly of some of the problems that undermined the stability of the antebellum slave family. "The family was, in short, an important survival mechanism," he concluded. "Although it was weak, although it was frequently broken" (1979, p. 191). Genovese included several warnings in his discussion,

---

[8] Gutman here wrote specifically about the Virginia slave experience but concluded similarly about slave family life throughout the South.

[9] Fogel asserted that 64 percent lived in nuclear families, 21 percent lived in one-parent families, and 15 percent lived in nonfamily households (1989, p. 150, Table 5).

including his suggestion that claims to the slave's positive familial experiences "must be read within limits—as a record of the countervailing forces even within the slavocracy but especially within the slave community" (1974, p. 451). And although Gutman clearly was more comfortable than Blassingame or Genovese with characterizing slave families as "stable," he made brilliant suggestions for future revision, maintaining that one must not "underestimate" the "adaptive capacities of the enslaved" or their "cultural difference" when trying to understand slave kinship (Gutman, 1976, p. xxi).

Colonialists were some of the first historians to take on the challenges for future scholarship that Gutman and other revisionists posed. Mechal Sobel (1987), Darrett Rutman and Anita Rutman (1984), Cheryll Ann Cody (1987), Allan Kulikoff (1986), and Phillip Morgan (1987) are among the most successful to do so. Focusing his attention on the tidewater counties of Virginia and Maryland, for example, Kulikoff in a series of articles and later in his book-length study, *Tobacco and Slaves: The Development of Southern Cultures in the Chesapeake, 1680–1800* (1986), persuasively described a relationship between the various stages of southern African American cultural development and slave kinship organization. Although conceding that the "religious beliefs, kinship systems, and forms of social organization differed substantially" among African slaves in the Chesapeake, Kulikoff assured his readers that "West Africans did share some values and experiences" (p. 317) that in some ways affected the social institutions they fashioned for themselves. Not surprisingly, his findings, which emphasize the importance of variables such as plantation size and cultural background of the slave, were different from those of revisionists. Kulikoff discovered that on large plantations only about half (47 percent) of the slaves lived in nuclear households and that on small plantations only about 18 percent did. He also documented substantial diversity in household membership, noting that the majority of slaves on either size plantation usually lived in: single-parent–child units; only with other siblings; in a number of versions of extended kin arrangements; or with no kin at all (18 to 41 percent) (1986, pp. 317, 370–372).

Historians writing about the antebellum era also have begun to qualify further, if not fundamentally challenge, some of the basic contentions of revisionist slave scholars. Jo Ann Manfra and Robert Dykstra's work, centered on the late antebellum slave experience, for example, provocatively amends the Gutman thesis. In their 1985 groundbreaking study, "Serial Marriage and the Origins of the Black Stepfamily: The Rowanty Evidence," they focused their attention on the revisionist's assumption of long-term slave monogamy. Centering their research on the domestic relationships of the last generations of slaves in Dinwiddie County, Virginia, their findings emphasized the significant rate of family breakage and remarriage that led to a large incidence of serial marriage and stepfamily formation. For the last generations of Virginia slaves residing in this southside, tobacco-producing county, long-term monogamous marriages and the nuclear families derived from them were not widely normative (Manfra and Dykstra, 1985).

Whereas Manfra and Dykstra gathered evidence of multiple marriages, family breakage, and reconstruction, in my 1990 article, "Distress and Discord in Virginia Slave Families, 1830–1860," I explored the subtleties of slave domestic conflict. Canvassing numerous sources, including slave autobiographical accounts, slave inventories, and fertility statistics gleaned from reconstructed slave family listings and census records, I questioned the dominance and functional capacity of nuclear slave families by not only documenting widespread matrifocality among late antebellum Virginia slaves, but also by tracing its impetus to both legal and logistic roots in the South as well as the sociocultural prerequisites of both slave and slaveholder. The study also reopened a discussion of slave family stability, exposing both external and internal destabilizing forces. I argued that slave families and marriages often were complicated by conflicts derived from slave owner interference (e.g., indiscriminate marriage and family breakage, the removal of black adolescents and males from their kin networks, forced breeding, and usurpation of parental control) as well as inappropriate slave social behavior (e.g., color prejudice and domestic violence).

The upper South was the focus of the Manfra and Dykstra and Stevenson studies of the antebellum era, but historians of the deep South also have contributed to this new discourse. Of particular importance is Ann Patton Malone's meticulously researched and constructed analysis of slave kinship and household composition, *Sweet Chariot: Slave Family and Household Structure in Nineteenth-Century Louisiana* (1992). Malone garnered information from an impressive 155 slave communities in Louisiana as well as from a host of other sources in order to document family relationships and structure, how they might have changed over time, and under what circumstances they did change. Malone masterfully argued that slaves lived in a variety of households and contributed to numerous kinds of kin-based relationships, both of which were subject to tremendous change over time. But she also did much more. She created from her data base a developmental model that purports to predict slave family change and stability. Her contribution to the historiography, therefore, was not just to provide new conclusions about the antebellum slave family, but also to create a new methodological approach.

Malone's findings parallel, to a certain extent, the conclusions about the Virginia slave family that are presented in this chapter. Both studies emphasize in particular the variability of slave family structure. Clearly, many conditions of the antebellum South greatly affected the family life of slaves. Location—for example, whether blacks resided in a border, deep South, or southwestern state or territory; whether they lived in a settled or frontier region; whether they had an urban or rural experience—was a very important factor. So too were demographic characteristics, work conditions, and the generation in which a slave lived. All of these variables could have a significant impact on slave marriage and family. Despite the change over time, place, and space, however, there were certain behavioral patterns and perspectives that continuously threatened slave kinship. Blacks responded to these phenomena and their own cultural difference in ways that ultimately defined their kin and social relationships as unique from those of European Americans. Herein lies the basis for the difference between the findings of this study and those of Malone.

Regardless of an innovative methodology and a sophisticated, subtle reading of her data, many of Malone's most significant conclusions still are those of the revisionists. She conceded, for example, that "all recent historians of slavery, including myself, agree that the two-parent nuclear family was the societal ideal; that the dominant household type was the simple family; and that within the simple family category, the two-parent nuclear family usually prevailed" (p. 258). The findings gleaned from this study of Virginia slave life, however, do not support Malone's notion of the "nuclear ideal" and the assertion that the "parents (or parent) and child unit was the vital core of the slave community—the model for other relationships within the larger corporate body" (p. 258).

The familial history of slaves in colonial and antebellum Virginia offers compelling evidence that many slaves did not have a nuclear structure or "core" in their families, and there is little evidence that suggests that a nuclear family was their sociocultural ideal. Virginia slave families, although demonstrating much diversity in form, essentially were not nuclear and did not derive from long-term monogamous marriages. The most discernible ideal for their principal kinship organization was a malleable extended family that provided its members with nurture, education, socialization, material support, and recreation in the face of the potential social chaos the slaveholders' power imposed. Matrifocality; polygamy; single parents; abroad spouses; one-, two-, and three-generational households; all-male domestic residences of blood, marriage, and fictive kin; single- and mixed-gender sibling dwellings—these, along with monogamous marriages and co-residential nuclear families, all comprised the familial experiences of Virginia slaves. Beneath this overwhelming record of diversity, the extended slave family remained the most consistent norm and the most clearly identifiable ideal.

Even when there existed the physical basis for a nuclear family among slaves—the presence of a husband, a wife, and their children—as it did for a significant minority, this type of family did not function as it did for blacks in precolonial Africa or whites in the colonial and antebellum South. Slave husbands never provided the sole or most significant means of financial support for their wives and children. Husbands had no legal claim to their families and, accordingly, could not legitimately demand their economic resources or offer them protection from abuse or exploitation. The primary role of the slave mother, if compared to mainstream American gender convention, also was deeply compromised, for she never was able to give the needs of her husband and children great priority. Even though most slave children were part of matrifocal families, the slave woman's most important daily activities encompassed the labor that she performed for her owner, not her family. This responsibility claimed so much of her time and energy that childbearing was limited, whereas childrearing necessarily was a task she shared with a number of females, within and outside of her blood and marriage-related family.

Likewise, although slave couples committed to monogamy may have been devoted to and able to sustain feelings of love and respect for one another over time—feelings sufficient to lead them to marry legally after emancipation—many did not have the opportunity to express such feelings for more than a few years while enslaved. Across time and space, the frequent and indiscriminate separation of slave spouses, temporarily and permanently, denied them the opportunity to live together, to share the responsibilities of their households and children, and to provide each other with sociosexual outlets.

Let us consider one example from antebellum Virginia—the family of Caroline Hunter, who was a slave in Suffolk, Virginia. Hunter lived as a small child with her mother, free black father, and three brothers. The entire family lived in "one room back of" her master's home where they all "et, slep an' done ev'ything in jus' dat one room." Although Hunter's description of her family's composition indicates a monogamous marriage and a nuclear kin group, neither the marriage nor the family remained intact very long nor ever really functioned like those of European American marriages and families of the time (Perdue, Barden, and Phillips, 1976, pp. 149–151).

The first to leave the Hunter clan was Caroline's father. "My papa didn't stay wid us ve'y long," she noted. "He left 'cause my massa beat him." Mr. Hunter was a free black who chose to live with his slave wife and children but refused to be treated as a slave. When his wife's owner beat him "till he bled" because his dog killed a sheep, Mr. Hunter left the family and went to reside in Norfolk. The nuclearity of this slave family, unlike that of southern whites, clearly did not presuppose a viable patriarchy erected on the superior economic resources of the husband and father. Mr. Hunter had no patriarchal claim to his wife or children and, once he went to live elsewhere, he was allowed to visit them only on Saturday evenings and Sundays, if at all (pp. 149–151).

Mrs. Hunter, as the head of this now matrifocal family, was left to rear her four children alone while her abroad husband resided some twenty miles away. Yet as family head, she had as little control over her destiny, much less that of her children, as her husband had had. "Many a day my ole mama has stood by an' watched massa beat her chillun 'till dey bled an' she couldn' open her mouf," Caroline Hunter added. Her adolescent brothers refused to obey their master and often received harsh whippings as a result. "I can' never forgit how my massa beat my brothers cause dey didn' wuk. He beat 'em so bad dey was sick a long time, an' soon as dey got a smatterin' better he sold 'em," she recalled.

Although Caroline Hunter's parents reunited after general emancipation, they never were able to find her oldest brother. The Hunters' postbellum status as a nuclear family and Mr. and Mrs. Hunter's monogamous marriage clearly did not indicate much of the reality of their antebellum lives (pp. 149–151).

Legal, Economic, and Cultural Factors Influencing Slave Marriage and Family

Colonial slave masters quickly established the right to define and structure the most intimate connections and activities of their slaves and servants, electing to control various aspects of their sexual behavior and family life through their power as lawmakers.[10] Legislation, which in part defined "family" for these blacks, both paralleled and contributed to the African's decline in status from that of indentured servant to that of slave. An act passed in 1662 that mandated that the children of a black female, regardless of the color or condition of their father, had to take the status of their mother had a profound effect on slave families for two centuries.[11] It not only placed a brand of perpetual servitude on the next several generations of Virginia blacks, but also provided the legal context for matrifocal kinship groups among succeeding generations of slaves.[12] As such, slaveholders not only identified a slave child's status with that of his or her mother, but routinely identified the child's parentage solely with the mother, often denying any acknowledgment of the father's role—biologically, emotionally, socially, or materially.

Within the owner's perception of an ordered domestic world, the legal association between slave mother and child reinforced the cultural dictates of their society with regard to gender-differentiated responsibility. Owners believed that slave women, as childbearers, had a natural bond with their children and that it was their responsibility, moreso than that of the children's fathers, to care for their offspring. Many masters frowned upon separating mothers from their young children but refused to act similarly for fathers. Slave owners' preferential treatment of slave mothers made it difficult for slave men to have equal influence in the day-to-day activities of their families, particularly as many

---

[10] See, for example, the numerous, early laws established in Guild (1969, pp. 21–24).

[11] The 1662 statute read: "Whereas some doubts have arisen whether children got by any Englishman upon a negro woman should be slave or free, *Be it therefore enacted and declared by this present grand assembly*, that all children borne in this country shall be held bound or free only according to the condition of the mother, *And* that if any Christian shall commit fornication with a negro man or woman, he or she offending shall pay double the fines imposed by the former act" (Hening, 1823, p. 170).

[12] For a helpful discussion of matrifocality, see Tanner (1974, pp. 129–156). See especially Tanner's definition of matrifocality (p. 131).

of them did not live with their children. It is not surprising, therefore, that among a compilation of reminiscences of Virginia former slaves, the large majority spoke of the importance of their mothers while they were growing up, but less than half referred to their fathers. Matrifocality was a fundamental characteristic of most slave families, even when fathers were present.[13]

Matrifocal slave families were not inherently problematic. Found throughout the ancestral homes of southern slaves in western and central Africa, their reappearance in the colonial and antebellum South suggests an important relationship between the slave's indigenous cultural past and present, albeit within profoundly different social contexts. The lack of control that slave mothers had of their domestic affairs as a result of colonial southern legislation and customs, to say nothing of nascent sexism, did much to undermine the stability of matrifocal slave families. Designation of a child's status as a slave, based on the legal disposition of a mother who had no protective rights over her sexual being, her reproductive organs, or the inherent financial potential of her offspring, provided owners with a substantial economic incentive to support matrifocal slave families and various breeding schemes. Even the sexual abuse of female slaves ultimately meant a financial gain for owners. Both the law of 1662, which ascribed the connection between the slave child and mother, and a 1691 act, which instructed the courts to "banish forever" those whites, free or bond, who intermarried with a Negro, mulatto, or Indian, institutionalized the degradation of Virginia slave women and the bastardization of their children.[14]

One must also consider the demographic characteristics of colonial slave life. A seventeenth century population, negatively characterized by a severe adult gender imbalance, small numbers of persons dispersed over large areas, and a high mortality rate, permitted few opportunities for slaves to marry, remain married long enough to produce children, or to structure co-residential

---

[13]Of the former slaves discussed in Perdue et al. (1976), 82 percent spoke of the physical presence of their mothers during most of their childhood years, whereas only 42 percent recalled consistent contact with their fathers. Also, fully one-third of those who did make mention of the presence of their fathers during their childhoods noted that these men did not reside on the same farm or plantation with them but lived elsewhere. As "abroad" husbands and fathers, they only visited on weekend days or holidays (Perdue, Barden, and Phillips, 1976; Rawick, 1972, p. 30). For examples of attempts of antebellum Virginia masters to sell slave mothers and children as a unit, see Virginia newspapers: *Genius of Liberty,* October 26, 1818; *Washingtonian,* October 19, 1848; *Loudoun Chronicle,* March 1, 1850.

[14]The law of 1662 also mandated that those "Christians" who had sexual relations with "negroes" were to be fined. The 1691 statute stipulated that the mulatto children born of free or servant white women and black males were to be "bound out" by church wardens until the age of thirty. The Virginia colonial legislation lowered the ages of release in 1765 to twenty-one years for males and eighteen years for females. Further legislation passed in 1753 stipulated a six-month prison term and a fine of ten pounds for whites who intermarried with blacks or mulattos. An additional law of 1792 set the fine for intermarriage at thirty dollars (Guild, 1969, pp. 26–27).

marriages or nuclear families.[15] Poor physical health, psychological distress, and their age at the time of arrival meant that African women were scarcely able to reproduce the slave population. By the mid-eighteenth century, native-born slave women were beginning to improve the population's natural growth rate. Unlike African imports, Creole slave women usually began bearing children at an earlier age, could provide their infants with natural immunities to local illness, and are believed to have had superior physical and emotional health—all of which allowed them to have more live births and perhaps healthier children. A natural increase in the black population first became important in the Virginia Chesapeake during the 1720s and 1730s and continued to improve over the decades, a testament to the importance of family and children among eighteenth century slaves. It was only then that significant numbers of slaves had an opportunity to form families (Kulikoff, 1986, pp. 68–73; see also Gundersen, 1986).

Even then, with an adult sex ratio that still favored men at least two to one in some places, many continued to suffer a lonely sociosexual existence. Moreover, many of the households and communities that colonial slaves did help to form often were not defined by blood relationships, marriage, culture, or even race, but rather by economic and production necessities. Evidence suggests, however, that slaves did manage to create strong, companionable, codependent friendships with other servants and slaves who were African, Native American, and European. The documented examples of cooperation among colonial Virginia servants and slaves of various races in group escapes and other forms of resistance, as well as the creation of early laws that were meant to provide prohibitive punishments for interracial marriages and procreation, indicate close, kinlike relationships that these early residents attempted to form with one another across racial, cultural, and conventional lines. They created their kin networks with those with whom they felt if not cultural or blood affinity, then some political or "class" affiliation as well as social and emotional compatibility. The extended family ideal, a common trait of numerous indigenous African cultures from which slaves derived, took on its broadest interpretation during the first generations of colonial southern slaves.[16]

Natural increase among the numbers of slaves eventually produced an equal adult sex ratio. This "balance," effected during the relatively long colonial era,

[15] By the end of the seventeenth century, the colony had a black population estimated between six and ten thousand, of whom males were the clear majority. The numbers arriving increased tremendously during much of the eighteenth century. Approximately 100,000 blacks, mostly Africans, entered the Chesapeake regions of Virginia and Maryland between 1690 and 1770 (Kulikoff, 1986, p. 67; Morgan, 1975, pp. 421–423; Writer's Program, 1940, p. 8).

[16] Regarding the cooperative activities of fugitive slaves and servants of various races and ethnicities, see Windley (1983); also see Mullin (1975). Regarding the African cultural heritage of groups represented among Virginia slaves, see Adaba et al. (1978), Busia (1954, pp. 196–207), Douglas (1954, pp. 2–7, 13–15), Kulikoff (1978), Little (1954, pp. 111–113, 115–135), Mbiti (1990), Mercier (1954, pp. 210–233), Paulme (1974), Piage and Piage (1981), Sargent (1982), Smith (1964), Thornton (1992).

suggested to revisionist scholars the basis for monogamous marital relationships and nuclear families among late eighteenth and nineteenth century slaves. Some emphasized the availability of slave spouses among large slaveholdings.[17] Certainly the rise in the number of slave women and the overall increase in slave population density caused a flourishing of slave marriage and family formation. However, the question of what kinds of marriages and families emerged, structurally and functionally, remains to be resolved. For example, a review of late eighteenth century and antebellum slave lists reveals that, even among large slaveholdings, many adult slaves did not marry; and among those who did marry, many did not reside daily with their spouses. Consequently, neither a majority of slave children nor adults lived in nuclear families. These were the realities of Virginia slave family life that economic, social, and cultural circumstances imposed.

Residential Patterns

Virginia colonial and antebellum planters traditionally divided their agricultural enterprises among a number of locations, establishing working farms often distributed over long distances. Slave masters staffed each farm with the slave personnel they believed best suited that farm's particular needs, rarely considering the impact of their decisions on a slave's marital or familial relationships. Evidence in the form of slave lists, which indicate residential patterns, substantiates that large Virginia slaveholders with several tobacco or grain farms to operate were not any more likely to shift the residence of a slave from one of their farms to the next in order to keep slave couples or families united than smaller slaveholders were willing to buy family members of their slaves. Both wealthy and middling slave owners routinely based such decisions on economic feasibility or necessity, not their concerns for slave family life. Thus, the assumptions by some revisionist scholars about the availability of slave spouses and the feasibility of monogamous marriages and nuclear families within large slaveholdings are not informed by the reality of slave work assignments and consequent residential patterns. The economic priorities of large slaveholders usually helped to ensure numerous abroad marriages and often eliminated favorable opportunities for permanent marital relationships, nuclear families, and uninterrupted reproduction cycles among their slaves, even after their adult sex ratio was even.

George Washington, for example, was the largest slaveholder in the northern tidewater county of Fairfax, Virginia, at the end of the eighteenth century.

---

[17] See, for example, Blassingame (1979, pp. 77–78). Kulikoff (1986, pp. 352–380), however, took into account the continued spatial distribution of colonial slave families even after there is an even sex ratio established. I concur with Kulikoff and assert here the continuation of this trend in Virginia throughout the antebellum era.

The details of the physical distribution of his slave property, as well as his wife's, are illuminating because of the size of their slaveholdings and the meticulous description Washington left of the slaves themselves—their marriages, ages, familial composition, and residential and occupational designations. According to his own compilations, Washington controlled 188 slaves in 1783, 216 in 1786, and 316 in 1799, whom he distributed among the five farms that comprised his Mount Vernon estate. The overall adult sex ratio for his slave population was excellent for a holding as large as his—1.03 in 1786 and .90 in 1799, representing a slight shift from a male to a female majority (eighty-seven men, ninety-six women) as the eighteenth century came to a close.[18]

It is clear from his diaries, correspondence, and last will and testament that Washington was aware of slave family ties and was sympathetic to them, perhaps more so than most of his peers. Yet whereas it is certain that Washington was opposed to destroying slave families through sale, it also is obvious that he routinely determined the residences of his slaves based on his labor and production needs, rather than his concern that slave couples or families share the same residence. His priorities, in turn, helped create an expansive slave community across his property—a slave community characterized by a diversity of marriage styles and family and household structures. Particularly prevalent were examples of abroad marriages, residential matrifocality, and significant numbers of single parents and adults. The patterns of family life among the Washington slaves that persisted on his farms deny that there was a preponderance of residentially nuclear families and bring into question the functional importance of monogamy even when it did exist, because many "monogamous" couples did not live together.

Among George Washington's five farms, the Mount Vernon or "home" plantation had the largest slaveholdings (see Table 2.1). Its size and the nature of the work of the house, yard, and skilled slaves, which would have brought them physically and perhaps emotionally "close" to their master, might have provided a conducive atmosphere for the maintenance of residentially nuclear families among the slaves. To some extent it did—there were six families comprised of at least a father, a mother, and their children living together at Washington's Mansion House property in 1799. But these six families characterized

---

[18] George Washington owned several thousand acres of land in Fairfax, Frederick, Loudoun, and Hampshire counties. His slave property had grown greatly over the years, constructed through purchase, slave procreation, and his marriage. Washington principally grew tobacco until the era of the Revolution and then almost abruptly began to produce wheat and other grains. Like many of the other planters in the area, he divided his slave property among his various farms and business operations, hiring some out when possible, renting some himself when necessary. He also had white indentured laborers and hired several overseers and underoverseers to supervise his slaves. Washington also sometimes used black men as overseers on his Dogue Run, River, and Muddy Hole farms ("Black Mount Vernon"; "Housing and Family Life"; "Negroes Belonging to George Washington"; "List of George Washington's Tithables"; Fitzpatrick, 1925, pp. 15–22; Padover, 1955; Ritter, 1931; Wall, 1980, pp. 55–61).

TABLE 2.1

Slave Family Household Types: Mount Vernon, 1799

Household Type	Mansion House	Muddy Hole Farm	Dogue Run Farm	Union Farm	River Farm
Nuclear	6	2	3	0	4
Couple	2	0	1	0	2
Abroad couple	0	2	2	2	3
Wife and children (husband abroad)	4	4	4	3	6
Husband (wife and children abroad)	21	1	0	0	0
Single mother, children	2	3	2	2	2
Single father, children	0	0	0	0	0
Single women	9	1	2	5	1
Single men	15	1	1	4	6
Adolescents	0	3	2	1	3
Siblings	1	0	0	0	1
Children	0	0	0	4	3

Source: "Negroes Belonging to George Washington in His Own Right and by Marriage," 1799.

the familial experiences of only a minority, or 27 percent, of the ninety-six slaves in residence at the time. The remaining persons lived quite differently. There are two obvious reasons Washington's slaves did not form more co-spousal, residential, nuclear households. First, the adult men at the Mansion House outnumbered the women by almost two to one (forty-four men, twenty-three women), allowing few of the men to marry the women who worked and resided on this part of the Washington estate. More than one-third of the Mansion House slave men were not married, and 60 percent of the married men had abroad wives. Second, Washington dispersed the members of the slave families that did exist over quite a distance, some as far as seventeen miles away and across the Potomac River on his River Farm. Others lived at the homes of friends, kin, and business acquaintances. Altogether, 61 percent of the married men (twenty-one) and women (four) at Washington's home plantation did not live with their spouses but had abroad husbands or wives. There also were two single mothers. Consequently, more slave children lived in households with only their mothers present than with both parents. Moreover, a substantial number of resident men (fifteen, or 34 percent) and women (eleven, or 48 percent) were not married at all. These single adults usually lived with extended family members, their families of birth, or in gender-segregated housing ("Negroes Belonging to George Washington").

Collectively, the other four farms that Washington owned represented even more exaggerated conditions of residential and complete matrifocality, abroad marriages, and single adults. Union Farm, Washington's last acquisition whose slaveholdings included many blacks he hired from Mrs. Daniel French, had the largest number of nonnuclear families and abroad marriages. The slave household composition on this farm is important because it exemplifies slave domesticity on newly established farms—a low incidence of co-residential marriage or of nuclear families altogether. Of the thirty-six slaves who resided at Union Farm in 1799, none lived together as a married couple or within a nuclear-structured family. There were four women with abroad husbands, three of whom were mothers residing with their children; only one married man, whose wife lived elsewhere; five single women, three of whom were mothers; four single men; three children whose mothers were abroad; and one orphan child, named Jesse.

Thus, of the 183 men and women who resided on all of Washington's five farms in 1799, only thirty lived together as married couples, whereas as many as fifty-eight (66 percent) of all those who were identified as married had abroad spouses. Many of Washington's slaves who were married, therefore, may have had monogamous relationships, but they routinely did not live with their spouses and could not provide each other with regular emotional or sociosexual support. Moreover, a sizable number of adult slaves were not married at all—32 percent of the slave men and women who resided on Union Farm, for example, were single, as were 30 percent of all the adults at Mount Vernon. Significantly, as many as 75 percent of those slave families with children did not have fathers present on a daily basis—44 percent of the slave mothers had abroad husbands, whereas 30 percent were single or had no identifiable spouses. The majority of slave mothers, therefore, raised their children in residentially or complete matrifocal structured households, without the daily support and input of fathers. Two-parent dwellings were more myth than reality on the Mount Vernon estate in 1799.

The residential patterns of George Washington's slaves provide a compelling example of the physical context in which black slaves developed their marital and familial relations. So too do the patterns of the slaves belonging to William Fitzhugh. Like Washington, Fitzhugh was a descendant of a prestigious line of Virginia planters who arrived during the seventeenth century, patented large tracts of tidewater property, imported servants, bought slaves, and established prosperous tobacco plantations. Although the emphasis of the family's business shifted over time from tobacco to grain and corn production, and Fitzhugh owned considerably more slaves than his ancestor—224 by the beginning of the nineteenth century—his blacks were quartered on three farms that comprised the Ravensworth estate.[19] Although the majority (70 percent)

---

[19] Regarding the ancestral line of William Fitzhugh and the family's life-style in seventeenth century Virginia, see Davis (1963).

lived in kin groups in 1801, 71 percent of the slave mothers on his farms lived with their children but not with their husbands. Fitzhugh's slave men, like Washington's, were much more likely to live outside of kin groups. Fully 69 percent of the sixty-eight slaves belonging to Fitzhugh who did not live in family groups, for example, were adult males, many of whom were either single or had abroad wives, or families who belonged to someone else (Sweig, 1982, pp. 116–131).

The next generation of Fitzhugh slaves, most of whom then were the property of the younger William Henry Fitzhugh, lived somewhat differently. The dwindling size of Fitzhugh's slaveholdings due to death, sale, and inheritance suggests serious consequences for this slave community that are obvious when one reviews the changes in slave family and household membership. There were only eighty-three slaves residing on the Ravensworth estate in 1830, 63 percent fewer than in 1801. Within the context of this greatly diminished slave community, the toll to slave family life is clear: although a slight majority still lived in family groups, fully 46 percent did not. Moreover, less than half of those who lived with at least one family member lived in nuclear households. The majority lived in a variety of household types, including matrifocal units, homes with only grandparent(s) and grandchildren present, and extended family groups that included varied married and blood-related kin. Thus, although the representation of nuclear families among the Fitzhugh slaves increased slightly from 1801 to 1830, the majority of his slaves still did not live in nuclear households. Moreover, the numbers of persons who lived with any blood or marriage kin at all decreased significantly (24 percent) over just twenty-nine years, a haunting indictment of what could and did happen to slave marriages, families, and communities over time (Sweig, 1982, pp. 116–131).

Slave lists from later years of the antebellum era overwhelmingly substantiate the persistence of earlier trends of diversity in slave domestic structures that physically resulted from large, and perhaps growing, numbers of abroad slave marriages, single mothers, and absent adolescent and adult males. Likewise, slave lists from Virginia counties as geographically diverse as Sussex and Gloucester in the southeast, Nottoway and Charlotte in the southern piedmont, Essex in the central tidewater region, Frederick in the north, Madison in the mountainous west, and the city of Richmond provide conclusive documentation of these kinds of domestic situations for slaves throughout the state.[20]

---

[20] Slave lists surveyed include: Fitzhugh List (Madison Co.), 1853, Ambrose Powell Hill Papers, Virginia Historical Society, Richmond, Virginia (hereafter referred to as Va. Hist. Soc.); Ledger of William and Samuel Vance Gatewood (Essex and Bath Cos.), 1772–1863, Va. Hist. Soc.; Robert and Charles Bruce Slave Lists (City of Richmond and Charlotte Co.), 1798–1859, Bruce Family Papers, Va. Hist. Soc.; William H. Gray List (Loudoun Co.), 1839–1865, Gray Family Papers, Va. Hist. Soc.; Joshua Skinner Slave List, 1785–1835, Va. Hist. Soc.; List of the Bryan Family Slaves (Gloucester Co.), 1845–1865; Grinnan Family Papers, Va. Hist. Soc.; Slave Lists of Col. C.W. Gooch (Richmond), 1830, 1839, 1852, Gooch Family Papers, Va. Hist. Soc.; Slave List of Sarah Fitzgerald (Nottoway Co.), 1864, Fitzgerald Family Papers, Va. Hist. Soc.; Digges Slave List, 1770–1860 (Frederick Co.), Digges Family Papers, Va. Hist. Soc.

Continued and perhaps increased variability among Virginia slave kinship groups is not surprising given the high volume of slaves exported from the state as part of the domestic slave trade. Slaveholders and traders shipped hundreds of thousands (almost 68,000 between 1850 and 1860 alone) of Virginia slaves to the lower South and Southwest during the pre–Civil War nineteenth century. The majority of those slaves left without spouses, children, parents, or other kin.[21] Virginia former slave Lorenzo Ivy provided a typical scenario:

> My master was very good to his slaves, and they thought a great deal of him. But all of our happy days were over when he went South and caught the cotton fever. . . . He tuk two of my aunts an' lef dere husbands up heah an' he separated all tergether seven husbands an' wives. One 'oman had twelve chillun. Yessuh! Separated dem all an' tuk 'em south wif him to Georgey an' Alabamy (Blassingame, 1979, pp. 736–737; see also Perdue, Barden, and Phillips, 1976, pp. 151–152).

When the consequences of the domestic slave trade or other economic priorities of the slave master did not disrupt slave marriages and families, the "natural" cycle of a slaveholding often did. Time and time again family fortunes dwindled and masters sold slave property to pay off debts. Slaves died from accidents, diseases, and natural causes. Owners died, too, and their slave property was divided among heirs. In every instance, slave marriages, families, and communities were threatened. Remembering the death of his master, Henry Box Brown of Louisa County, Virginia, stated: "It mattered not how benign might have been our master's conduct to us, it was to be succeeded by a harrowing scene. . . . [W]e must now be separated and divided into different lots, as we were inherited by the four sons of my master." Brown was only thirteen years old at the time, but he vividly recalled the 1829 scene that separated him and all his siblings, except the youngest, from his mother. "It is a difficult matter to satisfactorily divide the slaves on a plantation," he explained, "for no persons wishes for *all* children, or for *all* old people. . . . There is no equitable way of dividing them, but by allowing each one to take his portion of both children, middle aged and old people; which necessarily causes heart-rending separations" (Brown, 1851, p. 34).[22]

Slave registers retained in the Fitzhugh family papers and those of Colonel Claiborne William Gooch of Richmond provide an opportunity to view the kind of impact on slave family life that these changes had over time. Three Gooch family slave registers have survived: One from 1830 lists thirty-five

[21] For a discussion of the domestic slave trade, see Sutch (1975). Regarding Virginia specifically, see Manfra and Dykstra (1985, pp. 32–34), Stevenson (1990, pp. 103–124, 293–297), and Sweig (1982, pp. 189–261).

[22] Brown was born in 1816 in Louisa County but escaped to freedom in 1848. Regarding his escape, see Still (1872/1968, pp. 81–86).

slaves; another from 1839 indicates twenty-seven; and the last, dated 1852, names forty (slave lists of Colonel Gooch, 1830, 1839, 1852). The slave list from 1830 does not designate family groups; those dated 1839 and 1852 do (see Table 2.2). When one analyzes the Gooch documents, general patterns of matrifocal structures in children-inclusive, nonnuclear households appear. For example, whereas 70 percent of the Gooch slaves lived in blood-related kin groups in 1839, three of the five residential family units among these slaves were comprised only of a mother and her children. Remarkably, the numbers of Gooch slaves living with family members (i.e., blood relations or spouses) increased by the next generation (represented by the 1852 list) to include virtually everyone. Yet, out of the nine discernible family households, only one-third were two-parent inclusive or residentially nuclear.[23] Six, or the remaining two-thirds, were households that included only one parent and his or her children— five were mother-present, again indicating the prevalence of matrifocal families, and only one included a father and his children (slave lists of Colonel Gooch, 1830, 1839, 1852).

What perhaps is even more indicative of challenges to and change of family life among these slaves, however, is evidence of slave community dispersal and possible destruction. Comparing the Gooch list of 1830, for example, to those of 1839 and 1852 suggests such a pattern. Of the thirty-five Gooch slaves listed in 1830, twenty-one (60 percent) did not reappear on the slave registers of 1839 or 1852. Over half of the Gooch slave community, nine males and eleven females, disappeared between 1830 and 1839. Sale and high mortality rates undoubtedly produced this extreme loss in the Gooch slave community and families during this nine-year period. A note written on the 1830 list provides details of the fate of some of these slaves: "Sell Juliet and child and Milly and put two boys in their places. . . . Sell William and replace him with a likely Tractable boy for the house—hire some of the young females out—and put out others for their victuals and clothes" (slave list of Colonel Gooch, 1830).

It is clear that such monumental losses over a relatively short period of time (twenty-two years) not only placed a tremendous burden on slave marriages and families as well as the general slave community, but forced slaves to continuously restructure their families and communities in order to respond to these losses and the addition of other slaves that owners bought or rented to meet new and changing labor needs. Under such circumstances, no other kinship structure than the malleable, broadly inclusive extended family was available to slaves that could provide a modicum of persistent stability. Certainly, extended slave families experienced extreme pressures, but they persisted to support those

---

[23]There also was a two-generational parent-inclusive household noted in the 1852 list: the elderly couple Aaron and Sukey, their three children—Lavinia, Julia, and Richard—and the youngest generation of their family, Lavinia's unnamed child of nineteen or twenty months (Slave Lists of Colonel C.W. Gooch, 1839, 1852, Gooch Family Papers, Va. Hist. Soc.).

remnants of slave marriages and nuclear families that did not survive or those abroad marriages, matrifocal families, single adults, and orphans who needed greater institutionalized familial support.

Slave Marriage and Family Ideals

The preponderance of evidence drawn from the slave registers and from the autobiographical accounts of slaves substantiates that Virginia slaves had a variety of marriage and family structures, especially matrifocality, abroad spouses, and extended family networks. The data also identify the problematic nature of slave domestic relations and some of the sources of those problems. What remains to be investigated is the question of slave marriage and family ideals. Although it is difficult to prove conclusively, some slaves may have willingly,

TABLE 2.2

Slave Families, Unattached Adults, Adolescents, and Children
Among Holdings of Colonel Claiborne Gooch, Richmond, Virginia

1830 (family ties not available)

Females (age)	Males (age)
Old Eve (about 62)	Prince (49)
Jane (59)	William (30)
Nelly (30)	Turner (25)
Sarah (30)	Tom (21)
Aggy (26)	Nelson (18)
Aggy's two [children]	Dick (17)
Juliet (21)	Patrick (14)
Lydia (19)	William (11)
Lydia's one [child]	Lewis (?)
Anna (14)	Dixon (?)
Patty (?)	Davy (1)
[?]bira (12)	Solomon (3)
Lavinia (12)	Hunter (3)
Milly (11)	Henry (1)
Harriet (8)	
Apphia (7, daughter to Sarah)	
Patsy (6)	
Betsy (5)	
Georgianna (4, daughter to Sarah)[a]	
Sophia (1, daughter to Nelly)	

[a]Georgianna and Georgiana refer to same person. Spelling was recorded differently in the two lists.

1839 (family groups indicated)

John (32) and Polly (30)
  Vinny (daughter, 7)
  Caroline (daughter, 6)

Sarah (about 39)
  Apphia (daughter, 15)
  Georgiana (daughter, 13)[a]
  Mary (daughter, 8)
  Matilda (daughter, 3)

Lydia (28)
  Hardenia (daughter, 6)
  Mahala (daughter, 1)

Children and adolescents without designated family ties
  Emanuel (12)
  Solomon (12)
  Horace (10)
  Peter (?)

Adults without designated family ties
  Turner (about 32)
  Nelson (27)
  Anthony (36)
  Tom (30)

Patrick (23) and Anna (22)
  George (son, few days old)

Nelly (38)
  Sophia (daughter, 9)
  Margaret (daughter, 6)
  Ellen (daughter, 1)

1852 (family groups indicated)

Patrick (37) and Anna (35)
  Mary Jane (12)
  Tom Princer (10)
  Charles (6)
  Beverly (4)
  Adeline (2)
  Edward (4 months)

Mary (44)
  Sarah (20)
  Solomon (18)
  Joe (16)
  Fanny Ellen (16)
  Mary Ann (14)
  Linsy (12)
  Elisabeth (9)
  Jane (6)

Matilda (36)
  Henry (15)
  Laura (12)
  Robert (10)
  Alice (7)

Aaron (62) and Sukey (56)
  Julia (15)
  Richard (12)
  Lavinia
  Lavinia's child (19 or 20 months)

Nelson (43 [or 40?]) and Judy (33)
  Jim (son, 2)

Turner (45)
  Evelyn (7)

Sarah (50)
  George (27)
  Big Solomon (23)

Milly (33)
  William (12)

Sophy (20)
  Molly (10)

or willfully, "chosen" marital or familial structures other than those that could be termed monogamous or nuclear. For example, regard for rules of exogamy aside, it is known that many slave men chose to marry women who did not live on their farm or plantation, ostensibly because it allowed the owner less control and it protected either spouse from witnessing the other's abuse (Blassingame, 1979, pp. 164–165). Many examples of abroad marriages and the matrifocal households that resulted, therefore, did not all exist solely because of an owner's interference. Neither did the substantial rate of serial marriage nor did rare examples of polygamy persist throughout Virginia slave history because blacks lacked control of their domestic lives. For example, Manfra and Dykstra's (1985, p. 32) survey of late antebellum slave couples who resided in the southside of Virginia indicates that of those slave marriages terminated before general emancipation, 10.1 percent ended as a result of mutual consent, and another 10.8 percent ended because of spousal desertion. Blassingame concluded similarly for slave couples living in Mississippi, Tennessee, and Louisiana (1972/1979, Tables 1 and 2). Certainly, these voluntary breaks—attributable to incompatibility with one's partner, feelings of betrayal, or a host of other problems that might plague any marriage—supported the development of some serial slave marriages. They also support the assertion that slaves exercised choice in their private lives, and some chose not to have monogamous marriages or nuclear families (Blassingame, 1972/1979, Tables 1 and 2, p. 90; Manfra and Dykstra, 1985, p. 32).

Consider, for example, former slave Israel Massie's insistence that Virginia slave men and women "understood" and sought out polygynous marital relationships. Polygyny, where it occurred, did not foster the development of nuclear families, but rather matrifocal households and a broad-based extended family network such as found throughout Virginia slave communities. "Naw, slaves didn't have wives like dey do now. I'll tell ya de way we useta do. Ef I liked ya, I jes go an' tell marster I wanted ya an' he give his consent—dat's on de same plantation ef both slaves wuz his," Massie began his description. "Ef I see another gal over dar on another plantation, I'd go an' say to de gal's marster, 'I want Jinny fer a wife'. . . . I got two wives now, ain't I? Hit may be still another gal I want an' I'll go an' git her. Allright now, dars three wives an' slaves had as many wives as dey wanted. Do ya kno' women den didn't think hard of each other? Got 'long fine together." Massie went on to illustrate late antebellum slave polygyny with an example from his own farm. "When Tom died," he added, "dar wuz Ginny, Sarah, Nancy, an' Patience. All four dar at de grave crying over dat one man. Do ya kno' . . dem women never fou't, fuss, an' quarrel over dem men folks? Dey seemed to understood each other. Yes siree! Not any bit of hit" (Perdue, Barden, and Phillips, 1976, p. 209).

Polygyny, or something akin to it in which a slave man had long-standing, contiguous intimate relationships with more than one woman, probably was a much more popular alternative to monogamy than has been realized. The unavailability of marriageable slave men in those slave communities that were hit particularly hard by the domestic slave trade provided the physical conditions for such behavior. Minimal knowledge of ancestral domestic arrangements (in Islamic and many traditional religious groups) also could have provided its cultural sanction among some slaves. Yet, few records remain of polygyny practiced among antebellum slaves, probably because these kinds of marriage arrangements could not be legalized after general emancipation.

Given the predilection of local churches, northern missionaries and teachers, and Freedmen's Bureau representatives in the postbellum South to establish monogamy as the only choice of marriage relationships among freed slaves, it is not surprising that "recorders" of freedmen's domestic relations ignored postbellum polygynous or polygamous relationships. More than a few probably appear in the official records of that day as mere "promiscuous couplings" of one kind or another, "immoral" behavior, or adultery. Likewise, black men and women who were recently freed undoubtedly felt pressure to change this aspect of their lives, or at least to camouflage it from public view.

Massie again is instructive in his description of what became of polygamous relationships once slaves were freed at the end of the Civil War: "Now, out of all dem wives, when Lee surrendered, ya choose from dem one 'oman an' go an' git a license an' marry her. Some turned all dey wives loose an' got a new wife from some t'other place." Although he offered no real explanation of why postbellum Virginia slaves abandoned polygyny as a viable marital structure, he (and probably many others) clearly was aware that it was illegal for free men to have more than one wife. Former slaves hoping to legitimize their domestic world through acquisition of the marriage license had to publicly abandon polygyny. Regardless of the reason for this postbellum change, it is clear that Massie and the slaves he referred to acted as if monogamy, or even serial monogamy, were not the only marriage alternatives they had (Perdue, Barden, and Phillips, 1976, p. 209).

The slave's cultural heritage, complex rules of exogamy operative among African American slaves, a desire to extend one's social world beyond one's residential community, and the psychological need to establish some "emotional distance" between oneself and one's loved ones all contributed to the "choices" slaves made about their domestic lives given the rigid constraints their masters imposed. They also inform us about possible marriage and family ideals.

The slaves' intense concern not to marry a close blood relation, for example, probably also greatly influenced the numbers of abroad marriages that existed. On the farms and plantations where generations of intermarriage and procreation had created intricate and complex kinship ties, probably only discernible to a member of that slave community, black men and women could find few choices for a spouse because they had to avoid marriage with a close blood relation. This kind of avoidance is practically undetectable by scholars who have to rely on slave lists produced by owners or overseers who rarely would concern themselves with the minute details of these kinds of slave intimacies. Yet, clearly many masters realized that their slaves were upholding stringent rules of exogamy. Georgia Gibb recalled that her master "never sell none of his slaves, but he'd always buy more. . . . [D]at keeps de slaves from marrying in dere famblies" (Perdue, Barden, and Phillips, 1976, p. 105). Thus, she identifies her owner's knowledge of his slaves' respect for such rules. Numerous stories circulated among slaves about the shame and horror associated with someone marrying a close blood relation likewise expressed explicit rules of exogamy that were at play in Virginia slave communities and that inspired slaves to marry someone abroad.[24]

The practice of male slaves marrying a woman who did not live close by also can be linked to African American conventions of manhood that both free blacks and slaves shared. Black men in Virginia viewed travel and the "adventure" associated with it as a "natural" desire and activity of a "man." "In the year 1827, a spirit of adventure, natural to most young men, took possession of me, and I concluded to leave Virginia and go to Ohio," John Malvin, a Virginia free black, confessed. "Slaves always wanted to marry a gal on 'nother plantation 'cause dey could git a pass to go visit 'em on Saddy nights," former slave Tom Epps recalled. Massie's description of polygamous marriages that allowed some slave men to have two or three wives on different farms not only suggested the sociosexual pleasure men gained from polygamy and the "freedom" to enjoy it that abroad marriages allowed, but also the delight they gained from the "travelling" necessary to maintain multiple intimate relationships.[25]

Conclusions

Whereas the issue of "force" versus "choice" and all the sociopolitical and cultural variables that are involved obscure an unimpeachable decision as to the slaves' marriage and familial ideals, three conclusions have been substantiated. First, neither monogamous marriages nor nuclear families dominated slave family forms. Matrifocal families, abroad spouses, and extended families were very prevalent. Second, slave marriages and families exhibited a diversity of form and relationship that marked them substantially different from those of European

---

[24] Slaves often taught each other rules of exogamy through the stories they told of "mistaken" marriages between two persons too closely related by blood.

[25] Masters allowed abroad husbands, not wives, to visit their spouses, usually one day a week (Saturday evening through Sunday evening), if the woman did not live a great distance away (Malvin, 1879/1988, p. 37; Perdue, Barden, and Phillips, 1976, pp. 89, 209; Rawick, 1972, p. 45).

Americans. Even when slaves did live in nuclear households and sustained monogamous marriages, these institutions did not function similarly to those of contemporary whites. Third, the slaves' ideals of marriage and family were not imitative or necessarily sanctioned by European Americans. Rather, they were variable, uniquely multifaceted, and complexly derived culturally and socially.

REFERENCES

ADABA, G., BEKOMBO-PRISO, M., MOGEY, J., AND OPPONG, C., eds. 1978. *Marriage, fertility and parenthood in West Africa.* Canberra: Australian National University.

Black Mount Vernon. From the collection at the Mount Vernon Library, Fairfax County, Virginia.

BLASSINGAME, J.W. 1972. *The slave community: Plantation life in the antebellum South.* New York and London: Oxford University Press.

BLASSINGAME, J.W. 1977. Introduction. In J.W. Blassingame, ed., *Slave testimony: Two centuries of letters, speeches, interviews and autobiographies,* pp. xvii–lxv. Baton Rouge: Louisiana State University Press.

BLASSINGAME, J.W. 1979. *The slave community: Plantation life in the antebellum South* (revised and enlarged edition). New York and Oxford: Oxford University Press.

BREEN, T.H., AND INNES, S. 1980. *"Myne owne ground": Race and freedom on Virginia's Eastern Shore, 1640–1676.* New York: Oxford University Press.

BROWN H.B. 1851. Narrative of Henry Box Brown. Philadelphia: Rhistoric Publications (1969).

BUSIA, K.A. 1954. The Ashanti. In Daryll Forde, ed., *African worlds: Studies in the cosmological ideas and social values of African peoples,* pp. 190–209. London: Oxford University Press.

CASHIN, J.E. 1990. The structure of antebellum planter families: "The ties that bound us was strong." *Journal of Southern History,* 56:55–70.

CLINTON, C. 1982. *The plantation mistress: Women's world in the Old South.* New York: Pantheon.

CODY, C.A. June 1987. There was no "Absalom" on the Ball plantation: Slave-naming practices in the South Carolina low country, 1720–1865. *American Historical Review* 92,2:563–596.

DAVIS, R.B., ed. 1963. *William Fitzhugh and his Chesapeake world, 1676–1701: The Fitzhugh letters and other documents.* Chapel Hill: University of North Carolina Press.

DEGLER, C. 1980. *At odds: Women and the family in America from the Revolution to the present.* New York: Oxford University Press.

DOUGLAS, M. 1954. The Lele of Kasai. In Daryll Forde, ed., *African worlds: Studies in the cosmological ideas and social values of African peoples,* pp. 1–26. London: Oxford University Press.

ELKINS, S. 1959. *Slavery: A problem in American institutional and intellectual life.* Chicago: University of Chicago Press.

FITZPATRICK, J.C., ed. 1925. *The diaries of George Washington, 1748–1799.* Vol. 3, *1786–1788.* Boston: Houghton Mifflin.

FOGEL, R. 1989. *Without consent or contract: The rise and fall of American slavery.* New York: Norton.

FOX-GENOVESE, E. 1988. *Within the plantation household: Black and white women of the Old South.* Chapel Hill: University of North Carolina Press.

FRAZIER, E.F. 1939. *The Negro family in the United States.* Chicago: University of Chicago Press.

FRIEDMAN, J.E. 1985. *The enclosed garden: Women and community in the evangelical south, 1830–1900.* Chapel Hill: University of North Carolina Press.

GENOVESE, E. 1974. *Roll, Jordan, roll: The world the slaves made.* New York: Vintage.

GUILD, J., ed. 1969. *Black laws of Virginia: A summary of the legislative acts of Virginia concerning Negroes from the earliest times to the present.* Reprint. New York: Negro Universities Press.

GUNDERSEN, J.R. 1986. The double bonds of race and sex: Black and white women in a colonial parish. *Journal of Southern History,* 52:351–372.

GUTMAN, H. 1976. *The black family in slavery and freedom, 1750–1925.* New York: Pantheon.

HENING, W.W., ed. 1823. *The statutes at large of Virginia (1619–1682).* Vol. 2. New York: R. & W. & G. Bartow.

Housing and family life of the Mount Vernon Negro. From the collection at the Mount Vernon Library, Fairfax County, Virginia.

JONES, J. 1985. *Labor of love, labor of sorrow: Black women, work, and the family from slavery to the present.* New York: Basic Books.

KULIKOFF, A. 1978. The origins of Afro-American society in Tidewater Maryland and Virginia, 1700 to 1790. *William and Mary Quarterly* (3rd series), 35:226–259.

KULIKOFF, A. 1986. *Tobacco and slaves: The development of Southern cultures in the Chesapeake, 1680–1800.* Chapel Hill: University of North Carolina Press.

LEBSOCK, S. 1984. *The free women of Petersburg: Status and culture in a southern town, 1784–1860.* New York: Norton.

A list of George Washington's Tithables in Fairfax County in June 4th 1761, 1762, 1763, [. . .] 1774, 1786–1789. From the collection at the Mount Vernon Library, Fairfax County, Virginia.

LITTLE, K. 1954. The Mende in Sierra Leone. In Daryll Forde, ed., *African worlds: Studies in the cosmological ideas and social values of African peoples,* pp. 111–137. London: Oxford University Press.

MALONE, A.P. 1992. *Sweet chariot: Slave family and household structure in nineteenth-century Louisiana.* Chapel Hill: University of North Carolina Press.

MALVIN, J. 1988. *The autobiography of John Malvin, free Negro, 1795–1880.* Allan Peskin, ed. Kent, OH: Kent State University Press. (Original work published 1879.)

MANFRA, J.A., AND DYKSTRA, R.P. 1985. Serial marriage and the origins of the Black stepfamily: The Rowanty evidence. *Journal of American History,* 72:18–44.

MBITI, J.S. 1990. *African religions and philosophy.* 2nd ed. Oxford: Heinemann International.

MCMILLEN, S. 1985. Women's sacred occupation: Pregnancy, childbirth, and early infant rearing in the antebellum south. Unpublished Ph.D. dissertation, Duke University.

MERCIER, P. 1954. The Fon of Dahomey. In Daryll Forde, ed., *African worlds: Studies in the cosmological ideas and social values of African peoples,* pp. 210–234. London: Oxford University Press.

MORGAN, E.S. 1952. *Virginians at home: Family life in the eighteenth century.* Williamsburg, VA: Colonial Williamsburg Foundation.

MORGAN, E.S. 1975. *American slavery, American freedom: The ordeal of colonial Virginia.* New York: Norton.

MORGAN, P. 1987. Three planters and their slaves: Perspectives in slavery in Virginia, South Carolina and Jamaica, 1750–1790. In W.D. Jordan and S. Skemp, eds., *Race and family in the colonial south,* pp. 37–79. Jackson, MS: University of Mississippi Press.

MOYNIHAN, D.P. 1965. *The Negro family: The case for national action.* Washington, DC: U.S. Dept. of Labor, Office of Policy Planning and Research.

MULLIN, G. 1975. *Flight and rebellion: Slave resistance in eighteenth-century Virginia.* New York: Oxford University Press.

Negroes belonging to George Washington in his own right and by marriage, 1799. From the collection at the Mount Vernon Library, Fairfax County, Virginia.

PADOVER, S.K. 1955. *The Washington papers: Basic selections from the public and private writings of George Washington.* New York: Harper.

PAULME, D. 1974. *Women of tropical Africa.* Berkeley: University of California Press.

PERDUE, C.L., BARDEN, T.E., AND PHILLIPS, R.K., eds. 1976. *Weevils in the wheat: Interviews with Virginia ex-slaves.* Charlottesville: University Press of Virginia.

PIAGE, J., AND PIAGE, K. 1981. *The politics of reproductive ritual.* Berkeley: University of California Press.

RAWICK, G.P., ed. 1972. *American slave: Vol. 16, Virginia.* Westport, CT: Greenwood.

RITTER, H.L. 1931. *Washington as a business man.* New York: Sears.

RUTMAN, C.B., AND RUTMAN, A.H. 1980. "Now-wives and sons-in-law: Parental death in a seventeenth century Virginia county." In T.W. Tate and D.L. Ammerman, eds., *The Chesapeake in the seventeenth century: Essays on Anglo-American society,* pp. 153–182.

RUTMAN, C.B., AND RUTMAN, A.H. 1984. *A place in time: Middlesex county, Virginia 1650–1750.* New York: Oxford University Press.

SARGENT, C. 1982. *Maternity, medicine and power: Reproductive decisions in urban Benin.* Berkeley: University of California Press.

SCOTT, A. 1970. *The southern lady from pedestal to politics, 1830–1930.* Chicago: University of Chicago Press.

SMITH, D.B. 1980. *Inside the Great House: Planter family life in eighteenth century Chesapeake society.* Ithaca, NY: Cornell University Press.

SMITH, M. 1964. *Baba of Karo: A woman of the Moslem Hausa.* New York: Praeger.

SOBEL, M. 1987. *The world they made together: Black and white values in 18th century Virginia.* Princeton: Princeton University Press.

STAMPP, K. 1956. *The peculiar institution: Slavery in the ante-bellum South.* New York: Random House.

STEVENSON, B. 1990. Distress and discord in Virginia slave families, 1830–1860. In C. Bleser, ed., *In joy and in sorrow: Women, family and marriage in the Victorian South,* pp. 103–124, 293–297. New York: Oxford University Press.

STILL, W., ed. 1968. *The underground railroad: A record of facts, authentic narratives, letters, etc.* New York: Arno. (Original work published 1872.)

SUTCH, R. 1975. The breeding of slaves for sale and the westward expansion of slavery, 1850–1860. In S.L. Engerman and E.D. Genovese, eds., *Race and slavery in the western hemisphere*, pp. 173–210. Princeton: Princeton University Press.

SUTCH, R. 1982. *Northern Virginia slavery: A statistical and demographic investigation.* Unpublished Ph.D. dissertation, College of William and Mary.

SWEIG, D.M. 1982. Northern Virginia slavery: A statistical and demographic investigation. Ph.D. dissertation, College of William and Mary.

TANNER, N. 1974. Matrifocality in Indonesia and Africa and among black Americans. In M.Z. Rosaldo and L. Lamphere, eds., *Woman, culture and society*, pp. 129–156. Stanford: Stanford University Press.

THORNTON, J. 1992. *Africa and Africans in the making of the Atlantic World, 1400–1680.* Cambridge: Cambridge University Press.

WALL, C.C. 1980. *George Washington: Citizen-soldier.* Charlottesville: University Press of Virginia.

WHITE, D. 1983. Female slaves: Sex roles and status in the antebellum plantation South. *Journal of Family History*, 3:248–261.

WHITE, D. 1985. *Ar'n't I a woman?: Female slaves in the plantation South.* New York: Norton.

WINDLEY, L.A., ed. 1983. *Runaway slave advertisements: A documentary history from the 1730s: Vol. 1. Virginia and North Carolina.* Westport, CT: Greenwood.

WOODWARD, C.V. 1974. History from slave sources: A review article. *American Historical Review*, 79:470–481.

Writer's Program of the Work Projects Administration in the State of Virginia (Comp.). 1940. *Negro in Virginia.* New York: Hastings.

WYATT-BROWN, B. 1982. *Southern honor: Ethics and behavior in the Old South.* New York: Oxford University Press.

SECTION TWO

Sociological Antecedents of African American Marital Patterns

3

THE EFFECT OF EMPLOYMENT ON MARRIAGE AMONG BLACK MALES IN INNER-CITY CHICAGO

Mark Testa
and
Marilyn Krogh

A PROMINENT explanation for the declining level of marriages among blacks is the growing joblessness of black males. A long literature in sociology links rates of marital disruption (divorce, separation, and desertion) with the inability of fathers to provide stable financial support to their families (Moynihan, 1965; Scanzoni, 1982). Recent writings hypothesize a similar link between male joblessness and never-married parenthood (Cherlin, 1981; Wilson, 1987). Although initial evidence for these relationships appeared mixed (Lerman, 1989), recent empirical investigations demonstrate a robust association between male employment and marriage (Ellwood and Rodda, 1990; Fossett and Kiecolt, 1993; Lichter, LeClere, and McLaughlin, 1991; Lichter et al., 1992; Testa et al., 1989). The findings are less conclusive for nonmarital parenthood (Plotnick, 1988; South and Lloyd, 1992), and a number of studies question the overall importance of male joblessness as an explanation for recent trends in marriage and nonmarital fertility (Vinovskis, 1988; Mare and Winship, 1991; Testa, 1991).

This chapter provides new evidence on the relationships among male employment, nonmarital parenthood, and marriage. It draws on retrospective event-history data collected by the National Opinion Research Center (NORC) for the 1987 Urban Poverty and Family Structure (UPFS) survey in Chicago. The sample frame was restricted to census blocks (primary sampling units) in which 20 percent or more of the 1980 residents of the tract had family incomes below the federal poverty line. The geographical area encompassed by these poverty tracts constitutes for the purposes of this study the inner city of Chicago. This paper focuses on the 415 black men in the sample.

The large number of black men in the sample who fathered their first child out of wedlock ($N = 247$) enables us to estimate the effect of employment on marriage after conception (legitimation) as well as on marriage before conception (conventional marriage). We estimate these models for the entire sample of black men born between 1941 and 1969 and for separate birth cohorts. We also estimate a model of the relationship between employment and premarital conception. We use hazards regression methods to explore the effects of employment and other variables on these marital and parental transition rates.

The chapter begins by considering alternative hypotheses of variation in the relationship between male employment and marriage over time. We discuss the sample data and methods of analysis in the third section and present our results in the fourth section. We find that while the age-specific rate of marriage has declined for successive cohorts of black men, the age-specific rate of fatherhood has remained constant. As a result, successively larger fractions of cohorts of black fathers are unmarried at the conception of their first child. During this same period, successively smaller fractions of cohorts of black men are stably employed. Compared to men who are out of work and not in school or the military, men in stable employment are substantially more likely to marry. While marriage rates have declined across cohorts, cohort-specific analyses show that the decline in marriage has been much more precipitous among nonemployed men than among employed men. As a consequence of the diverging marriage rates between working and nonworking men, the relationship between male employment status and marriage is strengthening over time. Although these results are consistent with theories of the ghetto underclass (Wilson, 1987), they should be regarded as provisional. Replications of these findings with other samples will be necessary to assess whether they are artifacts of sample selection or indicators of valid trends. We discuss some public policy implications of these findings later in the chapter.

Theoretical Perspectives

Until recently, most men and women could be expected to marry and then have children. Consequently, most theoretical discussions of marriage have focused on conventional marriage (before conception of a child) and on marital stability. Two theories explicitly predict a positive relationship between male employment and marriage. Economic theories posit that the initiation and continuation of marriage depend on the advantages of marriage relative to nonmarriage (Becker, 1981). Social exchange theories posit that marital stability depends on each partner's fulfilling his or her expected roles (Scanzoni, 1982). Under a "traditional" division of market and domestic labor, earnings support from the man increases the financial advantages of marriage for the woman and fulfills traditional role expectations for the man. From either partner's perspective, male joblessness decreases the attractiveness of their marrying and staying together.

Less systematic consideration has been given to the effects of male employment status on marriages which occur during pregnancy or after the child's birth. Even studies of blacks, whose rates of premarital pregnancy have long exceeded whites, frequently neglected the factors affecting post-conception marriages. This was understandable when most black single-parent families were the consequence of divorce, separation, or desertion. But now that most black single-parent families result from never-married parenthood, and white out-of-wedlock childbearing has increased, greater consideration must be given to the factors affecting marriage after a premarital conception.

Figure 3.1 charts trends in the percentage of firstborn black children who were conceived out of wedlock and the percentage of these pregnancies that resulted in marriage before the child's birth. Estimates are derived from the responses of women in the 1980 and 1982 Current Population Surveys (O'Connell and Rogers, 1984) and in the 1987 UPFS survey. There is remarkable similarity between the two samples. The differences reflect the higher concentration of poor people in the Chicago sample. Since the early 1960s the percentage of out-of-wedlock conceptions among blacks has risen nationally and in Chicago, while the percentage of premarital pregnancies that are legitimated prior to the child's birth has declined. Both trends have contributed to the rise in the percentage of black single-parent families.

Trends in post-conception marriages can readily be studied within existing theoretical frameworks. However, neither economic nor social exchange theories provide explicit guidance on how economic and noneconomic factors possibly interact when the birth of a child is impending. Even though male joblessness is expected to reduce post-conception marriage rates, changes in other factors, such as the stigma of illegitimacy, the availability of welfare, and the mother's access to extended familial support, can interact with male employment to strengthen or dilute the effects on marriage over time.

We now discuss five hypotheses concerning variation over time in the relationship between male employment and post-conception marriage which have some validity in theory or empirical studies. These five alternatives are diagrammed in Figure 3.2. We assess the validity of these alternative hypotheses with our sample data in our Discussion section.

No Relationship
Between Male Employment and Declining Marriage Rates

The first alternative is the null hypothesis of no relationship between male employment and marriage. It asserts that expectant couples decide to marry or

FIGURE 3.1

Firstborn black children conceived out of wedlock and proportion resulting in marriage before child's birth (based on responses by women).

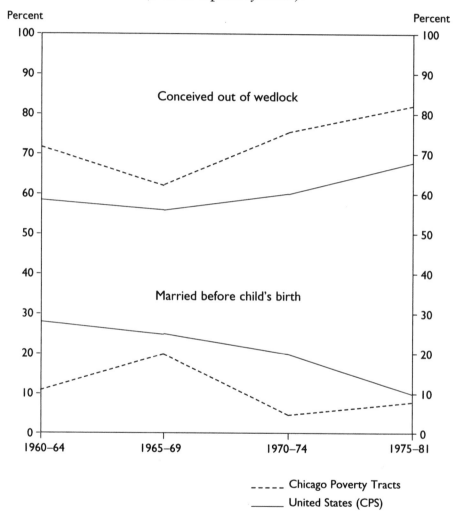

Percent   Percent

Conceived out of wedlock

Married before child's birth

1960–64   1965–69   1970–74   1975–81

- - - - - Chicago Poverty Tracts
————— United States (CPS)

FIGURE 3.2

Hypothetical relationships between marriage and male employment.

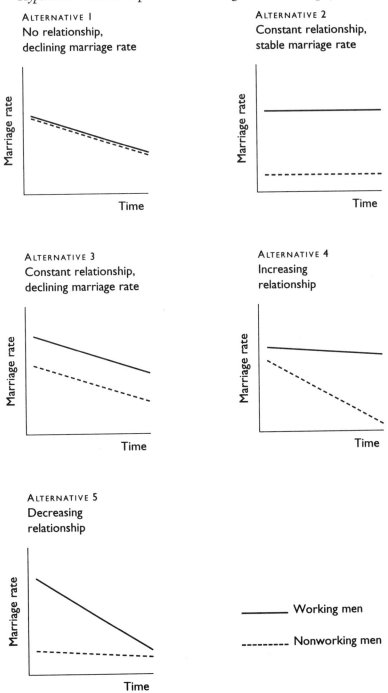

ALTERNATIVE 1
No relationship,
declining marriage rate

ALTERNATIVE 2
Constant relationship,
stable marriage rate

ALTERNATIVE 3
Constant relationship,
declining marriage rate

ALTERNATIVE 4
Increasing
relationship

ALTERNATIVE 5
Decreasing
relationship

——— Working men

--------- Nonworking men

to remain single for reasons that are largely separate from the employment status of the father. If true, it would mean that the decline in post-conception marriage rates must depend on factors other than increased male joblessness. Although there is little theoretical backing for this hypothesis, there is empirical support for considering it further. For example, in studies from the 1960s, Scanzoni (1982) found that couples who faced a premarital pregnancy tended to marry earlier than those who did not, regardless of social class. This suggests that the social pressure to legitimate a premarital pregnancy probably outweighed counterbalancing financial concerns. Whether the man was employed, in school, or out of work, the couple was expected to marry and do their best to make ends meet while raising their child. Any effect of male employment on marriage was presumably felt after the fact.

A recent review of the literature by Lerman (1989) lends additional credibility to the null hypothesis by raising doubts about the relationship between male employment and never-married parenthood. Research by Plotnick (1988) shows no relationship between the likelihood of a woman's becoming a never-married mother by the age of nineteen and the state-level ratio of single employed men to single women of the same race. Lerman's own investigations show no effects of area unemployment rates and past jobholding on the likelihood that young men remain childless, live with their children, or become absent fathers (Lerman, 1986). The only evidence of a positive relationship between male employment and marriage which Lerman cited is a previous study of ours (Testa et al., 1989). It shows that inner-city fathers in stable employment were twice as likely to marry the mother of their first child as fathers without a job.

Since Lerman's review, a number of empirical studies have appeared that examine the relationships among male employment, nonmarital parenthood, and marriage (Ellwood and Rodda, 1990; Fossett and Kiecolt, 1993; Lichter et al., 1992; Lichter, LeClere, and McLaughlin, 1991; South and Lloyd, 1992). Most report a positive association between employment and marriage, but the findings are less conclusive on the relationship between employment and nonmarital parenthood. A major problem with comparing these studies is that different social processes are examined. For example, our previous study examined flows into marriage after pregnancy and childbirth; Plotnick (1988) examined flows into parenthood before marriage; and Lerman (1986) looked at differences in the stocks of absent parents at a given time. Because the probability of premarital parenthood can be viewed as the product of two successive probabilities—(1) conceiving a child out of wedlock and (2) not marrying prior to childbirth—it is quite possible that male employment exerts little effect on the unconditional probability of premarital conception but a strong effect on the conditional probability of legitimation. A "reduced form" model of childbirth out of wedlock might show a small cumulative effect of employment on premarital parenthood even if the conditional effect of male employment on legitimation is large. In addition, by ignoring flows into marriage after a child is born, one runs the risk of seriously underestimating the causal significance of male employment status on overall marriage rates.

Constant Relationship, Stable Marriage Rates

The second alternative is the obverse of the null hypothesis. It posits a positive relationship between male employment and marriage. Moreover, it posits that the rates of marriage for employed and jobless men have remained constant over time. If true, it would mean that increased male joblessness fully accounts for the decline in post-conception marriage.

As mentioned above, the first part of this hypothesis is supported by numerous studies which show a positive effect of male employment on marriage rates. The second part of the hypothesis stands up less well to empirical scrutiny. Available data indicate that the magnitude of the male employment effect would have to be implausibly large in order to account fully for the decline in black marriage rates (Schoen and Kluegel, 1988). Either marriage rates had to decline equally for both working and nonworking men or the rates had to decline much more steeply for one group than for the other. These alternatives lead us to consider three final hypotheses of variation over time in the relationship between male employment and marriage.

Constant Relationship, Declining Marriage Rates

Alternative 3 (Figure 3.2) is a synthesis of the first two alternatives. It assumes a constant relationship between male employment and marriage but posits that marriage rates have declined just as much among working men as among nonworking men. If true, it would mean that the decline in black marriages is partly due to increased black male joblessness but mainly due to other factors. For example, the hypothesis that black women have become less inclined to marry as their earnings potential has converged with that of black men (Farley, 1988) belongs in this category. So does Ehrenreich's (1983) argument that men generally have become more reluctant to take on family responsibilities even when they can afford to do so. Economic theory also predicts a drop in inner-city marriage rates as a result of the decline since 1974 in real wages for non-college-educated men. To some extent, this effect may have been offset by the decline in the real value of AFDC benefits during this same period.

The early evidence in support of these views comes mostly from comparing trends in black marriages, controlling for work status or educational level. For example, Jencks (1989) reported that the decline between 1960 and 1980 in the proportion of black men who were married and living with their wives was almost as large among black men who had worked throughout the previous year as the decline among black men in general. Lerman (1989) reached similar conclusions by comparing increases in the fraction of college and non-college-educated men who are still single (that is, never married). Between 1970 and 1980, the fraction of black men who were unmarried by age twenty-nine rose nearly as much among those with some college (19 to 29 percent) as among high school dropouts (24 to 38 percent).

More recent investigations lend additional support to the hypothesis of equal declines in marriage among working and nonworking men. Examining decennial census data, Mare and Winship (1991) found that employment trends had relatively small effects on declines in rates of marriage. Only about 20 percent of the changes in marriage rates for black men from 1960 to 1980 were attributable to decreasing employment rates. In a more direct test of the hypothesis, Ellwood and Rodda (1990) modelled the effects of work and earnings on transitions into marriage using two panels from the National Longitudinal Surveys of Labor Market Experiences of Youth (NLS). They found no evidence of change in the proportional impact of work and earnings on marriages between the 1967–71 and 1980–86 observation periods. This is consistent with the hypothesis of equal declines.

Because both studies involved national samples, it is uncertain whether these same patterns hold for ghetto-underclass populations. Also because they lacked information on parental status, it is uncertain whether recent cohorts of working and college-educated men have become more reluctant to marry even when they face childrearing responsibilities. The drop in black marriages reflects declines in conventional marriage as well as decreases in rates of legitimation. Modelling only those flows into marriage that occur after the conception of a child might show diverging trends between working and nonworking fathers.

A Strengthening Relationship
Between Male Employment and Marriage

One type of divergence is diagramed as Alternative 4 in Figure 3.2. It shows the differences in post-conception marriage rates widening between jobless and stably employed men. Nearly all of the decline is confined to jobless men. If correct, the relationship between male employment and post-conception marriage should be strengthening over time.

There are several plausible reasons for predicting a divergence in marriage trends between jobless and stably employed men. One is that the reduced stigma of out-of-wedlock childbearing may have relieved low-income couples from the social pressure to legitimate a premarital pregnancy when the man is unemployed. Another is that expanded legal entitlements to public assistance may have enabled more pregnant women to forgo marrying the father if he is not working.[1] A third reason comes from Wilson's (1987) theory of the ghetto underclass.

According to Wilson, major shifts in the urban economy have greatly devalued the labor of men without a college education or craft skills. These shifts in labor demand have disproportionately affected blacks living in ghetto neighborhoods, creating, in effect, an economic underclass. Moreover, the movement of middle-class and working-class blacks out of older inner-city neighborhoods has isolated the remaining ghetto residents (largely women and children) from mainstream norms and behaviors. As a consequence, the behavior of inner-city residents has sharply diverged from mainstream conventions. This is reflected in increased levels of out-of-wedlock births, welfare dependency, crime, and drug abuse.

Wilson and Neckerman (1986) use statistics on blacks to draw inferences about the ghetto underclass, since inner-city poor are disproportionately represented among blacks. Wilson and Neckerman observe that the rising proportion of black single parents mirrors the declining ratio of employed black males per one hundred females (the male marriage pool index—MMPI). By comparison, there is little correspondence between the slowly rising levels of white single parenthood and changes in the white MMPI. They infer that the large decline in black married-couple families can be linked to the employment problems experienced by black men, while the smaller decline in white married-couple families is probably due to the increased employment of white women. They acknowledge that more direct measures at the individual level are necessary to test their inferences.

A Weakening Relationship Between Male Employment and Marriage

Alternative 5 is the obverse of Alternative 4. It posits that most of the decline in marriage rates has occurred among working men rather than nonworking men. If correct, the relationship between male employment and marriage should be getting weaker over time. The assertion that the relationship between male employment and marriage is becoming weaker follows from arguments about the pauperization of the working class. According to Murray

---

[1]Between 1968 and 1971, the United States Supreme Court struck down numerous rules and regulations that had restricted a single mother's eligibility for AFDC benefits, including local residency requirements, the "man-in-the-house" rule, and regulations that had denied assistance to "employable mothers." In addition, the Court required welfare agencies to give fair hearings and proper notice to recipients threatened with termination of benefits. According to Patterson, these changes heightened eligible families' awareness of their entitlements under the law and led to a large jump in the AFDC participation of eligible families from about 33 percent in the early 1960s to more than 90 percent in 1971 (Patterson, 1986).

(1984), eligibility changes made to the AFDC program between 1961 and 1969 gave employed, low-income fathers a financial incentive to avoid marriage. Specifically, he argues that the 1968 Supreme Court decision striking down the "man-in-the-house" rule made it advantageous for employed, low-income fathers to cohabit rather than marry. If the man married, his family would become ineligible for AFDC benefits. If he lived with his partner out of wedlock, they could combine her welfare grant with his minimum-wage earnings and in effect double their household income. To the extent that people's behaviors were consistent with this logic, these changes in AFDC eligibility rules increased the rate of out-of-wedlock births[2] (U.S. Congress, House Committee on Ways and Means, 1985).

Murray cites the sharp rise in AFDC caseloads during the 1960s as offering strong circumstantial evidence in support of his arguments. There is a close correspondence between the timing of AFDC rule changes and the rise in AFDC recipients. Murray acknowledges, however, that the correspondence could be mere coincidence. A better test of his hypothesis is to compare the post-conception marriage rates of employed men with unemployed men from successive cohorts. As one reviewer of our previous study observed: "Since financial disincentives to marry are greatest for employed fathers, all other things equal, the decline in marriage resulting from the changes in welfare regimes should be greatest for employed fathers" (Daniel, 1989, p. 3). This prediction assumes an initial strong relationship between male employment and post-conception marriage rates which gradually weakens under the influence of liberal welfare rules. If low-income couples began to behave in a fashion consistent with Murray's argument, we should observe a sharp decline in the rate of legitimation after 1968 among employed fathers in the inner city. The comparable change among nonemployed men should be slight since the financial incentives for them remained unchanged.

Methods

To assess the empirical validity of these five alternative hypotheses, we drew on retrospective data collected by the National Opinion Research Center (NORC)

---

[2] It is worth noting that Murray's hypothesis, as stated here, is often confused with other notions about the presumed effects of AFDC on family life. Most often, it is confused with assertions that women have babies in order to collect AFDC benefits or that state variation in illegitimacy is affected by differences in state AFDC-benefit levels. Murray disavows both of these interpretations (Murray, 1985). He emphasizes that AFDC affords pregnant women a broader array of choices about childbearing and marriage and not that welfare encourages poor women to become pregnant. He also contends that real differences in state-welfare packages are modest when food stamps, medicaid, and public housing benefits are included in the comparison. He says his argument is about nationwide changes in eligibility rules and not about modest differences in state-welfare packages.

on the employment, parental, and marital histories of 415 black men aged eighteen to forty-four who participated in the Urban Poverty and Family Structure (UPFS) survey. We use these data to estimate general and cohort-specific models of the effects of employment and other variables on age-specific rates of marriage. To the extent that the effect of male employment has been changing over time, these changes should be revealed by our estimation of marriage-rate models for separate birth cohorts. Before doing this, however, we first discuss our sample data, the methods for estimating rate models, and the statistical validity of our inferences.

Sample

NORC conducted the UPFS survey in 1987 with a multistage, stratified probability sample of 2,490 Mexican, Puerto Rican, non-Hispanic white, and black persons aged eighteen to forty-four years who resided in City of Chicago poverty tracts. At last census count, 40 percent of Chicago's three million residents resided in poverty tracts.

The UPFS sample was selected in multiple stages. In the first stage, blocks (primary sampling units) within poverty tracts were divided into four ethnic strata and then sorted by census tract. From this sorted file, a sample of block units (single blocks or groups of blocks) was selected with probabilities proportional to the number of households in each block unit. NORC then dispatched specially trained interviewers to list each dwelling unit on each block. From this list, individual dwelling units were selected for door-to-door screening interviews with probabilities inversely proportional to the prior stage of selection. The screening interviews were necessary to identify eligible respondents for the main survey.

Screening consisted of a brief interview with a representative of each selected dwelling unit. Interviewers spoke with a household member at least fifteen years old who could supply information about the composition of the household. The interview elicited the names of all household members, each member's sex and age and, for persons over fourteen years old, their ethnicity, marital status, number of children born, and number currently living with them. Persons eligible for the survey included Mexican, Puerto Rican, black, and non-Hispanic white mothers and fathers eighteen to forty-four years old. Also, a subsample of childless black men and women aged eighteen to forty-four was selected for interviews.[3]

---

[3] According to the screening interviews, the Chicago inner-city population aged eighteen to forty-four was 66 percent black, 13 percent Mexican, 6 percent Puerto Rican, 2 percent other Hispanic, 11 percent non-Hispanic white, and 2 percent other ethnic groups. In order to ensure adequate numbers of Mexican, Puerto Rican, and non-Hispanic white respondents, NORC mounted a second phase of block selection and household screening to identify additional age-eligible Mexican, Puerto Rican, and non-Hispanic white parents. Unlike the first-phase screening,

NORC completed personal in-depth interviews with a total of 2,490 persons. There were 291 completed interviews with black respondents who were screened as fathers and 124 completed interviews with black respondents who were screened as non-fathers.[4] The UPFS survey completion rates were 77 percent for black fathers and 79 percent for black non-fathers. These rates compare favorably to completion rates for other surveys of similar populations. The subsample of 415 black males aged eighteen to forty-four are the subjects of our analysis.

Model Estimation

The UPFS survey used a recent innovation in survey research, the life-history calendar (Freedman et al., 1988), to record major events in the lives of respondents. Use of the calendar improves recall of past events by enabling respondents to compare the dates of events with major milestones, such as births of children and marriage. With these retrospective data, we are able to conduct a quantitative analysis of life histories.

Analyses of life histories focus on changes from one state to another over time, such as a change in marital status from single to married (Kalbfleish and Prentice, 1980; Tuma and Hannan, 1984). The purpose is to gauge the causal significance of predictor variables, such as education, employment status, and family structure, on the rate of change. The rate of change is called a hazard or transition rate.

In event-history models, the transition rate is assumed to control the occurrence of an event (e.g., marriage) as well as the time until its occurrence (e.g., years remaining single). In formal terms, the transition rate is defined as the instantaneous probability of an event's occurring at a specific moment. It is calculated from the number of people experiencing an event at a specific time relative to the number of people "at risk" of experiencing that event up until that time. Intuitively, it indicates the level of risk to which a person is exposed. Once a person has experienced the event in question, he or she is no longer at risk.

---

which used an equal probability sample of dwelling units, the second-phase screening selected dwelling units disproportionately from poverty tracts with heavy concentrations of Mexicans, Puerto Ricans, or non-Hispanic whites. The sample data from both phases can be combined and, with the appropriate sample weights, used to produce unbiased estimates of population statistics.

[4] Subsequent face-to-face interviews with respondents did reveal some errors in the screening of race and parental status. Two fathers who were mistakenly screened as nonblack were later reclassified as black during the interview. Also, one percent of fathers were later reclassified as nonparents because they were determined during the interview to be step- or adoptive parents. Five percent of black fathers were reclassified as nonparents and 19 percent of black male nonparents were reclassified as fathers as a result of the survey. There were no other reclassifications of parental status among the other ethnic groups. Most of the errors in the black sample appeared to be concentrated among the older respondents who had a child at younger ages. The final classification showed 793 biological fathers, 9 adoptive or stepfathers, and 116 black male nonparents.

Event-history models solve several analytic problems associated with the quantitative study of life histories. In particular, they offer a way to deal with censored observations and competing events. For instance, in the UPFS survey some respondents had never been married at the time they were interviewed. Their marriages may happen at some time in the future, if at all. Consequently, our knowledge of their marital history is incomplete or "censored." In ordinary regression analysis, censored observations are sometimes dropped from the study, assigned a maximum value, or truncated at an arbitrary cutoff date (Allison, 1982). Hazards regression analysis avoids these ad hoc solutions by retaining censored observations in the risk pool for the calculation of transition rates up until the time of the interview. In this way, all the information known about a censored case is used. That is, up until the date of the interview, the event in question did not happen.

Event-history models also provide a way to analyze competing events. For instance, the event of becoming an unmarried father precludes marrying before childbirth (conventional marriage). To analyze these competing events, we use an approach recommended by Allison (1984). It involves dropping cases out of the risk pool when a competing event occurs, much like dropping a case out of the risk pool when an observation is censored. For example, when we are examining the rate of conventional marriage, a man is dropped from the risk pool when he conceives a child before marriage. Similarly, when we are examining the rate of marriage to the mother of the first child, a man is dropped from the risk pool when he marries another woman. Event-history analysis also provides a way to analyze conditional events. For instance, the only men "at risk" of a post-conception marriage (legitimation) are men who conceived a child before marriage. Men who did not conceive a child before marriage are not included in the risk pool for legitimation.

In event-history models, transition rates are posited as varying as a function of age or time and as a function of predictor variables. The time function can be defined explicitly or left to vary freely as a "nuisance function." Because we have no a priori sense of the functional form of time dependence in the case of marriage, we chose the latter approach, commonly known as proportional hazards regression. This approach is partially parametric because only the effects of the exogenous variables are estimated explicitly. The transition rate is the product of a baseline hazard function, which varies freely with time, and a set of predictor variables, some of which are fixed and others of which vary with time.

Statistical Inference

Statistical inference from complex sample surveys, such as the UPFS survey, requires the use of different computational procedures from the default procedures found in standard statistical packages, such as SAS, SPSS, and BMDP. These packages assume that the data come from a simple random sample. While these packages can produce unbiased sample estimates of means, proportions, and other statistics by using the appropriate sample weights, the standard errors these packages generate for constructing confidence intervals and for assessing statistical significance will almost always be too small. As a result, the associated confidence intervals and statistical tests will be incorrect.

Several procedures are available for computing the correct standard errors for means, proportions, and other statistics based on complex survey designs. In this study, we employ the Taylor series method of variance estimation using computer software written by C. Dennis Carroll of the Office of Educational Research and Improvement, Department of Education (Carroll, 1988). These Taylor series estimates from a complex sample vary considerably more than estimates from a simple random sample of comparable size. We find, however, that the ratios of the corrected variance to the simple random sample variance (the design effect, or deff) in the UPFS are not very large. The only exceptions are those variables that are highly clustered by census tract, such as residence in public housing.[5]

It should be noted that we use sample weights and make adjustments for design effects only when estimating population statistics, such as proportions and means. We do not use sample weights in our hazards regression analysis and instead treat the sample as unweighted. If one does employ sample weights, the asymptotic theory upon which significance tests are based collapses. Because there is disagreement over the appropriateness of using sample weights in event-history analyses (Hoem, 1987), we have chosen to ignore the weights in order to obtain approximate test statistics.

Results

In this section, we present the results of our hazards regression analysis of the effects of employment and other variables on rates of marriage. Our variable of employment is taken from a monthly measure of activity status which we constructed for each respondent based on information he supplied for the life-history calendar. We coded one activity per month: work, school, or military service. Work took precedence over both school and military reserves. Persons who were neither employed, in school, nor in the military were coded as "inactive" for that month. Because only jobs lasting six months or longer were recorded on the life-history calendar, the category of inactive sometimes includes a small proportion of working men in jobs of brief duration.

Besides activity status, we also include in our hazards regression models the following predictor variables: fatherhood status, cohort indicators for the

[5]We are grateful to Martin Frankel, Roger Tourangerou, and Kenneth Rasinski of NORC for helping us to obtain the necessary computer software and for reviewing our results.

year of the man's birth, whether fatherhood was intended or unplanned, period of military service (draft or volunteer army), high school graduation, incarceration in jail or prison, and family structure at age fourteen.[6] With the exception of birth cohort and family structure, all of the remaining predictor variables can change values over time.

In the following sections, we present descriptive statistics on the dependent variable of marriage and the predictor variables of fatherhood and activity status for four birth cohorts of black men aged eighteen to forty-four living in inner-city Chicago in 1987. We then present the results of our hazards regression analysis of the effects of activity status and the other variables on general and cohort-specific marriage rates.

Marital and Parental Events

Figure 3.3 diagrams the distribution of marital and parental events for black men in the UPFS survey. The Taylor series estimates of the standard errors are shown in parentheses.[7] An estimated 41 percent of black men aged eighteen to forty-four reported never having fathered a child or never having been married by the time of the NORC interview. Another 13 percent reported marrying prior to the conception of their first child, and 46 percent reported conceiving their first child prior to marriage.[8] Thus nearly one-half of the black male respondents are estimated to have become fathers before marrying.

Approximately one-half of the premarital fathers eventually married. An estimated 5 percent of premarital fathers legitimated the child's conception

[6] Most of the men in this sample (71 percent) were born in Chicago. About 19 percent were born in Mississippi or Arkansas and the remainder in other Southern states. The percentage born in Chicago rose from 37 percent for the 1941–49 cohort to 83 percent for the 1961–69 cohort. In spite of the lower percentages born in Chicago among the older cohorts, most Southern-born men attended high school and began their working lives in Chicago. The average age of migration north was twelve and a half. Overall, 76 percent of the men in this sample had mothers who completed at least an eighth-grade education. This percentage increases from 51 percent for the oldest cohort to 88 percent for the youngest, which parallels the rise in the percentage of men born in Chicago. Also, about 44 percent of the men reported living with their mother only at age fourteen. This percentage was about the same for all four cohorts. About half of the men came from large families with at least five brothers and sisters (including half-siblings). And about 41 percent of the men reported that their mother worked outside the home while they were growing up. The percentage of men whose families ever received public aid while they were growing up increased from 15 percent in the oldest cohort to 43 percent in the youngest. Again this increase corresponds to the rising percentage of men born in Chicago. We explored these background variables for inclusion in our hazards regression models, but, with the exception of living in a mother-only family at age fourteen, we found that they were not related to marriage rates.

[7] An approximate 95 percent confidence interval can be constructed by adding and subtracting twice the Taylor corrected standard error from each estimate.

[8] Throughout this chapter, conception of a first child refers to the first conception that resulted in a live birth. We do not have any information for men on conceptions that resulted in an abortion or miscarriage.

FIGURE 3.3

*Marital and parental transitions of black men aged 18–44
in Chicago poverty tracts, 1986.*

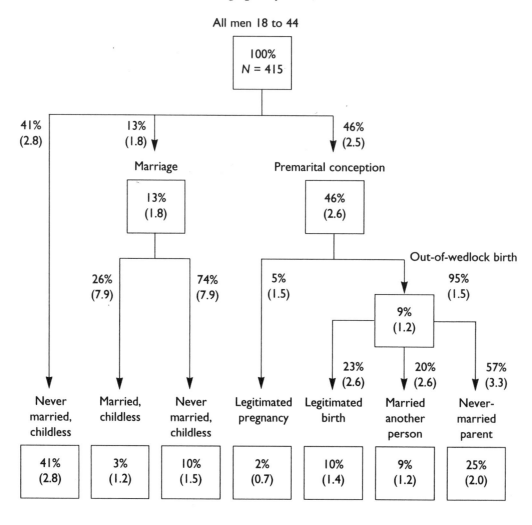

before its birth. Overall, 2 percent of all respondents married during their partner's pregnancy, and an additional 10 percent married after the child's birth. Some 9 percent of respondents conceived their first child out of wedlock but reported marrying a woman other than the mother of their first child. An estimated 25 percent of respondents were never-married parents. These data show that over one-half of the marriages among black men occurred after the conception of their first child.

Marital and Parental Events by Birth Cohorts

Figure 3.3 combines data from several cohorts of black men which obscure important differences in marriage rates when marital events are classified by birth cohort. Table 3.1 shows that the proportion married at selected ages has declined significantly for successive cohorts. To take account of censoring, we computed these estimates from the Kaplan-Mier survival distributions of age at first marriage. The Breslow and Mantel-Cox tests of the equality of the distributions across birth cohorts are also shown.

An estimated 48 percent of black men born between 1941 and 1949 had married by age twenty-five, compared to 21 percent of black men born between 1961 and 1969. Similar cohort differences exist at other ages, and the hypothesis of equal distributions is rejected at the 0.01 significance level. These cohort differences are consistent with a rising age at first marriage. The same holds true for pre-conception marriages, except that the hypothesis of equal distributions cannot be rejected.

Table 3.2 displays similar information from the Kaplan-Mier survival distributions of age at first fatherhood. The data show only slight differences in the percentages of cohort members who become fathers. An estimated 62 percent of black men born between 1941 and 1949 conceived their first child by age twenty-five, compared to 57 percent of black men in the youngest cohort. The hypothesis of equal distributions cannot be rejected at the 0.20 significance level. These cohort similarities imply a stable age at first fatherhood.

A generally rising age at first marriage in conjunction with a stable age at first fatherhood means that successively larger fractions of recent cohorts of black fathers are unmarried at the birth of their first child. If we compute the ratio of premarital fathers to all fathers at age twenty-five in Table 3.2, we find that two-thirds of the oldest cohort of fathers were unmarried at their child's birth, compared to nine-tenths of the youngest cohort.

Activity Status by Birth Cohorts

In order to assess the effects of male employment on transition rates into first marriage, we need to consider how the activity status of different cohorts has changed over this same period of time. The top panel of Table 3.3 presents

TABLE 3.1

Proportion Married at Selected Ages, by Birth Cohort:
Black Males Aged 18–44 in Chicago Poverty Tracts, 1986

Marital Status Birth Cohort	Age					*n*
	19	22	25	28	31	
First marriage						
1941–49	8.8	29.0	47.6	55.5	63.2	98
1950–55	5.4	21.0	35.1	41.4	47.6	90
1956–60	1.8	10.2	23.5	31.7	—	99
1961–69	1.9	10.9	20.5	—	—	128
All cohorts	3.5	16.4	30.3	38.4	45.9	415
	p-values: Breslow 0.001; Mantel-Cox 0.005					
Pre-conception marriage						
1941–49	3.5	14.0	21.2	23.7	24.6	98
1950–55	1.6	7.0	14.8	16.3	16.9	90
1956–60	1.0	2.8	7.4	10.4	—	99
1961–69	0.8	5.9	14.8	—	—	128
All cohorts	1.1	6.5	12.9	15.5	16.3	415
	p-values: Breslow n.s.; Mantel-Cox n.s.					

TABLE 3.2

Proportion Parents at Selected Ages, by Birth Cohort:
Black Males Aged 18–44 in Chicago Poverty Tracts, 1986

Marital Status Birth Cohort	Age						*n*
	16	19	22	25	28	31	
First fatherhood							
1941–49	2.9	17.7	46.9	62.0	67.7	77.0	98
1950–55	2.1	27.4	52.1	62.9	67.7	71.0	90
1956–60	2.6	18.6	39.7	48.1	58.5	—	99
1961–69	1.7	18.1	32.6	56.5	—	—	128
All cohorts	2.0	19.7	41.1	55.1	62.3	67.6	415
	p-values: Breslow n.s., Mantel-Cox n.s.						
Premarital fatherhood							
1941–49	2.6	13.2	32.0	39.8	42.3	49.6	98
1950–55	1.2	24.5	42.7	51.6	53.9	56.1	90
1956–60	1.9	16.6	33.8	42.1	47.5	—	99
1961–69	0.9	12.9	30.2	52.6	—	—	128
All cohorts	1.2	15.6	33.6	44.2	48.0	52.0	415
	p-values: Breslow n.s.; Mantel-Cox n.s.						

the percentage of each cohort of black men who were inactive on the birthdays listed. The bottom panel of Table 3.3 presents the percentage of each cohort who were in school, in the military, or at work. The percentages of each cohort who are inactive and active sum to 100 percent.

The data show that on their sixteenth birthday, less than 10 percent of each of the cohorts were inactive. Most were still in high school. On their nineteenth birthday, 33 percent of each cohort were inactive. On their twenty-second birthday, large cohort differences begin to emerge. The inactive proportion declines to 21 percent for the 1941–49 cohort and to 31 percent for the 1950–55 cohort. By contrast, the inactive proportion rises to 42 percent for the 1956–60 cohort and to 37 percent for the 1961–69 cohort. These disparities narrow only slightly at later birthdays.

The United States military build-up in Vietnam between 1966 and 1969 accounts for some of the oldest cohort's lower levels of inactivity at ages nineteen and twenty-two. At later ages, the largest source of the differences comes from the decline in the proportion of each cohort in stable work. Table 3.4 shows that the percentage engaged in stable work at each age is lower for each successive cohort. At age twenty-two, almost fifteen points separate the employment percentages of the 1941–49 and 1956–60 cohorts. At age twenty-eight, the employment gap widens to nearly eighteen percentage points.

Table 3.4 also shows that the inactivity levels of the youngest cohort would have been even higher at ages nineteen and twenty-two were it not for their higher school enrollments. The percentage of the 1961–69 cohort in school is twelve points higher at age nineteen, and seven points higher at age twenty-two than the 1941–49 cohort. Since students can be considered semi-dependent on families and government for support, the percentages of students and inactive youth may be combined to estimate the magnitude of social dependency among inner-city black youth. In the youngest cohort, students and inactive youth constitute about 62 percent of inner-city black youth at age nineteen and about 48 percent at age twenty-two. This compares to a social dependency ratio, two decades earlier, of a little under 47 percent at age nineteen and 26 percent at age twenty-two for the oldest cohort.

The prolonged social dependency of inner-city youth parallels similar trends among middle-class youth. The critical difference, however, is that most nonemployed, middle-class youth are enrolled in college while most nonemployed, inner-city youth are "on the street." Efforts by out-of-school youth to obtain blue-collar jobs in the industries that once employed their fathers have been hurt by massive shifts in city economies from centers of manufacturing to centers of service, administration, and information exchange (Kasarda, 1989). The effects of these shifts are clearly evident in the changing occupations held by successive cohorts of young men.

The most common occupation reported by respondents at ages nineteen to twenty-eight changed from operative and assembler jobs among the oldest cohort to service jobs (waiters and janitors) among the youngest cohort. The

TABLE 3.3

Percentage Inactive and Active (in School, Military, or Work) at Selected Ages,
by Birth Cohort: Black Males Aged 18–44 in Chicago Poverty Tracts, 1986

Activity Status Birth Cohort	Age						*n*
	16	19	22	25	28	31	
Inactive							
1941–49	9.7	29.4	21.4	29.0	29.0	18.5	98
1950–55	11.2	33.8	30.6	32.2	37.9	42.7	90
1956–60	10.2	37.7	42.3	43.0	43.4	—	99
1961–69	6.4	32.3	36.8	—	—	—	128
All cohorts	8.8	33.4	33.6	35.2	36.4	29.6	415
	p-values: Breslow n.s.; Mantel-Cox n.s.						
Active							
1941–49	90.3	70.6	78.6	71.0	71.0	81.5	98
1950–55	88.8	66.2	69.4	67.8	62.1	57.3	90
1956–60	89.8	62.3	57.6	57.0	56.6	—	99
1961–69	93.6	67.7	63.2	—	—	—	128
All cohorts	91.2	66.6	66.4	64.8	68.5	70.4	415
	p-values: Breslow n.s.; Mantel-Cox n.s.						

Note: Taylor series estimates of standard errors for separate cohorts vary from 4 for 10 percent and 90 percent to 6 for 50 percent. For all cohorts, the standard errors vary from 2 for 10 percent and 90 percent to 3 for 30 percent and 70 percent.

second most common occupation changed from clerical and administrative jobs to handlers and laborers. Altogether, operative and assembler jobs, clerical jobs, driving jobs, labor jobs, and service jobs accounted for about 65 percent of all the occupations reported by each cohort at each age. The modal occupation for each cohort was generally the same at each age. The only obvious change was the loss of operative and assembler jobs by the two older cohorts.

As occupations shifted from manufacturing to service employment, the jobs also became more irregular. With the exception of the youngest cohort at age nineteen, the median number of months worked by jobholders decreased for each cohort. Between ages twenty-two and twenty-five, one-half of the 1941–49 cohort worked thirty-three months or more. At later three-year age intervals, one-half of the oldest cohort worked the full thirty-six months. By comparison, the younger cohorts fared less well. Between ages twenty-two and twenty-five, one-half of the 1950–55 cohort worked for only eighteen months or more, and one-half of the 1956–60 cohort worked for only thirteen months or more.

TABLE 3.4

Percentage in Type of Activity at Selected Ages, by Birth Cohort:
Black Males Aged 18–44 in Chicago Poverty Tracts, 1986

Activity Type Birth Cohort	Age						*n*
	16	19	22	25	28	31	
Work							
1941–49	10.0	43.2	57.4	67.4	70.0	80.6	98
1950–55	8.9	36.5	49.3	58.2	54.9	54.1	90
1956–60	7.7	31.4	42.9	51.9	52.3	—	99
1961–69	7.1	34.4	49.6	—	—	—	128
All cohorts	8.1	35.6	49.2	59.3	59.3	68.4	415
	p-values: Breslow n.s.; Mantel-Cox n.s.						
School							
1941–49	80.3	17.6	4.4	0.9	0.9	0.9	98
1950–55	79.9	20.9	10.4	6.4	7.2	3.2	90
1956–60	82.1	20.9	8.9	1.9	4.3	—	99
1961–69	86.5	29.7	11.2	—	—	—	128
All cohorts	83.1	23.6	8.9	2.6	4.2	2.0	415
	p-values: Breslow n.s.; Mantel-Cox n.s.						
Military							
1941–49	—	9.8	16.9	2.7	—	—	98
1950–55	—	8.8	9.7	3.2	—	—	90
1956–60	—	10.8	5.8	3.2	—	—	99
1961–69	—	3.6	2.4	—	—	—	128
All cohorts	—	7.4	8.3	2.8	—	—	415
	p-values: Breslow n.s.; Mantel-Cox n.s.						

Note: Taylor series estimates of standard errors for separate cohorts vary from 4 for 10 percent and 90 percent to 6 for 50 percent. For all cohorts, the standard errors vary from 1 for 2 percent and 98 percent to 3 for 50 percent.

Marital Transitions by Activity Status and Birth Cohorts

The above data show that during the period of time that marriage rates of black men have declined, there has been a corresponding increase in the proportion of black men who are inactive. To examine the relationship between activity status and marriage, we present in this section the results of the hazards regression analysis of the effects of activity status and other variables on rates of first marriage. We examine four categories of marriage. The first is all first marriages, regardless of the woman's relationship to the man's first child. The second is limited to only those first marriages that were to the mother of the man's first child. It includes both marriages that preceded the child's conception and marriages that followed the child's conception. Cases involving a first marriage to another woman are censored at the date of the marriage. The third and fourth categories are pre-conception and post-conception marriages treated separately.

We estimate three separate models for each category of marriage. Model 1 estimates the effects of activity and fatherhood status on rates of marriage. Model 2 adds the cohort indicators for the year of the man's birth. Model 3 adds the remaining variables: period of military service (draft or volunteer era), whether or not the pregnancy was unwanted, high school graduation, incarceration, and family structure at age fourteen.

Table 3.5 displays the results of the three models for all first marriages. Model 1 provides an initial test of the null hypothesis of no relationship between employment status and rates of marriage. The exponentiated coefficients for activity status in Model 1 show how engagement in work, school, or military service increases (greater than 1.0) or decreases (less than 1.0) the likelihood of marriage at each age. The reference category is men who are inactive.

The results indicate that the null hypothesis can safely be rejected. The exponentiated coefficient for work under Model 1 reveals that men who are employed are twice as likely to marry at each age compared to men who are inactive. School and military service can be interpreted in similar fashion. Model 1 shows that single men who are attending high school or college are no more or less likely to marry than inactive men. By contrast, single men who enter the military are over three times more likely than inactive men to marry. Model 1 also controls for out-of-wedlock fatherhood. Men who conceived a child out of wedlock are over twice as likely to marry at a given age compared to men who remain childless.

Model 2 provides a test of the second hypothesis. According to this hypothesis, cohort differences in rates of marriage are attributable entirely to cohort differences in the proportions of black men who are stably employed. We showed in Table 3.4 that the proportions of black men in stable employment at selected ages declined for each successive birth cohort. The results in Table 3.5 show, however, that these declines in stable employment do not fully explain the secular decline in marriage rates among black males. The exponentiated coefficients for birth cohorts under Model 2 show that regardless of activity and fatherhood status, black men born during the 1940s were more likely to marry than men born during the 1960s (the reference group).

In Model 3, we distinguish between military service that began during the draft and military service that began after 1974 with the introduction of the volunteer army. The results show that men who served during the draft were no more likely to marry than men who were inactive. The exponentiated coefficient for the draft is not significantly different from 1.0. Conversely, men who entered the service after the introduction of the volunteer army were much more likely to marry at a given age than inactive men. The exponentiated coefficient is larger than 7.0. This difference agrees with our intuitive sense of how military service affects the chances of a man's remaining single or marrying.

TABLE 3.5

Hazards Regression Estimates of Effects on Age-Specific Rates of First Marriage:
Black Males Aged 18–44 in Chicago Poverty Tracts, 1986

Variables	Model 1		Model 2		Model 3	
	exp(b)	b/s.e.	exp(b)	b/s.e.	exp(b)	b/s.e.
Activity status						
Work	2.30	4.46	2.15	4.24	1.93	3.50
School	1.28	0.73	1.29	0.75	1.09	0.26
Military	3.54	4.28	3.10	3.78		
Draft					1.19	0.39
Volunteer					7.51	5.71
Fatherhood	2.34	5.43	2.44	5.63	4.25	6.51
Unplanned pregnancy					0.55	−2.88
Birth cohorts						
1941–49			2.03	2.62	2.60	3.47
1950–55			1.66	1.86	1.87	2.27
1956–60			1.25	0.80	1.35	1.07
High school graduate					1.41	2.18
Incarceration					0.69	−1.24
Mother-only family at age 14					0.87	−0.94

Note: n = 413; censored = 52.5 percent.

Men who entered the armed services during the draft were more likely to be shipped overseas for combat. Men who enlisted in the volunteer army were more likely to be in noncombat duty. The better pay and benefits of the volunteer army also made it easier to support a family.

Under Model 3, we also attempt to distinguish between premarital pregnancies that were intended from those that were unintended. We code a pregnancy as being intended if the respondent reported that he was trying to have a baby when his first child was conceived. Otherwise, we code it as being unintended. Approximately 80 percent of the fathers reported that their first child was conceived unintentionally. This percentage was about the same for all four cohorts. We acknowledge that this retrospective distinction between intended and unintended pregnancies is problematic. Still, we include this indicator under Model 3 to explore whether unwilling fathers were just as likely to legitimate a premarital pregnancy or birth as willing fathers.

In Table 3.5, the coefficient for fatherhood under Model 3 refers to fathers who reported having intentionally conceived their first child. They were over four times more likely to marry at a given age compared to men who had not yet conceived a child. In order to estimate how an unintended pregnancy affects the age-specific rate of marriage, we multiply the coefficient for fatherhood by the coefficient for unintended pregnancy. This reduces the fatherhood effect to 2.33 (4.25×0.55). These results show that fathers who reported that their first child was unintended were less than half as likely to marry compared to fathers who reported that the pregnancy was intended. While we cannot rule out the possibility that married fathers are more prone to recall that their first child was intentionally conceived than never-married fathers, these results strongly suggest that whether a pregnancy is planned or unplanned affects the likelihood of marriage.

The last three variables included under Model 3 are high school graduation, incarceration, and family structure. Family structure is coded as a fixed variable. It is coded 1.0 if the respondent lived in a mother-only family at age fourteen or 0.0 if he resided with both his parents, stepparents, or another adult. Both high school graduation and incarceration are coded month by month as time-varying variables. Once a respondent graduates, we switch the graduation variable from 0.0 to 1.0; otherwise we leave it fixed at zero. We do the same for incarceration. Once a respondent spends a month or longer in a detention center, jail, or prison, we switch the incarceration variable from 0.0 to 1.0. If he has never been incarcerated, we leave the indicator fixed at zero. By including these time-varying indicators in our hazards regression analysis, we can explore if having a high school diploma or a prison record affects a single man's chances of marrying. The exponentiated coefficients show that graduation from high school increases the age-specific rate of marriage and that incarceration and living in a mother-only family at age fourteen decreases the rate of marriage. Although all three coefficients are in the expected direction, the ratio of the coefficient to its standard error for both incarceration and family structure is less than 2.0.

Table 3.6 displays the results of the same three models for those first marriages which were to the mother of the man's first child. This includes conventional marriages even if the couple has not yet had a child (only 3 percent of respondents). Table 3.6 tells much the same story as Table 3.5. Employed men and men serving in the military are more likely to marry the mother of their first child at each age than men who are inactive. Men from the 1941–49 cohort are more likely to marry than men from the 1956–60 cohort. The coefficients and levels of significance in Table 3.6 are generally a little smaller than in Table 3.5. The most notable change is the drop in the coefficient for unplanned pregnancy. Men who unintentionally conceive a child are only 1.46 times as likely to marry (3.66×0.40) the mother of their first child as single men who have not yet conceived a child out of wedlock. This compares to 2.33 in Table 3.5. Apparently, men who unintentionally conceive a child out of wedlock are only slightly more likely to marry the mother of their child, even though they are at somewhat higher risk of eventually marrying.

TABLE 3.6

*Hazards Regression Estimates of Effects on Age-Specific Rates of Marriage
to Mother of First Child: Black Males Aged 18–44 in Chicago Poverty Tracts, 1986*

	Model 1		Model 2		Model 3	
Variables	exp(b)	b/s.e.	exp(b)	b/s.e.	exp(b)	b/s.e.
Activity status						
Work	1.98	3.34	1.84	2.95	1.63	2.29
School	1.04	0.09	1.05	0.11	0.88	−0.31
Military	3.56	4.09	3.09	3.58		
Draft					1.26	0.50
Volunteer					7.06	5.19
Fatherhood	1.59	2.63	1.68	2.91	3.66	5.29
Unplanned pregnancy					0.40	−3.63
Birth cohorts						
1941–49			1.96	2.32	2.56	3.18
1950–55			1.42	1.17	1.61	1.58
1956–60			1.05	0.16	1.14	0.43
High school graduate					1.38	1.80
Incarceration					0.53	−1.55
Mother-only family at age 14					0.82	−1.15

Note: $n = 413$; censored = 68.4 percent.

Table 3.7 presents the results of the three models for pre-conception (conventional) marriages. Model 1 shows the familiar effects of activity status. Employment and military service increase the likelihood of conventional marriage at each age relative to inactivity and school. There is no fatherhood coefficient for pre-conception marriages because cases are censored at the occurrence of a premarital conception. The coefficients for birth cohort, while successively decreasing, are much smaller than the coefficients in the prior tables. This suggests that changes in activity status account for a large amount of the secular decline in conventional marriage rates. However, the inclusion of the remaining predictor variables under Model 3 brings the birth cohort coefficients into closer alignment with the results in previous tables. While the effect of employment status under Model 3 remains positive, the ratio of the coefficient to its standard error is just below 2.0. This drop in significance level is due largely to the small proportion of conventional marriages in the sample data (13 percent).

Table 3.8 shows the three models of post-conception marriage. Model 1 shows the familiar effects of work and military service, while Model 2 shows that the likelihood of post-conception marriage drops sharply over time. Men

TABLE 3.7

*Hazards Regression Estimates of Effects on Age-Specific Rates
of Pre-Conception Marriage: Black Males Aged 18–44 in Chicago Poverty Tracts, 1986*

Variables	Model 1		Model 2		Model 3	
	exp(b)	b/s.e.	exp(b)	b/s.e.	exp(b)	b/s.e.
Activity status						
Work	2.12	2.47	2.01	2.28	1.84	1.91
School	1.08	0.15	1.05	0.09	0.91	−0.18
Military	3.33	3.34	2.96	2.30		
Draft					0.51	−0.64
Volunteer					6.70	3.74
Birth cohorts						
1941–49			1.27	0.63	1.72	1.35
1950–55			1.21	0.46	1.38	0.78
1956–60			0.73	−0.72	0.82	−0.45
High school graduate					1.58	1.54
Incarceration					0.81	−0.79
Mother-only family at age 14					0.81	−0.79

Note: n = 413; censored = 83.8 percent.

born between 1941 and 1949 were over three times as likely to legitimate the premarital conception of their first child as men born between 1961 and 1969. Model 3 shows the familiar positive effect of volunteer military service and the dampening effect of unintentional pregnancy. As in the previous tables, the exponentiated coefficient for volunteer service is about 7.0, and men reporting unintended pregnancies are half as likely to marry as men reporting intended pregnancies. Unlike the previous tables, however, in this case the introduction of the final control variables in Model 3 reduces the significance level of the employment coefficient to well below twice its standard error.

This reduction in the significance of the employment coefficient suggests either that employment is irrelevant to the decision to legitimate a premarital pregnancy, or that the relationship between employment and legitimation is changing over time. It is plausible to think that the employment effect may be increasing as the stigma of single parenthood diminishes. This would strengthen the importance of economic considerations. On the other hand, the relationship between employment and legitimation may be weakening in response to changed AFDC rules. In the following section, we explore the possible interactions between employment and cohort on marriage rates by fitting separate models to each birth cohort.

TABLE 3.8

*Hazards Regression Estimates of Effects on Rates of Post-Conception Marriage
to Mother of First Child: Black Males Aged 18–44 in Chicago Poverty Tracts, 1986*

	Model 1		Model 2		Model 3	
Variables	exp(b)	b/s.e.	exp(b)	b/s.e.	exp(b)	b/s.e.
Activity status						
Work	1.96	2.36	1.69	1.80	1.44	1.24
School	0.90	−0.21	0.84	−0.32	0.76	0.54
Military	3.57	3.05	3.13	2.71		
Draft					1.87	1.18
Volunteer					6.89	3.22
Birth cohorts						
1941–49			2.83	2.44	3.50	2.90
1950–55			1.84	1.38	1.93	1.47
1956–60			1.57	1.00	1.58	1.01
Unplanned pregnancy					0.43	−3.29
High school graduate					1.29	1.05
Incarceration					0.34	−1.76
Mother-only family at age 14					0.85	−0.67

Note: $n = 413$; censored $= 68.4$ percent.

Activity Status and Birth Cohort Interactions

Examining the interactions between employment and birth cohort specified in hypotheses three to five requires estimating separate models of marriage for each cohort. Tables 3.9 and 3.10 present such cohort-specific models. Incarceration is not included in any of these models because we found it was often monotonic over time with uncensored cases of marriage, which prohibits event-history estimation. Since the cohort-specific samples are small ($n < 100$), we regrouped intentional and unplanned pregnancies together into the one variable of fatherhood to reduce the number of predictor variables.

The top half of Table 3.9 displays separate models by cohort for all first marriages. In these models a case is censored when a man enters the military. Consequently, the comparison category for employed men is the same as in previous models: men who are out of school, not at work, and not in the military. The exponentiated coefficient for work increases steadily from 1.64 for the 1941–49 cohort, to 2.10 to 3.36, and finally to 5.98 for the 1961–69 cohort. Moreover, the exponentiated coefficient for the fatherhood variable decreases over the four cohorts from 3.70 for men born between 1941 and

TABLE 3.9

*Hazards Regression Estimates of Effects on Initial Marital Transitions, by Birth Cohort:
Black Males Aged 18–44 in Chicago Poverty Tracts, 1986*

Variable	Work		High School Graduation		Mother-Only Family at 14		Fatherhood		*n*
	exp(b)	b/s.e.	exp(b)	b/s.e.	exp(b)	b/s.e.	exp(b)	b/s.e.	
All first marriages									
1941–49	1.64	1.57	1.63	1.73	0.73	−1.05	3.69	4.27	97
1950–55	2.10	2.22	1.86	1.89	0.95	−0.17	1.98	1.99	90
1956–60	3.36	3.03	1.31	0.73	0.64	−1.26	2.34	2.18	98
1961–69	5.98	2.61	1.55	0.71	1.16	0.27	1.36	0.53	128
Marriages to mother of first child									
1941–49	1.45	1.03	1.60	1.44	0.79	−0.69	2.18	2.26	97
1950–55	1.49	1.06	1.84	1.57	0.86	−0.39	1.31	0.68	90
1956–60	5.15	2.89	1.54	0.90	0.67	−0.89	1.52	0.91	98
1961–69	7.40	2.48	1.29	0.40	0.80	−0.36	1.17	0.25	128

1949 to a statistically insignificant 1.36 for men born between 1961 and 1969. Across birth cohorts, the effect of employment on all first marriages increases, and the effect of fatherhood on all first marriages decreases.

The bottom half of Table 3.9 displays separate models by cohort for marriage to the mother of a man's first child. Again, the coefficient for the work variable increases steadily over the cohorts. Compared to the coefficients for all first marriages, the work coefficient for marriage to the mother of a first child starts out smaller and ends up larger. As before, the coefficient for the fatherhood variable decreases over cohorts. Unlike before, the coefficient for fatherhood is statistically significant only for the oldest cohort.

Like Table 3.9, the top half of Table 3.10 presents models of all first marriages and marriages to the mother of a first child. In these models, however, the two older and the two younger cohorts are combined in order to estimate a coefficient for military service. For the two older cohorts, military service occurred almost entirely during the draft, while for the two younger cohorts, it occurred during the volunteer army. Table 3.10 shows that military service during the draft does not affect the likelihood of either all first marriages or marriages to the mother of a first child, but volunteer service in the military dramatically increases the likelihood of both. Otherwise, Table 3.10 tells the same story as Table 3.9. The effect of employment on both types of marriage

TABLE 3.10

Hazards Regression Estimates of Effects on Initial Marital Transitions

Variable	Work		Military Service		High School Graduation		Mother-Only Family at 14		Fatherhood		n
	exp(b)	b/s.e.	exp(b)	b/s.e.	exp(b)	b/s.e.	exp(b)	b/s.e.	exp(b)	b/s.e.	
All first marriages											
1941–55	1.48	1.98	0.91	−0.22	1.38	1.77	0.93	−0.42	2.70	5.14	187
1956–69	4.15	4.21	>9.99	6.24	1.35	1.09	0.79	−0.92	1.77	2.09	226
Marriages to mother of first child											
1941–55	1.15	0.64	0.93	−0.15	1.27	1.49	0.89	−0.57	1.76	2.62	187
1956–69	6.30	4.06	>9.99	6.02	1.46	1.18	0.71	−1.12	1.31	0.87	226
Pre-conception marriages											
1941–55	1.35	0.95	0.32	−1.09	1.16	0.48	0.80	−0.70	na	na	187
1956–69	4.70	2.34	>9.99	4.93	2.60	1.79	0.58	−1.22	na	na	226
Post-conception marriages											
1941–55	1.00	0.02	1.53	0.83	1.27	0.83	0.97	−0.10	na	na	123
1956–69	7.88	3.26	>9.99	3.47	1.11	0.26	0.96	−0.10	na	na	118

increases over cohorts, and the effect of fatherhood decreases. These trends are especially pronounced for marriages to the mother of a first child. For men born between 1941 and 1955, the likelihood of marriage to the mother of the man's first child was only slightly larger among stably employed men than among nonemployed men. For men born between 1956 and 1969, the likelihood among employed men was six times larger.

The bottom half of Table 3.10 displays models for conventional marriages and legitimations. Again, military service during the volunteer army increases the likelihood of these marriages. Also, high school graduation increases the likelihood of conventional marriages for the younger cohorts. But most significantly for our analysis, the effect of employment on these marriages increases dramatically over the cohorts. The effect of employment is especially pronounced for legitimations in the younger cohorts. While employment has no effect on legitimation for men born between 1941 and 1955, it increases the likelihood of legitimation by eight times for men born between 1956 and 1961.

Table 3.11 displays these same results in a simpler form than the event-history models. The top half compares the percentages of employed and nonemployed men who ever married before the child's conception or by the child's third birthday, ignoring marriages to women other than the mother of their first child. The bottom half compares the percentages of single fathers who eventually married the child's mother by the child's third birthday. In both cases, employment status is fixed at the date of the child's conception. Hence, it is a cruder indicator than the time-varying indicator we used in the event-history analysis. Despite its simplicity, the results are striking. Across the four cohorts, the percentage of employed men who ever married declined only slightly from 56 percent for men born between 1941 and 1949 to 43 percent for men born between 1961 and 1969. Similarly, the percentage of employed single fathers who eventually married by the child's third birthday stayed relatively constant at around 30 percent. By contrast, the marriage rates among men who were not employed at the time of the child's conception dropped sharply. Whereas 55 percent of the oldest cohort of nonemployed men ever married, only 10 percent of the youngest cohort did. Also, 46 percent of the oldest cohort of nonemployed fathers legitimated the conception of their child by their child's third birthday compared to 4 percent of the youngest cohort. These cross-tabulations exclude men who were observed for less than three years after the conception of their first child, which accounts for the small number of observations in the youngest birth cohort. In spite of the small numbers, these cross-tabulations clearly show that marriage rates among employed and nonemployed black men in inner-city Chicago have been diverging over time. It is this divergence in marriage rates which accounts for the strengthening relationship between employment and marriage over cohorts in the event-history models. The ratio of marriage rates of employed to nonemployed men rises from approximately 1.0 in the older cohorts to between 4.0 and 8.0 in the younger cohorts.

TABLE 3.11

Marriages to Mother of First Child by the Child's Third Birthday,
by Employment Status at Child's Conception:
Black Males Aged 18–44 in Chicago Poverty Tracts, 1986

	Employment Status at Child's Conception			
	Employed		Not Employed	
Marriage Type Birth Cohort	Percent Married	*n*	Percent Married	*n*
Marriages to mother of first child				
1941–49	56	50	55	37
1950–55	46	31	30	42
1956–60	50	22	14	44
1961–69	43	7	10	26
Post-conception marriages				
1941–49	32	34	46	29
1950–55	22	21	22	38
1956–60	33	18	8	39
1961–69	33	6	4	24

Premarital Conceptions

So far our analysis has estimated the effects of activity status and other variables on marriage. We now turn to an analysis of premarital conceptions. Previous studies find little relationship between male employment status and the likelihood of fathering a child before marriage (Lerman, 1989). We think this makes some sense. Except for possible variation in contraceptive practice, there is little reason to believe that a young man's activity status (in school, work, military, or idle) has any direct bearing on his sexual behavior or risk of early fatherhood. On the other hand, once he has conceived a child out of wedlock, our previous analysis shows that his ability to support a family strongly affects the likelihood of his marrying. Collapsing the two processes and estimating a "reduced form" model is apt to obscure the actual effect of employment on marriage.

Table 3.12 displays three models predicting the likelihood of premarital conceptions at each age. Model 1 shows that employment is unrelated to age-specific risks of premarital fatherhood, even though military service is associated with a higher risk. Model 2 shows no trend by birth cohort in the likelihood of conceiving a child premaritally. This agrees with our estimates from the Kaplan-Mier survival distributions (see Table 3.2). Model 3 shows that men

TABLE 3.12

*Hazards Regression Estimates of Effects on Age-Specific Rates of Premarital Conception:
Black Males Aged 18–44 in Chicago Poverty Tracts, 1986*

Variables	Model 1		Model 2		Model 3	
	exp(b)	b/s.e.	exp(b)	b/s.e.	exp(b)	b/s.e.
Activity status						
Work	1.18	1.10	1.20	1.20	1.27	1.52
School	1.08	0.41	1.08	0.39	1.13	0.60
Military	1.71	2.05	1.77	2.15		
Draft					2.15	2.33
Volunteer					1.45	0.87
Birth cohorts						
1941–49			0.85	−0.85	0.82	−1.03
1950–55			1.02	0.08	0.99	−0.03
1956–60			0.96	−0.24	0.94	−0.32
High school graduate					1.02	0.13
Incarceration					1.65	2.11
Mother-only family at age 14					0.95	−0.41

Note: n = 413; censored = 68.4 percent.

with a prison record are at greater risk of conceiving a child premaritally than men who stayed out of jail. Also, only military service during the draft increases the risk of premarital fatherhood. In sum, variables which strongly affect the likelihood of marriage, especially employment and cohort, do not affect the age-specific risks of premarital conception.

Discussion

This study provides evidence showing that black male employment is positively related to marriage rates. The null hypothesis of no relationship is rejected for all categories of marriage. Black single men who are in stable employment are twice as likely to marry as single men who are inactive. Increases in black male joblessness, however, do not fully explain declines in the incidence of marriage. The hypothesis of stable marriage rates, controlling for employment status, is rejected. Single men born between 1941 and 1949 were far more likely to marry than men born between 1961 and 1969 regardless of employment. During this same period of time, rates of premarital conception remained approximately stable for all four birth cohorts. An estimated 44 percent of all respondents fathered their first child out of wedlock by their twenty-fifth birthday. There was no relationship between employment status and the risk of premarital fatherhood.

This study shows that marriage rates are declining in accordance with hypothesis three. Moreover, cohort-specific analyses indicate that the fifth hypothesis of converging marriage rates for working and nonworking men can also be rejected. According to these data, employed black men in the inner city have not shunned marriage in order to combine women's AFDC benefits with their earnings. Instead, the marriage rates of working and nonworking black men appear to be diverging over time in accordance with hypothesis four. Consequently, the relationship between male employment and marriage appears to be strengthening over time. This finding is consistent with Wilson's underclass hypothesis linking male marriageability with the ability to support a family.

Both sample size limitations and the possibility of sample-selection biases prevent us from definitely rejecting hypothesis three in favor of four. Because the UPFS sample was restricted to poor census tracts, estimates of the magnitude of the employment effect among older cohorts may be biased downward due to the migration of working- and middle-class families from inner-city neighborhoods. Since the likelihood of out-migration most probably increases with age, black men who were employed when they got married may be systematically underrepresented among the older cohorts in our sample. Consequently, our estimate of the employment effect for the older cohorts in our sample could be misleadingly small.

Another study (Testa, 1991) attempted to replicate these results with data from the National Survey of Families and Households (NSFH), which was conducted with a national sample of adults at the same time the UPFS survey was underway. The similarity in findings was striking for the main two results. Employment status was unrelated to the likelihood of fathering a child out of wedlock in both samples, but was strongly predictive of marriage rates. Where the results differed was with respect to the intensity of the employment effect over time. Whereas the Chicago sample showed a clear strengthening of the employment effect, the result was only partially replicated with the national data. The more parsimonious model of equal declines (Alternative 3) fit the national data; therefore, we are inclined to attribute the Chicago trend as most likely an artifact of the selective migration of working- and middle-class families out of inner-city neighborhoods. Nonetheless, the hypothesis of strengthening employment effects (Alternative 4) should not be completely dismissed. The validity of the national findings is hampered by the lack of a sufficient number of observations. It will be important to continue pursuing this line of inquiry with much larger samples of single fathers.

One additional qualification to the findings should be made. All of the inferences we have drawn assume that employment status influences marriage.

But it could be otherwise: the intention to marry could motivate the search for work. If the correct causal order is indeed from marriage intention to employment, rather than the other way around, the policy implications would be quite different. Still, a reversal of the causal order does not obviate the fact that employment is strongly associated with marriage. Even if stable employment only enables marriage, improving the employment status of men would still be a necessary, if not sufficient, intervention to reduce levels of single parenthood.

In reflecting on these findings, we are reminded that most first births and marriages occur during early adulthood. Over one-half of the black men in our sample became fathers before their twenty-fifth birthday. This percentage has not changed very much for successive cohorts of black men. What has changed dramatically is the proportion who are working or serving in the military. Presently, almost two-thirds of inner-city black males are either in school or idle between ages nineteen and twenty-two. They depend fully, or in part, on government assistance, family help, or illicit activities for support. Few young men at this age are in a position today to support a family.

It appears to us that public policy can take two directions in response to the prolonged social dependency of inner-city youth. One direction is to renew efforts to prevent unwanted pregnancies. Our finding that 80 percent of fathers reported that the conception of their first child was unintended suggests the need for improved male contraceptive practice. Also, raising the costs of absent fatherhood through more vigorous child-support enforcement might help to lower rates of premarital fatherhood.

A second direction is to create alternative roles for out-of-school youth who are presently idle. Aside from military service, there are currently few ways for out-of-school youth to reliably secure adult roles. The strong positive effect of voluntary military service on marriage suggests to us that young men joining the military find a secure role as productive adults. Their experience of sustained work and decent pay is quite different from the irregular jobs and low wages currently experienced by many young people, not just black males, when they leave high school. Some groups are calling for the creation of alternative routes to adulthood through a combination of national service, paid apprenticeships, and cooperative school-employment training (William T. Grant Foundation, 1988). Dependable access to adult roles could mitigate the social isolation of poor and minority youth. It strikes us as no coincidence that black men in stable employment or military service are more likely to marry than youth who are detached from the labor force. Establishing more such pathways to adulthood could provide not only the means to raise a family, but also the reason to wait to have a family.

Conclusion

This study shows that black male employment is positively related to marriage rates. Overall, we find that black men in stable employment are twice as likely to marry as black men who are not in school, in the military, or at work. Moreover, black men in voluntary military service are also more likely to marry than men who are inactive.

Cohort-specific models reveal that the relationship between male employment and all first marriages in inner-city Chicago has strengthened over cohorts. The relationship strengthens especially for marriages to the mother of the man's first child. Cohort-specific models also show that the relationship between premarital fatherhood and marriage has weakened over cohorts, especially for marriages to the mother of the man's first child. This is consistent with a weakening of normative pressures on couples to legitimate a premarital conception. Although these results are consistent with theories of the ghetto underclass (Wilson, 1987), they should be regarded as provisional. Replications of these findings with other samples will be necessary to assess whether they are artifacts of sample selection or indicators of valid trends.

These models also underscore the importance of distinguishing the effect of male employment on marriage from its effect on the conception of a child before marriage. Male employment has virtually no impact on the latter. In fact, none of our models fit the data on premarital conceptions very well. Premarital conception may be random or related to variables not specified in our models. Consequently, increasing the employment of men would not necessarily decrease premarital conceptions, even though it might increase the proportions of pregnancies resolved through marriage. Preventing unplanned pregnancies, in addition to increasing the employment of men, appears to be crucial to increasing levels of married fatherhood.

REFERENCES

ALLISON, P. 1982. Discrete-time methods for the analysis of event histories. In S. Leinhardt, ed., *Sociological Methodology 1982*, pp. 61–98. San Francisco: Jossey-Bass.

ALLISON, P. 1984. *Event history analysis: Regression for longitudinal event data* (Sage University Paper Series on Quantitative Applications in the Social Sciences Series 07-001). Beverly Hills: Sage Publications.

BECKER, G.S. 1981. *A treatise on the family.* Cambridge, MA: Harvard University Press.

CARROLL, C.D. 1988. *Tabulation routines for means and percentages with Taylor standard error estimates* (Version 3.1). Washington, DC: Department of Education, Office of Educational Research and Improvement.

CHERLIN, A.J. 1981. *Marriage, divorce, and remarriage.* Cambridge, MA: Harvard University Press.

DANIEL, K. 1989. A note on Mark Testa et al. *Employment and marriage among inner-city fathers* (ERC 89-3). Chicago: NORC/University of Chicago, Economics Demography Group, Economics Research Center.

EHRENREICH, B. 1983. *The hearts of men.* New York: Doubleday.

ELLWOOD, D.T., AND RODDA, D. 1990. The hazards of work and marriage: The influence of employment on marriage. Unpublished paper, Harvard University.

FARLEY, R. 1988. After the starting line: Blacks and women in an uphill race. *Demography,* 25:477–495.

FOSSETT, M.A., AND KIECOLT, K.J. 1993. Mate availability and family structure among African Americans in U.S. metropolitan areas. *Journal of Marriage and the Family,* 55:288–302.

FREEDMAN, D., THORNTON, A., CAMBURN, D., ALWIN, D., AND YOUNG-DEMARCO, L. 1988. The life history calendar: A technique for collecting retrospective data. In C. Clogg, ed., *Sociological methodology 1988,* pp. 37–68. Washington, DC: American Sociological Association.

GRANT, THE WILLIAM T. FOUNDATION COMMISSION ON WORK, FAMILY, AND CITIZENSHIP. 1988. The forgotten half: Pathways to success for America's youth and young families. Washington, DC: The William T. Grant Foundation Commission on Work, Family and Citizenship.

HOEM, J.M. 1987. *The issue of weights in panel surveys of individual behavior* (Stockholm Research Reports in Demography 39). Stockholm: University of Stockholm, Section of Demography.

JENCKS, C. 1989. What is the underclass and is it growing? *Focus,* 12:14–26.

KALBFLEISH, J., AND PRENTICE, R. 1980. *The statistical analysis of failure time data.* New York: Wiley.

KASARDA, J.D. 1989. Urban industrial transition and the underclass. *The Annals of the American Academy of Political and Social Science,* 501:26–47.

LERMAN, R.I. 1986. Generating poverty: Why do young men become absent fathers? Paper presented at the annual meeting of the Association of Public Policy and Management, Seattle, WA.

LERMAN, R.I. 1989. Employment opportunities of young men and family formation. *American Economic Review Papers and Proceedings,* 79:62–66.

LICHTER, D.T., LeCLERE, F.B., AND McLAUGHLIN, D.K. 1991. Local marriage markets and the marital behavior of black and white women. *American Journal of Sociology* 96:843–867.

LICHTER, D.T., McLAUGHLIN, D.K., KEPHART, G., AND LANDRY, D.J. 1992. Race and the retreat from marriage: A shortage of marriageable men? *American Sociological Review,* 57:781–799.

MARE, R.D., AND WINSHIP, C. 1991. Socioeconomic change and the decline of marriage for blacks and whites. In C. Jencks and P. Peterson, eds., *The urban underclass,* pp. 175–202. Washington, DC: The Brookings Institution.

MOYNIHAN, D. 1965. *The Negro family: The case for national action.* Washington, D.C.: U.S. Department of Labor, Office of Policy Planning and Research.

MURRAY, C. 1984. *Losing ground: American social policy, 1950–1980.* New York: Basic Books.

MURRAY, C. 1985. Have the poor been "losing ground"? *Political Science Quarterly,* 100:427–445.

O'CONNELL, M., AND ROGERS, C.C. 1984. Out-of-wedlock births, premarital pregnancies and their effect on family formation and dissolution. *Family Planning Perspectives,* 16:157–162.

PATTERSON, J.T. 1986. *America's struggle against poverty 1900–1985.* Cambridge, MA: Harvard University Press.

PLOTNICK, R.D. 1988. Determinants of out-of-wedlock childbearing: Evidence from the National Survey of Youth (mimeo). Seattle: University of Washington, Graduate School of Public Affairs and School of Social Work.

SCANZONI, J. 1982. *Sexual bargaining: Power politics in the American marriage.* 2nd ed. Chicago: University of Chicago Press.

SCHOEN, R., AND KLUEGEL, J.R. 1988. The widening gap in black and white marriage rates: The impact of population composition and differential marriage propensities. *American Sociological Review,* 53:895–907.

SOUTH, S.J., AND LLOYD, K.M. 1992. Marriage markets and nonmarital fertility in the United States. *Demography,* 29:247–264.

TESTA, M. 1991. Male joblessness, nonmarital parenthood, and marriage. Paper presented at the Chicago Urban Poverty and Family Life Conference, Chicago, IL.

TESTA, M., ASTONE, N.M., KROGH, M., AND NECKERMAN, K.M. 1989. Employment and marriage among inner-city fathers. *The Annals of the American Academy of Political and Social Science,* 501:79–91.

TUMA, N.B., AND HANNAN, M.T. 1984. *Social dynamics: Models and methods.* New York: Academic Press.

U.S. CONGRESS, HOUSE COMMITTEE ON WAYS AND MEANS. 1985. *Children in Poverty,* p. 118. Washington, DC: U.S. Government Printing Office.

VINOVSKIS, M. 1988. Teenage pregnancy and the underclass. *The Public Interest,* 93: 87–96.

WILSON, W.J. 1987. *The truly disadvantaged: The inner city, the underclass and public policy.* Chicago: University of Chicago Press.

WILSON, W.J., AND NECKERMAN, K.M. 1986. Poverty and family structure: The widening gap between evidence and public policy issues. In S.H. Danziger and D.H. Weinberg, eds., *Fighting poverty: What works and what doesn't,* pp. 232–259. Cambridge, MA: Harvard University Press.

COMMENTARY

Sheldon Danziger

I N AN IMPORTANT paper, first presented at a conference in 1984, William Julius Wilson hypothesized that "the increasing inability of many black men to support a family is the driving force behind the rise of female-headed families" (Wilson and Neckerman, 1986, p. 258). He expanded on this theme in his influential book, *The Truly Disadvantaged* (Wilson, 1987) and launched a major research project—The Chicago Urban Family Life Project—to test this and other relationships among employment, family structure, and social isolation in the inner city. The chapter by Testa and Krogh utilizes data gathered as part of Wilson's Chicago project and evaluates Wilson's hypothesis and several others concerning the relationship between male joblessness and female family headship.

Before beginning the discussion, let me briefly review the national data that provide some perspective for this Chicago study. Table C3.1 shows the living arrangements of American children in 1960 and 1990. Several points are relevant. First, the trends for whites and blacks are quite similar. Children of both races are now more likely to live in mother-only families, especially with never-married mothers. Despite similar trends, however, female headship among white children in 1990 was quite similar to what it was for black children in 1960—about one-sixth of all white children lived in mother-only families, and fewer than one in thirty lived with a never-married mother. Finally, because of the rapid changes in living arrangements, more than half of black children lived in mother-only families in 1990. The single most rapid change was in the percentage living with never-married mothers. Only about one in fifty black children lived with never-married mothers in 1960, as compared to more than one-fourth by 1990.

An important contribution of the Testa/Krogh chapter is its focus on non-marital parenthood. Many earlier studies of the causes of female family headship

TABLE C3.1

Living Arrangements of Children, 1960 and 1990

	White Children		Black Children	
	1960	1990	1960	1990
Percentage of children living with				
Two parents	90.9	79.0	67.0	37.7
Mothers only	6.1	16.2	19.9	51.2
Never married	0.1	3.0	2.1	27.3
Divorced, separated, or widowed	6.0	13.2	17.8	23.9
Fathers only	1.0	3.0	2.0	3.5
Other relatives	1.4	1.4	9.6	6.5
Nonrelatives only	0.5	0.4	1.5	1.0

Source: U.S. Bureau of the Census (1991).

have not distinguished between the different types of female-headed families—those headed by never-married as opposed to ever-married women.

Table C3.2 shows that all of these trends are associated with rising child poverty. Children in two-parent families have much lower poverty rates than children in mother-only families; children living with never-married mothers have much higher poverty rates than those living with ever-married mothers. Living arrangements are now more important than race when it comes to child poverty—black children in two-parent families have a much lower poverty rate than white children living in mother-only families. For both white and black children, but particularly for blacks, changes in marital status and living arrangements have contributed to increasing poverty.

TABLE C3.2

Poverty Rate of Children, by Living Arrangements and Marital Status of Parents, 1990

Poverty Rate	All Children	Two Parents	Mother Only				Father Only
			Divorced	Separated	Widowed	Never Married	
White children	14.5	8.7	33.4	51.7	32.6	57.2	17.1
Black children	42.7	18.1	46.2	59.2	54.1	67.9	37.4

Source: U.S. Bureau of the Census (1991).

Given the importance of premarital conception in explaining the well-being of black children, and having reviewed Chapter 3, it is easy in hindsight to argue that the most interesting question that emerges from the chapter differs from the one which motivated it. The chapter was directly motivated by and does address Wilson's "male marriageable pool hypothesis" about the effect of employment on marriage. However, I wish the authors had focused instead on trying to understand what economic, social, and psychological factors explain this increased premarital childbearing. In particular, why do so many African American children whose fathers are employed live only with their never-married mothers?

Almost half of their sample, men aged eighteen to forty-four, had fathered a child out of wedlock. Testa and Krogh's finding in this regard actually foreshadows my critique and suggests an avenue for further research:

> . . . none of our models fit the data on premarital conceptions very well. Premarital conception may be random or related to variables not specified in our models.

The data gathered by the Chicago project can shed light on this issue and commend it to the authors for further research. But in this new research they should rectify another problem mentioned in their conclusion—their use of a very limited number of variables from a rich data set. Indeed, the authors mention some of the omitted variables in the introductory section—the stigma of out-of-wedlock birth, the availability of welfare, mother's access to extended familial support. I would add a range of variables that were gathered as part of the Urban Poverty and Family Structure survey—religiosity, participation in community organizations, social networks, attitudes toward marriage, aspirations, and so forth. The significance of the cohort variables in most of the models suggests that they may be proxies for trends in these unmeasured variables.

In addition, the authors proxy the economic status of the men by their employment status at a point in time, by whether or not they are working. No distinction is made between men who have stable versus sporadic work histories, men who have high-status versus low-status occupations, men who have above-average versus very low earnings. I suspect that these dimensions of employment may be significantly related to marital behaviors.

The authors sacrificed the richness of the data to the elegance of the hazard model, which requires contemporaneous information on employment and marital status. I would suggest a compromise. The authors could also provide the reader with descriptive tables that address simpler questions. For example, were men who were stably employed at "good jobs" in their early twenties more likely to have married and less likely to have fathered a child out of wedlock?

Of course, neither their hazard models nor such tables can reject an alternative view—that the causality runs not from male employment to marriage, but in the reverse direction. That is, men who desire to marry the mother of their child, or men who feel strong pressure to do so, are more likely to seek employment. Such data may be available from the Chicago project, and it would be worth investigating.

In some ways, the neglect of the broader range of noneconomic variables is not surprising, as the key goal was to test Wilson's view that male joblessness was a prime determinant of female headship. However, this study and others (reviewed in Testa, 1991) have concluded that

> the magnitude of the male employment effect would have to be implausibly large in order to account fully for the decline in black male marriage rates.

In other words, by 1991 a number of papers had tested Wilson's original male marriageable pool hypothesis, and their findings led Wilson (1991) himself to this modification:

> Finally, our data show a strong relationship between male employment status and marriage. However, the data also suggest that the stronger the norms against premarital sex, out-of-wedlock pregnancy, and single parenthood, the less economic considerations affect decisions to marry. Our ethnographic data show that inner-city black single parents feel little pressure to consummate a marriage. They emphasize the importance of having secure jobs and financial security before seriously considering matrimony. Ethnographic data suggest these responses reflect a linkage between evolving cultural arrangements, changing norms, and new structural realities. The result has been increased out-of-wedlock births, a weaker family structure, the growth of persistent poverty, and a rise in welfare receipt.

My reading of the literature, including Testa (1991) and Wilson (1991), led me to sketch the complicated model shown in Figure C3.1. This model is much easier to outline than to estimate, so it is not surprising that Testa and Krogh focused only on the link between male joblessness and marriage. A more complex model requires information on the mothers as well as on the fathers, particularly the mothers' own opportunities for economic independence, attitudes toward welfare and marriage, and the kinds of variables discussed in Wilson (1987, 1991)—limited aspirations, negative social dispositions, casual work habits, constrained class networks, and limited access to jobs.

This model also posits a role for some general societal views on commitment to marriage, sanctions for out-of-wedlock birth, the stigma of welfare, as well as the "ghetto-specific norms" discussed by Wilson. The model notes that there are common factors to the common trends—increasing female headship

FIGURE C3.1

Model of factors influencing recent trends in patterns of family formation.

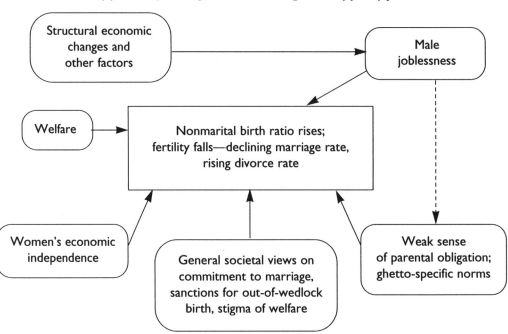

for both whites and blacks—but additional factors that are presumed to operate only within "underclass areas."

Testa and Krogh do estimate that marriage is twice as common among men who were employed or in the military as among those who were inactive. Unfortunately, they do not translate their hazard rates back into expected marriage rates, so it is difficult to evaluate the absolute magnitude, as opposed to the relative importance, of their main effect. For example, we are told that if the probability that an unemployed man is married is X, then the probability for an employed man is 2X, but we are never told X, the underlying rate. From Figure 3.3, we learn that 66 percent of the sample never married, so I infer that X is rather low for employed as well as unemployed men. This reinforces my view that we should try to understand the low rate among employed men, particularly employed men who have fathered children out of wedlock.

Jencks (1992) does offer some descriptive tables that are consistent with the Testa/Krogh conclusion. Jencks uses the 1960 and 1980 census data for black men in different cohorts. For those between the ages of twenty-five and twenty-nine, the probability of marriage declined by more than 23 percentage points over the two decades (from 69.8 to 46.1 percent). Marriage was much more likely in any year for those working full time than for those not working at all during the year, but the marriage rate actually fell by a greater amount for the former. In this cohort, the rate for full-year workers fell by 20 percentage points (from 75.9 to 55.7 percent), while it fell by only 8 points (from 31.2 to 23.5 percent) for nonworkers. Ellwood and Crane (1990) make a similar point, using data on employed and unemployed men in other cohorts over the 1960 through 1988 period. What these studies do not report, which Testa and Krogh could present, are the changes across cohorts in out-of-wedlock fatherhood by the employed and unemployed.

Wilson has called attention to three distinct problems—the inability of an increasing percentage of black males to support a family; an increasing percentage of children who live in female-headed families; and the extent of economic hardship and poverty in the inner city, especially the dire prospects for children living there. Even if male joblessness is not the primary cause of increased female family headship, each trend is important in its own right. Testa and Krogh are clearly correct in their policy conclusions—renewed efforts to prevent unwanted pregnancies and to promote self-sufficiency among young men (and I might add, young women), such as paid apprenticeships, national service, or other training and work opportunities. Unfortunately, as we all know, it will take much more than this to resolve the economic and social crises in the inner city.

REFERENCES

ELLWOOD, D.T., AND CRANE, J. 1990. Family change among black Americans: What do we know? *Journal of Economic Perspectives,* 4 (4):65–84.

JENCKS, C. 1992. *Rethinking social policy: Race, poverty and the underclass.* Cambridge, MA: Harvard University Press.

TESTA, M. 1991. Male joblessness, nonmarital parenthood, and marriage. Paper presented at the Chicago Urban Poverty and Family Life Conference, Chicago, IL, October.

U.S. BUREAU OF THE CENSUS. 1991. *Marital status and living arrangements: March 1990. Current Population Reports,* series P-20, no. 450. Washington, DC: U.S. Government Printing Office.

WILSON, W.J. 1987. *The truly disadvantaged: The inner city, the underclass, and public policy.* Chicago: University of Chicago Press.

WILSON, W.J. 1991. Poverty, joblessness, and family structure in the inner city: A comparative perspective. Paper presented at the Chicago Urban Poverty and Family Life Conference, Chicago, IL, October.

WILSON, W.J., AND NECKERMAN, K.M. 1986. Poverty and family structure: The widening gap between evidence and public policy issues. In S.H. Danziger and D.H. Weinberg, eds., *Fighting poverty: What works and what doesn't,* pp. 232–259. Cambridge, MA: Harvard University Press.

4 THE WIDENING GAP BETWEEN BLACK AND WHITE MARRIAGE RATES: CONTEXT AND IMPLICATIONS

Robert Schoen

M ARRIAGE RATES in the United States, and in a number of other Western countries, have been declining for some time. Among American women born around 1940, whose marriages were concentrated in the years 1960–65, 97.3 percent of those surviving to age 15 married, and their average age at first marriage was 21.1 years (Schoen et al., 1985). However, rates in the United States observed in 1983 imply that only 89.7 percent of those surviving to age 15 will ever marry, and their average age at first marriage will be 24.5 years (Schoen, 1987).

Declines in marriage have been particularly large for blacks (Cherlin, 1981), and the growing divergence in black-white patterns has led some commentators to speak of a "crisis" or a "deterioration" in contemporary black family life (Staples, 1985; Wilson, 1978). At the same time, others have noted that there are substantial compositional differences between the black and white populations. In particular, black females face a marriage market with fewer eligible males of the same race than do white females (Spanier and Glick, 1980). As a result, black females may be experiencing a "marriage squeeze" that depresses their marriage rates and exaggerates black-white differences.

This chapter examines black and white patterns using propensities to marry, measures which reflect the mutual attraction for marriage independent of population composition. Focusing on previously unanalyzed data for Wisconsin in 1980, it looks at marriages by age, race, and educational attainment, and compares black and white marriage levels and patterns of marriage choice.

A Theoretical Perspective

The recent decline in marriage rates in the United States has been well documented, though much less attention has been given to changes in the characteristics of persons who marry one another. That is unfortunate, because an analysis of "who marries whom" can shed considerable light on the nature of the marriage bargain and how marriage is responding to social and economic change.

Traditional marriage has been seen as the exchange of a male's economic resources for a female's social and domestic services. Homogamy (i.e., marriage between people with similar characteristics) has been considered the traditional norm (Blau and Duncan, 1967; Carter and Glick, 1976). Edwards (1969) related homogamy to exchange theory by taking a utility maximization perspective. The essence of his argument is that marriageable persons seek partners who will maximize their rewards from marriage. Persons with similar characteristics are likely to maximize each other's rewards, as both are likely to reject persons with resources inferior to their own, and persons with equivalent resources are likely to have similar characteristics. Schoen and Wooldredge (1989) extended Edwards's reasoning, arguing that couples with equivalent resources need not be similar on all characteristics relevant to marriage choice because overall equivalence could result from exchanges between relative strengths in different areas. Exchanges are apt to take place because husbands and wives have traditionally filled different roles. Even though the traditional division of labor by sex has been substantially eroded by women's increased labor-force activity, the socioeconomic status of the husband is still more important than that of the wife in determining a couple's status (Leslie, 1982; Nock and Rossi, 1978). As a result, women are more likely to stress their partner's socioeconomic characteristics, men are more likely to stress their partner's noneconomic (or social) characteristics, and both may be able to gain from an exchange.

With regard to interracial marriage, the classic exchange arguments are found in the studies of Kingsley Davis (1941) and Robert Merton (1941). They theorized that most black-white marriages in the United States would be between black males and white females, because those marriages could embody exchanges between the groom's higher socioeconomic status and the bride's "caste" status. Studies have shown that most black-white marriages do involve black grooms, though whether that is due to the exchanges envisioned by Davis and Merton remains in dispute (Monahan, 1976; Schoen and Wooldredge, 1989).

The theoretical considerations described above also relate to black-white differences in *intra*racial marriage behavior, because the social and economic context in which the marriage exchange takes place differs by race. At all socioeconomic levels, black men hold more traditional beliefs about the role of women than do white men, while black and white women hold similar views

(Ransford and Miller, 1983). At the same time, black women are more econom-ically active than white women, and the wage gap between males and females is much smaller for blacks than for whites (Farley, 1988). Comparing the hourly earnings of blacks relative to whites for persons aged twenty-five to thirty-four in 1980, Farley (1984, p. 126) found that black women earned 98 percent of the amount earned by white women, while black men earned only 81 percent of the amount earned by white men. Thus, with respect to the traditional marriage exchange, black men, relative to white men, are likely to expect more in terms of role behavior while being able to offer less in terms of economic benefits, making the traditional marriage exchange less advantageous to black women than to white women.

That perspective leads to three hypotheses regarding black-white marriage patterns. First, blacks are expected to have a lower propensity to marry because they stand to gain less from the marriage exchange. Second, black women are expected to marry a man with more education than their own less often than white women, because the economic role of black women, relative to black men, is greater than the economic role of white women relative to white men. Third, interracial marriages are expected to involve more black grooms than white grooms because black male/white female marriages offer the possibility of exchanges between a male's higher socioeconomic status and a female's race.

Past research on marriage patterns has provided only equivocal support for the exchange perspective. However, those inconsistent findings may be only a reflection of the methodological complexities involved in measuring intergroup marriage. Much of the work done in the past only examined data on marriages, and thus did not take into account the population at risk of marrying. The population at risk is important because, other things equal, one would expect more marriages between persons who share a common characteristic than be-tween persons who share an uncommon one. The study by Schoen and Wool-dredge (1989), which applied the exchange perspective described above to 1969–71 and 1979–81 data on blacks and whites in North Carolina and Vir-ginia, found the results hypothesized here. The present analysis of data for Wisconsin in 1980 examines whether similar results can be found in a northern state.

Measuring the Propensity to Marry

Since every monogamous marriage involves one male and one female, an indi-vidual's chance of marrying is influenced by population composition. To control for compositional effects, including the marriage squeeze, and to obtain compo-sition-independent measures of marriage behavior, this chapter makes use of the approach developed in Schoen (1981, 1986).

Consider a male marriage rate of the form

$$W_m(A,B) = C(A,B)/M(A) \tag{4.1}$$

where $W_m(A,B)$ represents a male marriage rate for males with characteristics A marrying females with characteristics B,

$C(A,B)$ represents the number of marriages between males with characteristics A and females with characteristics B, and

$M(A)$ represents the number of males with characteristics A.

The rate in equation (4.1) is sensitive to the composition of the male population, but not to the composition of the female population. The analogous female marriage rate is of the form

$$W_f(A,B) = C(A,B)/F(B) \tag{4.2}$$

where $W_f(A,B)$ represents a female marriage rate for females with characteristics B marrying males with characteristics A, and

$F(B)$ represents the number of females with characteristics B.

The rate in equation (4.2) is sensitive to the composition of the female population, but not to the composition of the male population.

Schoen (1981, 1986) derived an expression for the *propensity to marry* (or the magnitude of marriage attraction), a measure analogous to a hazard rate that reflects the underlying mutual attraction for marriage between males with characteristics A and females with characteristics B independent of population composition. Denoted by $H(A,B)$, the propensity can be written as

$$H(A,B) = u W_m(A,B) + v W_f(A,B) \tag{4.3}$$

where u is the length of the male age interval and v is the length of the female age interval. As a sum of male and female marriage rates, it is sensitive to the risk of marriage for both sexes.

To see how the propensity remains independent of population composition with respect to the characteristics recognized, consider the following example. A certain population initially has m males, f females, and c marriages. Its marriage propensity is thus given by $H = c/m + c/f$. Now assume that the number of males increases to m' while the number of females and the propensity to marry remain the same. It is reasonable to expect that the number of marriages will increase, say to c', but that the proportional increase in the number of marriages will be less than the proportional increase in the number of males. That implies that the new male marriage rate c'/m' will be less than c/m. Furthermore, the new female marriage rate c'/f will be greater than c/f because the number of marriages increases while the female population remains the same. Since the propensity to marry does not change, equation (4.3) states that $H = c'/m' + c'/f$, and thus the decline in the male rate is exactly offset by the increase in the female rate. In short, the marriage propensity is independent of ·population composition because compositional changes lead to counterbalancing changes in male and female marriage rates.

The Data

To analyze marriages specific to the age, race, and educational level of the bride and groom, information on both marriages and the population at risk of marriage are needed. For the year 1980, data on 39,991 marriages were taken from machine-readable data files provided by the state of Wisconsin (Wisconsin Bureau of Health Statistics, 1983). Data on the unmarried population of Wisconsin in 1980 were taken from the 5 percent Public Use Microdata tapes issued by the Census Bureau (U.S. Bureau of the Census, 1983).

The number of marriages available is sufficient to allow a detailed breakdown by age. For both males and females, seventeen age groups are recognized, specifically ages 14–17, 18, 19, 20, 21, 22, 23, 24, 25, 26–27, 28–29, 30–32, 33–35, 36–39, 40–44, 45–49, and 50–59. There are no marriages under age 14, and the few marriages at ages 60 and over are ignored. Race is a dichotomous variable, black and nonblack. There are only a small number of marriages involving persons who are neither white nor black, and it seems most appropriate to include them with the larger white group.

The educational levels of the bride and groom are available by single years of schooling completed, but the analysis employs four categories that emphasize the major credentialing points. Those categories are "less than four years of high school," "four years of high school," "some college," and "four or more years of college." Education, while not an ideal measure, provides an objective indication of the socioeconomic status of the couple at the time of marriage.

Results and Discussion

Equation (4.3) was used to calculate the matrix of marriage propensities by age, race, and education. With the categories employed, there are 18,496 [i.e., $(17 \times 2 \times 4)^2$] such propensities. The results by age are not shown, as age is used primarily to control for compositional differences between the various race and education groups. For convenience, expressions of the form (X,Y) will be used to refer to marriages involving a group X groom and a group Y bride, with B denoting blacks and N denoting nonblacks.

Table 4.1 presents numbers of marriages by race of the bride and groom. Nearly 97 percent of all marriages were between two nonblacks, but there were

TABLE 4.1

*Numbers of Marriages and Sums of Age-Specific Marriage Propensities,
by Race of the Bride and Groom: Wisconsin, 1980*

Groom's Race	Bride's Race		
	Black	Nonblack	Total
Black	3.26	.45	3.71
	(1,013)	(202)	(1,215)
Nonblack	.09	6.31	6.40
	(60)	(38,716)	(38,776)
Total	3.35	6.76	10.11
	(1,073)	(38,918)	(39,991)

Note: Figures in parentheses refer to numbers of marriages.

over a thousand (B,B) marriages. Only 262 marriages, 0.7 percent of the total, were interracial.

The marriage propensities shown in Table 4.1 represent sums of age-race-specific marriage propensities over all 289 (i.e., 17 × 17) possible combinations of age of bride and age of groom. For example, the figure of 3.26 shown for (B,B) marriages is the sum of all of the age of bride/age of groom specific propensities for (B,B) marriages. As the figure for (N,N) marriages exceeds that for (B,B) marriages, the propensity for marriage between two nonblacks is greater than the propensity for marriage between two blacks. Approximately 5 percent of all propensities in the table are for interracial marriage. (By way of comparison, the analogous figure for North Carolina-Virginia 1979–81 is 1 percent.) The sum of the propensities for (B,N) marriages is five times as large as the sum for (N,B) marriages, a finding consistent with the Davis-Merton hypothesis.

Table 4.2 shows sums of age-specific marriage propensities by education of the bride and groom, for all races combined. Educationally homogamous marriages—that is, marriages where the bride and groom are at the same educational level—are by far the most common, and account for 47 percent of the marriage propensities in the table. Among educationally heterogamous marriages, the marriage propensities are greater when the education of the groom is greater than the education of the bride, rather than when the education of the bride is greater than that of the groom. The ratio of the six propensities in the lower left portion of Table 4.2, where the groom's education exceeds the bride's, to the six propensities in the upper right portion, where the bride's education exceeds the groom's, is 1.27. If we only consider combinations with an educational difference of two or three categories, that is, if we compare the

TABLE 4.2

Numbers of Marriages and Sums of Age-Specific Marriage Propensities,
by Education of the Bride and Groom: Wisconsin, 1980

Groom's Education	Bride's Education				
	Less than Four Years of High School	Four Years of High School	Some College	Four or More Years of College	Total
Less than four years of high school	1.66 (2,058)	1.70 (2,507)	.47 (420)	.13 (91)	3.96 (5,076)
Four years of high school	1.40 (2,376)	3.92 (11,875)	1.62 (3,139)	.77 (905)	7.71 (18,295)
Some college	.70 (464)	2.20 (3,655)	2.35 (3,301)	1.11 (1,266)	6.36 (8,686)
Four or more years of college	.12 (90)	1.16 (1,487)	1.78 (2,168)	3.67 (4,189)	6.73 (7,934)
Total	3.88 (4,988)	8.98 (19,524)	6.22 (9,028)	5.68 (6,541)	24.76 (39,991)

Note: Figures in parentheses refer to numbers of marriages.

three lower left entries to the three upper right entries, the ratio is 1.45. Table 4.2 thus shows the expected pattern of women tending to "marry up" with respect to educational level, with the tendency more marked for greater educational differences.

Table 4.3 presents arrays of marriage propensities, summed over age, by both the race and educational level of the bride and groom. Among intraracial marriages, the propensity for an (N,N) marriage is greater than the propensity for a (B,B) marriage in thirteen of the sixteen education of bride/education of groom combinations. All three exceptions involve combinations where the education of the bride and groom differ by at least two categories. As these figures reflect marriage propensities, they are independent of the effects of any marriage squeeze related to the age, race, and education composition of the population.

Table 4.4 shows black/nonblack ratios for intraracial marriages by educational level, separately for brides and grooms. To put the results for Wisconsin 1980 in a comparative context, figures for North Carolina-Virginia 1979–81 are also shown (Schoen and Wooldredge, 1989). The upper left entry, .70, represents the ratio of all (B,B) marriage propensities for black grooms with less than four years of high school (2.89, in the first row of Table 4.3, Panel A) to all (N,N) marriage propensities for nonblack grooms with less than four

TABLE 4.3

*Numbers of Marriages and Sums of Age-Specific Marriage Propensities,
by Education and Race of the Bride and Groom: Wisconsin, 1980*

Groom's Education	Less than Four Years of High School	Four Years of High School	Some College	Four or More Years of College	Total
	Bride's Education				
	A. Black Groom and Black Bride				
Less than four years of high school	1.20 (120)	.99 (92)	.47 (32)	.23 (7)	2.89 (251)
Four years of high school	.79 (82)	2.10 (284)	1.05 (85)	.48 (21)	4.42 (472)
Some college	.20 (19)	1.48 (80)	1.81 (91)	.38 (24)	3.87 (214)
Four or more years of college	.15 (4)	.41 (13)	1.20 (28)	1.61 (31)	3.37 (76)
Total	2.34 (225)	4.98 (469)	4.53 (236)	2.70 (83)	14.55 (1,013)
	B. Black Groom and Nonblack Bride				
Less than four years of high school	.12 (15)	.14 (21)	.07 (8)	.01 (1)	.34 (45)
Four years of high school	.07 (7)	.18 (34)	.13 (17)	.04 (7)	.42 (65)
Some college	.01 (2)	.09 (13)	.30 (20)	.10 (9)	.50 (44)
Four or more years of college	.03 (2)	.38 (11)	.48 (11)	.74 (24)	1.63 (48)
Total	.23 (26)	.79 (79)	.98 (56)	.89 (41)	2.89 (202)

Note: Figures in parentheses refer to numbers of marriages.

years of high school (4.14, in the first row of Table 4.3, Panel D). It is clear that black marriage propensities are substantially less than nonblack marriage propensities for both sexes, both areas, and all educational levels. Overall, there does not seem to be any clear pattern by educational level. Neither well-educated nor poorly educated blacks exhibit any distinct differences relative to similarly educated nonblacks. That finding is consistent with the expectation that blacks at all educational levels have less to gain from the marriage exchange.

TABLE 4.3 *(continued)*

Groom's Education	Bride's Education				
	Less than Four Years of High School	Four Years of High School	Some College	Four or More Years of College	Total
	C. Nonblack Groom and Black Bride				
Less than four years of high school	.02 (3)	.02 (5)	.01 (2)	.07 (2)	.12 (12)
Four years of high school	.01 (4)	.03 (10)	.04 (5)	.12 (3)	.20 (22)
Some college	.00 (1)	.01 (3)	.04 (5)	.01 (1)	.06 (10)
Four or more years of college	0 (0)	.02 (4)	.03 (5)	.09 (7)	.14 (16)
Total	.03 (8)	.08 (22)	.12 (17)	.29 (13)	.52 (60)
	D. Nonblack Groom and Nonblack Bride				
Less than four years of high school	1.76 (1,920)	1.79 (2,389)	.46 (378)	.13 (81)	4.14 (4,768)
Four years of high school	1.56 (2,283)	4.02 (11,547)	1.65 (3,032)	.73 (874)	7.96 (17,736)
Some college	.76 (442)	2.26 (3,559)	2.38 (3,185)	1.14 (1,232)	6.54 (8,418)
Four or more years of college	.13 (84)	1.18 (1,459)	1.81 (2,124)	3.73 (4,127)	6.85 (7,794)
Total	4.21 (4,729)	9.25 (18,954)	6.30 (8,719)	5.73 (6,314)	25.49 (38,716)

Table 4.5 examines how the pattern of women marrying up with regard to education varies with the race of the bride and groom in both Wisconsin 1980 and North Carolina-Virginia 1979–81. The first two columns of the table show that, except for (N,B) marriages in Wisconsin, there is little variability in the proportion of marriages that are educationally heterogamous. The next two columns give ratios that relate propensities for educationally heterogamous marriages where the groom has more education to those where the bride has more education. In (N,N) marriages, the ratio is 1.31 in Wisconsin and 1.33

TABLE 4.4

Black/Nonblack Ratios of Sums of Age-Education-Specific
Marriage Propensities for Intraracial Marriages:
Wisconsin, 1980; North Carolina-Virginia, 1979–81

Educational Level	Wisconsin, 1980		North Carolina-Virginia, 1979–81	
	Males	Females	Males	Females
Less than four years of high school	.70	.56	.52	.44
Four years of high school	.56	.54	.49	.44
Some college	.59	.72	.59	.57
Four or more years of college	.49	.47	.52	.73
All	.57	.57	.53	.53

in North Carolina-Virginia, indicating that the sum of the propensities for marriages where the groom has more education is about a third larger than the sum of the propensities where the bride has more education. For (B,B) marriages, the results are less consistent. In Wisconsin, black women do marry up with regard to education, but in North Carolina-Virginia, men do. The last two columns of Table 4.5 show those ratios for marriages involving two- or three-category educational differences. In (N,N) marriages, the ratios show women marrying up by larger margins, but in (B,B) marriages both areas show men marrying up. Those results may be exaggerating the importance of the relative economic role played by black women or be signaling that there are problems with education as a socioeconomic indicator for blacks. In any event, they do support the hypothesis that black women marry up less than white women.

If the bride and groom are of different races, the last four columns of Table 4.5 show that chances of marrying up with regard to education are dramatically affected. In (B,N) marriages, women marry up while in (N,B) marriages men marry up, both to a much greater extent than in intraracial marriages. Those results are consistent with the Davis-Merton hypothesis, and strongly suggest the possibility of exchanges between the groom's educational level and the bride's race.

TABLE 4.5

Ratios of Educationally Heterogamous Marriage Propensities, by Race of the Bride and Groom: Wisconsin, 1980; North Carolina-Virginia, 1979–81

| Races of the Groom and Bride | Educationally Heterogenous Propensities as a Proportion of all Marriage Propensities | | Ratios of Sums of Educationally Heterogamous Marriage Propensities | | | |
| | | | (EDM > EDF)/(EDF > EDM) | | (EDM 2 or 3 Categories > EDF)/(EDF 2 or 3 Categories > EDM) | |
	Wisconsin, 1980	North Carolina-Virginia, 1979–81	Wisconsin, 1980	North Carolina-Virginia, 1979–81	Wisconsin, 1980	North Carolina-Virginia, 1979–81
Black, black	.54	.56	1.17	.85	.64	.72
Black, nonblack	.54	.57	2.19	2.56	3.62	5.37
Nonblack, black	.68	.56	.30	.54	.12	.33
Nonblack, nonblack	.53	.53	1.31	1.33	1.58	1.51
All	.53	.54	1.27	1.25	1.45	1.36

Note: EDM and EDF refer, respectively, to the educational categories of the groom and bride.

Summary and Conclusions

This study has examined marriage patterns in Wisconsin in 1980 by age, race, and educational level, using marriage propensities to focus on the underlying mutual attraction for marriage independent of compositional effects. It found that black marriage propensities were smaller than white marriage propensities at all educational levels, that black women married up with respect to educational level less than white women, and that there appeared to be exchanges between the educational level of the groom and the race of the bride.

The study adopted an exchange theory perspective, with traditional marriage viewed as the exchange of a male's economic resources for a female's domestic services. Even though that traditional division of labor by sex has been modified considerably, the socioeconomic status of the husband remains more important than that of the wife. Consequently, women are more likely to stress their partner's socioeconomic characteristics, men are more likely to stress their partner's noneconomic (or social) characteristics, and both may be motivated to exchange. The results are fully consistent with such a view.

Two final points should be made. First, the marriage propensities of blacks should be seen as quantitatively, not qualitatively, different from nonblacks. For blacks as well as nonblacks, the marriage exchange reflects the prevailing system of social stratification. The race/education exchange (as hypothesized by Davis, 1941, and Merton, 1941, to explain interracial marriage) found in Wisconsin and in North Carolina-Virginia has its counterparts in the ethnicity/education exchange found between Spanish-surnamed and non-Spanish-surnamed persons in California (Schoen, Wooldredge, and Thomas, 1989), the race/education exchanges found between Chinese, Japanese, Whites, Hawaiians, and Filipinos in Hawaii (Schoen and Thomas, 1989), and the mother tongue language/education exchanges found in the United States between persons whose first language is English, French, German, Italian, Polish, and Spanish (Stevens and Schoen, 1988).

Second, the key difference between black and nonblack marriage patterns seems to lie in the nature of the male-female relationship and how that affects the marriage exchange. There is apparently less consensus among black men and women on what constitutes appropriate sex-role behavior than there is among white men and women. Black women have traditionally been more economically self-sufficient than white women and, given their economic position, have less to gain from marriage. As Farley (1984, p. 170) and others have observed, in the future we are likely to see white marriage propensities move closer to the black pattern as white female labor-force participation continues to rise. The extraordinary increase in cohabitation suggests that the decline in women's economic dependence is heralding the spread of alternatives to marriage.

AUTHOR NOTES

This study benefited greatly from discussions with James R. Kluegel and the computational assistance of John Wooldredge. Support from the National Institute of Child Health and Human Development (DHHS) under grant 1 R01 HD19261 is gratefully acknowledged.

REFERENCES

BLAU, P.M., AND DUNCAN, O.D. 1967. *The American occupational structure*. New York: Wiley.

CARTER, H.N., AND GLICK, P.C. 1976. *Marriage and divorce: A social and economic study*. Rev. ed. Cambridge, MA: Harvard University Press.

CHERLIN, A.J. 1981. *Marriage, divorce, remarriage*. Cambridge, MA: Harvard University Press.

DAVIS, K. 1941. Intermarriage in caste societies. *American Anthropologist*, 43:376–395.

EDWARDS, J.N. 1969. Familial behavior as social exchange. *Journal of Marriage and the Family*, 31:518–526.

FARLEY, R. 1984. *Blacks and whites: Narrowing the gap?* Cambridge, MA: Harvard University Press.

FARLEY, R. 1988. After the starting line: Blacks and women in an uphill race. *Demography*, 25:477–495.

LESLIE, G.R. 1982. *The family in social context*. 5th ed. New York: Oxford University Press.

MERTON, R.K. 1941. Intermarriage and social structure: Fact and theory. *Psychiatry*, 4:361–374.

MONAHAN, T.P. 1976. The occupational class of couples entering into interracial marriages. *Journal of Comparative Family Studies*, 7:175–192.

NOCK, S.L., AND ROSSI, P.H. 1978. Ascription versus achievement in the attribution of family social status. *American Journal of Sociology*, 84:565–590.

RANSFORD, H.E., AND MILLER, J. 1983. Race, sex and feminist outlooks. *American Sociological Review*, 48:46–59.

SCHOEN, R. 1981. The harmonic mean as the basis of a realistic two-sex marriage model. *Demography*, 18:201–216.

SCHOEN, R. 1986. A methodological analysis of intergroup marriage. *Sociological Methodology*, 16:49–78.

SCHOEN, R. 1987. The continuing retreat from marriage: Figures from 1983 U.S. marital status life tables. *Sociology and Social Research*, 71:108–109.

SCHOEN, R., AND THOMAS, B. 1989. Inter-group marriage in Hawaii, 1969–71 and 1979–81. *Sociological Perspectives*. 32:365–382.

SCHOEN, R., URTON, W., WOODROW, K., AND BAJ, J. 1985. Marriage and divorce in twentieth century American cohorts. *Demography*, 22:101–114.

SCHOEN, R., AND WOOLDREDGE, J. 1989. Marriage choices in North Carolina and Virginia, 1969–71 and 1979–81. *Journal of Marriage and the Family*, 51:465–481.

SCHOEN, R., WOOLDREDGE, J., AND THOMAS, B. 1989. Ethnic and educational effects on marriage choice. *Social Science Quarterly*, 70:617–630.

SPANIER, G.B., AND GLICK, P.C. 1980. Mate selection differentials between whites and blacks in the United States. *Social Forces*, 53:707–725.

STAPLES, R. 1985. Changes in black family structure: The conflict between family ideology and structural conditions. *Journal of Marriage and the Family*, 47:1005–1013.

STEVENS, G., AND SCHOEN, R. 1988. Linguistic intermarriage in the United States. *Journal of Marriage and the Family*, 50:267–279.

U.S. BUREAU OF THE CENSUS. 1983. *Census of Population and Housing, 1980: Public Use Microdata*. Sample (A), Wisconsin [MRDF]. Washington, DC: U.S. Government Printing Office.

WILSON, W.J. 1978. *The declining significance of race*. Chicago: University of Chicago Press.

WISCONSIN BUREAU OF HEALTH STATISTICS. 1983. Marriage Records for 1980 [MRDF]. Prepared by Fred Krantz, Bureau of Health Statistics.

COMMENTARY

David M. Heer

FOR SOMEWHAT more than a decade, Robert Schoen has been concerned with what demographers call the two-sex problem. The two-sex problem is caused by "the fact that the observed behavioral rates of males and females cannot both be consistently incorporated into either life table or stable population models" (Schoen, 1981, p. 201). As a solution to the two-sex problem with respect to male and female marriage rates, Schoen has devised a measure he terms the propensity to marry. This measure reflects the "underlying mutual attraction for marriage between males with characteristics A and females with characteristics B independent of population composition" (Schoen, 1989). Schoen denotes this measure as $H(A,B)$. He defines it as the weighted sum of the rate of marriage of males of characteristic A to females of characteristic B and the rate of marriage of females of characteristic B to males of characteristic A. The weight for males is the length of the male age interval and the weight for females is the length of the female age interval. Where male and female age intervals are each single years of age, the propensity to marry reduces to the sum of the male and female rate.

Schoen's measure of propensity to marry allows researchers to solve many problems that were previously insoluble. First, use of the measure allows one to compare marriage propensities across populations that differ greatly in population composition. This was not previously possible in situations where a comparison of female rates presented a different pattern than a comparison of male rates. Second, use of the measure allows one to decompose a difference in rates over time or between populations into a component due to change in marriage propensities, a second component due to change in population composition, and a third component due to interaction between change in marriage propensity and change in population composition (Schoen and Kluegel, 1988).

In a recent paper Schoen and Wooldredge correctly state, "In one way or another virtually all work on marital choice is seriously flawed because the composition of the marriageable population was not taken properly into account" (1989, p. 467). This generalization can be illustrated by a previous paper I published (Heer, 1974). In that paper I attempted to test the Davis-Merton hypothesis that racial-caste hypogamy is associated with class hypergamy. I reported that the hypothesis received no support unless the availability of marriage partners by educational attainment was held constant. However, I had to admit that my own control for availability was inadequate. I concluded as follows: "Thus there is good reason to believe that the testing of the Davis-Merton theory (and its extension to racial-caste hypergamy) still suffers from inadequate control on the real availability of spouses by race at each educational attainment level. However, with the present data no more adequate control on availability is obtainable" (p. 256).

In his current paper, Schoen relies on exchange theory to explain his various findings. Exchange theory assumes that each individual in considering marriage wishes to optimize his utility. Persons will marry if they can find a particular partner who will provide them with more utility than they would have if they remained unmarried. Potential partners, in turn, are also seeking to maximize their own utility. The utility-maximizing strategies of all participants in the marriage market assure that most marriages will be homogeneous with respect to differentially evaluated characteristics. However, as pointed out by Schoen and Wooldredge (1989) and previously by the economist Gary Becker (1976), the gain in utility from marriage is most likely if each partner can gain from the relative strengths of the other. In the traditional marriage, women gained from the greater wage-earning capacities of men and men gained utility from enjoying the opportunity for sexual intercourse and procreation and a woman's superior parental and housekeeping abilities.

Unfortunately, most existing data on marriage propensities do not allow a full test of exchange theory. It can easily be shown that females show a propensity to marry men more educated than themselves rather than less educated, and hence to marry men more likely to be good economic providers. What existing data on marriage certificates cannot show well are the characteristics of women that are most attractive to men. In the traditional marriage, these were supposed to be superior physical beauty and superior parental and housekeeping abilities. Data on black-white marriage rates by whether the groom is black or nonblack and by educational attainment of both male and female are one of the few data sets that allow a more complete test of exchange theory. However, this more complete test is possible only if we assume that both men and women value a nonblack skin color more than a black skin color. If we make this assumption, then in a comparison of all marriages involving a black groom we can say that the groom exchanges his superior educational attainment for the privilege of having a bride of a superior skin color. The empirical data shown here by Schoen support exchange theory very well providing we make this assumption. The identical assumption concerning skin color was made by both

Davis (1941) and Merton (1941), the two sociologists who first considered black-white marriage in the light of exchange theory.

The major finding of Schoen's current paper is that in Wisconsin the propensity of blacks to marry is much lower than the propensity of nonblacks to marry. This finding is identical to a finding for North Carolina and Virginia reported in Schoen and Wooldredge (1989). Since in the United States the earnings capacities of black women relative to black men are far superior to the earnings capacities of white women relative to white men, these results are to be expected, given either the mathematically elaborate theory advanced by Gary Becker (1976) or the less mathematically elaborate assumptions of other exchange theorists.

Further research making use of Schoen's measure of propensity to marry should prove quite fruitful. For example, one might compare the marriage propensities of blacks and nonblacks in different states. I was disappointed to find out that no direct comparison is possible between Schoen's results for Wisconsin and his results for North Carolina and Virginia. This apparently results because Schoen used a greater number of age groups in his study of North Carolina and Virginia than in his study of Wisconsin. Hence his measures of marriage propensity in North Carolina and Virginia are greatly inflated relative to his measures for Wisconsin. However, this lack of comparability is very easily remedied. Considering the ongoing debate about the impact of public welfare on marriage behavior, it could be useful to compare marital propensities in states with very different AFDC benefit rates. The AFDC benefit rate in Wisconsin is one of the nation's highest whereas the AFDC benefit rates in both North Carolina and Virginia are quite low (U.S. Bureau of the Census, 1989). A valuable contribution would be made if further research were to correlate the marriage propensities of blacks in each state with the level of AFDC benefits. Also of interest would be research providing the correlation for all states between the black propensity for marriage and the relative mean wage of black women compared to that of black men. Finally, it would be interesting to have research demonstrating the multivariate relationship between the black propensity to marriage in each state, the level of AFDC benefits, and the relative mean wage of black women compared to that of black men.

REFERENCES

BECKER, G.S. 1976. A theory of marriage. In Gary S. Becker, *The economic approach to human behavior*, pp. 205–250. Chicago: University of Chicago Press.

DAVIS, K. 1941. Intermarriage in cast societies. *American Anthropologist*, 43:376–395.

HEER, D.M. 1974. The prevalence of black-white marriage in the United States, 1960 and 1970. *Journal of Marriage and the Family*, 36:246–258.

MERTON, R.K. 1941. Intermarriage and social structure: Fact and theory. *Psychiatry,* 4:361–374.

SCHOEN, R. 1981. The harmonic mean as the basis of a realistic two-sex model. *Demography,* 18:201–216.

SCHOEN, R. 1989. The widening gap between black and white marriage rates: Context and implications. Paper prepared for presentation at June 30–July 1 UCLA Conference on The Decline in Marriage among African-Americans: Causes, Consequences, and Policy Implications.

SCHOEN, R., AND KLUEGEL, J.R. 1988. The widening gap in black and white marriage rates: The impact of population composition and differential marriage propensities. *American Sociological Review,* 53:895–907.

SCHOEN R., AND WOOLDREDGE, J. 1989. Marriage choices in North Carolina and Virginia, 1969–71 and 1979–81. *Journal of Marriage and the Family,* 51:465–481.

U.S. BUREAU OF THE CENSUS. 1989. *Statistical abstract of the United States, 1989.* Washington, DC: U.S. Government Printing Office.

5 MATE AVAILABILITY AND MARRIAGE AMONG AFRICAN AMERICANS: AGGREGATE- AND INDIVIDUAL-LEVEL ANALYSES

K. Jill Kiecolt
and
Mark A. Fossett

THE IMPACT of the availability of potential mates on family formation and family structure among African Americans is receiving increasing attention. Recent theories (Guttentag and Secord, 1983; Heer and Grossbard-Schechtman, 1981) argue that the sex ratio, the number of men per hundred women, influences many aspects of male-female relations including marriage, divorce, fertility, sexual behavior, and gender roles. Supporting evidence is beginning to accumulate (Guttentag and Secord, 1983; South and Trent, 1988; South, 1988), and increasingly the sex ratio has been implicated as a determinant of black family formation and family structure (Cox, 1940; Darity and Myers, 1984; Guttentag and Secord, 1983; Jackson, 1971; Wilson and Neckerman, 1986). Indeed, some have suggested that the so-called "crisis in the black family" (Staples, 1985)—low marriage rates, high rates of divorce and separation, and the prevalence of female-headed families—may be linked to the low sex ratios for blacks (Darity and Myers, 1984; Guttentag and Secord, 1983; Jackson, 1971; Tucker, 1987; Wilson and Neckerman, 1986) which result from high rates of mortality and institutionalization for black men (Cox, 1940; Jackson, 1971; Passel and Robinson, 1985; Spanier and Glick, 1980).

The hypothesized effects of the sex ratio on black family formation and family structure have important implications for social theory. Low sex ratios are predicted to result in a lower prevalence of marriage for women, fewer husband and wife families, higher nonmarital fertility rates, higher proportions of children born to unmarried mothers, and greater percentages of children living in female-headed households. Until recently, explanations for such patterns in black family structure focused on factors such as the legacy of slavery, group subculture, class structure (especially the development of a permanent black underclass), and group differences in education and human capital. Now demographic factors are being added to this list.

The sex ratio hypothesis also has important implications for social policy. It implies that demands on some social services (e.g., Aid to Families with Dependent Children) will be closely linked to the sex ratio, as will the success of various programs for ameliorating social problems such as black nonmarital fertility. For example, if the sex ratio rather than the welfare state is the major cause of black nonmarital fertility and female headship of families (Darity and Myers, 1984), then policies that tighten welfare restrictions will simply increase human suffering rather than reduce levels of nonmarital fertility and female headship.

Given its potential significance for theory and policy, the impact of the sex ratio on black family formation and family structure should be carefully and systematically examined. We address this question in the present study by conducting both aggregate-level analyses and individual-level contextual analyses using data drawn from the National Survey of Black Americans (Jackson, Tucker, and Gurin, 1980) and the United States census. Our results support the sex ratio hypothesis at both levels of analysis. In the following sections, we discuss the sex ratio hypothesis and its relevance for black family formation and family structure, report the results of our tests of this hypothesis, and discuss the implications of our research.

The Sex Ratio, Marriage, and Family Formation

Drawing on social exchange theory (e.g., Emerson, 1962; Thibaut and Kelley, 1959), the sex ratio hypothesis asserts that members of the scarcer gender have a bargaining advantage in male-female relations because more alternative relationships are available to them (Guttentag and Secord, 1983; Heer and Grossbard-Schechtman, 1981). Guttentag and Secord (1983) term this advantage "dyadic" power. They argue that it is rooted in normative marital sex ratios, the number of "appropriate" men per hundred women, given normative patterns of marriage between men and women of different characteristics (e.g., the number of black men aged twenty-two to twenty-six per hundred black women aged twenty to twenty-four). Imbalances in the sex ratio shift the balance of dyadic power to members of the scarcer gender.

Bargaining between men and women is shaped not only by dyadic power, but also by structural power, the control of political and economic resources (Guttentag and Secord, 1983). In the United States as in virtually every society, men have greater structural power than women. Thus, the traditional marital relationship is one wherein men offer financial support and security to women in exchange for sexual, childrearing, domestic, and other services (Heer and Grossbard-Schechtman, 1981). Structural power must be taken into account when predicting the effects of the sex ratio.

Because of differential structural power, the effects of imbalances in the sex ratio should vary depending on which gender is scarce. For example, the sex ratio has a weaker effect on men's than on women's marriage rates (Cox, 1940), presumably because men are less dependent than women on a partner for economic support. The theory predicts that this asymmetry would diminish if gender differences in structural power were reduced. Thus, better economic opportunities for women should lead to lower female marriage rates given women's reduced dependence on men for economic support, and they should also be associated with a less steep slope of the effect of the sex ratio on female marriage rates (Becker, 1973; Ermisch, 1981; Preston and Richards, 1975; South, 1988).

The sex ratio hypothesis has several implications for marital status and marital outcomes. Individuals are assumed to search for the best match they can obtain, given their characteristics and those they desire in a partner (England and Farkas, 1986). Information about supply and demand for these characteristics is imperfect, but members of the scarcer gender have more potential partners (Guttentag and Secord, 1983). In interacting with members of the opposite gender, individuals gain information about their relative position in the marriage market, and they develop expectations concerning the "terms of exchange"—the kinds of partners that are available to them and what concessions (if any) they must make to secure a desirable partner.[1] Members of the scarcer gender should tend to develop higher expectations and make more demands of their partners, while members of the more abundant gender will be pressured to lower their expectations of partners or risk doing without a partner.

The lower the sex ratio (the scarcer men are), the more favorable the relationship outcomes men can negotiate because of their greater dyadic and structural power. Thus, men are predicted to be more reluctant to enter long-term relationships, partly because they can offer fewer incentives to induce women to enter sexual relationships. Conversely, women are predicted to receive fewer

---

[1] According to Guttentag and Secord (1983), members of either the advantaged gender or the disadvantaged gender need not be aware, and indeed are unlikely to be aware, of the extent to which their options are shaped by the sex ratio. Nevertheless, a person's attitudes, expectations, and negotiating positions in male-female relations should be influenced by the sex ratio even in the absence of precise knowledge of the sex ratio and how it shapes his or her choices, just as other aspects of social structure (e.g., city size or level of urbanization) influence attitudes and behavior without the person's conscious awareness (e.g., Fernandez and Kulik, 1981; reviewed by Kiecolt, 1988). Evidence from the popular press suggests that the public is somewhat aware of the sex ratio, however (e.g., Churchill, 1946; *Ebony*, 1947; Westoff and Goldman, 1984).

rewards for conforming to traditional familial roles and will be forced to consider nontraditional paths of marriage and family formation. Consequently, both men and women are predicted to be less likely to marry—men, because the wealth of alternative possibilities gives them the opportunity to avoid or postpone traditional familial responsibilities (Staples, 1985); women, because potential marriage partners are fewer in number and more reluctant to marry.

Some effects of the sex ratio may be stronger among unmarried people, but sex ratio effects are predicted among married persons as well (e.g., possible effects on the likelihood of divorce). A low sex ratio has been hypothesized to weaken husbands' commitment to marriage (Heer and Grossbard-Schechtman, 1981) by decreasing the value or utility that men place on marriage (Becker, 1973). As a result, husbands are hypothesized to provide fewer benefits and lower "compensation" to wives (Heer and Grossbard-Schechtman, 1981), resulting in less favorable subjective marital outcomes for women than for men (Guttentag and Secord, 1983). Ultimately this imbalance is predicted to heighten the risk of separation and divorce (Guttentag and Secord, 1983; Heer and Grossbard-Schechtman, 1981). At the individual level, this implies that the sex ratio should be negatively related to the likelihood of experiencing marital disruption.[2] At the aggregate level, all else equal, the sex ratio should be positively related to the prevalence of female marriage, the marital fertility rate, and the percentage of husband and wife families. Similarly, the sex ratio should be negatively related to the nonmarital birthrate and the percentage of nonmarital births, since female exposure to the risk of nonmarital pregnancy will be greater when the sex ratio is low. Moreover, these two effects should combine to create a negative relationship between the sex ratio and both the nonmarital fertility ratio and the proportion of children living in female-headed families.

Sex Ratio Research on Black Americans

Research on sex ratio effects on marital behavior among blacks is only beginning to accumulate (Cox, 1940; Guttentag and Secord, 1983; Jackson, 1971; Spanier and Glick, 1980; Tucker, 1987; Wilson and Neckerman, 1986), and quantitative analysis has usually been limited to bivariate correlations. Nevertheless, the evidence strongly suggests that the sex ratio has dramatic consequences for behavior related to family formation. For example, Cox (1940) reported strong correlations between the population sex ratio and the percentages of married men and women in a sample of cities in the United States in

---

[2]Low sex ratios also are predicted to increase the likelihood of wives' employment, because women presumably view employment as a hedge against the financial insecurity that could result from marital disruption (Guttentag and Secord, 1983; Heer and Grossbard-Schechtman, 1981). Indeed, South and Trent (1988) found that women's labor-force participation is negatively associated with the sex ratio at the societal level.

1930. Consistent with predictions of the sex ratio hypothesis, the sex ratio was strongly and positively related to the percentage of married black women in both southern and northern cities (r = 0.82 and 0.85, respectively) and negatively related to the percentage of married black men (r = −0.22 in southern cities and −0.50 in northern cities). Guttentag and Secord (1983, Chapter 8) have reported similar strong zero-order correlations (ranging from −0.67 to −0.87) between the population sex ratio and the separation rate, the divorce rate, and the proportion of single-parent families using state-level data in 1960 and 1970. Finally, a recent study using individual-level data indirectly supports the notion that mate availability (as indexed by age) determines whether men and women are married, as well as whether the unmarried have a main romantic involvement (Tucker and Taylor, 1989).

Individual-Level Analysis

Methods

Data for our individual-level analysis were drawn from the 1980 National Survey of Black Americans (Jackson, Tucker, and Gurin, 1980). This survey is a representative, national, cross-sectional sample of 2,107 blacks eighteen years of age or older in the continental United States (see Smith, 1987, for a discussion of the sample). Only respondents aged eighteen to forty-four were included in the analysis, as these are the ages at which the predicted effects of the sex ratio on family life should be the strongest. Data for computing sex ratios were drawn from published volumes of the United States census.

Measures

Marital status. An objective marital outcome, marital status, was categorized as legally married and living with spouse, divorced, separated, widowed, never-married, or being in a common-law marriage (volunteered by respondents). Respondents in either legal or common-law marriages were classified as married.

Sex ratio. We measured the sex ratio at the community level. Men and women meet in cities or local areas (Catton, 1964; Cox, 1940), and researchers studying the marriage market (Freiden, 1974; Goldman, Westoff, and Hammerslough, 1984; Westoff and Goldman, 1984) and the marriage squeeze (Akers, 1967; Ermisch, 1981) concur that marriage markets for most persons are local. Thus, sex ratios at the community level are likely to have greater effects on marriage than sex ratios at the national level. Community sex ratios vary considerably (Cox, 1940; Passel and Robinson, 1985; Ermisch, 1981;

Goldman, Westoff, and Hammerslough, 1984; Westoff and Goldman, 1984). Like national sex ratios, they reflect the sex ratio at birth, changes in fertility rates, and sex differences in mortality. Additionally, sex ratios in local areas also are affected by age and gender differences in migration rates. Since migration streams can involve large numbers of people and tend to change much more quickly than fertility rates and gender differences in mortality, sex ratios are likely to vary more across communities at a single point in time than do national sex ratios over time.[3] Analyses of metropolitan areas in 1980 (Passel and Robinson, 1985) and cities in 1930 (Cox, 1940) have documented substantial variation in sex ratios for the black population.

Using census materials, a community sex ratio was computed for each individual in the survey based on the age-sex structure of his or her SMSA (Standard Metropolitan Statistical Area) or nonmetropolitan county of residence as appropriate. After investigating several alternatives (Fossett and Kiecolt, 1991), we ultimately measured the sex ratio by the number of black men per hundred black women aged 15.0–44.9 in each community.[4]

Control variables. The models also included age, education, and income as control variables. Age was measured in years. The square of age also was included because previous research has shown that the relationship between age and marriage is nonlinear (Tucker and Taylor, 1989). Education was measured by recoding years of education into seven categories (1 = one to six years, 2 = seven to eight years, 3 = some high school, 4 = high school degree, 5 = some college, 6 = college graduate, 7 = graduate or professional school). Income was measured by respondent's (rather than family) income, coded to the category midpoints in thousands of dollars.

Results

We tested whether the effects of the sex ratio are detectable at the individual level by regressing on the sex ratio whether persons had ever been married and, if so, whether they were divorced or separated. The models were estimated using logistic regression. Age, the square of age, education, and income were entered as controls.

Table 5.1 shows that, as predicted, the sex ratio is positively related to the likelihood that women have ever married, and it is negatively related to the likelihood that women who have ever been married are currently divorced. That is, the greater the number of men in a local area, the more likely women are to have ever been married, and the less likely they are to be separated or di-

---

[3] One nonmetropolitan county was excluded from the analysis because of its extreme value on the sex ratio (226). Excluding this county left the significance of the effects of the sex ratio virtually unchanged.

[4] Data related to this point are presented in the aggregate-level analysis.

TABLE 5.1

Logit Coefficients from the Logistic Regression of Marital Status Variables on the Community Sex Ratio, by Gender

	Ever Married		Divorced[a]	
	Men	Women	Men	Women
Sex ratio	.020	.029*	−.017	−.029*
Age	1.041***	.709***	−.226	.467**
Age-squared	−.014***	−.009***	.005	−.007**
Education	.035	−.066	.155	−.227*
Income	.063**	.005	−.029**	.051**
Intercept	−20.143***	−14.505***	−3.987	−4.684
Model chi-square	253.70***	300.36***	61.33***	89.61***
n	412	673	246	446

[a] Analysis restricted to ever-married respondents.

p < .05. **p* < .01. ***p* < .001.

vorced. In contrast, the sex ratio did not have a statistically significant effect at the individual level on the likelihood that men have ever been married or that they are divorced.[5] This was not altogether surprising, because aggregate-level effects of the sex ratio on marriage rates for men have been found to be weaker than those for women (Cox, 1940), and individual-level effects typically are more difficult to detect. Perhaps larger sample sizes will be required to detect effects on men, inasmuch as these are predicted to be smaller due to men's greater structural power.[6]

[5] Following Cox (1940), we also estimated a model that included the square of the sex ratio to test for a nonlinear effect on marriage rates for men. Including this term did not significantly improve the fit of the model.

[6] Sex ratio effects are inherently much more difficult to detect in individual-level contextual analysis. This is because the goal of the survey is to provide a representative sample of individuals. Consequently, large communities contribute disproportionately (but representatively) to the sample. All else equal, the variance in the sex ratio (or any other community-level variable) will be compressed because a small number of large cities dominates the sample (e.g., the largest 10 percent of communities may contribute more than half of the sample, while the remaining 90 percent contribute the rest of the sample). When the variance on an independent variable is compressed in this way, there is less potential to detect effects in regression analysis, and the ability of the variable to contribute to explained variance is limited. Consequently, contribution to explained variance is not always the most meaningful indicator of a variable's effect. For example, the sex ratio can have important policy implications for local areas which experience dramatic effects due to an unbalanced sex ratio. This holds even when the sex ratio's contribution to explained variance in an individual-level sample is limited by the fact that the variability in the sex ratio for individuals is smaller than the variability in the sex ratio for communities.

The control variables behaved as expected. Age was positively related to the likelihood of ever having been married for both genders, although the negative coefficient for the squared term indicates that the relationship levels off with age. Age was positively related to being divorced for women, but not for men. Men's earning power significantly predicted whether they marry and remain married. The higher their income, the more likely men were to have ever been married and the less likely they were to be divorced. Income, by contrast, was unrelated to the likelihood of ever having married for women. The higher was ever-married women's income, the less likely they were to be divorced. Unfortunately, data limitations prevented us from determining whether women's as well as men's income enhances marital stability.

Aggregate-Level Analysis

Methods

The aggregate-level portion of our study drew on data for the seven metropolitan areas and forty-eight nonmetropolitan parishes (counties) of Louisiana in 1970 and 1980. Using these data provided significant advantages. First, no previous studies have examined sex ratio effects in nonmetropolitan areas. Second, many hypothesized determinants of family formation and family structure (e.g., regional subculture, welfare and public assistance policies and levels of support, levels of racism and discrimination, and so forth) do not vary substantially across areas of Louisiana and therefore did not need to be controlled in our analysis. Third, the choice of a single state simplified data collection. Finally, our familiarity with Louisiana parishes helped sensitize us to factors which might otherwise have distorted the measures (e.g., the location of state prisons and military installations). The major limitation of the data was that they were not a random sample of communities in the United States. Thus, while there is no reason to believe that the patterns observed for Louisiana differ from patterns for other states and regions, this ultimately must be confirmed with future research.

Measures

Dependent variables. We developed several measures of patterns of black family formation and structure. These were the percentage of women married with spouse present, the total, marital, and nonmarital birthrates per thousand women aged twenty to twenty-nine, the percentage of nonmarital births, the percentage of husband and wife families, and the percentage of children residing in husband and wife families. Many of these measures were computed separately for key subgroups. For example, in addition to computing the percentage married with spouse present for all black women aged sixteen and above, we also computed this percentage for women with young children (ages zero to five) and women with only older children (ages six to seventeen). Similarly, we measured the nonmarital fertility rate and the percentage of nonmarital births both for all women and for women in their twenties. Descriptive statistics for these measures are shown in Tables 5.2 and 5.3.

Sex ratio. We measured the sex ratio for black men and women aged sixteen and above, excluding inmates of institutions, who are not free to interact with members of the local community and are thus not part of the marriage market.[7] We selected this measure from several alternative measures of the sex ratio that could be computed given the data available for nonmetropolitan parishes. Other sex ratios were computed using different combinations of men and women from the total population, the population aged sixteen and above, the noninstitutional population aged sixteen and above, the labor force, and the employed labor force. We have discussed in detail issues relating to the measurement of the sex ratio elsewhere (Fossett and Kiecolt, 1991) and therefore will not repeat that discussion here. In brief, while the measure we used is simple, it is perhaps the best measure that can be obtained for nonmetropolitan parishes, given available data. It performed well as a predictor and was more than adequate for the purposes of our analysis.

Results

The variation in the sex ratio across areas was substantial for the key measures in our analysis. We particularly note the variation in the cross-sectional community sex ratio for blacks. It was considerably greater than the variation in the national sex ratio for whites over time, which has been viewed as potentially important by demographers and other social scientists (e.g., Heer and Grossbard-Schechtman, 1981; Schoen, 1983; Akers, 1967). To illustrate, Heer and Grossbard-Schechtman (1981) reported annual sex ratios between males aged 19.5–26.4 and females aged 17.0–23.9 with a standard deviation of 4.4 over the thirty-year period between 1955 and 1984. This can be compared with standard deviations of 7.61 and 6.20 for the ratios of noninstitutional adult males to females observed in 1970 and 1980, respectively. The variation in our data is not unusual. Passel and Robinson's (1985) metropolitan-level analysis using data for 1980, Guttentag and Secord's (1983) state-level analysis

---

[7] One nonmetropolitan parish (Vernon) was excluded from the analysis. Its extreme values on the sex ratio (452 in 1970 and 210 in 1980, due to a large military base) gave it inordinate influence on the regressions. When this parish was included, the effects of the sex ratio usually were exaggerated rather than diminished. We excluded two additional nonmetropolitan parishes (Jackson and St. James) from the analysis for 1980 because data to compute the sex ratio for the adult noninstitutional population were not available for them.

TABLE 5.2

Descriptive Statistics and Effects of the Sex Ratio on Selected Variables
for Fifty-Four Nonmetropolitan Parishes and Metropolitan Areas of Louisiana, 1970

Variable	Mean	S.D.	OLS[b] b	OLS[b] Beta	GLS[c] b	GLS[c] Beta
			Effect of Ratio of Adult Men to Adult Women (Noninstitutionalized)[a]			
Sex ratios for the black population						
Total population	94.39	25.18				
Adults (aged 16 and older)	88.31	31.78				
Noninstitutionalized adults	83.15	.61				
Males in labor force	50.20	9.31				
Births per thousand black women aged 20 to 29						
Marital births	157.46	53.42	.768	.109	3.155*	.346*
Nonmarital births	59.91	24.74	−1.934***	−.595***	−2.768***	−.610***
Percentage of nonmarital births						
All births	34.47	11.11	−.861***	−.590***	−1.585***	−.688***
Births to women aged 20 to 29	31.39	10.55	−.876***	−.632***	−1.319***	−.682***
Percentage of black women married with spouse present						
Women aged 16 and older	45.61	5.83	.651***	.851***	.754***	.833***
With children aged 0 to 5	70.76	8.78	.912***	.791***	1.157***	.807***
With children aged 6 to 17	67.54	6.87	.549***	.608***	.888***	.694***
Percentage of husband and wife families						
All families	69.72	4.01	.414***	.786***	.638***	.751***
With children aged 0 to 5	74.96	6.19	.491***	.603***	.971***	.731***
With children aged 6 to 17	66.41	5.30	.487***	.699***	.792***	.707***
Percentage of children living in husband and wife families						
Children aged 0 to 17	59.28	6.18	.484***	.596***	.924***	.742***

Note: Vernon parish was excluded from the analysis (see footnote [7]).

[a]The regression effects reported are net of controls for metropolitan status and average AFDC payments per family.
[b]OLS = ordinary least squares.
[c]GLS = generalized least squares. The GLS regressions are weighted to correct for heteroskedasticity.

*$p < .05$; ***$p < .001$ using a two-tailed test.

TABLE 5.3

Descriptive Statistics and Effects of the Sex Ratio on Selected Variables for Fifty-Two Nonmetropolitan Parishes and Metropolitan Areas of Louisiana, 1980

Variable	Mean	S.D.	OLS[b] b	OLS[b] Beta	GLS[c] b	GLS[c] Beta
			Effect of Ratio of Adult Men to Adult Women (Noninstitutionalized)[a]			
Sex ratios for the black population						
Total population	92.43	25.27				
Adults (aged 16 and older)	87.28	35.69				
Noninstitutionalized adults	80.76	6.20				
Males in labor force	49.29	9.08				
Births per thousand black women aged 20 to 29						
Marital births	90.67	22.03	1.550***	.436***	1.853***	.440***
Nonmarital births	66.05	19.10	−1.035*	−.336*	−1.592***	−.496***
Percentage of nonmarital births						
All births	50.30	9.46	−.887***	−.581***	−1.180***	−.707***
Births to women aged 20 to 29	48.64	10.66	−.927***	−.539***	−1.102***	−.634***
Percentage of black women married with spouse present						
Women aged 16 and older	37.86	4.62	.402***	.539***	.558***	.586***
With children aged 0 to 5	58.03	9.41	.959***	.632***	1.308***	.636***
With children aged 6 to 17	59.05	9.26	.732***	.490***	.892***	.541***
Percentage of husband and wife families						
All families	61.22	4.81	.597***	.759***	.721***	.583***
With children aged 0 to 5	63.24	7.20	.732***	.623***	1.077***	.587***
With children aged 6 to 17	59.45	6.92	.881***	.779***	.898***	.556***
Percentage of children living in husband and wife families						
Children aged 0 to 17	48.67	6.24	.683***	.679***	.913***	.641***

Note: Three parishes were dropped from the analysis (see footnote [7]).

[a]The regression effects reported are net of controls for metropolitan status and average AFDC payments per family.
[b]OLS = ordinary least squares.
[c]GLS = generalized least squares. The GLS regressions are weighted to correct for heteroskedasticity.

*p < .05; ***p < .001 using a two-tailed test.

using data for 1960 and 1970, and Cox's (1940) city-level analysis using data for 1930, have all documented substantial cross-area variation in sex ratios for the black population. Thus, comparative analyses such as these provide an excellent opportunity for assessing the potential effects of the sex ratio on aspects of family formation.

Tables 5.2 and 5.3 report correlation coefficients indicating the effects of the sex ratio on our measures of black family formation and family structure for our sample of metropolitan areas and nonmetropolitan counties in 1970 and 1980, respectively. The effects reported are net of controls for metropolitan status and AFDC payments. Consistent with previous comparative research on black sex ratios reported for cities (Cox, 1940) and states (Guttentag and Secord, 1983), we observed strong sex ratio effects. The sex ratio had strong positive effects on the percentage of black women who were married with spouse present, the rate of marital births per thousand black women aged twenty to twenty-nine, the percentage of husband and wife families, and the percentage of children living in husband and wife families, and it had strong negative effects on the nonmarital birthrate and the percentage of nonmarital births. All significant effects were in the expected direction, and most had probabilities of chance occurrence of .01 or less.

The effects of the sex ratio were very robust. They were estimated controlling for metropolitan status and average AFDC payments, and they were quite similar in 1970 and 1980. Additional analyses not reported here show that the effect of the sex ratio was also not significantly diminished when controls for city size, level of urbanization, and percent black were applied. Equally strong effects were observed when the regressions were performed using only the nonmetropolitan parishes or the metropolitan areas. Finally, as the tables indicate, the effects were virtually unchanged when they were reestimated using weighted least squares techniques (instead of ordinary least squares regression) to take account of heteroskedasticity associated with area differences in population size. Indeed, weighting to correct for heteroskedasticity tended to increase the magnitude of the unstandardized regression coefficients and to reduce their standard errors. In sum, we have reason to believe that the findings we observed are not artifacts of our sample, measures, or techniques of analysis.[8]

[8] In additional analyses not reported here, we found that the relationship between the sex ratio and most of our aggregate-level dependent variables could be described more accurately by using alternative measurement strategies. Specifically, the fit of our models was improved when we expressed the sex ratio as the natural logarithm of the ratio of males to females, and it improved further still when the percentage measured was similarly expressed as logits (e.g., the percentage of nonmarital births was expressed as the logarithm of the ratio of marital to nonmarital births). The improvements in prediction were observed both in the transformed metric for the variables and when the logit predictions were converted back to the original metric of percentages. Such improvements are to be expected in light of the advantages that logits can have over bounded measures such as percentages (Hanushek and Jackson, 1977). However, we present the results of the percentage versions of the variables, whose substantive implications are more readily interpretable.

Discussion

This study has examined whether the sex ratio affects marital outcomes and patterns of family formation for black men and women. The results from our individual-level data supported some but not all predictions of the sex ratio hypothesis (Guttentag and Secord, 1983; Heer and Grossbard-Schechtman, 1981), inasmuch as we found predicted effects of the sex ratio on women's, but not men's, marital status. Perhaps the absence of effects for men results because the sample size is small and the effects are likely to be more subtle and difficult to detect for men. All of the results from our analyses of aggregate-level data supported the predictions of the sex ratio hypothesis, even when the analysis was limited to nonmetropolitan areas. These effects reflect the aggregate-level consequences of sex ratio effects on individual marital outcomes. Aggregate level effects are probably easier to detect (see footnote 6). They demonstrate that effects that appear modest from the point of view of explained variance in individual-level models can have dramatic impacts at the aggregate level, as well as important implications for social policy.

Further work must be done to discover the causal connections between the sex ratio and family formation and family structure. Although Guttentag and Secord (1983) do not specify a full causal model of the attitudinal and behavioral consequences of imbalances in the sex ratio, they suggest that some of the sex ratio's effects on behavior are direct, while others are channeled through social-psychological processes. The sex ratio is predicted to influence the value or utility that men and women place on marriage and ultimately their satisfaction with marriage (Becker, 1973; Guttentag and Secord, 1983; Heer and Grossbard-Schechtman, 1981). To date, however, little previous research has rigorously examined the subjective effects of the sex ratio (except see Tucker and Mitchell-Kernan, in press).

For example, aside from objective search efficiency, beliefs about the number of available partners may intervene between the community sex ratio and attitudes and behavior surrounding male-female relationships (Oppenheimer, 1988; Tucker and Mitchell-Kernan, in press; Chapter 6 of this volume). Perceptions of marital opportunities may crucially influence how long persons are willing to search for a marital partner, as well as what they deem a minimally acceptable match (England and Farkas, 1986; Oppenheimer, 1988).

In conclusion, we have demonstrated at the individual level that the sex ratio affects the likelihood that black women have ever been married, and that ever-married black women are separated or divorced. We have also provided further evidence that the effects of the sex ratio on individual marital outcomes translate into dramatic consequences for black family formation and family structure. Future research at the individual level should attempt to identify the social-psychological mechanisms through which the sex ratio and other aspects of social structure influence marital behavior. Future research at the aggregate level should broaden the scope of analysis by including even more dependent variables and by investigating the impact of differential economic opportunities for men and women on the sex ratio.

AUTHOR NOTES

The analyses for this chapter were completed while Kiecolt was at Louisiana State University and Fossett was at the University of Texas, Austin. This research was supported by a grant from the Rockefeller Foundation. Any errors are solely the responsibility of the authors.

REFERENCES

AKERS, D.S. 1967. On measuring the marriage squeeze. *Demography*, 4:907–924.

BECKER, G.S. 1973. A theory of marriage: Part I. *Journal of Political Economy*, 81: 813–846.

CATTON, W.R. 1964. A comparison of mathematical models for the effect of residential propinquity on mate selection. *American Sociological Review*, 29:522–529.

CHURCHILL, J.C. 1946. Your chances of getting married. *Good Housekeeping*, 123: 38,313–319.

COX, O.C. 1940. Sex ratio and marital status among Negroes. *American Sociological Review*, 5:937–947.

DARITY, W.A., JR., AND MYERS, S.L., JR. 1984. Does welfare cause female headship? The case of the black family. *Journal of Marriage and the Family*, 46:765–780.

Ebony. 1947. Marriage: 800,000 Negro girls will never get to altar, experts predict. *Ebony*, 4:21.

EMERSON, R. 1962. Power-dependence relations. *American Sociological Review*, 27: 31–41.

ENGLAND, P., AND FARKAS, G. 1986. *Households, employment, and gender: A social, economic, and demographic view*. New York: Aldine.

ERMISCH, J.F. 1981. Economic opportunities, marriage squeezes, and the propensity to marry: An economic analysis of period marriage rates in England and Wales. *Population Studies*, 35:347–356.

FERNANDEZ, R.M., AND KULIK, J.C. 1981. A multilevel model of life satisfaction. *American Sociological Review*, 46:840–850.

FOSSETT, M.A., AND KIECOLT, K.J. 1991. A methodological review of sex ratio: Alternatives for comparative research. *Journal of Marriage and the Family*, 53:941–947.

FREIDEN, A. 1974. The U.S. marriage market. In T.W. Schultz, ed., *Economics of the family*, pp. 352–371. Chicago: University of Chicago Press.

GOLDMAN, N., WESTOFF, C.F., AND HAMMERSLOUGH, C. 1984. Demography of the marriage market in the United States. *Population Index*, 50:5–25.

GUTTENTAG, M., AND SECORD, P.F. 1983. *Too many women? The sex ratio question*. Beverly Hills: Sage Publications.

HANUSHEK, E.A., AND JACKSON, J.E. 1977. *Statistical methods for social scientists.* New York: Academic Press.

HEER, D.M., AND GROSSBARD-SCHECHTMAN, A. 1981. The impact of the female marriage squeeze and the contraceptive revolution on sex roles and the women's liberation movement in the United States, 1960 to 1975. *Journal of Marriage and the Family,* 34:49–65.

JACKSON, J.J. 1971. But where are all the men? *Black Scholar,* 3:30–41.

JACKSON, J.S., TUCKER, M.B., AND GURIN, G. 1980. National Survey of Black Americans [machine-readable data file]. Ann Arbor: Institute for Social Research [producer]. Interuniversity Consortium for Political and Social Research [distributor].

KIECOLT, K.J. 1988. Recent developments in attitudes and social structure. *Annual Review of Sociology,* 14:381–403.

OPPENHEIMER, V.K. 1988. A theory of marriage timing. *American Journal of Sociology,* 94:563–591.

PASSEL, J.S., AND ROBINSON, G. 1985. Factors associated with variation in sex ratios of the population across states and MSAs: Findings based on regression analysis of 1980 census data. In *Proceedings of the Social Statistics Section of the Annual Meetings of the American Statistical Association,* pp. 624–628.

PRESTON, S.H., AND RICHARDS, A.T. 1975. The influence of women's work opportunities on marriage rates. *Demography,* 12:209–222.

SCHOEN, R. 1983. Measuring the tightness of a marriage squeeze. *Demography,* 20: 61–78.

SMITH, A. W. 1987. Problems and progress in the measurement of black public opinion. *American Behavioral Scientist,* 30:441–455.

SOUTH, S.J. 1988. Sex ratios, economic power, and women's roles: A theoretical extension and empirical test. *Journal of Marriage and the Family,* 50:19–31.

SOUTH, S.J., AND TRENT, K. 1988. Sex ratios and women's roles: A cross-national analysis. *American Journal of Sociology,* 93:1096–1115.

SPANIER, G.B., AND GLICK, P.C. 1980. Mate selection differentials between whites and blacks in the United States. *Social Forces,* 58:707–725.

STAPLES, R. 1985. Changes in black family structure: The conflict between family ideology and structural conditions. *Journal of Marriage and the Family,* 47:1005–1013.

THIBAUT, J.W., AND KELLEY, H.H. 1959. *The social psychology of groups.* New York: Wiley.

TUCKER, M.B. 1987. The black male shortage in Los Angeles. *Sociology and Social Research,* 71:221–227.

TUCKER, M.B., AND MITCHELL-KERNAN, C. (in press). Mate availability among African Americans: Conceptual and methodological issues. In R. Jones, ed., *Advances in black psychology.* Hampton, VA: Cobb and Henry.

TUCKER, M.B., AND TAYLOR, R.J. 1989. Demographic correlates of relationship status among black Americans. *Journal of Marriage and the Family,* 51:655–665.

WESTOFF, C.F., AND GOLDMAN, N. 1984. Figuring the odds in the marriage market. *Money,* 13:32–42.

WILSON, W.J., AND NECKERMAN, K.M. 1986. Poverty and family structure: The widening gap between evidence and public policy issues. In S.H. Danziger and D.H. Weinberg, eds., *Fighting poverty: What works and what doesn't,* pp. 232–259. Cambridge, MA: Harvard University Press.

COMMENTARY

A. Wade Smith

AFRICAN AMERICANS have been participants in most of the major social trends which have swept this nation. At times, blacks have been at the crest of change; as a group, they were among the first to oppose the Vietnam War (Brink and Harris, 1967). In other instances, social change overswept black Americans. Lieberson (1980) demonstrated that the comparative success of European immigrants was due in part to the fact that the mostly rural and Southern black population was neither geographically nor competitively prepared to challenge other groups for the jobs coming into existence in the urban/industrial heydays of the late nineteenth and early twentieth centuries. Moreover, while African Americans have often been behind the trend of positive change, they have seldom enjoyed a position on the lee side of negative trends. For example, while virtually all major racial/ethnic groups in the United States are experiencing increases in the rates of both female-headed households and homicide, African Americans lead in both areas (Staples, 1985; Farley, 1986).

In this context, Kiecolt and Fossett posit the notion that a nontrivial portion of the decline in marriage among African Americans is a consequence of an imbalanced ratio of black males to females. Specifically, they argue that a shortage of viable black males in a given community simultaneously raises male expectations and lowers female expectations for mate selection.[1] As a consequence of these fluctuating sets of expectations, both black men and black women will be more reluctant (and less likely) to marry. In this view, both men and women are also more open to divorce because a husband's commitment to marriage is presumed weakened by the increased availability of unmarried fe-

---

[1] Only noninstitutionalized black men were considered viable. In their analysis, Kiecolt and Fossett's survey evidence included only those in the civilian residential population (i.e., no one living on college campuses, in prison, in the military, etc.); and for the aggregate data, they excluded two Louisiana parishes with high prison and military populations.

136

males around him. At the same time, wives are believed to receive less marital "compensation" from their husbands because men have more options outside of marriage. Examining both national survey (individual-level) evidence and statewide (aggregate-level) data from Louisiana, the authors confirm their expectations. At micro as well as macro levels, statistically significant relationships were established between black sex ratios and both marriage and divorce. To different degrees for men and women, these basic relationships persisted despite controls for personal attributes (age, education, income) and socio-ecological characteristics (countywide births, family living arrangements, etc.).

Kiecolt and Fossett are to be applauded for their innovative application of both micro- and macro-level analyses to the same research questions. Certainly, a great deal of the significance of their confirmation of the effects of a low black sex ratio on marital outcomes among African Americans stems from the redundancy of their findings. Moreover, Kiecolt and Fossett make a conceptual contribution via their introduction of socio-ecological measures of the community context in which markets actually exist. Recent theoretical work on marriage has overlooked the fact that marriage markets are local, as opposed to national, phenomena which may have different implications for different genders (Oppenheimer, 1988). For example, both men and women residing near a military base face a different sex ratio than their counterparts attending a large university. In my view, the application of this conceptual orientation is as significant a contribution as the authors' analytical strategy of cross-validation with micro- and macro-level data.

Despite these contributions, the Kiecolt and Fossett analysis fails to acknowledge the conceptual milieu in which the problem is imbedded. Furthermore, both the data sets and the analyses employed have serious weaknesses, the "national" or "aggregate" status of the data notwithstanding. These problems may not invalidate their basic conclusions. In fact, Kiecolt and Fossett may have actually understated some of the effects of sex ratios on African American marriage and divorce. But a recognition of the limitations of their analysis is in order.

Conceptual Context

Sex ratio theory asserts that the availability of potential mates affects not only premarital behavior, but propensity to marry, as well as willingness to maintain marriage (Guttentag and Secord, 1983). Using both macro- and micro-level data, Kiecolt and Fossett apply these concepts in an effort to examine marriage among African Americans. But what Kiecolt and Fossett have actually undertaken is a study of marriages of African Americans. The former occurs only when a black male enters a marital union with a black female. A union between a black and a nonblack involves an African American but is not an African

American marriage, per se. Neither the personal interview surveys nor the aggregate data used by Kiecolt and Fossett specify that the black participants are married to other blacks. This distinction has two important implications for Kiecolt and Fossett's analysis.

First, to the extent that African Americans are willing to marry outside of their race, the sex ratio and its impact on pre- and within-marital behavior, which Kiecolt and Fossett attribute to it, are severely altered. As a result, they may be simultaneously overestimating (for black men) and underestimating (for black women) the influence of the *black* sex ratio on marital outcomes. For those black men willing to engage in interracial marriage—especially to the extent that a corresponding number of nonblack men are unwilling to marry black women—there is a dramatically increased pool of available mates. By Kiecolt and Fossett's reasoning, this should further exaggerate their mate selection criteria and premarital behavior, make them less likely to marry early, less likely to marry an African American woman (given their percentage of the population), and less likely to remain in any marriage. Since a substantial number of potential partners exist "outside" of marriage, black women who are willing to marry nonblacks will also have a wider selection in terms of both the number of men available, as well as the personal characteristics they value in a relationship. These women should also be less willing to marry early. In short, for those African American men and women willing to marry outside of their race, the black sex ratio may have little impact on their marital or mate-selection behavior. Instead, their behavior may be governed primarily by the sex ratio for American society in general—which Kiecolt and Fossett cannot use in their analyses, since the overwhelming majority of blacks marry within race.

Thus, the Kiecolt and Fossett analysis holds *only* if the number of black men willing to undertake interracial marriages equals the number of nonblack men willing to marry black women; *and, only* if those black women willing to marry nonblacks are replaced by equal numbers of nonblack women. These specific conditions are unlikely to be met since, in all probability, more African American men than women outmarry (see Tucker and Mitchell-Kernan, 1990).

Another unmeasured factor in this research—and one generally unacknowledged in discussions involving either the sex ratio or marriage—is the extent of homosexual orientation in both the general population and within a specific subgroup such as African Americans. Unless there are equal numbers of black male and female homosexuals, the effects of the black sex ratio are further reduced. For instance, every black male-homosexual couple reduces, by two, the number of possible mates for those black women seeking black mates. Of course, there is a reverse effect from black lesbian couples. In other words, compared to those black men who marry nonblacks, to the extent that black male homosexuals seek black partners, they have twice the effect on black female mate selection. To the extent that there are gender differences in homosexual orientation among blacks, this would further exaggerate the mate availability imbalance by lowering the potential pool of black mates for the opposite sex.

In general, the problem with Kiecolt and Fossett's approach is that there is an unknown degree of imprecision in the extent to which their *concept (mate availability) is actually represented by their measure (sex ratio)*.[2] In this light, it is not surprising that Kiecolt and Fossett did not obtain significant zero-order sex ratio effects on the marital behavior of black men, unlike that obtained for black women (see Table 5.1). By including unknown numbers of black men married to nonblack women (and vice versa), as well as black male and female homosexuals, they were probably fortunate to have obtained any of those higher-order effects for men; and even here there are gender differences in the impact of the independent variables. To the extent that black homosexuals and/or African Americans willing to marry nonblacks are present in the data employed by Kiecolt and Fossett, their analysis probably overstates the impact of the imbalance in the black sex ratio on the marriage-forming behavior of black men, and understates its effect on black women.

A second problem with Kiecolt and Fossett's conceptual approach concerns their analysis of marital outcomes. Suppose that African Americans involved in interracial marriages have significantly different rates of marital stability. To the extent that black/nonblack unions have higher (or lower) rates of divorce, then research using data only from black respondents (as opposed to respondents from, or commited to forming, all black dyads) may overstate (or understate) the dissolution of marriages involving two African Americans. Again, to the extent the black men and women outmarry at different rates, and/or have differential rates of disruption of those unions, there may be spurious gender differences in the impact of the black sex ratio on marital disruption. This is precisely what Table 5.1 shows. While there are direct sex ratio effects for women on both marriage and divorce, there are none for men. The authors attribute both of these differences in the findings to a need to increase the chances for statistical significance. Yet there are sufficient cases of both married and divorced African American men and women to make even small effects robust.

Since sex-role theory predicts the mate selection and marital behavior of both men and women, some suspicion should be aroused when results conform to the theory for one gender, but not the other. In fact, Kiecolt and Fossett's theoretical application of the sex ratio framework to men is more straightforward than it is for women. For example, it does not follow, a priori, that (as stated by the authors) "because" potential marriage partners are fewer in number (women are) "more reluctant to marry." Kiecolt and Fossett's interpretation is that a decrease in the supply of available mates may lead some women to accept mates with less competitive characteristics, and others may not marry at all rather than take an unacceptable mate.

However, some women might also marry earlier (e.g., at the first viable

---

[2]This is not just Kiecolt and Fossett's problem. It is one shared by all researchers who use an *unadjusted* sex ratio as their *singular* measure of mate availability. Other research presented in this volume is compromised by this same problem.

opportunity) rather than wait for a more desirable male who may never come (Oppenheimer, 1988). This would account for the lower (but still positive) relationship between age and ever-marriage which Kiecolt and Fossett observed for black women, but not black men. [Since, as the authors observe, previous research has demonstrated that age has a curvilinear relationship with both marriage and marital outcomes, future researchers might be wise to employ a cohort concept. It would seem to be another measure of the local marriage market milieu in which individuals exist.] In the final analysis, more conceptual clarity is needed if the application of sex ratio theory to African Americans is to realize its full potential.

Methodological Issues

By assembling survey research and aggregate demographic data for their investigation, Kiecolt and Fossett have demonstrated the potential fruitfulness of combining micro- and macro-level approaches within the same investigation. But these data are not without some faults, especially in their application to the issues of concern to Kiecolt and Fossett. Moreover, the weaknesses in the evidence do not necessarily invalidate the conclusions reached here (they may, in fact, undermine their robustness), nor are they necessarily irrevocable.

When Kiecolt and Fossett used the National Survey of Black Americans (NSBA), they may not have realized (or at least they did not inform their readers) that the NSBA has been subject to some criticisms, including the use of a sampling strategy that I find somewhat unsynchronous with the demographic realities of African Americans (Smith, 1987). The Kiecolt and Fossett study should therefore be replicated with other data sets. While there are fewer cases involved, the black oversamples of the (1982 and/or 1987) General Social Survey (GSS) or the entire National Black Election Study (NBES) may serve to confirm their findings. The major drawback to the immediate comparisons of the GSS or NBES data with Kiecolt and Fossett's data set is that the former lack those community-specific characteristics for each respondent which were grafted on to the NSBA by the authors. Thus, in spite of the conceptual and measurement problems I have cited, Kiecolt and Fossett's methodological contribution lies as much in the quality and character of the individual-level data they have brought to bear on the issue, as in any specific analytical technique.

Then, there are unique aspects to the aggregate data based on Louisiana that Kiecolt and Fossett employ to augment their micro-level findings. The authors readily admit that the state may be atypical but assert that its use here is an advance over previous research that failed to include rural areas, and call for confirmation based on data from other areas. I am troubled, however, by the curious absence of a measure of "urbanness" from their analyses. What is unusual about Louisiana is something for which no official data exist—in this state or any other. That is, the extent to which the prevalence of Catholicism in Louisiana, and specifically among blacks in the state, may affect marital behavior. At the very least, the authors should acknowledge the higher proportion of Catholics among blacks in this state (relative to others). Since official Catholic doctrine opposes divorce, the incidence of marital disruption in these data may reflect, in part, distinctive religious principles.

Conclusion

In the final analysis, Kiecolt and Fossett have presented an interesting depiction of the potential influence of the black sex ratio on the marital behavior of African Americans. These analyses are problematic in some respects; however, they serve to underscore the importance of linking micro- and macro-level investigations of marital behavior in general, and of blacks in particular. Perhaps the most salient contribution of the Kiecolt and Fossett analysis is their sensitivity to variations in local community marriage market conditions. They are among the first and the few contemporary sociologists to articulate (relevant to issues of family formation) the heterogeneity of experiences and responses to contextual forces among African Americans.

REFERENCES

BRINK, W., AND HARRIS, L. 1967. *Black and white: A study of U.S. racial attitudes today.* New York: Simon & Schuster.

FARLEY, R. 1986. Homicide trends in the United States. In D.F. Hawkins, ed., *Homicide among black Americans,* pp. 13–28. Lanham, MD: University Press of America.

GUTTENTAG, M., AND SECORD, P.F. 1983. *Too many women? The sex role question.* Beverly Hills: Sage Publications.

LIEBERSON, S. 1980. *A piece of the pie: Black and white immigrants since 1880.* Berkeley: University of California Press.

OPPENHEIMER, V.K. 1988. A theory of marriage timing. *American Journal of Sociology,* 94:563–591.

SMITH, A.W. 1987. Problems and progress in the measurement of black public opinion. *American Behavioral Scientist,* 30:441–455.

STAPLES, R. 1985. Changes in black family structure: The conflict between family ideology and structural conditions. *Journal of Marriage and the Family,* 47:1005–1013.

TUCKER, M.B., AND MITCHELL-KERNAN, C. 1990. New trends in black American interracial marriage: The social structural context. *Journal of Marriage and the Family,* 52:209–218.

SECTION THREE

Consequences
and Correlates
of African American
Marital Decline

-

6

MARITAL BEHAVIOR AND EXPECTATIONS: ETHNIC COMPARISONS OF ATTITUDINAL AND STRUCTURAL CORRELATES

M. Belinda Tucker

and

Claudia Mitchell-Kernan

RECENT DRAMATIC changes in marital patterns in the United States generally, and among African Americans most particularly, have given rise to a renewed emphasis on the determinants of marital behavior and family formation more generally. As certain of the changes first became evident in the black population in the early 1960s, earlier discussions focused on the seemingly distinctive nature of African Ameican family organization, and included suggestions of "pathology" (e.g., Moynihan, 1967). Such a focus in effect shifted the research agenda of many to defense of the African American family rather than an empirical analysis of the roots of what was actually a very recent change in black family formation patterns. As these patterns now characterize the American population generally, although they are more strongly evident among blacks, we have chosen to examine the correlates of marital behavior and expectation in distinct sociocultural groupings. In this manner we might discern whether the same structural conditions are associated with specific marital trends in all groups, whether culturally distinctive attitudinal patterns are more prominent correlates, or whether a combination of structural and sociocultural factors is associated with marital behavior and expectation. We might also determine whether such groups differ in their perceptions of marital opportunities and constraints.

In both the earlier and the current periods of focus, theory and research on the problem have been dominated by a focus on macro-level constructs. Key issues have been the economic viability of men (which, if unhealthy, would discourage marriage) and the demographic characteristics of groups (in particular a shortage of men most pronounced at middle and older ages)—both directly influencing the marriage market. It remains to be seen, however, whether individual perceptions of the marriage market bear a relationship to structural assessments. Also unknown is the extent to which determinants of marital behavior, as perceived by the actors themselves, conform to notions developed through macro processes. Furthermore, analysis of the individual attitudinal components of marital expectations and behavior, in the context of mate availability considerations, has not been conducted. The intent of this chapter is to address these lacunae through a focus on attitudinal level data obtained on three racial/ethnic groups through the 1989 Southern California Social Survey.

The immediate objectives are: (1) to examine the differential relationship between perceived mate availability and more objective assessments of sex ratio in broadly distinctive sociocultural groupings; (2) to determine whether major theoretical conceptualizations concerning the role of mate availability in family structure are differentially relevant for those groups; and (3) to examine the contributions of structural versus attitudinal components to marital expectations and marital status.

Background

Changing marital behavior.   As documented in Chapter 1, American patterns of family formation have undergone remarkable change in recent times. Americans now marry later, are less likely to stay married, and are less likely to marry after divorce than in previous times. Between 1970 and 1990, the percentage of women married by age twenty to twenty-four decreased from 64 percent to 37 percent, and the percentage of men married by that age declined from 45 percent to 21 percent. The divorce rate nearly tripled between 1970 and 1990 (from 60 per 1,000 to 166 per 1,000 married women) (U.S. Bureau of the Census, 1991a). Notably, the proportions of both women and men who *ever* married (that is, married at least once) did not change substantially over this twenty-year period. The cumulative data, therefore, suggest that in recent years Americans have been as likely to marry eventually as before—but spend significantly greater portions of their lives as unmarrieds, due to later age of first marriage and a greater likelihood of divorce. Still, based on current trends in marital incidence, some demographers and economists have predicted substantial decreases in the likelihood of being ever married for American women (Rodgers and Thornton, 1985; Bloom and Bennett, 1985).

Group specific trends.   Although American trends in family formation are pervasive, reflecting (and perhaps driving), in part, worldwide changes, these transitions have not been equally experienced across ethnic groups. In particular, the transformations evident in the family formation patterns and living arrangements of African Americans, and some Latino groups, have been more substantial along certain dimensions. Prior to 1950, African Americans displayed a long-established tendency to marry earlier than whites. That pattern is now reversed (Cherlin, 1981). Between 1970 and 1990, the proportion of women who had ever married declined sharply from nearly 83 percent to 63 percent among blacks, while there was virtually no change in the extent of being ever married among either whites or women of Spanish origin (Norton and Moorman, 1987; U.S. Bureau of the Census, 1991a—Asian breakdown not reported and figures for 1970 unavailable). [As we observed in Chapter 1, however, marriage among younger cohorts of white women has declined very dramatically, indicating either greater marital delay or real generational differences in the tendency to marry.] It has been estimated that only 70 percent of black women born in 1954 will ever marry, compared to 86 percent of black men and 90 percent of whites of both sexes (Rodgers and Thornton, 1985). Of black women born in the 1930s, 94 percent eventually married.

Although Latino marriage patterns overall had been relatively stable through 1985, a nearly nine-point drop in marital prevalence occurred over the next five-year period—at a time when African American and white patterns had begun to stabilize. Futhermore, for certain indicators, within-group differences among Latinos are quite substantial. Although in 1990 only 16 percent of Mexican-origin households were being maintained by females without males, that figure was 21 percent for Central and South Americans, and 31 percent for Puerto Ricans (U.S. Bureau of the Census, 1991b).

Although this discussion has focused on changes over very recent decades, as is made clear in Chapter 1, the fifties and sixties were quite distinctive in terms of family formation patterns. When trends over the last fifty years are considered, some changes no longer seem as dramatic, due to substantial fluctuations in marital patterns over time. Nevertheless, later marriage and more divorce are two very significant changes evident among all Americans, and the decline in African American marital prevalence is substantial, regardless of whether the comparison point for current behavior is 1970 or 1940. These trends raise questions about the underlying attitudinal components, as well as the structural underpinnings, of marriage behavior and marital expectations. Do Americans still want to marry? Do they expect to marry? Are the desire and expectation to marry among African Americans significantly less than that observed in other American populations? What are the perceived constraints on marriage? What are the attitudinal correlates of marriage and marital expectations and do they differ among the groups that evidence differential marriage patterns?

Conceptual Perspectives

In Chapter 1, we reviewed a number of the broad conceptual perspectives that have been offered to explain current marital trends, including those that have served to frame the study presented in this chapter. In our research program, we have focused specifically on the demographic and economic arguments because such causes, in our view, offer the greatest potential for influence through social policy. The perspectives that have been most influential in our research are briefly outlined below.

Sex ratio imbalance. Several theorists have argued that a shift in the availability of marriage partners affects family formation patterns and family values (Glick, Heer, and Beresford, 1963; Guttentag and Secord, 1983; Rodgers and Thornton, 1985; Schoen, 1983). Because the number of males, relative to females, in the African American population has declined steadily since the 1920s, and has become increasingly divergent from white sex ratios, some believe that sex ratio imbalance is a significant factor in black marital decline (Guttentag and Secord, 1983; Staples, 1981a,b). Epenshade (1985) has argued that since decreases in black marriage have only been evident since the 1960s, sex ratio declines could not be the primary cause of this change. However, as demonstrated in Table 6.1, the most dramatic sex ratio declines have been evident only in recent decades. It is also possible that the inconsistencies noted by Epenshade (1985) stem from Guttentag and Secord's (1983) narrow focus on the demographic variable of sex ratio, rather than the range of issues related to marital opportunity.

Male economic viability. Economic factors have been cited by a number of theorists as central contributors to marital decline (e.g., Darity and Myers, 1986/87; Ross and Sawhill, 1975; Wilson, 1987; Wilson and Neckerman, 1986). These arguments have taken various forms and focus on different economic processes including declining male economic power, increasing female economic power, and a declining differential between male and female economic power, among others. Testa and Krogh in Chapter 3 outline a number of the major competing economic hypotheses concerning marriage among inner-city minorities. Also included among these theories is Oppenheimer's (1988) assertion that increasing marital delay is a function of an elongated search strategy in which more time is required to assess male economic prospects. All of these arguments suggest that societal shifts in marriage patterns are related to the fact that the economic incentives to marry and remain married have undergone change.

Other explanations of marital change. Clearly, the above conceptualizations cannot fully explain the substantial shifts in family formation and living arrangements that characterize either the American population generally or African Americans. As noted in Chapter 1, it seems clear that some ideological shifts are factors, including significant shifts in views of the roles of women and greater acceptance of cohabitation and childbirth out of wedlock. Also, significant improvements in contraception have certainly provided a freedom of choice for women unparalleled in human history.

TABLE 6.1

Sex Ratios from Raw Census Data
for Blacks and Whites: 1830–1990

Year	Race	
	Blacks	Whites
1990	88.2	96.0
1980	89.6	95.3
1970	90.8	95.3
1960	93.4	97.4
1950	94.3	99.1
1940	95.0	101.2
1930	97.0	102.9
1920	99.2	104.4
1910	98.9	106.7
1900	98.6	101.5
1890	99.5	105.4
1880	97.8	104.0
1870	96.2	102.8
1860	99.6	105.3
1850	99.1	105.2
1840	99.5	104.6
1830	100.3	103.7

Sources: U.S. Bureau of the Census (1960, 1964, 1973, 1982, 1983, 1992).

Toward synthesis through microanalysis. As detailed more fully in Chapter 1, a number of studies have attempted to compare and test various explanations of marital change and ethnic differences in marriage behavior. The results have been varied and inconclusive, although it seems clear that both demographic and economic factors are implicated in recent trends in family formation.

We propose theoretical integration in several respects. First, the economic and demographic theories are not incompatible. As separable issues, each is more or less salient depending on the circumstances of the population under study. In earlier work, we presented a detailed discussion of the factors affecting mate availability (Tucker and Mitchell-Kernan, in press). Depending in part on geographic location, the marriage pool may be influenced to a lesser or greater extent by true demographic imbalances (i.e., an absence of "warm bodies"), compromised eligibility (which could be due to economic limitations or institutionalization, as two examples), or sociocultural unavailability (e.g., persons of other races have not normally been available as potential partners). Locational variations of a related sort would include differential inclinations to out-marry (e.g., between 1970 and 1980, one out of six black men in the western states who married for the first time wed a woman of another race, although the black female tendency was only one-quarter that rate; during the same time period in the South only 2.5 percent of black men out-married compared to less than 1 percent of black women—U.S. Bureau of the Census, 1985).

Using the demographic and economic factors as anchoring points, it seems plausible that different groups are differentially affected by these factors. In particular, we would argue that white American marital behavior and expectations are influenced to a greater extent by the demographic forces cited by marriage squeeze theorists (per the "baby boom" effect); that local Latino marital behavior and expectations are more influenced by economic forces than by demographic forces (i.e., a shortage of economically viable men, but no shortage of men per se); and that African American marital behavior and expectations are a function of both economic and demographic phenomena. If the impact of these forces is at least additive (i.e., first fewer men, then those remaining men are economically compromised), we would therefore expect black marriage rates to be more constrained than either of the other groups.

The second level of integration involves the examination of attitudinal data in conjunction with structural variables such as age, education, and income. As long as we have no indication that macro-based notions of mate availability, either in demographic or economic terms, are detected and/or incorporated on the individual level, our understanding of the process of mate selection and marital decision is incomplete. This point is particularly compelling in light of some of the more recent studies attempting to explain the black-white difference in marital behavior. That is, the failure to more fully explain ethnic differences in marriage behavior on the basis of demographic and economic factors may reflect the attitudinal consequences of different situations. In particular, if black men are in greater demand by their female counterparts than white men (due to their more chronic numerical shortage and greater access to alternatives), social exchange theory would suggest that black men would adopt more stringent criteria for mate selection, thereby *decreasing* their inclination to marry. Aggregate-level studies cannot account for such phenomena.

Method

Procedures

The Southern California Social Survey (SCSS) was administered to 1,116 residents of Los Angeles, Ventura, and Orange counties during a six-week period in February and March, 1989. The sample was a stratified random-digit-dialed telephone sample. Predominantly black and Hispanic areas were oversampled at a factor of thirteen to one in order to provide sample sizes sufficient for analytical purposes. Data from the 1980 census were used to establish the sampling frame.

All call scheduling and questionnaire administration were handled by the Computer Assisted Telephone Interviewing (CATI) system operated by the Institute for Social Science Research of UCLA. A single respondent at least eighteen years of age was randomly selected among all reported adults in each household.

Sample Characteristics

Data used here are taken from the unweighted sample which was 44 percent white, 27 percent black, 20 percent Latino, 5 percent Asian, and 4 percent other. Only the white, black, and Latino samples were used in the analyses to be presented. The overall gender breakdown was 55 percent female and 45 percent male. As shown in Table 6.2, the three ethnic groups differed rather dramatically on the basis of age. Whites were somewhat older than blacks, and Latinos were substantially younger than the other two ethnic groups. Nearly 64 percent of the male Latino respondents were between eighteen and twenty-nine years of age. To some extent, the age breakdown is a reflection of the true age distribution of the three groups in this area. However, both Latino and black men under age thirty are overrepresented, with a corresponding underrepresentation of older Latinos (note population distribution in Table 6.2). Young white women are also somewhat underrepresented. In view of these skewed representations and the striking differences between the age structures of the three ethnic groups, age was entered as a control variable in all of the multivariate analyses that we conducted.

One factor that could possibly account for the youthfulness of our Latino sample is the absence of Spanish-language interviewing. Younger Latinos may be more likely to speak English. Overall, only 36 percent of our Latino sample was foreign born. United States census figures indicate that in 1990, 53.3 percent of the Los Angeles County "Spanish-origin" population was foreign born (U.S. Bureau of the Census, 1993). Since the SCSS also includes Ventura and Orange counties (although only minimally represented in the unweighted sample), the actual foreign-born figure for the Southern California population probably lies somewhere between these two figures.

Household income by sex and ethnicity indicates that black women were substantially less well off economically than any of the other groups, while white men were generally in the best economic circumstances. Black and Latino men were somewhat similarly situated economically, although there were twice as many black men in households making less than $10,000. Women overall were in poorer households than were men. It should be noted that the limitation of English-only interviewing probably resulted in an underrepresentation of very low-income Latinos.

TABLE 6.2

Demographic Characteristics of Sample, by Ethnicity and Gender

	Blacks		Whites		Latinos	
	M	F	M	F	M	F
Sample size	94	176	218	229	102	100
Age (%)						
18 to 29 years	41.3	30.8	30.3	21.6	63.7	42.0
30 to 49 years	33.7	39.6	38.1	44.1	29.4	40.0
50 to 64 years	15.2	18.3	20.6	15.4	5.9	9.0
65 years and older	9.8	11.2	11.0	18.9	2.9	9.0
Population distribution for persons over age 19 from 1990 census: L.A.-Long Beach PMSA (%)						
20 to 29 years	27.9	25.6	21.4	19.2	41.5	35.1
30 to 49 years	44.5	43.0	42.9	38.6	42.8	43.7
50 to 64 years	17.6	17.6	19.4	19.0	10.7	13.1
65 years and older	10.1	13.8	16.3	23.3	5.0	8.1
Household income (%)						
<$10,000	9.4	23.3	5.3	10.6	4.3	9.0
$10,000–19,999	25.9	25.8	8.3	14.9	26.1	29.2
$20,000–29,999	16.5	16.0	16.0	14.9	15.2	23.6
$30,000–39,999	22.4	16.6	22.8	17.8	26.1	20.2
$40,000–49,999	11.8	7.4	13.1	9.6	15.2	7.9
>$50,000	14.1	11.0	34.5	32.2	13.0	10.1
Neighborhood income level (%)						
Poor	5.4	15.1	1.9	1.3	2.0	11.3
Working-class	48.4	54.1	32.7	22.0	58.4	53.6
Middle-class	37.6	26.7	38.8	41.6	34.7	33.0
Upper-middle-class	12.5	4.1	23.8	27.9	5.0	2.1
Wealthy	0.0	0.0	2.8	2.2	0.0	0.0

Measures

Two dependent variables were used in the analyses to follow: married versus nonmarried (including single, separated, divorced, and widowed) and marital expectation. The latter was measured by the question, "On a scale of one to ten, how likely do you think it is that you will ever marry/remarry?" Response categories ranged from "extremely unlikely" to "extremely likely."

Structural variables used in the study included age, education, income, and number of children. Age was measured by reported age at last birthday. Education was a five-point scale in which 1 = less than high school diploma, 2 = high school diploma, 3 = some college, no degree, 4 = associate of arts degree, vocational or technical degree, 5 = bachelor's degree, and 6 = at least one graduate degree. The measurement of income was somewhat problematic. Since the core Southern California Social Survey did not include a measure of personal income, household income and the respondent's assessment of the economic level of her or his neighborhood were used in the present analyses. In the multivariate analyses, all analyses were run with one indicator, then the other, and the variable that was most predictive of the variable in question was used in the final models. Household income was measured by six response categories: (1) < \$10,000; (2) \$10,000–19,999; (3) \$20,000–29,999; (4) \$30,000–39,999; (5) 40,000–49,999; (6) > \$50,000. The neighborhood income question was: What kind of people mainly live in your neighborhood—mostly very poor, working-class, middle-class, upper-middle-class, or mostly wealthy people? Number of children was represented by the reported number of live births or children fathered plus those adopted.

The attitudinal questions include a series of items concerning marriage and family values (only those specifically related to marriage are used in these analyses). The issue of mate availability was addressed in several ways. Single persons were asked specifically about their dating experiences and whether it was very difficult or easy to find suitable dates. All persons were asked whether there were not enough, enough, or more than enough persons of the opposite sex for persons like themselves, similar with respect to education and social background. Additionally, we also asked for a sex ratio equivalent—an estimate of how many men there were for every ten women. The three mate availability items were designed to tap different aspects of the availability. It should be noted that our mate availability questions incorporate notions of demography as well as some sort of respondent-defined notion of suitability, in the context of the respondent's sense of his or her own personal capital (i.e., one's own marketability, so to speak). This is indeed how the real world operates. Our perceived pool of eligibles is a function of both objective and subjective factors.

The attitudinal variables also included items and factors derived from a set of questions about marital values (all answered on a ten-point scale from not very to extremely important). Areas assessed included the importance of being married, the importance of having children (in general), and the importance of being married when you have children. The importance of each of the following for a "successful" marriage was also assessed: similar social/cultural background, same religion, love, "being faithful," life-long commitment, being of same race/ethnic group, similar likes/dislikes, adequate income, good sex, being good friends, and having children.

Three indicators were formed from the marital values items: romantic (love, fidelity, lifelong commitment), background (sociocultural, religion, race) and practical factors (friends, income, sex). The indicators were formed by summing scores obtained on the composite items.

Data Analysis

The primary multivariate analytical procedures employed were logistic regression and multiple linear regression. Logistic regression analysis was developed specifically to handle the problems created by regressing a dichotomous dependent variable (Berkson, 1953; Theil, 1970). The technique enabled us to assess the probability of an individual being married versus unmarried as a function of a set of predictors that includes both categorical and continuous variables. Multiple linear regression was used to determine the correlates of marital expectation, a continuous variable.

On theoretical grounds, the significance of economic versus demographic/availability concerns is expected to differ by gender. In fact, our previous analyses have revealed gender differences in correlates of relationship status in the general black population (Tucker and Taylor, 1989). Because of these factors, and the fact that marital prevalence differs by gender, most of the analyses that follow were conducted separately for women and men.

Results and Discussion

Perceived Mate Availability

Table 6.3 presents the 1990 Los Angeles-Long Beach PMSA (Primary Metropolitan Statistical Area) sex ratios for persons aged eighteen and over for blacks, non-Hispanic whites, and Latinos, as well as two indicators of perceived mate availability by gender: the perceived number of men for every ten women (sex ratio), and whether there were "not enough," "enough," or "more than enough" women/men for "people like yourself." [We recognize the limitation of census data and the fact that black men and Latinos in general were undercounted. This would only indicate, however, that the shortage of black men is less than indicated by these figures. Furthermore, as we have argued elsewhere, many of the men who are not counted by the census are essentially out of the marriage market anyway because of severely compromised economic situations—the homeless, for example (Tucker and Mitchell-Kernan, in press).]

The results indicate that both black men and women perceive a substantial shortage of men. Whites and Latinos also see shortages, but to a lesser extent than blacks. A fair degree of consistency across gender for all races exists. The perceived mate availability item reflects the same trend with black women feeling the most substantial limit on partner availability (nearly 70 percent of black women believed that not enough men are available). Black men confirmed this perception with 60 percent of them believing that there are more than enough women. A similar but less dramatic pattern was observed among whites, but the pattern was much less extreme among Latinos.

TABLE 6.3

Family/Relationship Characteristics and Attitudes, by Ethnicity and Gender

	Blacks		Whites		Latinos	
L.A.-Long Beach PMSA sex ratio (1990 census)	85.2		96.0		107.4	
	M	F	M	F	M	F
Perceived sex ratio (ten-point scale)	4.7	4.8	7.0	6.0	5.2	4.8
Perceived mate availability (%)						
Not enough	15.4	69.4	20.0	59.0	14.1	54.3
Enough	26.4	20.0	38.5	32.5	46.5	32.6
More than enough	58.2	10.6	41.5	8.5	39.4	13.0
Marital status (%)						
Married	26.9	23.4	48.1	47.6	32.4	43.0
Separated	6.5	13.7	2.3	1.8	2.9	8.0
Divorced	15.1	17.1	9.7	13.2	10.8	13.0
Widowed	3.2	11.4	4.6	13.2	0.0	8.0
Never married	48.4	34.3	35.2	24.2	53.9	28.0
Married or romantically involved (%)	61.4	53.0	65.0	67.8	73.4	62.0
Want to marry/remarry[a] (%)	81.3	72.4	79.0	71.8	93.8	76.0
Importance of long-term involvement[b]	7.9	7.6	8.3	8.3	8.0	8.3
Importance of marriage[b]	7.0	7.1	7.3	7.1	7.3	7.6
Marital expectations[a,b]	6.6	6.3	6.7	5.7	8.1	6.1

[a] Asked of single persons only.
[b] Ten-point scale.

Overall, black and white perceptions tended to reflect their relative "realities" as indicated by the census-derived sex ratios for the two races. Although the Latino perceived sex ratio did not reflect the census figure, fewer Latinas (than observed with either black or white women) felt that there are "not enough" men and fewer Latino men believed that there are "more than enough" women. At least in relative terms, then, individual mate availability perceptions of these distinct sociocultural groupings did indeed reflect the census-derived "reality."

Notably, however, despite their demographically favorable position, the Latina perspective on mate availability seemed more similar to that of black and white women. The fact that their perceptions were somewhat removed from the objective "reality" as measured by the sex ratio lends support to the notions we have presented in earlier writings (Tucker and Mitchell-Kernan, in press). That is, personal perceptions of mate availability are not determined solely by the existence of "warm bodies," but by the perceived availability of potential partners with socially desired features. Latina assessments of availability were most likely a function of their perceptions of the economic viability of potential Latino mates—an area in which their eligibility is greatly compromised—rather than numerical representation.

Relationship Involvement

Marital status. As shown in Table 6.3, marital status differed substantially among the three groups, with the greatest extent of marriage evident among white men and the lowest among black women. Table 6.3 also shows that the greatest source of nonmarriage for black women is marital dissolution through separation, divorce, or widowhood (42.2 percent), rather than never having been married (34.3 percent). Also, despite the fact that a substantial proportion of the Latino sample was Catholic, divorce and separation were fairly substantial among Latinas (21 percent). Marital dissolution is therefore highest among women married to the most economically disadvantaged groups of males. (Since all men are more likely to remarry, their dissolution rates are *artifactually* deflated.) It must also be noted, however, that black women and Latinas remain the *most* economically disadvantaged of all groups and that marital dissolution is often the source of further economic decline (U.S. Bureau of the Census, 1991c). It therefore seems unlikely that the primary source of marital breakdown is the increased economic fortunes of these women. A more likely source is the strain caused by financial difficulties, which is amplified among blacks by the actual shortage of men. Previous research has provided fairly unambiguous evidence of a relationship between husband-specific economic factors and black separation and divorce (Hampton, 1979; Ross and Sawhill, 1975).

Latino men were the most likely to be never married, which is probably the result of the age structure differences among the groups. The dominance of young men in the Latino population in particular, but across all groups, inflates the never-married rates among men; while the relatively larger number of older white women and relative absence of young white women inflates the widowed category.

Nonmarital romantic involvement. When those who were involved in "long-term" romantic relationships were added to those who were married, the extent of relationship involvement across groups becomes more approximately equal with most individuals in all groups involved in a long-term relationship of some kind. Nevertheless, black female relationship involvement is lowest.

Taken together with the marital status figures, the dominant form of relationships for both black and Latino men is *nonmarital* romantic involvement.

This last point is particularly notable in terms of the economic eligibility framework. In the two clearly economically compromised groups of men, nonmarital romantic involvements predominate. Although it could be suggested that the youthfulness of the Latino male sample explains the absence of marriage among them, over 70 percent of the Latinas (who were nearly as young as the men) were either currently or previously married. These findings are supported by an earlier study conducted by Tucker and Taylor (1989). In that study, National Survey of Black Americans data showed that marriage as opposed to nonmarital romantic involvement was related to male personal income.

Desire to Marry or Remarry

Given the great variation in the extent of marriage among these groups, is "desire for marriage" similarly distinctive? When asked whether "you ever want to marry or remarry," respondents across all races indicated a strong willingness to become legally attached. Although gender differences characterized all races, with men consistently being *more* desirous of marriage, the greatest discrepancy between men and women was evident among Latinos (with Latino men being exceptionally desirous of marriage relative to all other groups). Also, black women were least likely to express a desire to marry—a view that may be tempered by the reality of their circumstances. Still, there existed relative consistency within race, with Latino men being more desirous of marriage than other men, and Latinas wanting to marry more than other women. Whites were least likely to want to marry or remarry.

Importantly, these findings contradict the commonplace stereotypical implication that blacks simply do not want to marry. We do not believe that "social desirability" any longer demands a positive response to the question. It would seem that Americans are freer than ever before to reject marriage. The fact that blacks were more likely to express a desire to marry than whites strongly suggests that the reasons for not marrying may be structural, rather than the result of a fundamental change in the way they value the institution of marriage. This result also conflicts with the Guttentag and Secord (1983) predictions concerning the consequences of male shortage, namely, that when men are in short supply they devalue the institution of marriage.

Marital Values

When asked directly about the importance of long-term relationships and marriage, there was again considerable similarity in the responses supplied by the three ethnic groups. As shown in Table 6.3, responding on a scale of one to ten, with ten being extremely important, means for all three groups averaged between 7 and 8.3. There were no significant differences on the basis of either ethnicity or gender.

In order to determine whether ethnic similarities and differences in perspectives on marriage and family might be due to differences in the compositions of the three populations (e.g., on age), we used Multiple Classification Analysis (Andrews et al., 1973) to compute adjusted means for all of our marriage and family value items—controlling for age, gender, and neighborhood income level. Table 6.4 shows the results of those analyses. It is clear that there are very few differences between the ethnic groups in terms of the marriage and family values assessed here. The only clear patterns of distinction are: (1) the tendency for Latinos to view children as more important for a successful marriage and for whites to see them as substantially less important, and (2) the tendency for blacks to view adequate income as more central for marital success than other groups. These responses provide further indication that, despite current distinctive African American marital patterns, the underlying values concerning marriage held by blacks do not differ from those held by groups with greater proportions of intact marriages.

Reasons for Not Marrying

All single persons (i.e., those never married, separated, divorced, or widowed) were asked why they had not married or remarried (see Table 6.5). Although, as was expected, all groups indicated that having "never found the right person" was the primary reason (and for that reason, this response category was presented last in the interview), the next most dominant reasons are more instructive. Women in general believed, more than men, that there are not enough persons of the opposite sex who meet their standards, although black women were most likely to feel this way. Latinas (who enjoy a favorable sex ratio) were least likely among women to report availability concerns as reasons for not marrying. Interestingly, however, nearly half of black men also reported that there were not enough women who met their standards.

"Not ready to settle down" was cited more by men than by women, but may be more a reflection of the fact that the men in this sample were younger than the women (since this reason would seem on the face to be more associated with youth). Men, overall, were also more likely to indicate that not having enough money to support a family was a reason for not getting married, with over half of all Latino men and over 40 percent of black men giving that response. Over a quarter of black women also felt that financial concerns were reason for not marrying, compared to much lesser percentages for white women and Latinas. Significant percentages of men in all groups also cited concentration on school or work as factors in their staying unmarried, with women in

TABLE 6.4

Multiple Classification Analysis: Adjusted Means for Marriage and Family Values, by Ethnicity (controlling for age, gender, and income)

Blacks (n = 247)	Latinos (n = 192)	Whites (n = 418)	Eta
Importance of long-term involvement			
7.71	8.06	8.28	.10
Importance of being married			
7.17	7.55	7.10	.05
Importance of similar sociocultural background for successful marriage			
6.96	7.39	6.62	.07
Importance of same religion for successful marriage			
6.71	7.52	6.02	.21
Importance of love for successful marriage			
9.17	9.21	9.30	.03
Importance of "being faithful" for successful marriage			
9.36	9.36	9.59	.06
Importance of lifelong commitment for successful marriage			
9.07	9.29	9.50	.11
Importance of having children for successful marriage			
7.77	8.39	6.40	.29
Importance of being of same race/ethnic group for successful marriage			
5.55	6.46	5.99	.07
Importance of similar likes/dislikes for successful marriage			
7.64	7.47	7.41	.07
Importance of adequate income for successful marriage			
8.70	8.22	7.96	.18
Importance of good sex for successful marriage			
8.80	8.94	8.62	.11
Importance of being good friends for successful marriage			
9.56	9.68	9.59	.04
Importance of having children			
8.22	8.57	7.76	.11
Importance of being married when you have children[a]			
8.50	8.50	8.44	.01

Note: All value scores are based on ten-point scales, with one being "not very important at all" and ten being "extremely important."

[a] Asked only of childless respondents.

TABLE 6.5

Reason for Not Marrying Among Unmarried Persons, by Ethnicity and Gender: Percentage Indicating Reasons

	Blacks		Whites		Latinos	
	M	F	M	F	M	F
Devoted energies to school or work	40.3	22.9	57.1	31.3	63.1	37.5
Not enough men/women who meet standards	47.5	55.6	27.6	51.4	18.5	46.7
Do not want to lose freedom	25.8	26.9	30.7	23.9	41.5	32.6
Do not believe in marriage	6.5	7.3	12.5	5.3	16.9	19.1
Not ready to settle down	48.3	34.6	53.9	41.6	76.9	39.6
Having fun playing the field	16.1	10.1	20.6	15.9	44.6	10.4
Not enough money to support a family	41.9	25.7	36.5	15.9	52.3	18.8
Never found the right person	68.9	66.7	77.0	73.6	55.6	77.1

Note: Since respondents could indicate more than one reason, the columns do not sum to 100 percent.

each group only half as likely to indicate the same. Latinos were most likely and blacks were least likely to give this reason.

Importantly, only relatively small percentages of all groups did not believe in marriage; but those percentages were lowest overall among blacks and highest among Latinos. With the exception of the Latino men (who are relatively young), few persons indicated that "having fun playing the field" was a reason for not marrying.

In general then, in this sample, nonmarriage is not a function of "not believing in marriage." Economic factors figured prominently for all groups of men, more so than for the women in those groups—and particularly so among Latino men. Women's concerns in all groups centered on the issue of availability, although availability was an important dimension of nonmarriage among black men as well.

These findings lend support to our notions about the salience of the different structural constructs for different groups—that is, economic versus demographic/availability factors. Latinos, among men, were most concerned about financial readiness for marriage but basically believed that there were enough available women who met their standards. In contrast, although black men were also concerned about economic readiness, they did not believe that there are enough suitable women. Stated in theoretical terms: numerical scarcity inflates male value while economic deficiency deflates male marital capabilities. As seen in this sample, black men whose marriage market value has been enhanced by their scarcity apparently believe that they can be "choosier" in terms of mate selection [which would fit the Guttentag and Secord (1983) social exchange model predictions—in situations of scarcity, the alternatives available to the sex in short supply increase and their selection standards are raised]. Because of their economic constraints, black men are less able to enter into marriage, but also due to the greater availability of alternatives for them, black men would have less need to commit to marriage. On the other hand, Latino men are not a scarce commodity and could therefore not afford to be too "choosy," but were also not financially "ready" for marriage.

On the basis of these frequencies alone, it would appear that black men are less likely than Latino men to view economic factors as marital constraints. However, we believe that this represents a theoretically consistent pattern of "exchange." In an objective sense, black men's overt concerns about economics as a marital inhibitor may be diminished by their numerical advantage.

Multivariate Analyses

The relationships above were then examined from a multivariate perspective, looking first at predictors of marriage versus nonmarriage and, second, examining marital expectations. In each set of analyses, the models presented are final versions that, in the interest of parsimony, do not include certain indicators that were determined from previous analyses to be inconsequential for the relationship at issue. The sets of variables considered for marital status and marital expectations are therefore not parallel—although the initial models tested were essentially the same.

Marital status. Logistic regressions of marital status on structural and attitudinal variables for all three ethnic groups are presented in Table 6.6. Among the structural variables, age and economic level of neighborhood were significant correlates of marital status among both whites and blacks, but not among Latinos (older age and higher income were correlated with being married). The significance of the age^2 (squared) factor among white and black women indicates that young as well as older respondents were least likely to be married. For the most part, education played only a minimal role in predicting marital status.

Among the attitudinal variables, the importance of long-term involvement, as well as the importance of marriage, emerged as significant predictors of marriage among all groups (although the long-term relationship value was not significant for Latino men). Placing a high value on the romantic aspects of marriage (i.e., love, commitment, sexual fidelity) was related to being married among both black women and Latinas. Black women who were married also valued similarity of background (i.e., sociocultural, religion, race) more than those who were single. The practical aspects of marriage (i.e., income, being good friends, sex) were more highly valued by married than single Latino men. Mate availability also proved to be significant across all groups (with the

TABLE 6.6

Logistic Regression Coefficients (Betas):
Married (1) versus Single (0) Status on Structural and Attitudinal Variables, by Gender and Race

	Blacks		Whites		Latinos	
	M	F	M	F	M	F
Structural variables						
Education	0.44	1.23*	-0.78*	-0.07	0.36	-1.14
Age	0.22	0.37**	0.37****	0.29***	1.86	0.08
Age²	-0.000	-0.003*	-0.03****	-0.002***	-0.02	-0.001
Economic level	1.43***	1.54***	0.62*	0.29	-0.16	0.19
Age × education	-0.02	-0.03*	0.004	-0.000	-0.02	0.04
Attitudinal variables						
Importance of long-term involvement	0.58**	0.58**	0.33*	0.42****	-0.15	0.54**
Importance of marriage	0.43**	0.43**	0.90****	0.36****	1.00****	0.46***
Importance of romantic factors for marriage	-0.14	-0.19*	-0.08	-0.07	-0.07	-0.39*
Importance of practical factors for marriage	0.02	0.04	0.03	-0.08	-0.33**	0.04
Importance of background factors for marriage	-0.06	0.08*	-0.04	-0.002	0.03	-0.02
Perceived availability of opposite sex	1.45**	0.11	0.72*	0.66*	-0.02	1.17*
Perceived sex ratio	0.13	0.17*	0.08	-0.06	0.24	0.007
Intercept	-19.20***	-17.33***	-17.66***	-9.64***	-28.00***	-1.63
Model chi-square	38.40****	60.22****	133.18****	84.46****	64.31****	36.23****
Predictive ability of model						
Structural variables only						
c	.76	.70	.72	.71	.78	.63
Somer's D$_{yx}$	.53	.39	.43	.41	.59	.26
Total model						
c	.92	.90	.94	.88	.95	.86
Somer's D$_{yx}$	.83	.80	.87	.75	.90	.73

$*p < .10.$ $**p < .05.$ $***p < .01.$ $****p < .001.$

exception of Latino men), but in different ways. Whether there were not enough, enough, or more than enough persons of the opposite sex was related to marital status among black men, all whites, and Latinas (i.e., married persons perceiving greater availability). However, the variable of sex ratio itself was the more important availability indicator for black women. In all cases, married persons believed that there was greater availability of the opposite sex, and more men relative to women than did single persons.

When prediction by models containing only structural variables was compared to predictability with a combination of structural and attitudinal variables (see Table 6.6), it was clear that predictability was significantly enhanced for all groups by the combined models. The Latina model was least effective.

Overall, then, marriage among the three ethnic groups was differentially affected by the structural variables, with economic issues being most salient among blacks and age being most salient for whites. No structural variables were prominent among Latinos. In terms of the attitudinal variables, the value placed on marriage by the respondent was, not surprisingly, universally predictive of marital status; but the perceived sex ratio indicators also emerged as significant correlates.

Expectations of marriage. Table 6.7 presents the results of linear multiple regressions of structural and attitudinal variables on expectations of marriage or remarriage by ethnic group. For the same reason cited earlier, analyses were conducted separately for men and women. In these analyses, only single persons (i.e., not currently married) were included. Also, it was possible to include a third indicator of mate availability that was not asked of married persons: ease in finding dates. Since the three indicators of marital success used in the marital status analyses (romantic, practical, background) were not found to be significant predictors in earlier runs, they were not included in the final versions. However, one item on the "practical" measure did prove to be an important indicator—"importance of adequate income for marital success"—and was therefore included in the analyses presented. Finally, household income proved to be a more effective indicator than neighborhood income level in these analyses.

Among all groups, except Latino men, age was significantly related to expectations of marriage, with older respondents more apt to believe that marriage or remarriage was unlikely. The structural variable of household income was also related to expectations of marriage for black men (with higher-income men having greater expectations of marriage). The income variable was unrelated to marital expectations for white and Latino men. However, the income variable was *negatively* related to marital expectations among white women. Those with higher incomes were less likely to expect to marry. Number of children also emerged as a significant predictor for black women only, with greater numbers of children associated with lower expectations of marriage.

TABLE 6.7

*Regression of Expectations of Marriage on Structural and Attitudinal Variables,
by Gender and Ethnicity*

| | Beta Coefficients | | | | | |
| | Blacks | | Latinos | | Whites | |
	F	M	F	M	F	M
Structural block						
Age	−.22***	−.27***	−.49****	−.20	.60****	−.49****
Income	−.05	.15*	.16*	.05	−.08	.003
Number of children	−.27****	−.03	.03	.05	−.04	−.04
R^2 change	.14	.08	.24	.03	.29	.22
Attitudinal block						
Date availability	.12*	.06	.07	−.10	.18***	.11*
Perceived sex ratio	−.09	.07	−.09	.21**	.03	−.11*
Availability of opposite sex	−.01	−.02	−.13	−.05	−.03	−.06
Importance of being married	.41****	.53****	.19*	.26**	.21***	.34****
Importance of adequate income for marriage	.12*	.20**	−.03	.06	.11	.08
Importance of being married for having children	−.20***	.02	−.06	−.07	.01	−.04
Importance of religion	.14**	−.02	−.02	−.07	−.03	−.11*
R^2 change	.18	.31	.05	.13	.10	.16
R^2	.38	.49	.34	.17	.47	.38
Adjusted R^2	.34	.42	.27	.08	.45	.35

*$p < .10$.　**$p < .05$.　***$p < .01$.　****$p < .001$.

The attitudinal variables displayed some similarity in the patterns of association among the groups. For all ethnic groups and both sexes, expectations of marriage were distinctly associated with highly valuing the state of marriage. Among the mate availability measures, date availability—whether one had an easy or a hard time finding dates—was the most effective predictor for black and white women and white men. However, perceived sex ratio was a better predictor of marital expectations for Latino and white men. No availability measures were significant predictors of marital expectations among black men.

In other respects, black attitudes showed distinctive predictive patterns. The belief that having an adequate income was an important factor in marital success (one of the variables included in the "importance of practical aspects of marriage" factor) was a significant predictor of marital expectation for black men as well as black women. Those who believed that an adequate income was important were *more* likely to expect to marry. One additional, somewhat puzzling finding is that black women who believed that it was important to be married when one had children were *less* likely to expect to marry. (We initially thought it might have been the result of an age interaction, in which older women with lower marital expectations would be more likely to believe that marriage was necessary for having children. However, the interaction term did not contribute significantly to the model.) One highly speculative explanation may be that believing that marriage is necessary for having children may be part of a "traditional" values complex that makes women who hold such beliefs feel disadvantaged in the highly competitive black marriage market and pessimistic about their marital prospects. This notion is actually supported by the religiosity finding. Among black women, a belief in the importance of religion is *negatively* related to marital expectancy. For all other groups, and significantly so among white men, religiosity is positively related to marital expectancy.

As with the marital status analyses, the attitudinal variables made substantial contributions to the regression models (with the sole exception of Latinas). The best models, in terms of explanatory power, were the black male and white female models which explained 42 percent and 45 percent, respectively, of the variance in marital expectation. The least effective model was the Latino male model which explained less than 10 percent of the variance in expectations of marriage.

In summary, age was by far the most dominant overall predictor of marital expectancy for whites, but attitudes concerning mate availability and the importance of relationships were also significant indicators. For blacks, a more complex array of predictors emerged; but, compared to other groups, income-related variables were more central factors in marital expectations for both men and women. Although age was the primary predictor of marital expectations among Latinas, as a whole, the remaining structural and attitudinal variables were not very effective predictors for Latino men and women. In addition, marital behavior seemed to be reflective of a more balanced contribution of structural and attitudinal correlates. However, in a manner that was not entirely consistent, for marital expectations, the influence of structural variables was greater than that of attitudinal variables for certain ethnic-gender groups, but not for others. Among white women and Latinas, the structural variable contribution was greater (reflecting perhaps the extremely powerful impact of age on marital expectations for these groups), while the attitudinal contribution was greatest for black and Latino men (perhaps a function of the relative insignificance of age as a marital inhibitor for these groups).

Conclusions

This study has provided evidence that certain global conditions, determined on the basis of aggregate-level assessments, are accurately perceived by individuals. For the most part, the assessments of mate availability by men and women in the three ethnic groups reflected their particular demographic and socioeconomic realities.

Overall, this research has demonstrated that economic and mate availability concerns are differentially related to marital behavior and marital expectancy among socioculturally distinct groups. As predicted, economic as well as availability indicators were salient for blacks (both structurally and attitudinally). Economic factors were not as salient for whites, but perceived availability played a significant role as a correlate of both marital behavior and expectation. While the multivariate analyses did not provide support for the primacy of economic indicators for Latino marital behavior and expectations, the bivariate comparisons did indicate a very dominant male concern with economic readiness for marriage. Although the results of the multivariate analyses indicated that the variables used in this study were less predictive of Latina behaviors and expectations than for other groups, there were some interesting indicators of what may be Latina trends. The bivariate comparisons indicated a similarity between Latina responses and those of black and white women that was not evident among the men. Latino male responses were quite distinct from those of black and white men. Although age structure differences may be a partial explanation, the increased Latina economic viability and new sex-role conflicts cited in the emerging Latina literature may partially explain the Latino gender differences. That is, the discrepancy between Latina and Latino desire to marry may reflect a growing Latina ambivalence about marriage in the face of the conflicts generated through increased women's economic power and traditional sex-role beliefs (Melville, 1980; Pesquera, 1984; Vasquez and Gonzalez, 1981).

The study also provided support for Wilson and Neckerman's (1986) contention that changes in marital patterns among whites are more linked to women's economic advances than would be the case for blacks. Unlike black women or Latinas, the more financially advantaged white women in our sample did have lower expectations of marriage. (This may also reflect the fact that although there is a subgroup of white women who have substantial economic resources, few black women or Latinas are in comparable financial positions.) Clearly, these data on the whole show that the dynamics of marriage vary quite substantially by group, depending on the situational characteristics of that group.

We conclude that economic and demographic factors separately and jointly affect marital status and marital expectations, acting alternatively as constraints and incentives at different historical moments. It should be kept in mind, however, that the impingement of such structural factors as marital attitudes and behavior also requires examination within the context of sociocultural background factors which may differ for the groups under study and which may produce internal dynamics that result in the changes in marital behavior observed today.

We should also note that although a causal ordering is implied by the economic findings (i.e., that poor economic circumstances constrain marital opportunity), no such ordering is suggested for certain of the attitudinal relationships. It is quite likely that marital status and/or constrained marital opportunity may lead to changes in attitudes concerning the value of marriage. A woman in her late thirties or early forties who previously valued marriage quite highly may reassess those values if she has not married and views her prospects of marriage as limited.

An indication of the clarity with which individuals view their marital opportunities is the relationship between perception of marital chances and the existence of marital constraints. In particular, the fact that black women with children had lower expectations for marriage likely stems from their own realization that the competition for economically viable black men really is stiff and that women with children are disadvantaged (whether in terms of first or later marriages). Such personal resource factors may be more important for marriage among black women than for either white women or Latinas. There is evidence that black women are the least likely of all groups to remarry—whether after divorce or widowhood (U.S. Bureau of the Census, 1992).

These findings must be interpreted within the context of change. We have placed what may be an artificial constraint on these analyses by assuming that mate selection and marriage occur primarily within ethnic groups. Certainly, intermarriage data for whites, African Americans, and Latinos presently support such an assumption. However, there has been significant change in this regard in recent decades (Tucker and Mitchell-Kernan, 1990). Two-thirds of the respondents in this survey indicated that they had dated persons of another race; the same proportion stated that they would be willing to marry a person of another race. Although interracial marriage rates in the West are higher than those observed in other regions, the increase in interracial unions is a nationwide trend (Tucker and Mitchell-Kernan, 1990). If this is indicative of a fundamental change in societal attitudes concerning intermarriage, it may be that persons who find themselves in severely constrained marriage markets will broaden their eligibility criteria to include persons of other ethnic groups.

A related issue is the function of changing sex-role ideology. Jessie Bernard (1981) argued that the "good-provider" role has undergone change in American society generally, resulting in greater emphasis on the nonprovider roles of husband. Secord and Ghee (1986) have discussed the implications of these notions in the context of the black marriage market, arguing that in situations where men are constrained in attempts to act as provider, marital roles must be reevaluated. To be sure, the basis of marriage is not solely economic. Some women choose to marry poor men; some poor men choose to marry. In this regard the marital search construct may prove valuable for understanding declining marriage rates and increases in marriage age—although in our view, the paradigm suffers from an overreliance on the economic uncertainty factor. One of our tasks is to locate economic considerations in the complex of factors leading to prolonged marital search and marital decline. Economic uncertainty and changes in economic incentives not only affect women and men differentially, they may entail further sequelae by elevating other mate-selection criteria to new levels of importance. In particular, black women and Latinas who are less likely to expect economic benefits from marriage may begin to give greater emphasis to other eligibility factors, such as the ability to care for children and emotional supportiveness. This suggests that marriage as an institution may be taking on a different meaning for such women—although still highly valued.

Another purpose of this study was to examine the relative efficacy of structural versus attitudinal variables. It seems clear that both are operative, in the case of marital behavior as well as marital expectations.

This study was undertaken in part to examine the relative explanatory significance of two dominant theoretical paradigms. However, an additional interpretive task demanded by the study's results is that of explaining the gap between marital attitudes and behavior in the African American population. The theories that form the basis of this study would suggest that several factors—in particular, economic and mate availability concerns—constrain behavior that would conform with the stated values. However, there are other theoretical contexts for consideration of this issue. The social psychological theory of reasoned action (Fishbein and Ajzen, 1975; Ajzen and Fishbein, 1980) holds that the intention to act is a function of one's attitude toward the behavior as well as perceived social pressure to perform the behavior. (The theory is more complex than is evident from the previous statement, and explicitly considers other factors including beliefs about the consequences of the behavior, the motivation to conform, and beliefs about the expectations of specific others. A host of studies have sought to further clarify the model.)

One could therefore argue that despite African Americans' favorable attitudes toward marriage, there has been a decline in the social pressure on blacks to marry, thus accounting for the decline in marriage. This is probably true, to a certain degree. However, one would still have to explain why social pressure to marry has lessened. Kiecolt (1988) has reviewed the sociological research that examines the influence of the social structure on attitude formation and the connection between attitude and behavior, and cites the work of Liska as one particularly promising direction for further work. Liska (1984) takes the Fishbein and Ajzen (1975) conceptualization as a point of departure and explicitly considers the role of the social structure in a revised model. He especially takes issue with the Fishbein and Ajzen assumption that most behaviors of interest are under volitional control—which is precisely the point that concerns us with respect to marriage—and argues that most behavior is contingent on the cooperation of others, a number of environmental resources, and one's position in the social structure. Obviously, such a conceptual framework requires a linking of macro theory (e.g., the economic and demographic theories of marriage) and micro theory (e.g., the attitude-behavior theories) with new methodological strategies. Recently, several procedures have been proposed for this purpose (Entwisle and Mason, 1985; Liska, 1990) and may hold the key to a more complete understanding of changing marital behavior.

Future research on African American marriage and family formation must go beyond the necessary focus on economic factors and consider other marital facilitators and inhibitors. Work in this area must also consider individual-level decision making and its relationship to macro phenomena in a more specific manner. While we would hope for a new economic order that provides black men as well as women with the means to provide an emotionally as well as materially supportive family atmosphere, in the short run, we must bolster those mechanisms that support marital bonds despite financial constraints.

Author Notes

This investigation was supported in part by a Research Scientist Development Award to Dr. Tucker from the National Institute of Mental Health, grant K01 MH 00681. Additional support was provided by the UCLA Afro-American Studies Program in Interdisciplinary Research, a program grant from the Ford Foundation to Drs. Mitchell-Kernan and Tucker. The Southern California Social Survey was sponsored by the UCLA Institute for Social Science Research.

REFERENCES

AJZEN, I., AND FISHBEIN, M. 1980. *Understanding attitudes and predicting social behavior.* Englewood Cliffs, NJ: Prentice-Hall.

ANDREWS, F.M., MORGAN, J.N., SONQUIST, J.A., AND KLEM, L. 1973. *Multiple classification analysis: A report on a computer program for multiple regression using categorical predictors.* 2nd ed. Ann Arbor: University of Michigan.

BERKSON, J. 1953. A statistically precise and relatively simple method of estimating the bioassay with quantal response based upon the logistic function. *Journal of the American Statistical Association,* 48:565–599.

BERNARD, J. 1981. The good-provider role: Its rise and fall. *American Psychologist,* 36 (1):1–12.

BLOOM, D.E., AND BENNETT, N.G. 1985. Marriage patterns in the United States. National Bureau of Economic Research Working Paper Series. No. 1701. Cambridge, MA: National Bureau of Economic Research.

CHERLIN, A.J. 1981. *Marriage, divorce, remarriage*. Cambridge, MA: Harvard University Press.

DARITY, W., AND MYERS, S.L. 1986/87. Public policy trends and the fate of the black family. *Humboldt Journal of Social Relations*, 14:134–164.

ENTWISTLE, B., AND MASON, W.M. 1985. Multilevel effects of socioeconomic development and family planning programs on children ever born. *American Journal of Sociology*, 91:616–649.

EPENSHADE, T.J. 1985. Marriage trends in America: Estimates, implications, and underlying causes. *Population and Development Review*, 11:193–245.

FISHBEIN, M., AND AJZEN, I. 1975. *Belief, attitude, intention and behavior*. Reading, MA: Addison-Wesley.

GLICK, P.C., HEER, D.M., AND BERESFORD, J.C. 1963. Family formation and family composition: Trends and prospects. In M.B. Sussman, ed., *Sourcebook in marriage and the family*. New York: Houghton Mifflin.

GUTTENTAG, M., AND SECORD, P.F. 1983. *Too many women: The sex ratio question*. Beverly Hills: Sage Publications.

HAMPTON, R.L. 1979. Husband's characteristics and marital disruption in black families. *The Sociological Quarterly*, 20:255–266.

KIECOLT, K.J. 1988. Recent developments in attitudes and social structure. *Annual Review of Sociology*, 14:381–403.

LISKA, A.E. 1984. A critical examination of the causal structure of the Fishbein/Ajzen attitude-behavior model. *Social Psychology Quarterly*, 47:61–74.

LISKA, A.E. 1990. The significance of aggregate dependent variables and contextual independent variables for linking macro and micro theories. *Social Psychology Quarterly*, 53:292–301.

MELVILLE, M.B. 1980. *Twice a minority: Mexican American women*. St. Louis: C.V. Mosby.

MOYNIHAN, D.P. 1967. The Negro family: The case for national action. In L. Rainwater and W.L. Rainwater, eds., *The Moynihan report and the politics of controversy*. Cambridge, MA: MIT Press.

NORTON, A.J., AND MOORMAN, J.E. 1987. Current trends in marriage and divorce among American women. *Journal of Marriage and the Family*, 49:3–14.

OPPENHEIMER, V.K. 1988. A theory of marriage timing. *American Journal of Sociology*, 94:563–591.

PESQUERA, B.M. 1984. "Having a job gives you some sort of power": Reflections of a Chicano working woman. *Feminist Issues*, 4:79–96.

RODGERS, W.L., AND THORNTON, A. 1985. Changing patterns of first marriage in the United States. *Demography*. 22:265–279.

ROSS, H.L. AND SAWHILL, I. 1975. *Time of transition: The growth of families headed by women*. Washington, DC: The Urban Institute.

SCHOEN, R. 1983. Measuring the tightness of the marriage squeeze. *Demography*, 20(1): 61–78.

SECORD, P.F., AND GHEE, K. 1986. Implications of the black marriage market for marital conflict. *Journal of Family Issues*, 7:21–30.

STAPLES, R. 1981a. Race and marital status: An overview. In H.P. McAdoo, ed., *Black families*, pp. 173–175. Beverly Hills: Sage Publications.

STAPLES, R. 1981b. *The world of black singles*. Westport, CT: Greenwood Press.

THEIL, H. 1970. An estimation of relationships involving qualitative variables. *American Journal of Sociology,* 76:103–154.

TUCKER, M.B., AND MITCHELL-KERNAN, C. 1990. New trends in black American interracial marriage: The social structural context. *Journal of Marriage and the Family,* 52:209–218.

TUCKER, M.B., AND MITCHELL-KERNAN, C. In press. Mate availability among African Americans: Conceptual and methodological issues. In R. Jones, ed., *Advances in black psychology.* Hampton, VA: Cobb and Henry.

TUCKER, M.B., AND TAYLOR, R.J. 1989. Demographic correlates of relationship status among black Americans. *Journal of Marriage and the Family,* 51:655–665.

U.S. BUREAU OF THE CENSUS. 1960. *Historical statistics of the United States, colonial times to 1957.* Washington, DC: U.S. Government Printing Office.

U.S. BUREAU OF THE CENSUS. 1964. *U.S. census of population: 1960,* Vol. I, *Characteristics of the population,* Part I, United States Summary. Washington, DC: U.S. Government Printing Office.

U.S. BUREAU OF THE CENSUS. 1973. *U.S. census of population: 1970,* Part 1, United States Summary—Section 2. Washington, DC: U.S. Government Printing Office.

U.S. BUREAU OF THE CENSUS. 1982. *Statistical abstract of the United States: 1982–83.* 103rd ed. Washington, DC: U.S. Government Printing Office.

U.S. BUREAU OF THE CENSUS. 1983. *U.S. census of population: 1980,* Vol. I, *Characteristics of the population,* Chapter B: General Population Characteristics, Part 1, United States Summary. Washington, DC: U.S. Government Printing Office.

U.S. BUREAU OF THE CENSUS. 1985. *U.S. census of population: 1980, Vol. 2, Subject reports: Marital characteristics.* Washington, DC: U.S. Government Printing Office.

U.S. BUREAU OF THE CENSUS. 1991a. Marital status and living arrangements: March 1990. *Current Population Reports,* series P-20, no. 450. Washington, DC: U.S. Government Printing Office.

U.S. BUREAU OF THE CENSUS. 1991b. The Hispanic population in the United States: March 1990. *Current Population Reports,* series P-2, no. 449. Washington, DC: U.S. Government Printing Office.

U.S. BUREAU OF THE CENSUS. 1991c. Family disruption and economic hardship: The short-run picture for children. *Current Population Reports,* series P-70, no. 23. Washington, DC: U.S. Government Printing Office.

U.S. BUREAU OF THE CENSUS. 1992. Marriage, divorce, and remarriage in the 1990s. *Current Population Reports,* series P-23, no. 180. Washington, DC: U.S. Government Printing Office.

U.S. BUREAU OF THE CENSUS. 1993. Population and housing characteristics for census tracts: 1990. CP-H3. Washington, DC: U.S. Government Printing Office.

VASQUEZ, M.J.T., AND GONZALEZ, A.M. 1981. Sex roles among Chicanos: Stereotypes, challenges, and changes. In A. Baron, Jr., ed., *Explorations in Chicano psychology.* New York: Praeger.

WILSON, W.J. 1987. *The truly disadvantaged.* Chicago: The University of Chicago Press.

WILSON, W.J., AND NECKERMAN, K.M. 1986. Poverty and family structure: The widening gap between evidence and public policy issues. In S.H. Danziger and D.H. Weinberg, eds., *Fighting poverty: What works and what doesn't.* Cambridge, MA: Harvard University Press.

COMMENTARY

James S. Jackson

TUCKER AND MITCHELL-KERNAN have addressed a long-standing debate in the field regarding marital behavior. The chapter is a significant contribution because it clarifies a number of issues related to level of analysis, structural versus personal tastes, and the role of sociocultural factors in contributing to the complex and poorly understood social psychological phenomenon of marriage.

In many ways, the concept of marriage, as an institution, is a peculiar one. In the United States, and I suspect in most other societies, the nature and form of marriage vary substantially—across and within class and culture. Preferred age of marriage ranges widely by socioeconomic status and ethnicity. The motivation for, and what is defined as, appropriate marital behavior also differ dramatically, across multiple dimensions. There is nothing so openly displayed as marriage, when we affirm our relationships and undying devotion in public ceremonies. Yet, there is nothing so private as marriage—in which childrearing behavior, sexual behavior, and various forms of familial abuse are conducted well outside of the public eye. In other parts of the world, and at different historical moments, societies have been more forthright in arranging and specifying the economic priorities of marriages designed to unite geographic, national, and ethnic groups or families. Thus, both historically and contemporaneously, we have and do ask a great deal of the marital union.

Tucker and Mitchell-Kernan have addressed important social and psychological issues at both group and individual levels. They are cognizant of the fact that marriage-related behaviors are fundamentally social psychological in nature, and that we must focus on how macroeconomic and demographic forces play a role at the individual and group levels. The authors point out that greater scientific attention must be paid to how demographic and structural factors, separately and in concert (in the context of sociocultural processes), come to influence individual and micro-social associative behaviors. They conclude, quite correctly I believe, that "future research on African American marriage and family formation must go beyond the necessary focus on economic factors and consider other marital facilitators and inhibitors. Work in this area must also consider individual-level decision making and its relationship to macro phenomena in a more specific manner."

Their work, then, contributes in two important ways to the conceptualization of research in this area. First, it moves the field beyond an emphasis on single explanations for complex social and individual behavior. Second, it demands a consideration of ethnic and cultural factors. Tucker and Mitchell-Kernan raise complex questions about historical time, socialization, and period events, all of which can influence the orientation that men and women have toward romantic associations and marital partnerships. I found the chapter satisfying in addressing the issues that I have summarized thus far, but also provocative in raising a number of issues for future theorizing and research. First, the authors assume that attitudes toward romantic associations develop in response to structural, economic, and social realities. How does this come about? It is possible that comparison level and comparison level for alternatives theory, considered within the context of the complex economic networks in which people are imbedded, may play a major role in the transformation of macro-level phenomena to the micro-level issues of concern here.

Second, personality-like factors—such as risk taking, schemas—may be important elements with respect to demographic realities. For example, what are the individual-level schemas for marriage that individuals hold; how do people conceive of marriage in both cognitive and affective terms; and how do these cognitive and affective schema then direct behaviors? How do partners in marriage come to share schemas of marriage and the appropriate behaviors of the other? Are these schemas developed as part of the socialization process or through direct observation of marriages of parents and families? How do these schemas adapt and change over time as a function of the experience of the interpersonal relationship in the marriage dyad?

Demographic and economic factors make it more or less difficult for marriages to work. In fact, the failure to change, or to incorporate schemas with environmental realities, can indeed be self-handicapping. For example, a schema for marriage that would have a rose-covered cottage as the setting may come face to face with the reality of apartment living in a central city environment. Thus, such personality-like schemas, which both guide and motivate behavior, may serve to provide the basis for the expectation and either the fulfillment or the frustration of those expectations over time.

Third, I believe that there should be greater attention paid to the larger familial context in which ostensibly individual decision making about romantic associations takes place. While the dominant ethos of this society is to view the decision to romantically associate and marry as a personal one, it is not a decision which is independent of family approbations nor the cultural context of a person's socialization. Too often in this society, these decisions are treated as independent ones. How the larger family, and even community, context plays a role in marital formation, maintenance, and disintegration, needs greater attention in theory and research. For example, Tucker and Mitchell-Kernan did not include acculturation level in the Latino models. It is possible that acculturation, beyond the requirement of English-speaking that defined the sample, could have resulted in the increased efficiency of those models.

Another limitation of previous work is the absence of never-married women and men as appropriate comparison points. Do the social and psychological processes for never-married persons change with historical time and social events? These may be particularly crucial concerns for mate-selection criteria. For example, whether someone is a good dancer or dresser may play a role in earlier pairings, but may give way to other kinds of issues at later points in the life span. And we must consider how these factors, which may contribute to selection, are themselves related to the basis of stability and retention in romantic associations and marriage over time. Clearly, there is a need for greater attention to the studies of the role of expectations in marital formation and disintegration. It is possible that marriages at relatively young ages are, for the most part, never based on expectations of long-term economic viability and stability. How do such current issues as the fear of AIDS affect the marriage schema that I have discussed?

Finally, in many ways, we have been studying issues of romantic association and marital behavior in a relative cross-cultural vacuum. While the findings on black and Latino groups contributed by this chapter provide some needed cultural heterogeneity, I believe that such a comparison is simply not enough. It may be necessary to do cross-national studies on this topic, simultaneously focusing on the countries of origin of racial and ethnic groups, as well as the individuals from those countries who now reside in the United States. This would allow us to begin to disentangle cultural from what may be opportunity and structural factors. Although the findings of this study strongly suggest an important role of attitudes and expectations in the behavioral intentions and desired statuses related to romantic association and marriage, the causal interrelationships are as yet unexplored.

In sum, I find that Tucker and Mitchell-Kernan have raised a number of excellent issues in their chapter. The researchers are to be commended for their work. Their research brings a micro and macro focus to the study of marital behavior and expectations in an attempt to test competing theoretical formulations of romantic associations and marital decision making. The comparative focus on blacks, Latinos, and whites is also noteworthy. They also stress the need for a larger cultural context and cross-national work. In my comments, I have noted some issues that, in my view, require further attention. For example, not including degree of value, behavioral and attitudinal acculturation as measured variables may have contributed to the lack of efficiency of some of their models, particularly for the Latino group. I have also noted that greater attention should be paid to personality-like variables as potential mediators and contextual factors for the micro behavior of individuals in romantic associations and marital dyads. Finally, I noted the importance of the study of marital formation, maintenance, disintegration, and expectation within the larger cultural and extended family context, as well as the need to extend our analyses and conceptualizations to considerations of time, cohort, and period events. This larger contextual and dynamic approach may allow us to understand changes in romantic association, marital decision making, and marital behavior as a function of secular changes in the larger familial and economic spheres. I believe that this approach would be consistent with the important work initiated by Tucker and Mitchell-Kernan and the directions they envision for their future research and writing.

7 MARITAL INSTABILITY AMONG BLACK AND WHITE COUPLES IN EARLY MARRIAGE

Shirley Hatchett
Joseph Veroff
and
Elizabeth Douvan

G ETTING MARRIED and staying married may become relatively rare events among black Americans if current trends in family organization, and in the economic marginalization of young black men, continue. As a result of a trend which began at the end of World War II and gained momentum in the 1960s and 1970s, nearly half of all families among blacks are now headed by women (Farley and Allen, 1987). Although such households have also increased among whites (as documented in Chapter 1), the change has been more dramatic for blacks. The underlying dynamics of this trend suggest that the ceiling has yet to be reached in the transformation of black family organization.

Widowhood was the primary contributor to female headship among both races in earlier periods. However, marital dissolution and out-of-wedlock births have become major driving forces in the changing structure of American families. This is particularly true for blacks whose rates of separation and divorce as well as out-of-wedlock births are much greater than those for whites (Farley and Allen, 1987; Sweet and Bumpass, 1984). The growing number of "never married" adult women also contributes to the rise in female-headed households. The proportion of single women increased from 30 percent in 1960 to 69 percent in 1980 among blacks and from 29 percent to 47 percent among whites (Wilson, 1987). Among whites, this increase is due in significant degree to the greater tendency among both women and men to delay marriage to pursue education and careers (Glick, 1977). For black women, this trend appears to derive more and more from the decreased availability of prospective marriage partners (Tucker and Taylor, 1989; Farley and Allen, 1987). Wilson and Neckerman (1986) suggest that the decreased pool of marriageable black men is a function of an imbalanced sex ratio and the increased economic marginality of black men. This marginality is also seen as a factor in black marital dissolution (see Elder and Caspi, 1988, for a general discussion of the effects of unemployment and economic stress on family relations).

The implications of these trends for black Americans are worrisome. Household composition per se is not problematic for family functioning. However, female-headed families are more likely to be impoverished. And the immediate quality of life for black men, women, and children, as well as for future generations, depends on the economic well-being of families. The economic marginality of blacks, particularly men, appears to be tied to both family formation and family breakup. Given these critical issues, the major aim of this chapter is to more fully understand marital instability among blacks.

We explore economic and other factors which may predict marital instability in the early years of marriage among blacks and whites using data from a longitudinal study of urban newlyweds. The First Years of Marriage Study (FYM) is an ongoing research project at the University of Michigan's Institute for Social Research. This four-year prospective study assumes that the early years of first marriage are complicated times because couples must negotiate the task of blending their individual lives and social networks into a coherent couplehood and a stable bond. This negotiation will be successful for most couples but not for others. We expect to find racial similarities and differences in the factors which determine marital success and instability.

What hinders the establishment of a harmonious marriage? Research on this question has been scant with very little emphasis on racial differences. Most of the literature in this area addresses either social and demographic factors from cross-sectional studies or psychological factors from retrospective accounts of divorced people. Two important longitudinal studies (Raush et al., 1974; Huston, McHale, and Crouter, 1986) include only white samples. Demographic analyses (Norton and Glick, 1979) have revealed the following: divorce is especially likely to occur among poorer, less educated, and younger respondents; there is a much higher rate of divorce among blacks than whites; and premarital pregnancy greatly increases the probability of divorce. Unemployment has also been found to be related to marital dissolution. Cherlin (1979) found that the relationships of income, employment, and dual earnership to marital success are complex. For example, if a wife's wages are low relative to those of the husband, even in low-income families, there is less likelihood of marital dissolution. Overall, these demographic results seem to be as true for black marriages as they are for white marriages. However, one set of findings is different for blacks and whites. There is evidence of greater intergenerational transmission of divorce among white couples than among black couples (Duncan and Duncan, 1969).

The two prospective studies of marriage mentioned above suggest that styles of communication are among the most critical indicators of psychological functioning to be considered in studies of marital disharmony. The results, however, have been contradictory. Raush et al. (1974) found that it was not the amount of communication per se that was a factor in marital harmony, but the particular ways in which people handle marital conflict. Huston, McHale, and Crouter (1986), however, found that the more couples communicated about their personal feelings and talked about problems, the more likely they were to be satisfied in the relationship eighteen months later.

A General Framework for Studying Marital Instability

Cross-sectional studies of marital quality have been more likely than prospective studies to focus on psychological processes. Therefore, the general conceptual framework we use to guide our analysis is derived largely from marital quality research (see Lewis and Spanier, 1979). Various levels of analysis have been used by researchers considering the contribution of psychological processes to marital quality—beyond the demographic factors listed earlier. Some researchers focus on interpersonal interactions, some on psychological feelings and attitudes, and others on more specific behaviors in the context of spousal and parental roles. We believe that each of these has some relevance to marital instability and therefore have included measures that reflect each of these factors. Our conceptualization of the relationships among these variables is shown in Figure 7.1. In this framework, the social context of marriage—from both premarital experiences and the early experiences of marriage—set the stage for various types of processes of marital interaction among newlyweds. These, in turn, set the stage for specific feelings about marital functioning during the first year which affect the overall marital well-being experienced by the couple. These affective experiences about marriage per se, plus experiences of stressful life events and role conflict during the first few years, generally contribute to marital stability in subsequent years.

Although our framework implies sequential causation, we recognize that the connections between these sets of factors may indeed be bidirectional, especially those directly involving the first year of marriage. We argue that the effects in the reverse direction are weaker than effects indicated by the major arrows in the figure. However, the analyses presented in this chapter do not explicitly test the causal patterns implied in this framework. Below we discuss each set of factors outlined in Figure 7.1.

FIGURE 7.1

Potential factors in the first years of marriage affecting the development of marital instability.

First Year

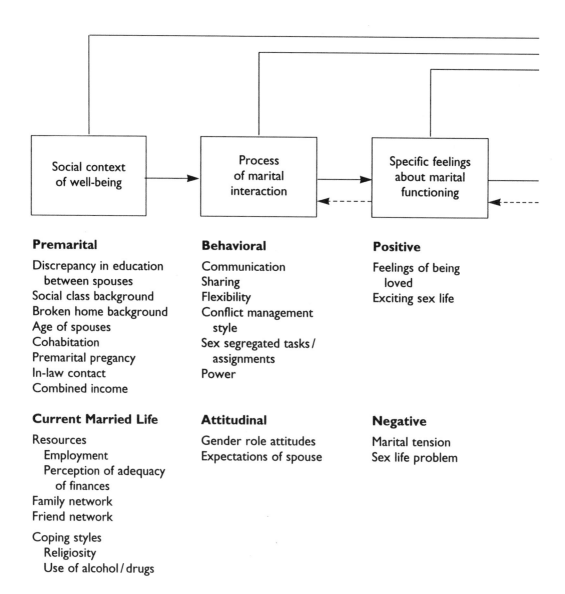

Premarital

Discrepancy in education
  between spouses
Social class background
Broken home background
Age of spouses
Cohabitation
Premarital pregancy
In-law contact
Combined income

Behavioral

Communication
Sharing
Flexibility
Conflict management
  style
Sex segregated tasks /
  assignments
Power

Positive

Feelings of being
  loved
Exciting sex life

Current Married Life

Resources
  Employment
  Perception of adequacy
    of finances
Family network
Friend network

Coping styles
  Religiosity
  Use of alcohol / drugs

Attitudinal

Gender role attitudes
Expectations of spouse

Negative

Marital tension
Sex life problem

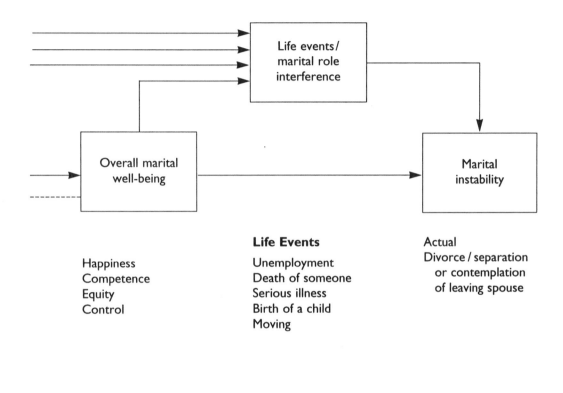

Second / Third Year

Life events/
marital role
interference

Overall marital
well-being

Marital
instability

Life Events

Unemployment
Death of someone
Serious illness
Birth of a child
Moving

Happiness
Competence
Equity
Control

Actual
Divorce / separation
  or contemplation
  of leaving spouse

**Role Interference
from:**

Work
Own family
In-laws
Friends

The Premarital Social Context

Even before a couple marries, they have had experiences in their families of origin and the social world in general that predispose them to risks of marital instability. We have already noted a number of these sociodemographic risk factors. Both lower socioeconomic background and youth are associated with greater marital instability, perhaps because both could be related to problematic marital interaction and, hence, lower marital well-being. Other factors may also be salient. Growing up in an intact family is related to marital stability among whites but not blacks. Greater integration with future in-laws can ease the transition into marriage. Also, a number of studies suggest that living together before marriage is associated with greater marital instability, although the specific factors involved have not been clearly identified. People who live together tend to be less religious and are more likely to have had a premarital pregnancy—both of which may affect marital interaction and well-being in the first and subsequent years of marriage. Each of these factors is included in our analyses.

The Social Context of the First Year of Marriage

The first year of marriage presents a number of challenges to newlyweds. They must combine two individuals' lives in a manner that both promotes harmonious couplehood yet preserves individuality. One aspect of life that is very much related to these potentially competing demands is the couple's social networks. Hatchett, Veroff, and Beyers (1989) found that a workable balance between the separation from and the amalgamation of individual family and friend networks appears to be important to marital happiness in early marriage. In our analyses, we have included measures which tap the affective, structural, and functional aspects of social networks (both positive and negative). Consistent with Surra (1988), who noted that global indicators of interference from networks have the clearest impact on intimate relationships, Hatchett, Veroff, and Beyers (1989) found that reports of negative, rather than positive, social support influenced marital happiness.

There are other resources that affect marital adjustment in these early years, including economic well-being and the coping styles employed by couples together and individually. As noted earlier, low economic well-being and male unemployment have been consistently linked to marital instability. We have included measures of two general coping styles that may be employed by couples as they confront financial and other challenges of marriage and everyday living. Religion can be an important mode of coping especially if shared by spouses. Also examined is the use of alcohol or drugs to relieve tension—an adaptive behavior that has been found to be problematic for couples.

Processes of Marital Interaction: Behavior

Clearly, the way in which wives and husbands interact is important for marital well-being. In addition to communication (discussed earlier), other interactional factors related to marital adjustment are the degree to which couples share activities and interests, flexibility in responsibility for familial tasks such as childcare and housework, and the management of disagreements. The latter factor can be highly prognostic of harmony in marriage (see Crohan, 1988, and Oggins, Veroff, and Leber, 1993). In addition, the extent to which gender issues, particularly in regard to power, are egalitarian or male centered may assume greater importance in marital harmony during this period of normative change. Pinderhughes (1988) notes that these issues are especially crucial in black marital relations.

Processes of Marital Interaction: Attitudes

We have isolated two sets of attitudes that may affect marital negotiation during the initial year of marriage: traditionality of views of gender roles and couples' expectations for each other. The first set included in our analyses measures the extent of traditionalism in gender role attitudes across a number of domains. (Went, Sutherland, and Douvan, 1988, and Sutherland, 1989, examined gender and race differences in traditionality and their impact on marital well-being.) The second set contains measures of discrepancies between real and ideal characteristics of one's spouse. In some instances, marital experience does not meet the idealized premarital appraisals of couples. The resulting disappointment may threaten marital harmony. Ruvolo (1988) found that a wife's report of discrepancies between real and ideal characteristics of her husband affected her husband's marital happiness but his perception of her was unrelated to her marital happiness.

Specific Feelings about Marital Functioning

Divorced persons or those seeking divorce often state that they simply no longer experienced love in the relationship. Thus, the particular feeling of being cared for by the spouse should be examined as a major indicator of marital functioning. Marital tension—upsetting feelings about the way a couple gets along—has been found by Bradburn (1969) to be independent of positive feelings. Therefore, we examine negative and positive feelings separately. We additionally assess positive and negative aspects of the couple's sexual life, including excitement and passion experienced, as well as the degree to which a respondent's sexual life is viewed as problematic. Greenblatt (1983) found that the quality rather than the frequency of sexual encounters was most important during the early years of marriage.

Overall Marital Well-Being

In previous analyses for this study, Crohan and Veroff (1989) determined four different factors of overall marital well-being: general happiness; sense of competence in dealing with the spousal role; perceptions of equity in the marital relationship; and the perceived ability (control) to make things right in the relationship. These factors are also used in the present examination of marital instability.

Second- and Third-Year Situational Experiences

Many occurrences after the first year of marriage can affect marital stability. Two sets of situational factors are included in this study: critical life events and role conflicts. Key life events that can potentially affect marital well-being include unemployment, birth of a child, moving, health problems, and death of loved ones. Role conflicts can emerge from family and friend pressures, or work and leisure demands away from the family. These second- and third-year events are no doubt a function, in part, of premarital and first-year marital experiences, as indicated by the arrows in Figure 7.1. In turn, the stresses of life events and role conflicts can combine with marital evaluations to influence marital stability.

Marital Instability

Booth, Johnson, and Edwards (1982) proposed two measures of marital instability: certainty that the relationship will last and contemplations of leaving the relationship. In each wave of the study, we used these assessments. In the third year, an additional measure was used: "In the last few months, how often have you considered leaving your (wife/husband)?" The highest response value given by one or the other spouse about such instability is used as the couple's level of instability. All of the analyses are performed at the couple level. Couples that became separated or divorced during the second or third year are assigned the most extreme value on this measure of marital instability.[1] Thus, our measure of marital instability combines psychological orientation to maintaining a marriage with the behavioral fact of divorce or separation.

The framework we have outlined includes factors that occur premaritally, and across the panel's first three years of marriage, although the majority of the variables are from the first year. Our primary concern is the predictability of these factors for marital instability as assessed in the third year. The specific items used to construct measures assessing the factors shown in Figure 7.1 are summarized in the Appendix to this chapter.

---

[1]The categories and values of this variable are: often (4); sometimes (3); rarely (2); and never (1). Separated and divorced couples were assigned a value of "5."

Methods

Our data are derived from face-to-face interviews with black and white wives and husbands in the metropolitan Detroit area. In the first year of the study (1986), 373 couples—199 black, 174 white—were interviewed in their homes three to seven months after they were married. Respondents had been randomly selected from couples applying for marriage licenses in Wayne County within a three-month period—April through June 1986—who met our eligibility criteria: first marriage for each spouse and bride no older than thirty-five years of age.[2] We used the latter criterion in order to maximize the possibility of childbearing during the study. Couples were notified by mail of their selection and contacted at their residences for the interviews.

The overall response rate for the interview was 66 percent,[3] which is relatively high for this kind of study given that the joint cooperation of the husband and the wife was needed. Our retention of the sample for Year 2 and Year 3 was excellent for the white couples, but less than ideal for black couples. Once they agreed to participate in this study, we found very few actual refusals to participate in subsequent years.[4] Couples found to be separated or divorced during a given study year were interviewed for that wave and then dropped from subsequent ones. A major factor in black attrition, aside from separation or divorce, was our inability to locate black couples. We were less able to find new addresses for blacks who had moved than for whites, and we also suspect that blacks were more geographically mobile than whites.[5]

Rates of Separation and Divorce

Table 7.1 presents changes in the marital status of our panel across the three years. Our estimate of marital status in Year 3 is actually one of marital status after two years of marriage, since interviews took place during the third year. Using data from the 1980 census, Sweet and Bumpass (1984) estimated that 8 percent of white first marriages and 11 percent of black first marriages ended in separation or divorce after two years. In comparison, our rates are lower for whites and much higher for blacks. The Sweet and Bumpass results

---

[2] Because of the relatively small proportion of blacks in Wayne County who were eligible, our three-month screening yielded just enough blacks to meet the sample *n* requirement. We, therefore, took all eligibles. Screening yielded a larger frame for whites.

[3] This is larger than what you would receive if you obtained an 80 percent response rate for each individual spouse. That joint probability would be .64.

[4] A good proportion of nonresponse coded as non-interviews resulted from missed appointments and the inability of interviewers to catch respondents at home. These were perhaps "subtle" refusals.

[5] A number of our couples moved to other parts of the state or the country. When possible we attempted to interview them by using staff or students travelling to those areas.

TABLE 7.1

Marital Status across Three Years
for Black and White Couples in First Years of Marriage Panel

Marital Status	Blacks (N = 199)			Whites (N = 174)		
	Year 1	Year 2	Year 3	Year 1	Year 2	Year 3
(Still) married	100%	84%	74%	100%	93%	90%
Separated/divorced	—	8%	17%	—	3%	6%
Not ascertained	—	8%	9%	—	4%	4%
		100%	100%		100%	100%

are for marriages that took place from 1965 to 1979. Our couples began their marriages in 1986. It is possible that conditions which foster black marital instability have become considerably more severe. We plan to use imputation techniques for nonresponse at a later date to predict the marital status of couples for whom we were unable to ascertain marital status in the second and third waves. We feel that such analyses will reveal a slightly higher overall rate of separation and divorce for both whites and blacks. Black separation and divorce rates have been estimated at one and one-half to two and one-half times those for whites. In our panel, the rate is 2.8 times greater for blacks than for whites.

Profile of Panel

Table 7.2 shows selected socioeconomic and demographic characteristics of our couples in their first year of marriage.[6] One can see from Table 7.2 that blacks were more likely than whites to enter the marriage with children and to have lived together for a longer period of time. On the average, black wives and husbands were a year older than their white counterparts, but there was little racial difference in mean years of education. Black wives had slightly more education than black husbands and white husbands had somewhat more education than white wives, but these patterns are consistent with those found for the general population.

Confirming other such data, black couples in our study were less well-off economically than white couples. They were eight times more likely than whites to have total family incomes below ten thousand dollars. However, there was

---

[6] Because discrepancies were often found between wives' and husbands' reports, the total household income reported in Table 7.2 is that reported by the husband; the length of time the couple lived together before marriage and the number of children are from the wife's interview.

little difference in the employment status of black and white husbands. The economic well-being differences appear to stem from fewer dual-earner black families and a greater tendency of working black husbands and wives to occupy low-paying jobs.

The Interview

In the first and third years of the study, spouses were interviewed separately and then together. The race of respondent and interviewer was matched in both types of interview. Individual interviews lasting an average of eight minutes were conducted with a standard structured questionnaire containing both open- and fixed-response questions. In the couple interview, the respondents were asked to tell a very open-ended story of their relationship (see Chadiha and Ortega, 1988, for a discussion of this technique). Data from these joint narratives are still being analyzed. Another feature of the couple interview was a task where couples resolved differences they had in judgments of the importance of a list of rules for marriage. All of the couple interviews were tape-recorded. Only data from the individual spouse interviews are used in the present analyses. For their cooperation, each couple received twenty-five dollars after the couple interview was completed. During the second year of interviewing, brief telephone interviews were conducted.

Analysis

Two strategies were followed in our analyses. First, we examined the ability of the sets of factors presented in Figure 7.1 to predict marital instability. Separate measures for husbands and wives were obtained for most factors. For example, both husbands and wives reported on the degree to which they shared activities in the individual interviews. Although correlated, they are not identical and were entered into the regressions involving marital processes separately. Other factors like parental status and household income were measured at the couple level.[7] All analyses were conducted separately for blacks and whites.

In the second part of our analyses, we included predictors found to be significant in this first step in a hierarchical regression analysis to see which remain as important predictors in the overall models for each race. Our framework for understanding marital instability was used to guide the hierarchical analysis. We were particularly interested in similarities and differences in the predictive models for blacks and whites.

---

[7]Actually, we used the husband's report of household income and the wife's report of the number of children for these couple variables.

TABLE 7.2

First-Year Socioeconomic and Demographic Characteristics of Black and White Couples

	Blacks (N = 199)			Whites (N = 174)		
	Husbands	Wives	Couple	Husbands	Wives	Couple
Mean age	27.3	24.8		25.6	24.0	
Mean age difference			2.4			1.6
Mean education (years)	12.9	13.2		13.3	13.0	
Mean education difference			−0.3			0.3
Mean father's education	11.2	11.2		11.8	12.1	
Mean mother's education	11.9	12.3		11.8	11.9	
Mean number of months cohabited before marriage			14.7			6.9
Employment status						
Working	90%	63%		93%	72%	
Laid off	3	2		3	1	
Unemployed	5	16		3	1	
Homemaker	—	16		—	18	
Student	1	3		—	—	
Other	1	1		—	—	
	100%	100%		100%	100%	
Both work			56%			65%
Combined income						
$ 0–$ 9,999			16%			2%
$10,000–$19,999			21			14
$20,000–$29,999			25			21
$30,000–$39,999			16			25
$40,000–$49,999			11			19
$50,000+			11			19
			100%			100%

Results

First, we conducted regression analyses predicting marital instability from each set of factors, separately by race. Given that the analyses are quite extensive, the results are not detailed in this chapter (although they may be obtained from the authors). In Table 7.3, however, we present a descriptive summary of all predictors within each set of factors that were significant at the .05 level. Looking at this table, we see that results for black couples and white couples are similar in some ways and distinctive in others. Wives' and husbands' reports are similarly convergent, as well as divergent. There is far too much information

	Blacks ($N = 199$)			Whites ($N = 174$)		
	Husbands	Wives	Couple	Husbands	Wives	Couple
Occupation						
Professional/technical	11%	10%		20%	16%	
Managerial	6	5		11	5	
Sales	2	2		5	4	
Clerical	8	32		6	33	
Crafts	15	1		23	1	
Operatives	21	0		22	2	
Laborers	6	0		3	0	
Farmers	0	0		0	0	
Service	21	14		8	11	
(not working, missing data)	10	36		3	29	
	100%	100%		100%	100%	
Parental status						
No children			45%			78%
All by spouse			27			17
Some by someone else			28			5
			100%			100%
Number of children						
One			58%			82%
Two			26			18
Three or more			16			—
			100%			100%
Grew up with both parents	50%	41%		80%	71%	

here to summarize succinctly. Because the primary concern of this chapter is to better understand factors contributing to the much greater incidence of separation and divorce among blacks, we will discuss the results for black couples more fully than those for whites.

For simplification of presentation we will focus on only three types of significant predictors: (1) those that are significant for both black couples and white couples; (2) those significant for blacks but not whites; and (3) those significant for white couples but not blacks. Here, the main criterion is a significant difference between a given beta for blacks and that for whites. These predictors are listed in Table 7.4. Consequently, we will not discuss predictors for which the *comparison* of the betas for each group is not significant (even if one group's beta is significant while the other is not). We will return to some

TABLE 7.3

*Summary of Significant (p .05) Predictors of Marital Instability,
by Type of Factor × Race*

Type of Factor	Blacks		
	Wives	Husbands	Couples
Premarital social context	$(-)^a$ Age $(-)$ Father's education	$(-)$ Age Father's education $(-)$ Mother's education	$(-)$ Premarital children $(-)$ Combined income Premarital children × income
Current married life	$(-)$ R^b is employed Spouse's problematic drinking/drug use $(-)$ Spouse's disapproval of R's friends $(-)$ Church attendance	Worry about money Spouse's problematic drinking/drug use	—
Processes of marital interaction	Destructive conflict $(-)$ Role flexibility	Destructive conflict H-W power balance Woman's job hurts family	—
Specific feelings about marital functioning	Marital tension	$(-)$ Positive feelings	—
Overall marital well-being	$(-)$ Marital satisfaction	$(-)$ Marital satisfaction	—
Life events/marital role interference	Spouse's family interferes Spouse's friends interfere Someone close died R had a baby R was seriously ill	$(-)$ R's work interferes Spouse's family interferes Spouse's friends interfere Moved	—

^{a}A $(-)$ listed before a predictor indicates that this predictor predicts stability rather than instability.
^{b}R = respondent.

Whites		
Wives	Husbands	Couples
(−) Grew up with both parents Father's education (−) Mother's education	(−) Premarital acquaintance with in-laws	—
(−) Church attendance	(−) R is employed Church attendance	—
Destructive conflict	Destructive conflict (−) Egalitarian behavior	—
Marital tension	Marital tension	—
(−) Marital role competence	—	—
R's family interferes Spouse's friends interfere R had a baby	Spouse's friends interfere	—

TABLE 7.4

Significant Predictors of Marital Instability

Type of Factor	Predictors Significant[a] for Black and White Couples
Premarital social context	Age of husband
Current married life	(−) Wife: church attendance
Processes of marital interaction	Wife, Husband: destructive conflict
Marital feelings	Wife: marital tension
Overall marital well-being	
Life events/marital role interferences	Birth of a child Wife, Husband: role interference from friends

Note: Listed in this table are predictors that are significant in regressions of marital instability on the measures used to assess each type of factor separately. Summarized in the previous Tables 4–9 (−) listed before the predictor indicates that this predictor predicts stability rather than instability. If a predictor was significant for blacks and not whites (or vice versa) and comparing black and white betas revealed no significant difference, that predictor is not listed in this table.

[a] B standardized beta at least at .05 level.
[b] Difference between B's for white and black regression is significant at least at .05 level.

of these variables when we present results from the second part of our analyses as they emerge as predictors in the final total model of marital instability.

What does Table 7.4 reveal? First, there are more significant predictors of marital disruption for blacks than for white couples. Second, more significant differences between the two racial groups occur for situational factors (premarital social context, first year of married life context, and life events/marital role interferences) than for marital processes or feelings about marriage. That is, the internal processes associated with marital disruption were similar across race. Clearly, there may be situational issues that are similarly related to marital outcome for both blacks and whites (e.g., we found that among both races, childbirth during the early years was associated with instability). However, the experiences of most blacks and whites are sufficiently unique that we should expect to find racially distinct associations between situational circumstances

Predictors Significant[b] for Black Couples Only	Predictors Significant[b] for White Couples Only
Husband: father's education (−) Wife: mother's education	Wife: father's education
(−) Age of wife Husband: worry about money Wife: husband's disapproval of her friends	
(−) Wife: role flexibility Husband: power balance	
(−) Husband: marital satisfaction	(−) Wife: marital role competence
(−) Wife: interference from her family Wife: interference from husband's family (−) Wife: serious illness Husband: moving	Husband: interference from wife's friends Wife: interference from her family

and whether a marriage stabilizes during the early years. In the discussion that follows, we highlight a few of the more provocative results of our analyses.

Premarital factors. The most striking premarital result—one we did not anticipate—was that black men whose fathers had *more* education were more likely to be in unstable marriages in these early years than those whose fathers had less education. This was not true for white men, although it is curious that white women whose fathers had more education were also especially likely to be in unstable marriages.

We are unable to offer a convincing explanation of the result for white wives. However, we suspect that the finding for black husbands is related to the special pressures faced by educated black men, historically and presently. Since the ages of the black men in our study ranged from eighteen to forty-five years (the mean age was twenty-seven), their fathers were entering adulthood both before and during the significant black political movements of the 1960s. It should be pointed out that the mean number of years of education was eleven and that, for the most part, higher education means a high school diploma and, for a few, one or two years of some post-secondary education or training. Some of these more highly educated fathers were likely to have been underemployed. Those who were not underemployed probably held jobs that were unusual for blacks at that time. Research on social class among blacks has found that until recently, because of the enormous constraints on black occupational mobility before the Civil Rights movement, the black middle class encompassed a wider variety of occupations than did the white middle class (Landry, 1987; Frazier, 1962). For example, college-educated black men often held the positions of Pullman porter or mail carrier. Resentment about this underemployment or stress from being one of few blacks in a newly opened-up occupation may have led to familial tension. Black fathers' concerns about underemployment may also have influenced the socialization of their sons by conveying their feelings of inadequacy in the role of provider.

Another possibility is that this result reflects intergenerational mobility issues which may take on special significance in a postindustrial society. As high-paying, low-skill jobs in large manufacturing industries decline, so does the monetary value of a high school diploma. Marital stability may be a consequence of black husbands having less education than their fathers, as well as having the same, especially when that education is just a high school diploma. Both suggest an insecurity among black husbands about their ability to find and keep jobs that provide a liveable income for their families.

We have suggested both socialization and intergenerational mobility explanations in these relationships. When we entered a general mobility variable (husband's education minus father's education) into our analysis, we observed the same effect for husband's father's education. In addition, the mobility measure evidenced the predicted relationship with marital stability. So it appears that both socialization and intergenerational mobility may be involved in black marital instability.[8]

First-year factors. Consistent with these findings, black male provider role issues emerged clearly in the analysis of factors in the social context of the first year of marriage. The most dramatic result is that a black husband's perception of the adequacy of the couple's finances is a distinctive predictor of black marital instability. It was not a predictor for white couples. Nor is it the wife's concerns about finances that are prognostic. It should be noted that income is a significant predictor of stability for black couples as well, as indicated earlier in Table 7.3. Although this negative effect of income on marital stability was not significantly distinct from that found for white couples, the interaction of income and parental status was significant. This effect is discussed later in the presentation of results from the hierarchical analysis. It appears that it is not income level per se but the *anxiety that black husbands have about their income* that is related

---

[8] Half of the black husbands in this study grew up without a father in the home. We, therefore, did these analyses separately for couples where the husband grew up in an intact family and those where the husband's father was absent. The results were the same as those found for husband's father's education in the total black sample.

to marital commitment. This important finding underscores Wilson's (1987) speculations concerning the economic position of black men as key to understanding the structure and functioning of black families and the maintenance of underclass status among many African Americans. Black husbands may have very low expectations about their continued capacity to provide for a family. Leaving a marriage may be viewed as one way to maintain some sense of personal control. Black men's perceptions of their ability to assume the mainstream normative role of provider have been suggested for some time as an underlying dynamic in black husbands' and fathers' estrangement from their families [e.g., "street corner men" in Liebow's *Tally's Corner* (1967)].

Processes of marital interaction. Also of note are the findings on processes of marital interaction related to instability. Among blacks only, couples in which wives perceive role *inflexibility* in the assignment of household tasks and in which husbands report more equality in decision making (power balance) are more likely to be *unstable*. The fact that black marriages may depend particularly on role flexibility makes some sense with regard to the greater economic role that black wives have historically played. But the fact that having an equal say in decision making leads to marital instability in black couples makes sense if you consider historical limitations on black male power within families and in the society at large. There is some evidence that black males hold more traditional conceptions of gender roles than do white males (Ransford and Miller, 1983).

Marital well-being. For black couples, the husband's satisfaction with marriage is a significant predictor of marital stability. This is not so for the white couples. This suggests that the affective attachment that black husbands have for their wives may translate directly into marital commitment for them. Among white husbands there appears to be a greater separation of marital commitment from attachment. Whites seem more apt to maintain the institution of marriage even when marital satisfaction is lacking. It is also possible that the structural context of imbalanced sex ratio may provide a greater pool of alternatives for black men, thereby lessening commitment (as hypothesized by Guttentag and Secord, 1983). Factors which influence black husbands' marital satisfaction, then, may moderate the effect of the black sex ratio imbalance on marital instability.

Life events/marital role interferences. Finally, interference from in-laws, as reported by black wives, is clearly related to marital instability. It is much less the case for the white couples. A wife's family may be so dominant a family anchor among black couples that intrusions by the husband's family may be particularly disruptive of a couple's bonding. In fact, black wives' reports of *noninterference* by their own families seems distinctively problematic. Black women in our study were more likely to have children than their white counterparts and, consequently, may have lived as single parents on their own or with their parents. Therefore, before marriage, they were likely to have maintained a family life with their children that was closely linked with their kin network. Another surprising finding regarding social networks is that a black husband's disapproval of some of his wife's friends is predictive of stability rather than instability. This is contrary to a finding by Hatchett, Veroff, and Beyers (1988) that disapproval of some of one's spouse's friends leads to lower marital happiness. It is possible that maintaining a distinctive friend network apart from her husband's allows a wife to continue in a marriage regardless of her level of marital happiness.

We have not presented all of the findings distinctive to black marital instability as displayed in Table 7.4. However, those discussed depict the particular problems faced by black couples in negotiating the first years of marriage—problems having to do with the position of black men and women in the socioeconomic structure, and problems having to do with the way that black families have adapted their marriages to maintain family life.

Hierarchical Analysis

Next we performed a series of hierarchical regression analyses to determine which predictors remained significant in a general model of marital instability in the early years of marriage, and to assess the relative predictive power of the different sets of factors. In these analyses, we regressed each set of significant predictors (based on the earlier regressions summarized in Table 7.3) on marital instability in phases. Six sets of factors were entered in the following order: first, premarital factors of the social context of marriage; second, factors derived from the social context of the first year of married life; third, processes of marital interaction; fourth, specific marital feelings; fifth, overall marital well-being; and sixth, life events and perceived interferences in marital-role functioning from family, in-laws, friends, and work. The relative contribution of each set of factors to the explained variance of the marital instability model is shown in Table 7.5. The results of the fifth and the final phases of the regressions for blacks and whites are presented in Tables 7.6 through 7.9.

Overall, the factors included in these analyses were very predictive of marital instability. The proportions of variance explained in the final models were 62 percent for blacks and 58 percent for whites. For blacks, premarital factors appear to be the most predictive of marital instability (although this is in part a function of order of entry). Factors of processes of marital interaction and of life events and marital role interference follow, contributing an additional 7 percent and 8 percent in explained variance, respectively. Overall marital well-being contributed the least to the model. Marital processes and life events and role interferences appeared to be the most predictive sets of factors for marital

TABLE 7.5

Summary of Results from Hierarchical Regressions for Blacks and Whites

Phase	Variables Gaining Significance	Variables Losing Significance	Variance Explained[a]	Change in Variance (Previous − Current)[a]
Blacks				
Social context: premarital	—	—	28%	—
Social context: current life	—	Wife employed Wife's problematic drinking (husband) Wife's church attendance	41%	13%
Marital processes	—	Premarital children Husband's age Woman's job hurts family Power balance (husband)	48%	7%
Marital feelings/emotions	Premarital children	Wife's marital satisfaction	52%	4%
Overall marital well-being	—	Premarital children	54%	2%
Life events and role interference	Power balance (husband)	Combined income Husband worries about money Wife's destructive conflict Wife's tension Husband's work interference Wife's family interference (Husband) Death of someone close Serious illness	62%	8%
Whites				
Social context: premarital	—	Husband knew in-laws	10%	—
Social context: current	—	—	15%	5%
Marital processes	—	Egalitarian behavior Wife's father's education Wife's tension	32%	17%
Marital feelings/emotions	—	Husband's tension	33%	1%
Overall marital well-being	Wife's father's education	Husband employed Wife grew up with both parents	40%	7%
Life events and role interference	Husband employed	Wife's destructive conflict	58%	18%

[a] R^2 adjusted for number of predictors.

TABLE 7.6

Phase V Regression Results for Blacks: All Factors Except Life Events and Marital Role Interference

Factor	Wives β[a]	Wives B[b]	Husbands β	Husbands B	Couples β	Couples B
Social context						
Premarital children					-1.08	-.34*
Combined income					-.13	-.47**
Premarital						
Premarital children × income					.08	.50*
Age	-.09	-.22**	.04	.11		
Father's education	-.13	-.24***	.23	.37***		
Mother's education			-.20	-.27***		
First year						
Husband worries about money	.02	.01	.17*	.12*		
Wife employed	-.02	-.00				
Spouse's problematic drinking/drug use	.23	.11*	.06	.02		
Husband disapproves of wife's friends	-.17	-.21***				
Church attendance	-.03	-.03				
Marital processes						
Believes woman's job hurts family			.12	.08		
Destructive conflict	.38	.14*	.39	.15*		
Role flexibility	-.26	-.13*				
Power balance			.45	.12*		
Marital feelings						
Positive relations	.28	.13*				
Marital tension			-.51	-.13*		
Overall marital well-being						
Marital satisfaction	-.13	-.04	-.52	-.18*		
	Adj. R^2 = .54					

[a] β = the unstandardized regression coefficient.
[b] B = the standardized regression coefficient.

*$p < .05$. **$p < .01$. ***$p < .001$.

instability among whites. Among blacks, situational factors, reflective of their sociostructural position and the related adaptations of family life, overshadow the relational factors. Among whites, these factors appear to be more balanced in their impact on marital stability.

As shown in Table 7.7, premarital factors predictive of black marital instability are wife's age, the educational level of the fathers of both husbands and wives, and husband's mother's education. Marriages at risk are those where the wives are relatively young, where the educational level of wives' fathers is low, the educational level of husbands' fathers is high, and husbands' mothers' education is low. Factors pertaining to level of income, income in interaction with being a parent, and husband's perception of his ability to provide for his family remained significant until the last phase of analysis when life events and role interference factors were added. Low economic well-being and husband's concern over his role as provider were positively related to marital instability. In addition to the separate effect of income, there was a joint effect of income and parental status.

Figure 7.2 illustrates this interaction. Among low-income blacks, children have a stabilizing effect; the opposite is true for those with high income. Since these children were conceived premaritally, they may be part of the motivational factor for marriage among low-income blacks. When children are absent, there is less incentive for trying to make a marriage work. Among the more economically well-off, the presence of children, which often strains the relational aspect of marriage, may induce a couple to consider separating given that they have the resources to make this alternative viable. In all, it appears that the effects of these economic factors on marital stability may be mediated through events and outside pressures in the second and third years of marriage which evolve from earlier economic circumstances.

There were other contextual factors that continued to influence stability in the final model. These were a wife's report of her husband's disapproval of her friends and of her husband's drinking or drug use problem. These represent very different problems with regard to stabilizing marriages among black couples. The first is an issue of a balance between separation from and the amalgamation of networks; the second is the problem of potentially disruptive family experiences resulting from situational factors, both premarital and from the first year of marriage.

Three factors of marital processes and one of overall marital well-being remained significant in the total model. Husband's report of a destructive conflict style for the couple, husband's report of equal sharing of power, and wife's report of the lack of flexibility in gender-associated tasks increase marital instability. The first result for marital processes is one found for all marriages; the rest are peculiar to blacks for reasons discussed earlier. The affective attachment of black men to their marriages continued to influence stability, net of the effects of other factors.

TABLE 7.7

Final Regression Model: Factors Influencing Marital Instability Among Blacks

Factor	Wives β[a]	Wives B[b]	Husbands β	Husbands B	Couples β	Couples B
Social context						
Premarital						
Premarital children	-.07	-.17**	.04	.10	-.41	-.13
Combined income	-.13	-.24****	.22	.35****	-.06	-.21
Children × income			-.18	-.25****	.03	.18
First year						
Age			.11	.08		
Father's education	-.14	-.04				
Mother's education	.23	.11**	.11	.04		
Husband worries about money	-.19	-.24****				
Wife employed	-.06	-.05				
Spouse's problematic drinking/drug use						
Husband's disapproval of wife's friends						
Church attendance						
Marital process						
Believes woman's job hurts family	.15	.06	.02	.01		
Destructive conflict	-.23	-.11**	.41	.16***		
Role flexibility						
Power balance			.42	.12**		
Marital feelings						
Positive feelings	.15	.07	-.38	-.10*		
Marital tension						
Overall marital well-being						
Marital satisfaction	-.09	-.03	-.44	-.14**		
Life events and role interference						
Spouse's family interference	.39	.16***	.02	.01		
Spouse's friends' interference	.26	.12**	.35	.14**		
Own work interference			-.20	-.10*		
Death of someone close	-.06	-.07				
Had serious illness	.08	.08				
Changed residences						
Birth of child (year 2 or 3)	.10	.12**	.12	.14***		
		Adj. R^2 = .62				

[a] β = the unstandardized regression coefficient.
[b] B = the standardized regression coefficient.

*p < .10. **p < .05. ***p < .01. ****p < .001.

200

FIGURE 7.2

The interaction of parental status, income, and marital instability among blacks.

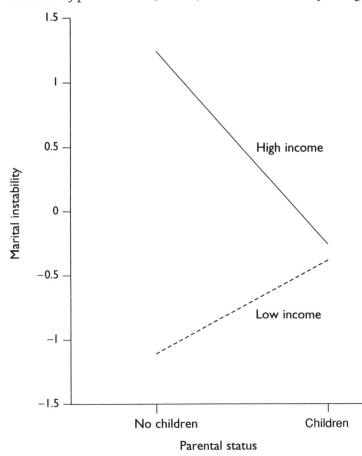

Five life-event and marital-role interference factors remained as significant predictors of instability and may have mediated the effect of economic worries noted above and of wife's perception of gender role flexibility, a husband's negative feelings about the relationship, a wife's report of the couple's destructive conflict, and wife's marital tension. These second- and third-year experiences are: wife's report of pressures from her husband's family and friends, a husband's report of interference from wife's friends, a husband's report of changing residences, and a wife's report of having a first child or an additional child. As discussed earlier, the wife's greater embeddedness in her family network may make relations with in-laws problematic, thus impairing the establishment of a stable marital bond. Similarly, a husband's perception of interference from his wife's friends may derive from both spouses' greater embeddedness in their own networks of friends. In other analyses of these data, we found that black couples had less integrated friend networks than white couples (Hatchett, Veroff, and Beyers, 1988).

While life events such as those examined in these analyses are often viewed as stressors on the individual level, they may have positive as well as negative effects on relationships. Although some events place marriages at risk, others may help solidify the relationship by requiring greater interdependence between partners. Those events that remained significant in this part of the analyses are of the former variety. We found that a wife's report of serious illness and birth of a child were negatively related to marital stability. The effect of having a child was also found for whites. Changing residences also appears to have a negative effect on marriage. Among black men, moving increased marital instability.[9]

Overall, these findings support those discussed earlier—the salience for marital stability of social networks and situational factors, especially economic, before marriage and during the early years of marriage.

Comparison of Models of Marital Instability Among Blacks and Whites

We have noted that our findings on factors influencing marital instability have been both convergent and divergent for blacks and whites as well as for wives and husbands. Here, we discuss several notable similarities and differences between races and genders that emerge in the final models of marital instability.

The role of social networks in the successful adaptation to marriage is different in character for wives and husbands and among blacks and whites. Overall, we have found that the potential supportive functions of social networks may be overshadowed by their potential to interfere in couple bonding in these early years. As indicated in our general framework for studying marital instability (Figure 7.1), we realize that marital-role interferences in the second and third years of marriage may be influenced by factors in the first year. How these social networks respond to or are marshaled in marital relationships gives us insight into their general characteristics. The same is true for the degree to which social network involvement is perceived as interference by one or both spouses. Earlier, we speculated that black wives' reports of noninterference from their family and interference by their in-laws, both positively related to marital

---

[9] It is possible that this result is partly artifactual, due to the inclusion of separated and divorced couples in the analyses.

instability, may derive from black wives' greater embeddedness in their own kin networks. In the final model for whites, shown in Table 7.9, we found that white wives' reports of interference from their families was positively related to marital instability. It seems that close kin involvement in married life may be less normative for whites than for blacks. Also, in their roles as kin keepers, both black and white wives may be more sensitive to how this involvement is negotiated than their husbands. All in all, it seems that, for different reasons, particularly close kin networks may be problematic for the marriages of *both* blacks and whites. Negotiation of the couple's relationship to each spouse's individual networks is an important task in these early years. Extremely close ties and obligations to one's own network may hinder network integration as well as interfere with the couple bond itself.

Among black and white wives, both family and friend network issues appear to be involved in marital instability. For black and white husbands, only friend network issues emerge as being particularly predictive. These gender differences may reflect women's greater sensitivity to family issues noted above. Reports of interference from spouse's friends from both wives and husbands, blacks and whites, were positively related to marital instability. Perceived interference from each other's friends may indicate a lack of integration of friend networks. These findings further underscore the importance of coming to a workable integration of social networks in the early years of marriage. The fact that black couples are less likely to share friends puts these marriages at greater risk.

We had expected that two factors in the first year of marriage which tapped marital resources and styles of coping—family networks and religiosity as measured by church attendance—would mediate problematic experiences resulting from situational factors. These factors have been seen as strengths in African American family life (Hill, 1972). Black families are more likely than white families to be extended at the household level (Farley and Allen, 1987), and they evidence greater across-household interaction with kin (Martineau, 1977; Hays and Mindel, 1973; Aschenbrenner, 1978). This extended kin behavior is thought to moderate the negative effects of female headship and economic adversity (Stack, 1974). However, more systematic research has found that in spite of strong affective and structural ties to kin networks, blacks are less likely to report receiving instrumental aid, especially those with low incomes (Hatchett and Jackson, 1993; Ball et al., 1980, 1979; Heiss, 1975). Religiosity is seen as performing the same function for blacks who report higher church attendance than whites.

Our analyses here reveal that strong ties to kin may work against marital stability and that religiosity is not sufficient to weather the problematic situations faced by black couples. We have noted above how the lack of social network amalgamation puts black marriages at risk. Also, the earlier cited relationship between a wife's church attendance and increased marital stability dis-

TABLE 7.8

Phase V Regression Results for Whites: All Factors Except Life Events and Marital Role Interference

Factor	Wives β^a	Wives B^b	Husbands β	Husbands B	Couples β	Couples B
Social context						
Premarital						
Grew up with both parents	.10	.16***				
Father's education	.06	.16**				
Mother's education	-.12	-.25****				
First year						
Knew in-laws before marriage			-.00	-.00		
Husband employed			-.46	-.10		
Church attendance	-.19	-.22**	.18	.19**		
Marital process						
Destructive conflict	.26	.13*	.62	.26****		
Egalitarian behaviors			-.03	-.04		
Marital feelings						
Marital tension	.08	.05	.17	.11*		
Marital well-being						
Marital competence	-.52	-.28****				
	Adj. R^2 = .40					

[a] β = the unstandardized regression coefficient.
[b] B = the standardized regression coefficient.

$*p < .10.$ $**p < .05.$ $***p < .01.$ $****p < .001.$

TABLE 7.9

Final Regression Model: Factors Influencing Marital Instability Among Whites

Factor	Wives		Husbands		Couples	
	β[a]	B[b]	β	B	β	B
Social context						
Premarital						
Grew up with both parents	.05	.08				
Father's education	.07	.17***				
Mother's education	-.12	-.24****				
First year						
Knew in-laws before marriage			-.03	-.02		
Husband employed			-.74	-.16***		
Church attendance	-.13	-.15**	.22	.23***		
Marital processes						
Destructive conflict	.32	.15***	.52	.22****		
Egalitarian behavior			-.01	-.01		
Marital feelings						
Marital tension	.03	.02	.02	.01		
Overall marital well-being	-.30	-.16***				
Life events and role interference						
Own family interferes	.26	.15***				
Spouse's friends interfere	.32	.17***	.76	.34****		
Birth of child (year 2 or 3)	.12	.20**				
	Adj. R^2 = .58					

[a] β = the unstandardized regression coefficient.
[b] B = the standardized regression coefficient.

*p < .10. **p < .05. ***p < .01. ****p < .001.

appears when premarital factors, particularly economic ones, are introduced. A coping strategy that does appear to play a role in black marital instability is a husband's drinking or drug use. Among whites, church attendance has both negative and positive effects on marital stability. The frequency of a wife's church attendance increases marital stability while that of a husband's has the opposite effect. We speculate that "praying together" does not increase the possibility of staying together if the husband feels pressured into this behavior. Alternatively, such behavior among men may signify a behavioral or expectational set that may conflict with the orientation of other family members.

The role of relational factors also differed by race in the final models, with such factors being less predictive for blacks than for whites. One marital process factor and one overall well-being factor remained significant in the final models for both. Destructive conflict was damaging for both black and white marriages. Although the significant well-being factors were different in the two groups, the underlying similarity seems to be orientation toward marriage in general. Marital instability is associated with perceived lack of marital role competence among white women and lack of satisfaction in the marriage among black men. White women's assessments of their competence as wives appears to be an important component of white marital success, while for black men, their affective attachment to marriage keeps them committed to their relationships. These factors appear not to be *as* relevant to marital stability for white men and black women.

For the most part, contextual factors, premarital or those in the first year of marriage, were not only less predictive of marital instability for whites than for blacks but were different in nature. However, the effects of parental education were the same for black men and white women. Both findings were counterintuitive with education in fathers having a destabilizing effect while education in mothers tended to stabilize marriages. Further analysis and further study may be necessary to understand these results. Although blacks were more likely to come from single-parent homes, growing up in a nonintact family was an important predictor of marital instability only for white women. Since nonintact families are comparatively less common among whites, this kind of experience may have a greater impact on white wives' assumptions about the permanence of marriage. Such assumptions may facilitate leaving the relationship if things are not going well. The lack of a similar finding among blacks is notable, given speculations that the lack of positive role models reinforces underclass behavior (Wilson, 1987).[10] As noted in recent research and in these analyses, broader social structural factors have far greater impact on black family life than does family structure per se (Wilson, 1987; Farley and Allen, 1987).

As a predictor of marital instability, the most important of these social

---

[10] It is possible, however, that growing up in an intact family interacts with other variables in its impact on black marital instability. We are exploring this mediating role in other analyses.

structural factors was economic well-being. Although this is related to employment status of family members, employment per se was significant only for whites and only for husbands' employment. It is possible that this negative effect of white husbands' employment on instability is really a proxy for gender issues among whites, a concern about *who* is the provider. As noted earlier, gender role and power issues had explicit direct effects upon marital instability among blacks. An early negative relationship between black wives' employment and instability dropped out after income was controlled. Apparently for blacks, level of occupation and pay and their impact on anxiety about economic well-being were more salient for marital success than employment.

Summary and Discussion

What accounts for marital instability in black couples? These analyses have shed considerable light on this question. In this summary, we will concentrate on the major themes that have emerged from our results.

First, it is clear to us that a major factor in marital risk among African Americans is the anxiety felt by many black husbands about being able to provide adequately for their families. When a black husband has intense concerns about his role as provider, it is a good prognosticator of marital difficulties. We did not find this to be the case for white husbands. The long-term economic disadvantage that black men have experienced has generated legitimate and realistic worries about their earning capacity at dignified work. Such worries discourage entering marriage and, once married, cloud continued commitment. Indeed, Chadiha's (1989) analysis of the couple narratives from this study demonstrated that concerns about employment and being able to provide for a family are prominent themes in black men's courtship stories. Also, Bowman (1985) has shown how these issues produce role strain and affect the mental well-being of black fathers. Moving out of marriages where they feel inadequate may be a way of escaping a feeling of failure or reestablishing a sense of competence.

The fact that black couples are less stable when husbands are reported to have problems with drinking or substance use is further evidence of this pattern if we assume, as others have (e.g., McClelland et al., 1972), that in this society alcoholism is a means of coping with powerlessness. Our unexpected finding that marital instability was related to higher paternal education among black men can be interpreted within this same pattern. That is, if we assume that many of these better-educated fathers were either underemployed or highly scrutinized in upper-level jobs, then, as models for the young husbands in our study, they may have conveyed a fear of provider inadequacy. Also, if our young husbands have less or the same amount of education as their fathers, especially when that level is a high school diploma, the prospects for blacks in the current economic climate must amplify worries about fulfilling the provider role in their own families. At any rate, we are compelled to conclude, in accordance with Wilson (1987), that the position of black males in the economic opportunity structure of the United States makes them quite vulnerable to developing weak commitments to the institution of marriage.

A second related conclusion has to do with the forces that may strengthen these ties. It is clear from these data that, among blacks, male satisfaction with the marriage is especially critical for marital stability. One factor underlying that satisfaction may be a wife who is sensitive to the special character of gender issues among blacks. Black men and women have long experienced dissonance surrounding mainstream gender roles. They have lived in a society where men were supposed to have more power in both private and public spheres, and where women were to be provided for and protected. But this has not been their reality. For a long time, black men were symbolically, and at times literally, castrated by racial oppression. Power in the home, thus, became particularly important for black men. However, black women could often find work (although typically menial) when black men could not. As a consequence, black women have historically had a more significant economic role in families than their white counterparts. The fact that these more egalitarian patterns are now becoming acceptable has not lessened the significance of this gender issue among blacks. Perhaps the reason for this is that black familial arrangements emerged as a consequence of a wide-scale denial of basic rights and citizenship. For some blacks, it is possible that being able to assume "traditionally" pre-scribed family roles is part of the larger quest for equal opportunity.

Our analyses suggest that this issue is so central that it places black marriages at risk. Flexibility in familial task assignments seems to be a prerequisite for an adaptive dual-earner family. However, a wife's demands for this kind of flexibility could unwittingly compromise a husband's feelings of masculinity if he did not obtain some sense of greater power in other domains. How black couples address these issues in this period of changing norms will be a factor in marital success.

Another challenge for black marriages is the blending of premarital social networks. Black wives who reported that their families did *not* interfere in their marriage, and who reported interference from in-laws, were more likely to be in unstable marriages. As noted earlier, this may reflect greater embeddedness of wives in their own kin network. Also, as others have suggested, close kin involvement may be more normative for *both* black men and women. This kind of involvement is problematic for marriages when it hampers the development of a workable integration of the spouses' individual networks. These findings regarding the role of the social networks of blacks in marital stability are contrary to popular conceptions about the supportive role of black extended kin behavior. Instead of moderating the effects of the stresses and strains of being black on marital stability, the strong structural and affective ties of black kin networks, important for general survival, may work against this stability. Stack's work (1974) suggested a similar constraining effect on black courtships evolving into marriage. In our study, religion also did not moderate the impact of economic well-being and related concerns on marital stability.

We must interpret these data with several cautions in mind. First, we are analyzing instability in the earliest years of marriage. Other factors may emerge at later stages to disrupt black marriages. We have noted, for example, that while premarital children appear to stabilize marriage, the appearance of children in the first few years after marriage has a negative effect on marital stability. Premarital children may not continue to contribute to marital stabilization, particularly as they approach adolescence. Second, these analyses are somewhat general. For example, while we have conducted our analyses at the couple level and entered each spouse's responses separately, we have not explored how discrepancies between these responses influence marital instability. Also, we have not included all possible interactions between variables in these analyses. In our ongoing study of marital well-being and marital instability, various members of our research team are addressing these and other issues in greater depth. We feel, nevertheless, that these analyses have uncovered major issues in black marital instability.

Last, there are some critical features of marital relations that are important in the preservation of any marriage, regardless of race or ethnicity. The use of destructive conflict styles for resolving husband-wife disagreements can cause disaffection and alienation within any couple. There are other findings that are common for all couples. Feeling tension about how one is getting along as a couple is highly predictive of marital instability. So, while we are emphasizing the social structural features of African American life that may influence instability in young couples, we do not wish to underestimate the importance of more universal themes in couple relationships that contribute to marital success. We must conclude from this study, however, that key features of the social structure have such significant impact that they can overpower the relational resolve of many black couples, thereby placing their marriages at risk.

AUTHOR NOTES

The preparation of this chapter and the collection of data were supported by a grant from the National Institute of Mental Health. We want to thank Janet Malley and Doug Leber, as well as the rest of the research staff, for their valuable advice and comments. We appreciate the assistance of Halimah Hassan and Ann Ruvolo in the analysis of the data and the assistance of Darleen Maiden and Marina Barnett in the preparation of this chapter.

REFERENCES

ASCHENBRENNER, J. 1978. Extended families among black Americans. *Journal of Comparative Family Studies,* 47:319–334.

BALL, R.E., WARHEIT, G.J., VANDIVER, J.S., AND HOLGER, C.E., III. 1979. Kin ties of low income blacks and whites. *Ethnicity,* 6:184–196.

BALL, R.E., WARHEIT, G.J., VANDIVER, J.S., AND HOLGER, C.E., III. 1980. Friendship networks: More supportive of low income women. *Ethnicity,* 7:70–77.

BOOTH, H., JOHNSON, D., AND EDWARDS, J.N. 1982. Measuring marital instability. *Journal of Marriage and the Family,* 45:387–394.

BOWMAN, P.J. 1985. Black fathers and the provider role: Role strain, informal coping resources and life happiness. In A.W. Boykins, ed., *Empirical research in black psychology.* Rockville, MD.: Institute of Mental Health.

BRADBURN, N. 1969. *The structure of psychological well-being.* Chicago: Aldine.

CHADIHA, L.A. 1989. Narrating black newlywed courtships: A structural-functional and interactive-situational approach. Unpublished doctoral dissertation, University of Michigan. Ann Arbor, MI: University Microfilms.

CHADIHA, L.A., AND ORTEGA, R. November 1988. A narrative approach to the study of courtship and marriage. Paper presented at the 50th Annual Meeting of the National Council on Family Relations, Philadelphia, PA.

CHERLIN, A.J. 1979. Work life and marital dissolution. In G. Levinger and O. Moles, eds., *Divorce and separation: Contexts, causes and consequences.* New York: Basic Books.

CROHAN, S. 1988. The relationship between conflict behavior and marital happiness: Conflict beliefs as moderators. Unpublished doctoral dissertation, University of Michigan. Ann Arbor, MI: University Microfilms.

CROHAN, S., AND VEROFF, J. 1989. Marital well-being among white and black newlyweds. *Journal of Marriage and the Family,* 51:373–384.

DUNCAN, B., AND DUNCAN, O.D. 1969. Family stability and occupational success. *Social Problems,* 16:272–306.

ELDER, G.H., AND CASPI, A. 1988. Economic stress in lives: Developmental perspectives. *Journal of Social Issues,* 44:25–45.

FARLEY, R., AND ALLEN, W.R. 1987. *The color line and the quality of life in America.* New York: Russell Sage Foundation.

FRAZIER, E.F. 1962. *Black bourgeoisie.* New York: Free Press.

GLICK, P.C. 1977. Updating the life cycle of the family. *Journal of Marriage and the Family,* 39:5–13.

GREENBLATT, C.S. 1983. The saliency of sexuality in the early years of marriage. *Journal of Marriage and Family,* 45:289–299.

GUTTENTAG, M., AND SECORD, P.F. 1983. *Too many women? The sex role question.* Beverly Hills: Sage Publications.

HATCHETT, S., AND JACKSON, J. 1993. African American extended kin systems: An assessment. In H. MacAdoo, ed., *Family ethnicity: Strength in diversity.* Newbury Park, CA: Sage Publications.

HATCHETT, S., VEROFF, J., AND BEYERS, S. November 1988. The social networks of black and white newlyweds. Paper presented at the 50th Annual Meeting of the National Council on Family Relations, Philadelphia, PA.

HAYS, W., AND MINDEL, C. 1973. Extended kinship relations in black and white families. *Journal of Marriage and the Family*, 35:51–56.

HEISS, J. 1975. *The case of the black family: A sociological inquiry*. New York: Columbia University Press.

HILL, R.B. 1972. *The strengths of black families*. New York: Emerson Hall Publications.

HUSTON, T.L., MCHALE, S.M., AND CROUTER, A.C. 1986. When the honeymoon's over: Changes in the marriage relationship over the first year. In R. Gilmour and S. Duck, eds., *Key issues in personal relationships*. Hillsdale, NJ: Erlbaum.

LANDRY, B. 1987. *The new black middle class*. Berkeley: University of California Press.

LEWIS, R.A., AND SPANIER, G.B. 1979. Theorizing about the quality and stability of marriage. In W.R. Burr, R. Hill, F.I. Nye, and I.C. Reiss, eds., *Contemporary theories about the family*. Vol. 1, *Research based theories*. New York: Free Press.

LIEBOW, E. 1967. *Tally's corner*. Boston, MA: Little, Brown.

MARTINEAU, W. 1977. Informal social ties among urban black Americans. *Journal of Black Studies*, 45:347–358.

MCCLELLAND, D.C., DAVIS, W.N., KALIN, R., AND WANNER, E. 1972. *The drinking man*. New York: Free Press.

NORTON, A.J., AND GLICK, P.C. 1979. Marital instability in America: Past, present and future. In G. Levinger and O. Moles, eds., *Divorce and separation: Contexts, causes and consequences*. New York: Basic Books.

OGGINS, J.B., VEROFF, J., AND LEBER, D. 1993. Perceptions of marital interaction among black and white newlyweds. *Journal of Personality and Social Psychology*, 65: 494–511.

PINDERHUGHES, E.B. 1988. Treatment of black middle-class families: A systemic perspective. In A.R. Coner-Edwards and J. Spurlock, eds., *Black families in crisis: The middle class*. New York: Bruner/Mazel.

RANSFORD, H.E., AND MILLER, J. 1983. Race, sex and feminist outlooks. *American Sociological Review*, 48:46–59.

RAUSH, H., BARRY, W., HERTEL, R., AND SWAIN, A.A. 1974. *Communication, conflict and marriage*. San Francisco: Jossey-Bass.

RUVOLO, A.P. November 1988. Newlyweds' marital well-being of their spouses. Paper presented at the 50th Annual Meeting of the National Council on Family Relations, Philadelphia, PA.

STACK, C. 1974. *All our kin*. New York: Harper.

SURRA, C.A. 1988. The influence of the interactive network on developing relationships. In R.M. Milardo, ed., *Families and social networks*. Beverly Hills: Sage Publications.

SUTHERLAND, L.E. 1989. Sex-role attitudes and behaviors among black and white newlyweds. Unpublished manuscript, University of Michigan.

SWEET, J.A., AND BUMPASS, L.L. 1987. *American families and households*. New York: Russell Sage Foundation.

TUCKER, M.B., AND TAYLOR, R.J. 1989. Demographic correlates of relationship status among black Americans. *Journal of Marriage and the Family*, 51:655–666.

WENT, D., SUTHERLAND, L.E., AND DOUVAN, E. November 1988. Traditionalism and marital well-being among black and white newlyweds. Paper presented at the 50th Annual Meeting of the National Council on Family Relations, Philadelphia, PA.

WILSON, W.J. 1987. *The truly disadvantaged: The inner city, the underclass, and public policy*. Chicago: University of Chicago Press.

WILSON, W.J., AND NECKERMAN, K.M. 1986. Poverty and family structure: The widening gap between evidence and public policy issues. In S. Danziger and D.H. Weinberg, eds., *Fighting poverty: What works and what doesn't*. Cambridge, MA: Harvard University Press.

Appendix: Items Used to Construct Measures of Factors Included as Predictors of Marital Instability

Social Context

Premarital Factors

R's Education	What is the highest grade of school or year of college you have *completed*?
R's Parent's Education	What is the highest grade of school or year of college that your *mother* completed? What is the highest grade of school or year of college that your *father* completed?
Education Difference	R's education − spouse's education
Grew up with Both Parents	Did you always live with *both* of your natural parents up to the time when you were sixteen years old?
Good Marital Role Model	Thinking back to the time when you were growing up, whose marriage—good or bad—do you remember most from that time? Overall, would you say that relationship was *a good one, a fairly good one*, or one that was *not so good*?
Premarital Cohabitation	Some couples live together before they get married; others do not. Did the two of you live together for any length of time before you got married?
Premarital Children	How many children have you (given birth to/fathered)? (DO NOT COUNT STILLBIRTHS)
Combined Income	Please look at this page and tell me the letter of the income group that includes the income of what you think *all members of your family living in this household* will make in 1986 *before taxes*. This figure should include salaries, wages, pensions, dividends, interest, and all other income. (IF UNCERTAIN: What would be your best guess?)
Children × Income	

Appendix (*Continued*)

R's Age	1986 − year of birth
Premarital Acquaintance with Spouse's Family	How well did you know your (wife's/husband's) family before you were married? Would you say you knew them *very well, fairly well, not too well,* or *not well at all?*
Spouse's Premarital Acquaintance with R's Family	How well did your (wife/husband) know your family before you were married? Would you say (she/he) knew them *very well, fairly well, not too well,* or *not well at all?*

Current Married Life

Worry about Having Enough Money	Do you ever worry that your total family income will not be enough to meet your family's expenses and bills? How much do you worry?
Employed	Are you *working now for pay,* or are you *unemployed* (on *maternity leave,* a *homemaker*), a *student, disabled,* or what?
R's Problematic Drinking	How often has your drinking alcohol or getting high caused problems for family or friends?
Spouse's Problematic Drinking	How often has your (wife's/husband's) drinking alcohol or getting high caused problems for family or friends?
R's Closeness to Own Family	How close do *you* feel to *your own* family?
R's Closeness to Spouse's Family	How close do *you* feel to your (*wife's/husband's*) family?
Spouse's Closeness to Own Family	How close would you say your (*wife/husband*) feels to (*her/his*) own family?
Spouse's Closeness to R's Family	How close do you think your (*wife/husband*) feels to *your* family? Would you say (*he/she*) feels *very close, fairly close, not too close, not at all close* to your family?
R's Disapproval of Spouse's Friends	Does your (*wife/husband*) have friends that you would rather (she/he) not spend time with?

Appendix *(Continued)*

Spouse's Disapproval of R's Friends	Do you have friends that your (wife/husband) would rather you not spend time with?
R's Church Attendance	Would you say you attend religious services *every week, almost every week, once or twice a month, a few times a year,* or *never?*

Marital Processes

Behaviors

Communication	During the past month, how often did you: Reveal very intimate things about yourself or your personal feelings—*often, sometimes, rarely,* or *never?* Discuss and try to work out problems between the two of you—*often, sometimes, rarely,* or *never?* Talk about the quality of your relationship; for example, how good it is, how satisfying it is, or how to improve it?
Destructive Conflict	I am now going to read different things that sometimes happen when a couple disagrees. For each please tell me how true the statement is of the disagreement you mentioned: is it *very true, somewhat true, not very true,* or *not at all true* of what happened in your case? I calmly discussed the situation. I yelled or shouted at my (wife/husband). I insulted my (wife/husband) or called (her/him) names. I had to have the last word.
Share Interests	The following are statements married people have made about their lives together. How much does each describe your situation? For each, tell me whether the statement is *very true of your life together, somewhat true,* or *not true at all of your life together.* We share interests and hobbies with each other.
Role Flexibility	We sometimes shift household responsibilities from one of us to the other.
Husband-Wife Power Balance	In general, who has more say in your marriage—your (wife/husband) or you?

Appendix (*Continued*)

Spend Time Together	Now let's talk about the special pleasures and good feelings that come from being married. For each one of the feelings on this list, mark an "X" in the box telling *how often during the past month* or so you have had such feelings—*often, sometimes, rarely,* or *never*. Enjoy relaxed times just being with each other?
Egalitarian and Traditional Behaviors	Now let's talk about how you manage household responsibilities. For each of the following tasks or responsibilities, tell me who does it *most of the time*—is it *you, your (wife/husband), both* of you about equally, *someone else,* or *no one at all?* Prepares meals. Does laundry. Does housecleaning. Writes letters to families.

Attitudes

Should Share Child Care/ Tasks	Both men and women should share equally in child care and housework. Would you say you *strongly agree, somewhat agree, somewhat disagree,* or *strongly disagree?*
Should Share Provider Role	Both men and women should have jobs to support the family.
Woman's Job Hurts the Family	Having a job takes away from a woman's relationship with her husband and children.
Motherhood Fulfilling	The most fulfilling experience a woman can have is becoming a mother and raising a family.
Dissatisfied with Spouse	Summary of discrepancies between ideal and actual spouse traits. Here is a list of words that people use to describe their spouse. Please use them to describe your spouse—*the way he/she really is, not the way you would want him/her to be.* For each word, circle a number on the scale from one to ten which describes how much he/she is like that. *One* means that he/she is *not at all* like that; *10* if he/she is *a lot* like that; or any number in between. (Stubborn, can be trusted, easy-going, bossy, gentle, moody, impatient, likes to argue, considerate, selfish, ambitious, cooperative, independent)

Appendix (*Continued*)

Dissatisfied with Spouse   This time, using the same list, please describe your spouse—as *you would like him/her to be, whether or not he/she is that way now.* If your spouse could be the person you would like him or her to be, how would you rate him/her on these words? For the first word, *stubborn,* circle *1* if your want your spouse to be *not at all* like that; circle *10* if you want him/her to be *a lot* like that; or circle any number in between.
(Stubborn, can be trusted, easy-going, bossy, gentle, moody, impatient, likes to argue, considerate, selfish, ambitious, cooperative, independent)

Marital Feelings/Emotions

(A) Positive

Positive Relations   Now let's talk about the special pleasures and good feelings that come from being married. For each one of the feelings on this list, mark an "X" in the box telling *how often during the past month or so* you have had such feelings—*often, sometimes, rarely, never.*
Feel that your (wife/husband) felt especially caring toward you?
Feel that your (wife/husband) was someone you could count on in times of trouble?
Feel that your (wife/husband) made your life especially interesting and exciting?
Feel that your (wife/husband) made you feel good about having your own ideas and ways of doing things?
Feel pleased that you were thought of as a couple?
Feel your (wife/husband) made you feel good about the kind of person you are?

Positive Sex   Feel that your sexual life together was joyful and exciting?
Feel that your (wife/husband) felt your sexual life together was joyful and exciting?

(B) Negative

Negative Sex   Now please look at the next list which tells about troubles and complaints some married people have.
For each one, mark an "X" indicating how often during the past month you have had this trouble or these complaints—*often, sometimes, rarely,* or *never.*

Appendix (*Continued*)

Negative Sex	Feel upset about how you and your (wife/husband) were getting along in the sexual part of your relationship?
	Feel that your (wife/husband) was upset about how the two of you were getting along in the sexual part of your relationship?
Marital Tension	Feel irritated or resentful about things your (wife/husband) did or didn't do?
	Feel tense from fighting, arguing, or disagreeing with your (wife/husband)?

Overall Marital Well-Being

Marital Satisfaction

Marital Equity	Taking things altogether, how would you describe your marriage? Would you say your marriage is *very happy, a little happier than average, just about average,* or *not too happy*?
	When you think about your marriage—what each of you puts into it, and gets out of it—how *happy* do you feel? Would you say *very happy, fairly happy, not too happy,* or *not at all happy*?
	All in all, how satisfied are you with your marriage? Would you say you are *very satisfied, somewhat satisfied,* or *very dissatisfied*?
	All in all, considering how much each of you puts into your marriage, who would you say gets more out of being married—you, your (wife/husband), or both about equal?
	How do you think your (wife/husband) would answer that? Considering how much each of you puts into your marriage, who would (she/he) say gets more out of being married—you, (her/him), or both of you about equal?
Marital Role Competence	Since you've been married, how often have you felt you were not as good a (wife/husband) as you would like to be—*often, sometimes, rarely,* or *never*?
	When you think about what each of you puts into and gets out of your marriage, how *guilty* do you feel? Would you say *very guilty, fairly guilty, not too guilty,* or *not at all guilty*?

Appendix (*Continued*)

Life Events and Role Interference (YI-Y2 and Y2-Y3)

Marital Role Interference

R's Work Interfered	Here is a list of things that couples say interfere with their married life.
	In the *past year*, how often did the demands of your work interfere with your married life—*often, sometimes,* or *never*?
Spouse's Work Interfered	How often did the demands of your (wife's/husband's) work interfere with your married life?
Spouse's Family Interfered	How often did your (wife's/husband's) family or how either of you felt about them interfere?
R's Family Interfered	How often did your own family or how either of you felt about them interfere?
Spouse's Friends Interfered	How often did things your (wife/husband) did *with* or *for* (her/his) friends interfere?
R's Friends Interfered	How often did things you did *with* or *for* your friends interfere?

COMMENTARY

Hector F. Myers

T HE PROBLEM of marital instability and its impact on the health and
      well-being of African American families is an issue of growing social
      significance. Data from national surveys indicate that the majority of
black children are growing up in single-parent, female-headed households, and
that this family structure is implicated as a major risk factor for a variety of
negative social, economic, and health-related outcomes (Children's Defense
Fund, 1985; Gibbs, 1989). While there is continuing debate about how attenu-
ated family structures might contribute to these pathogenic outcomes, there is
little doubt that sociostructural factors which influence social status and social
mobility of black adults play a significant role in the stability of black families
(Bowser, 1989). The results reported by Hatchett, Veroff, and Douvan provide
additional support for this point. In their study of marital instability among
recently married black and white couples in Michigan, two general themes
emerge for blacks: first, that black marital instability is influenced by macrosocial
stresses which appear to operate cross-generationally to enhance feelings of
economic anxiety and vulnerability in black men, and second, that the impact
of these extrafamilial stresses are exacerbated by more microdynamic stresses
within the marriage, including such factors as conflicts with kin and friend
networks, patterns of dysfunctional spousal communication, tenuous marital
commitments, and the use of ineffective conflict management strategies. Their
results also illustrate important black-white differences in the importance
of these two broad domains of influences, as well as differences in which specific factors within each domain are the most important predictors of marital
instability.

The focus of this commentary is on several of the explanations offered by
Hatchett, Veroff, and Douvan for their results on black couples, and some
additional possible explanations will be suggested. An integrative, transactional
reformulation of their conceptual model of marital instability is also offered.

This model is based on a stress-coping perspective, and suggests several conditional and reciprocal relationships among the hypothesized risk factors for early marital instability in blacks. A comparative model for blacks and whites is not specifically offered but could be readily generated from the available data in this study. We suggest, however, that there is more to be gained at this time by focusing atttention on developing models of black marital instability than in pursuing additional hypotheses about black-white differences.

The Impact of Macrosocial Forces on Black Marital Relationships

Three findings in the study that illustrate the impact of sociostructural forces in undermining the stability of black marriages are particularly noteworthy. All three appear to exert their major effects on black males. These include the destabilizing effect of higher paternal education, higher black male anxiety over the economic well-being of the family, and the apparently more tenuous affective bonding of black men to their marriages. The authors make an eloquent case for cross-generational anxiety and self-doubt among black men about their ability to fulfill the provider role for their families, and suggest that the significant imbalance in the black male-female ratio which creates a "buyer's market" for black men is one factor that might account for their apparently tenuous commitment to marriage.

All of these suggested explanations are reasonable and very probable, but could be elaborated further. For example, the authors imply a cross-generational transmission of economic anxiety when they suggest that higher paternal education but greater underemployment during the period of radical social changes of the late 1950s and 1960s could have led to heightened anxiety in the sons about their ability to provide for their families. Despite their stifled occupational opportunities, these men were often able to support their families with some degree of success. In fact, we would venture a guess that a substantial number of the present generation of black professionals have fathers who fit this description. Therefore, while this argument is quite plausible, we suspect that a number of other equally reasonable explanations could be offered. For example, black men in this study may have reacted to their father's experiences of having to work long, hard hours for comparatively modest returns with anger and a determination not to suffer the same fate. In this case, their economic concerns would reflect conscious strivings for a better standard of living (i.e., high self-esteem and high aspirations) rather than anxiety over their ability as providers (i.e., low self-esteem). Unfortunately for them, the current economic climate demands greater marketable skills, and thus may make the subset of black men with only a high school education even less marketable than their fathers. For this group, any economic anxiety or anger they may experience is realistic.

It should also be noted that economic concerns of couples often get expressed in conflicts over decisional power. The previous generation of black fathers, although underemployed, were more than likely the "primary breadwinners" in their families even if their wives were also employed. The fact that employed black women typically held lower-paying jobs than black men further reinforced this gender status differential in the home. Also, and the myth of the black matriarchy notwithstanding, most students of the black family have argued that black two-parent families were more egalitarian and their gender roles were by necessity more flexible than in white families. However, there is little solid evidence to indicate that the "attitudinal norms" about gender lines of power and authority among black men and women within black families were any more egalitarian and less male-dominant than in white families of comparable socioeconomic status. The greater relative labor force participation of black women may have forced more equality in power decisions and greater flexibility in roles and functions within black families, but these adaptations were counternormative and were a chronic source of stress in black families. This conflict is a prominent theme in the popular literature on the black family. Consequently, we could speculate that the generation of black men in the present study probably grew up with relatively educated but underemployed fathers who were titular if not actual heads of their households.

Contemporary black men, on the other hand, especially those who have obtained a high school education from an inner-city public school, may not only be comparatively less well off than their fathers, but are also more out of step with the economic and social accomplishments of their more educated black contemporaries. Thanks to affirmative-action programs in education and employment, many of the institutional barriers that limited the occupational and social mobility of blacks in the previous generations have been reduced. As a result, educated black men and women today enjoy more options and greater opportunities for social mobility than their parents. At the same time, however, traditional notions of gender roles have been challenged and are being replaced by more egalitarian norms. Also, among the black underclasses where marital instability is the norm rather than the exception, family support programs for poor families (e.g., AFDC) have further eroded the power base of black men in their families by enhancing the economic independence of black women, but doing very little to improve the economic viability of low SES (socioeconomic status) black men (Jaynes and Williams, 1989). Consequently, the young black men in the study who had relatively limited education and marketable skills must cope with their more vulnerable economic status at the same time that they are trying to cope with both the ambiguity and conflicts around gender role relationships, as well as with the unintended consequences of social programs that undermine the viability of their families. Therefore, we could describe this group of black men as suffering from "compounded deprivation of social status and power." Not only do they have less marketable skills, but the rules of the game governing male-female relationships within families are also more ambiguous and conflict-prone.[1]

There are several factors that can be viewed as partially mitigating the crippling effect of this status of compounded deprivation on black men. One such factor is the favorable male-female ratio, which, as the authors noted, probably contributes to lower tolerance for conflicts in their relationships and a reduced commitment to working through the difficulties that emerge in all relationships. In addition, the proliferation of drugs in inner-city communities provides a ready escape from problems, as well as a lucrative economic alternative to regular employment for many young black adults. Thus, black men who face frequent failures in the mainstream labor market can opt out of the work force and seek the greater economic opportunities available in the underground drug economy, or they can seek the psychological escape drug use offers. In addition, those that cannot cope with the stresses of building meaningful relationships can opt out of any relationship and seek another. Unfortunately, however, the confluence of all of these forces results in institutionalizing marginality in large segments of the black male population, as well as creating greater marital instability among blacks today than probably at any other time in our history.

Two questions about this heightened financial anxiety among black husbands that were not addressed by Hatchett, Veroff, and Douvan come to mind. First, do black wives not share these concerns, and if so, why not? And second, how do black wives cope with their husbands' economic anxieties and fears? It is not clear from the data reported whether black wives did not raise similar concerns or whether their economic concerns were simply not as salient predictors of marital instability for them. In other words, black wives may have been no less concerned about economic issues than their husbands, but may have made more interpersonal causal attributions for their marital distress, while black husbands may have made more sociostructural attributions for their marital difficulties. If this is true, then the results may reflect some differences in gender response tendencies rather than true substantive differences in the salience of economic concerns as predictors of marital conflicts in black husbands and wives. The authors are encouraged to consider this possibility as they explore ways to further elucidate these intriguing results. In any event, these findings underscore the importance of cross-generational social status and economic issues in black marital instability, and suggest the need for research on black marriage and the family to take into account cross-generational influences

---

[1]The argument offered is not in support of traditonal male-dominated relationships, but rather underscores the fact that stable social norms about relationships provide stability and reduce ambiguity and anxiety. Recent challenges to traditional gender role norms and attitudes, although healthy and way overdue, have caused confusion and ambiguity for both men and women, and in turn, have increased the risk of relationship conflicts and stresses. This state of affairs can be expected to continue until the new attitudes become stabilized and incorporated as cultural norms.

on current family functioning (see Bowser, 1989, for a more detailed discussion of this issue).

Before we leave this topic, it is worth reiterating the authors' observation that contextual factors were less significant predictors of marital instability for whites than for blacks. This apparent "racial" difference, however, may be explained, at least in part, by SES differences in the samples. While 37 percent of the white couples reported annual incomes below $30,000 and 63 percent reported annual incomes above $30,000, 62 percent of black couples had incomes below $30,000 and only 38 percent had annual incomes above this figure. Thus, the white sample was largely a working-class to middle-class sample, while the black sample was largely a poor to working-class sample. Kessler and Neighbors (1986) argued quite correctly that race and social class should be viewed as operating interactively to affect distress, such that the greatest racial differential in distress should be observed in the lower-income groups. Thus, we should consider that the differences in the relative salience of sociostructural factors are not simply racial, but may reflect a race multiplied by social class effect. This alterative hypothesis would be worth exploring with this study sample.

Microsocial Dynamics
Implicated in Black Marital Instability

The Hatchett, Veroff, and Douvan study indicates that several factors within the spousal relationship and between the spouses and their social networks are important risk factors for marital distress and instability. Many of these factors have been noted for other families (Jacobson, Waldron, and Moore, 1980), and include such factors as spousal substance use, presence of children, ineffective conflict resolution styles, rigidity in spousal roles, and decisional power. With the exception of children, all of the other factors enhanced marital vulnerability regardless of social class.

The Impact of Children on New Marriages

The finding that the presence of children influenced marital stability in black families as a function of a social class was quite intriguing. It suggests, as noted by the authors, that children may be part of the reason for marriage among the lower SES black couples, and may also provide a justification for maintaining the family unit. However, this finding and its interpretation are somewhat counterintuitive given the low marriage rate and high separation/divorce rate among poorer blacks (Jaynes and Williams, 1989). In fact, the previous argument about enhanced economic anxiety and vulnerability among less educated younger black males, and the utility of addictive substances as both tools of escape and as a source of income suggest that the presence of children would pose an even greater economic hardship on less affluent blacks. Consequently, it would be very useful to explore through careful secondary analyses what attributes other than SES characterized those black low SES families for whom children were a stabilizing force.

The finding that children's presence is more destabilizing among more affluent black couples is somewhat more congruent and, as suggested by the authors, may be due to children's interference with spousal bonding. It is also possible that children could be seen as economic burdens that interfere with the achievement of economic and social status goals among more upwardly striving black couples. This perceived burden would be expected to be greater if the children were conceived premaritally. Research indicates that parent-child bonding in reconstituted families is one of the most difficult obstacles the family must overcome, and failure to do so is a major reason such families dissolve (Messinger, 1984). There is no reason to suspect that this task is any less difficult for black couples than for any other group. In fact, the evidence suggesting stronger ties between black wives and their kinship networks would be expected to make the task of effective family reconstitution an especially high-risk proposition for upwardly mobile black couples with children from previous marriages.

The authors are also encouraged to investigate possible differences in effects on marital stability of children living in the new household versus those living with ex-spouses or other relatives. The issues facing reconstituted families with stepchildren living in the home are likely to be different from those when the stepchild(ren) are living with the former spouse and may visit the new family household only periodically.

Kin and Friendship Networks as Risk Factors

The results related to the effects of kin and friendship networks on black marital instability are probably the most intriguing of all of the findings in this study. They indicate that the popular and uncritical view of black extended families as mainly supportive is overly simplistic. These results add to the growing body of evidence that indicates the need to look at black kinship networks more realistically, and to recognize that these kinship networks can serve as *both* sources of social support and sources of intrafamilial conflicts and stress. As noted previously, these kin-related strains may be especially problematic for new marriages that include children from previous relationships. The present results also suggest that the stronger the kinship network ties, the greater the potential access to needed support but the greater the risk of unwanted interference.

Gender Role Power Dynamics

Finally, and as expected, the issues of gender role inflexibility and shared decisional power emerged as important risk factors for marital instability. These issues are salient in the larger societal dialectic, and the ambiguity and confusion that are natural consequences of changes in social attitudes may prove more problematic for new black marriages. This exaggerated effect is expected for all of the reasons suggested by Hatchett and the others and discussed here. Personal power and status have always been tenuously held assets for both black men and women, and the black family has been the primary arena in which these struggles have been fought. Unfortunately, there is little indication from the present findings that these issues are being handled any more effectively by the current generation of young black adults. However, since some of the black couples in the study were not experiencing gender role conflicts, it would be useful to ascertain what is distinctive about them. We might suspect that these are the most educated and professional couples with minimal status differential between the husbands and wives.

An Integrative Model of Black Marital Instability

The findings reported by Hatchett, Veroff, and Douvan make an important contribution to the growing literature on marriage and the family among blacks. Their conceptualization of a five-domain model of influences over time adds conceptual sophistication to this field. However, they stop short of making full use of the conceptual richness available to them in their model. For example, many of the factors listed within their five domains are known to be correlated, and have been shown in other studies with whites to have predisposing, mediating, and reciprocal effects on a range of stress-related outcomes (Cronkite and Moos, 1985; McFarlane et al., 1983). These effects should be evident when the problem of black marital instability is reconceptualized within a stress and coping framework.

Most contemporary models of stress as a contributor to undesirable functional outcomes typically distinguish between two broad sets of factors as predictors. The first is a set of *external and internal precursors or risk factors,* which in this case would be the attributes the couple brings to the relationship (i.e., internal), and the social and economic context in which the relationship is currently evolving (i.e., external). These factors may serve as future assets or as vulnerabilities for the relationship. The second is a set of *internal and external mediators* that moderate or exacerbate the effects of the precursors on the outcome of interest (i.e., marital instability). There is a substantial body of evidence that the precursors or risk factors of undesirable outcomes exert their effects "conditional" on the mediators (e.g., stress enhances risk for psychological distress and dysfunction conditional on the availability of personal resources and social supports) (Frydman, 1981; Shumaker and Brownell, 1984), and that these effects may operate differently for men and women (Ilfeld, 1980), and for blacks and whites (Myers et al., 1986; Dressler, 1985). Other evidence has shown that stress mediators (e.g., personal control) can also influence future exposure to the risk factors (e.g., by reducing the number, severity, diffusion, and impact of life stresses) (Folkman, 1984; Kobasa, Maddi, and Kahn, 1982).

Using these concepts as a foundation, we propose the following as a reconceptualization of the Hatchett, Veroff, and Douvan model of marital instability (see Figure C7.1). First, we identify two sets of *premarital precursors,* those that are considered "socioecologic precursors" (e.g., attributes of families of origin, premarital children, etc.) and those that are "personal precursors" (e.g., prior relationship history, cognitive schemas about marriage and close relationships, psychological strengths and vulnerabilities, coping styles, etc.). Second, these precursors are then viewed as interacting to define a couple's *"degree of compatibility or fit."* This latent construct could be considered as either another precursor or as a mediator. Third, a host of factors could be construed as possible *marital process mediators.* Included would be those that are listed in the Hatchett et al. model as current marital life factors, marital interaction factors, specific feelings about the marriage, overall marital well-being, life change events, and chronic difficulties (e.g., role conflicts). For purposes of conceptual precision, we suggest grouping the marital life factors and interaction patterns into one category which we call *marital relationship factors and processes,* and grouping all of the life stress factors into a second category called *life strains.* Fourth, we then hypothesize that these relationship factors and life strains should interact to create the latent construct *degree of marital satisfaction and commitment.* This intermediate outcome is a by-product of the experiences shared by the couple over time and should not be misconstrued as an attribute of individuals (e.g., black males). Finally, fifth, we hypothesize that ultimately, marital satisfaction and commitment influence *degree of marital stability and instability.* A number of hypothesized reciprocal relationships are depicted in Figure C7.1 by bidirectional and reversed arrows. These arrows indicate feedback effects over time and acknowledge the fact of individual change and mutual adjustments that are part of establishing close relationships (i.e., developing a collective sense of "we-ness").

This more complex model obviously makes several assumptions about how these variables should interrelate, and these will need to be empirically verified. Fortunately, several statistical procedures appropriate to this task are available such as linear structural equation modeling with continuous variables using statistical packages such as the structural equation program, EQS (Bentler, 1985).

In conclusion, the present study makes a significant contribution to our understanding of the similarities and differences in the predictors of marital

FIGURE C7.1

Integrative model of marital instability in blacks.

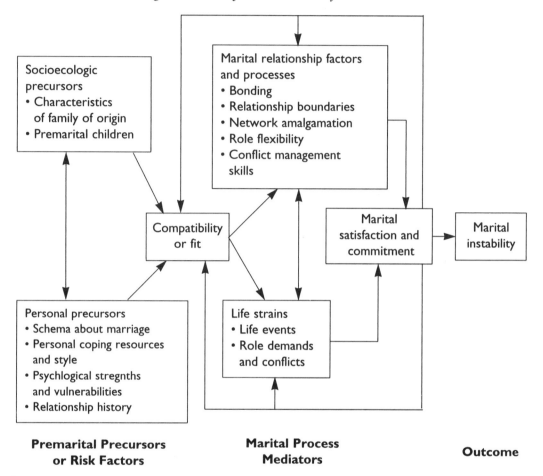

instability between blacks and whites. A more complex transactional model is offered to push us toward the next conceptual step and investigate how these predictors interact to produce the marital outcomes observed. Although the model is described as relevant to blacks, it is formulated in terms general enough to be potentially applicable to whites and to other ethnic groups. The ultimate goal of this integrative model is to differentiate pathways that predict marital stability from those leading to enhanced risk for separation and divorce. Ideally, we would hope that the results from testing such a model will help to inform the development of intervention programs that can reduce the risks of marital instability among young black adults.

REFERENCES

BENTLER, P.M. 1985. *Theory and implementation of EQS, a structural equations program.* Los Angeles: BMDP Statistical Software.

BOWSER, B.P. 1989. Generational effects: The impact of culture, economy and community across the generations. In R.L. Jones, ed., *Black adult development and aging,* pp. 3–30. Berkeley, CA: Cobb & Henry.

CHILDREN'S DEFENSE FUND REPORT. 1985. *Black and white children in America: Key facts.* Washington, DC: Children's Defense Fund.

CRONKITE, R.C., AND MOOS, R.H. 1985. The role of predisposing and moderating factors in the stress-illness relationship. *Journal of Health & Social Behavior,* 25: 372–393.

DRESSLER, W.W. 1985. The social and cultural context of coping: Action, gender and symptoms in a southern black community. *Social Science and Medicine,* 21(5):499–506.

FOLKMAN, S. 1984. Personal control and stress and coping processes: A theoretical analysis. *Journal of Personality and Social Psychology,* 46:839–852.

FRYDMAN, M.I. 1981. Social support, life events and psychiatric symptoms: A study of direct, conditional and interaction effects. *Social Psychiatry,* 16:69–78.

GIBBS, J.T. 1989. Black adolescents and youth: An update on an endangered species. In R. Jones, ed., *Black adolescents,* pp. 3–28. Berkeley, CA: Cobb & Henry.

ILFELD, F.W. 1980. Understanding marital stressors: The importance of coping style. *Journal of Nervous and Mental Diseases,* 168:375–380.

JACOBSON, N.S., WALDRON, H., AND MOORE, D. 1980. Toward a behavioral profile of marital distress. *Journal of Consulting and Clinical Psychology,* 48:696–703.

JAYNES, G.D., AND WILLIAMS, R.M., eds. 1989. Changing family patterns. In Committee on the Status of Black Americans, National Research Council, *A common destiny: Blacks and American society,* pp. 511–556. Washington, DC: National Academy Press.

KESSLER, R.C., AND NEIGHBORS, H.W. 1986. A new perspective on the relationships among race, social class, and psychological distress. *Journal of Health & Social Behavior,* 27:107–115.

KOBASA, S.C., MADDI, S.R., AND KAHN, S. 1982. Hardiness and health: A prospective study. *Journal of Personality and Social Psychology,* 42:168–177.

MCFARLANE, A.H., NORMAN, G.R., STREINER, D.L., AND ROY, R.G. 1983. The process of social stress: Stable, reciprocal, and mediating relationships. *Journal of Health & Social Behavior,* 24:160–173.

MESSINGER, L. 1984. *Remarriage: A family affair.* New York: Pergamon Press.

MYERS, H.F., ADAMS, L.A., MILES, R.E., AND WILLIAMS, J. 1986. Role strains, social support and depression in black women. Paper presented at the American Psychological Association Convention, Los Angeles, August 1986.

SHUMAKER, S.A., AND BROWNELL, A. 1984. Toward a theory of social support: Closing conceptual gaps. *Journal of Social Issues,* 40(4):11–36.

8 UNEMPLOYMENT AND IMBALANCED SEX RATIOS: RACE-SPECIFIC CONSEQUENCES FOR FAMILY STRUCTURE AND CRIME

Robert J. Sampson

CRIMINAL VIOLENCE and its relationship to structural features of the black underclass have been largely neglected in sociological research. As noted elsewhere (Wilson, 1984, 1987; Sampson, 1987), until recently there has been a general reluctance among social scientists to study behavior that could be construed as unflattering or stigmatizing to particular racial minorities. Indeed, the sharp criticisms aimed at scholars such as Rainwater (1966) and Moynihan (1965) in the 1960s led to a concentrated effort by liberal social scientists to insulate their work from the charge of racism or of "blaming the victim," hence limiting racially disaggregated research. Moreover, the research that does exist on black violence has been dominated by a focus on either individual-level factors (e.g., temperament, IQ) or subcultural explanations (for recent reviews, see Wilson and Hernstein, 1985, pp. 466–484; Messner, 1983). In particular, the prevailing viewpoint on black violence is the subculture of violence thesis (Wolfgang and Ferracuti, 1967; Curtis, 1975). Analogous to the culture of poverty thesis, this perspective asserts that high black crime rates reflect a cultural system unique to the black experience that condones and legitimates violence (Curtis, 1975).[1]

The lack of structural viewpoints and systematic empirical analysis of black violence has had serious consequences not only for theoretical development but for social policy and public opinion as well. As Wilson (1984) has noted, because there have been so few cogent explanations of social problems in the

---

[1]For a more complete review of subcultural theories and sociological research on black violence, see Kornhauser (1978), Sampson (1987), and Curtis (1975).

black underclass, racial stereotypes of life and behavior in the urban ghetto have not been sufficiently rebutted. Relatedly, the effort by liberal social scientists to ignore high rates of black crime appears to be self-defeating: conservative crime control policies account for an ever-increasing rate of black incarceration and execution (see Blumstein, 1982; Bureau of Justice Statistics, 1985b,c). In fact, at current incarceration rates a black male born in the United States today is estimated to have a one in five chance in his lifetime of serving a sentence in an adult state prison; further, in the period 1978–82 alone, the percentage of the adult black male population in the United States incarcerated in prison increased twenty-three percent (Bureau of Justice Statistics, 1985c). Perhaps most disturbing, black communities are plagued by persistently high levels of violent victimization—black males face a startling one in twenty-one lifetime chance of being murdered (Bureau of Justice Statistics, 1985a).

Recent Research

In an effort to address the imbalances of past research I recently presented a linkage of Wilson's (1987) theory of the structural determinants of black family organization with a macro-level perspective on communities and crime (see Sampson, 1987). First, Wilson's central thesis is that increases in black families headed by females may be tied to the increasing difficulty of finding a marriage partner with stable employment (Wilson, 1987; Wilson and Neckerman, 1985; see also Ross and Sawhill, 1975; Bishop, 1980). That is, independent of cultural values regarding out-of-wedlock births (e.g., an inherent matriarchal tendency or culture of poverty among blacks) and increases in funds available from welfare (cf. Murray, 1984), Wilson argues that an important structural source of black family disruption is the shortage of employed black males.

Second, I incorporated Wilson's theoretical perspective with a criminological focus on the macrosocial effects of family disruption on rates of crime and delinquency (Sampson, 1986a,b). High levels of family disruption (e.g., divorce rates; female-headed families with children) are posited to facilitate crime by decreasing community networks of informal social control (e.g., local networks of control of teenage peer groups). The resulting integrated hypothesis thus predicted that the effect of black adult male joblessness on black crime is mediated largely through its effects on family disruption.[2]

---

[2]Examples of informal social control include neighbors taking note of or questioning strangers, watching over one another's property, assuming responsibility for supervision of general youth activities, and intervening in local disturbances (see also Greenberg, Rohe, and Williams, 1985; Skogan, 1986). Two-parent families are probably effective not so much because they are able to intervene in actual criminal acts, but because they are better able to control those peer group activities (e.g., "hanging out," vandalism, truancy) that set the context for more serious crime, especially gang delinquency. For a more complete theoretical explication of the link between family structure and crime, see Sampson (1986a,b; 1987) and Sampson and Groves (1989).

My empirical test of this model departed from previous research by (*a*) racially disaggregating rates of robbery and homicide by juveniles and adults in over 150 cities in the United States in 1980; (*b*) explicitly focusing on the exogenous factors of marriageable (employed) black men and economic deprivation; and (*c*) examining the mediating effect of black family disruption on black urban violence. Overall, the results supported the main hypothesis and showed that the scarcity of employed black men relative to black women increased the prevalence of families headed by women in black communities. In turn, black family disruption substantially increased rates of black murder and robbery, especially by juveniles. These effects were independent of income, region, race and age composition, density, city size, and welfare benefits.

The consistent finding that family disruption had stronger effects on juvenile crime than on adult crime, in conjunction with the inconsistent findings of previous research on individual-level delinquency and broken homes (see Wilkinson, 1980; Ross and Sawhill, 1975), tends to support the idea that the effects of family structure are related to macro-level patterns of social control and guardianship, especially regarding youth and their peers (Sampson, 1986b; Felson and Cohen, 1980; Felson, 1986). Indeed, recent research shows that family disruption increases the prevalence of unsupervised teenage peer groups, which in turn increases crime rates (Sampson and Groves, 1989).

Perhaps most interesting, my results also revealed that despite a tremendous difference in mean levels of family disruption between black and white communities, the percentage of *white* families headed by a woman had a large positive effect on white juvenile and white adult robbery offending. In fact, the predictors of white robbery were shown to be in large part identical in sign and magnitude to those for blacks. Therefore, the analysis strongly pointed to the conclusion that the effect of family disruption on black crime is independent of commonly cited alternative explanations (e.g., poverty, region, urbanization, age/race composition), and cannot be attributed to unique cultural factors within the black community. Accordingly, I concluded that there is nothing inherent in black culture that is conducive to crime. Rather, persistently high rates of black crime were argued to stem from the structural linkages among unemployment, economic deprivation, and family disruption in urban black communities.

Although apparently supportive of a structural theory of urban black violence, my research was subject to four key limitations. The purpose of this chapter is to reassess my earlier findings by addressing these limitations.

A Reconsideration

According to Wilson (1987), the increasing rate of joblessness among black men is a major underlying factor in the rise of black single mothers and female-headed households (see also Wilson and Neckerman, 1985). Wilson's thesis is buttressed by a long line of demographic and ethnographic research linking unemployment to marital instability (see, e.g., Bishop, 1980; Liebow, 1967). To test the theory Wilson defined the *male marriage pool index* (MMPI)— employed men per hundred women of the same age and race (Wilson, 1987). Examination of the MMPI reveals long-term declines in the pool of economically stable black men, and levels much lower for blacks than for whites (see Wilson, 1987, pp. 81–90). Using a similar operational definition, I found a large negative effect of the black MMPI on black female-headed households, net of the effects of other important social-demographic factors (Sampson, 1987, p. 363).

Although intriguing, findings regarding the MMPI are ambiguous and confound two separate dimensions of urban structure—a demographic dimension (the sex ratio) and a socioeconomic dimension (the male employment rate). Specifically, the MMPI is mathematically an interaction term, the product of employment rates and sex ratio. This is seen in the following equation:

$$\frac{\text{Employed males}}{\text{Males}} \times \frac{\text{Males}}{\text{Females}} = \frac{\text{Employed males}}{\text{Females}}$$

Hence, a potential limitation of the MMPI is that it precludes identification of the distinctive effects of these two dimensions.

There are substantive reasons for disentangling the effects of sex ratio from employment rates on both family disruption *and* crime rates. First, gender is one of the most important individual-level predictors of violent criminality. For as long as data have been collected, men have exhibited higher rates of violence than women (Hindelang, 1979; Hindelang, Hirschi, and Weis, 1981). The strong relationship between gender and criminal activity at the individual level implies that sex ratios (males per females) may be an important determinant of variations in crime rates. Specifically, populations with relatively large numbers of males should, all else equal, exhibit higher violent crime rates than areas with low sex ratios. A positive relationship between sex ratios and aggregate crime would thus be produced through a "composition" effect. The MMPI fails to allow precise identification of this potentially important relationship.

Second, and perhaps more crucial, there is an important body of research suggesting that the sheer demographic force of imbalanced sex ratios will influence processes of family formation and dissolution (see especially Guttentag and Secord, 1983; South and Trent, 1988). In particular, a shortage of male marriage partners implied by a low sex ratio may decrease the likelihood of marrying while increasing rates of out-of-wedlock births and divorce. Thus, there is evidence to suggest that the sex ratio is inversely related to indicators of family disruption, which in turn positively influences the crime rate. Note the implications of the countervailing direct and indirect effects of sex ratio on crime. If sex ratio has indirect *negative* effects on crime through family disruption, but *positive* direct effects via composition, failure to control for family structure may suppress the positive effects and lead to null correlations between sex ratios and crime.

The third limitation of the MMPI is simply that it does not allow identification of the *socioeconomic* effect of male employment rates on either crime or family structure. If Wilson's arguments regarding the "suitability" of male partners is correct, then employment prospects of men should have effects independent of their sheer numbers. This distinction is similar to Schoen and Kluegel's (1988) separation of the purely compositional effect of numbers of males from "propensities to marriage" among potential partners. By disaggregating the MMPI into constituent parts, we can estimate not only the effect of employment (a dimension of propensity) on family structure independent of sex ratios, but its direct effect on crime as well. As might be expected, there is a long tradition of criminological research which posits a direct effect of employment on crime (see Freeman, 1983; Cantor and Land, 1985; Sampson, 1987).

Finally, Wilson's theory is consistent with the notion of an *interaction* of employment and sex ratios. Indeed, as shown above, the MMPI is in fact an interaction term, and much of Wilson's theory suggests that it is not just the numbers of men nor their employment prospects, but the joint interaction of the two that is central. If so, this should result in an affirmative answer to a simple question—does the MMPI add additional explanatory power to models containing the constituent terms of employment rates and sex ratio?

Other Limitations

My recent analysis of urban black violence (Sampson, 1987) suffered three additional limitations that I address in this chapter. First, my focus was primarily on explaining crime rates, and as a result I did not devote attention to the explanation of family dissolution among *whites*. This is a crucial limitation, since the viability of Wilson's theory hinges in large part on a differential effect of structural factors on black and white families. Quite simply, Wilson argues that the MMPI and, by implication, its component parts are chiefly responsible for high rates of black family disruption but relatively unimportant in explaining white family disruption. As Wilson states:

> Available evidence supports the argument that among blacks, increasing male joblessness is related to the rising proportions of families headed by women. By contrast, for whites, trends in male employment and earnings appear to have little to do with the increase in female-headed families. . . . That the employment status of white males is not a major factor in white single motherhood or female-headed families can perhaps also be seen in the higher remarriage among white women and the significantly earlier age of first marriage. By contrast, the increasing delay of first marriage and the low rate of remarriage among black women seem to be directly tied to the increasing labor-force problems of men. (Wilson, 1987, pp. 83–84)

In what might be termed a threshold effect, Wilson suggests that because unemployment is so low and relatively invariant across time for whites, it does not emerge as a salient force in understanding patterns of white family formation and dissolution. By contrast, levels of black unemployment are high and vary considerably, thus increasing their impact on family structure.

Wilson goes on to note the increasing incarceration rates and mortality among black males compared to white males. When joblessness is combined with their high mortality and incarceration rates, the proportion of black men in stable economic situations is thus exacerbated. Since the MMPI is composed of both demographic and employment factors, the hypothesis emerging from Wilson's theory is clear: the available pool of male marriage partners should have a much larger effect on black family disruption than white family disruption. This race-specific hypothesis derived from Wilson's (1987) theory of the black underclass is directly tested in the present study.

Another limitation of my previous research was the focus on one definition of family disruption—the percentage of female-headed households. As Wilson (1987) and others (see, e.g., Ross and Sawhill, 1975; Ellwood and Bane, 1984; Hogan and Kitagawa, 1985) make clear, the processes of family formation and dissolution cannot be fully understood by reference only to female-headed households. Age at first marriage, early childbearing, rates of divorce/separation, nonmarriage, and married-couple families with children are all dimensions of the general construct of family structure. For example, what is the effect of male employment on female marriage rates? Moreover, in terms of social disorder and crime it would seem that families with children in the delinquency-prone years (e.g., teenagers) would be most relevant—not childless couples. Also, for Wilson the true meaning of the underclass is tied to the concentration of poverty and family disruption (Wilson, 1987). Therefore, in this study I examine not only race-specific measures of family disruption (e.g., female-headed families; female nonmarriage rates; proportion of married-couple families among families with children) but a total measure of the proportion of families in poverty that are headed by females.

Finally, the central focus of my earlier research was the explanation of black violence—robbery and murder. Although important, this focus ignores the relative contribution of underclass family disruption to the overall, or aggregate, violence rate. The clear implication of Wilson's thesis is that the concentration of social dislocations in the underclass, especially family disruption, has been paramount in explaining rising crime rates in urban areas of the United States (Wilson, 1987, pp. 22–26). If true, the concentration of family disruption and poverty should have a salient effect on the overall crime rate, independent of race per se. I test this by examining the total effects of underclass family disruption on the aggregate violence rate.

In short, the goal of this chapter is to present new analyses that replicate and extend earlier research by addressing the four limitations noted above. I accomplish this by disaggregating the MMPI into the components of sex ratio and employment rates. These structural determinants are then assessed for potential race-specific effects on family disruption and violence. In testing the model I also examine the four measures that capture the diversity of family structure in the United States. And as a final test, the model is assessed not only with regard to black and white violence rates, but for overall crime as well.

Data and Method

The units of analysis for the present research are the 171 cities in the United States with a population greater than 100,000 in 1980. The mean black population in these communities is 85,344.[3] Raw data used to construct racially disaggregated measures of city characteristics were drawn from the U.S. Bureau of Census data tapes (Summary Tape File 3) and U.S. Bureau of the Census (1982).

A main theoretical interest is the mediating effect of an area's rate of marital and family disruption on both juvenile and adult crime. As noted earlier, to fully assess this relationship it is necessary to examine different conceptualizations and definitions of family structure. I thus examine three race-specific definitions that pertain to households, families with children, and females. First, I examine the percentage of *total black households* with a female head. The second definition is confined to the universe of families with children—specifically, the percentage of *black families with children aged six to seventeen* that are comprised of *married couples*. Third, I examine a race-age-specific proxy for female nonmarriage/divorce rates (census data do not allow race-age-sex specific measures of divorce and separation). The proxy measure is calculated as the percentage of *black females aged fifteen to fifty-nine* that are the head of a household and without a mate. Each of these three measures was then constructed for white households, white families with children, and white females aged fifteen to fifty-nine, respectively.

My original male marriage pool index (MMPI) was defined as the number of employed black males per hundred black females. The number of women was used as the denominator to reflect differences across cities in the situation of women in the "marriage market." Based on the reconceptualization outlined above, I disaggregate the MMPI measure into two component parts: the sex ratio and the black male employment rate. Again, these measures were also constructed for whites.

[3]A total population minimum of 100,000 was chosen to ensure the reliable estimation of serious offending rates in racially disaggregated analysis. For example, even though the present sample of cities has a mean total population of over 335,000 (mostly whites), the mean number of homicide arrests is only sixty-five. When disaggregated by race and age, offending estimates for serious crimes in smaller communities become unreliable.

The major indicator of variations in economic deprivation is black per capita income. A per capita measure rather than median family income is used to avoid differences across cities and races in family size (see, e.g., Ross and Sawhill, 1975). As noted by Ross and Sawhill (1975), welfare benefits also vary considerably across jurisdiction, a variation that may result in different forms of family structure (see also Honig, 1974). Murray (1984), for example, argues that relaxed restrictions and high welfare payments entice lower-class black women to bear children out of wedlock and encourage the breakup of existing families, since female headship is the major prerequisite for receiving Aid to Families with Dependent Children (AFDC) (for excellent reviews and analyses of this argument, see Ellwood and Bane, 1984; Ross and Sawhill, 1975). Therefore, to account for the possible effects of welfare on family disruption I collected the mean public assistance payment to black and white families receiving assistance for each city and entered it as a control variable (U.S. Bureau of the Census, 1982).[4]

In reviewing the demographic literature Wilson (1984, p. 98) notes the relationship between the age composition of racial groups and differences in fertility, out-of-wedlock births, and economic status (see also Ross and Sawhill, 1975; Hogan and Kitagawa, 1985; Bishop, 1980). Therefore, median ages of the black and white populations are included as control variables. Other measures of age composition (percent black females under eighteen years of age) and a proxy indicator of fertility (number of black children under five years of age per black female under age fifty-five) were highly correlated with median age ($-.78$ and $-.62$, respectively) and thus produced similar results.

The control variables that were not disaggregated were selected on the basis of past theory and research (see reviews in Byrne and Sampson, 1986).[5] First, region is controlled via dummy variables for both western and northern locations. The latter is related to levels of welfare payments and proportion of female-headed families (e.g., Ross and Sawhill, 1975), while the former has been shown to be associated with high crime rates in the 1980s (Sampson, 1986b) and high divorce rates (Ross and Sawhill, 1975, p. 51). Second, the natural log of population size is controlled (see Mayhew and Levinger, 1976). Third, the structural density of housing units is defined as the percentage of

---

[4]The welfare variable pertains to total public assistance payments (e.g., it includes aid to the blind) and not just AFDC payments because the latter measure was unavailable for all cities. AFDC constitutes the vast majority of public assistance, however, and the present data are consistent with previous research using AFDC (see, e.g., Ross and Sawhill, 1975). Also, DeFronzo (1983, p. 124) found that the correlation between AFDC and public assistance payments in SMSAs (Standard Metropolitan Statistical Areas) was .87, and that both measures yielded similar results in multivariate analysis. The evidence is thus strong enough to justify the use of mean public assistance as a proxy for mean AFDC payments across cities.

[5]Because the race-specific models of family disruption and crime rates are by definition racially disaggregated, racial composition (percent black) is not included as a predictor.

housing units located in structures of five or more units. As Wilson (1984) has argued, in densely settled ghetto areas, especially housing projects, residents have difficulty recognizing their neighbors and may be less willing to engage in guardianship behavior. In addition, high structural density offers more places (e.g., stairwells, hallways, underground garages) to carry out criminal acts such as robbery in the absence of capable guardians. To approximate the presence of housing projects and anonymity, the density measure includes *rental* units rather than home-owner units.

Finally, in analyzing *total* crime rates and family disruption I control for aggregate measures of sex ratios, employment rates, and median age. In addition, since the analysis of aggregate violence rates is by definition not race specific, I control for percent black.

Estimation of Offense and Offender Rates

The crime *offense* data consist of reported offense rates for the crimes of robbery and homicide. Although recorded police offense data are known to undercount the actual volume of crime, there is no evidence of systematic variation across cities in the reporting of serious crimes such as robbery and homicide (Gove, Hughes, and Geerken, 1985). Estimates of the causal effect of exogenous variables on the crime rate are unaffected by such absolute differences in the level of the dependent variable. Note also that the vast majority of homicides are reported to the police.

Offender rates were derived from data made available by the FBI in the form of unpublished arrest counts by crime type and demographic subgroup for each police jurisdiction of the 171 cities for the years 1980–82. These data were then merged with census files and used to estimate race-specific rates of criminal offending. Because arrest data have been the subject of numerous criticisms (see, e.g., Gove, Hughes, and Geerken, 1985), this section explains the assumptions and evidence underlying the procedure.

First, Hindelang (1978) has systematically compared national Uniform Crime Report (UCR) index arrest rates with offending rates estimated from National Crime Survey (NCS) victim surveys and found almost exact agreement. For example, Hindelang (1978) found that 62 percent of the robbery offenders reported by victims were black, compared with an identical 62 percent of blacks arrested for robbery in UCR arrest data for the same year. Since racial correlates of arrest rates are the same for offending rates measured from a data source independent of the criminal justice system, we can have increased confidence in the validity of arrest reports.

Second, a large body of research on police-citizen encounters has found that seriousness of the crime is the strongest predictor of arrest (see Gottfredson and Gottfredson, 1980; Gove, Hughes, and Geerken, 1985). Although racial and socioeconomic status (SES) factors appear to influence police contacts for common juvenile delinquency offenses such as vandalism and theft (Sampson, 1986c), there is no evidence of racial bias in police arrest decisions for robbery and homicide.[6] The present research thus limits testing to the most serious and reliably recorded of UCR index crimes—homicide and robbery—thereby reducing the likelihood of bias. One can still argue that official arrest data even for serious crimes may be contaminated with bias when compared *across* jurisdictions. Direct evidence on this issue is found in Messner and South (1986), who analyzed race-specific city-level victimization data from the NCS and FBI arrest data for twenty-six cities from the early 1970s. Although homicide cannot be studied in a survey of victims, and the twenty-six-city victimization data have validity problems of their own (Gove, Hughes, and Geerken, 1985), Messner and South (1986) report a high correlation of .81 between black arrest rates for robbery and black offending rates estimated from reports of robbery victims. Since homicide is a more serious crime and has a higher arrest probability than robbery, we can reasonably assume that homicide arrest rates are even more accurate than robbery arrest rates.

The available evidence clearly suggests, then, that for very serious crimes arrest data reflect the offending process. To account for remaining jurisdictional biases, I explicitly controlled variations across areas in arrest probability in the estimation procedures. Some police departments are simply more effective in making an arrest than are others (Sampson, 1986b). For example, in the present data the mean ratio of reported robbery offenses to robbery arrests is 4.18, ranging from a low of 1.33 to a high of 15.14. Some recent research also suggests that arrest probability may vary with structural characteristics such as inequality and racial composition (Liska, Chamlin, and Reed, 1985).

To account for these potential jurisdictional biases I multiplied each raw arrest rate by the offense/arrest ratio of its jurisdiction to achieve an estimate of *offending*. In other words, each demographic-specific arrest rate is scaled up to (i.e., transformed into) an offending rate by the ratio of crime-specific offenses to arrests. The procedure assumes that offense data are measured on a comparable basis across cities, and that there are no major differences among subgroups in arrest probability. The first assumption is valid because robbery and homicide offense data have been shown to be reliably and validly recorded across jurisdictions (Gove, Hughes, and Geerken, 1985). Furthermore, there are no important differences between black and white robbery victims in crimes reported to police (Flanagan and McLeod, 1983, p. 299). The second assumption is met by the findings noted above. Criticisms of arrest data are thus

---

[6]In probably the most recent effort to obtain direct evidence on arrest risk, Blumstein, Cohen, and Visher (1986) have examined self-reports of both crime and arrests in conjunction with actual arrest records for a sample of serious offenders. They reported that "no substantial differences in arrest risk were found by race, age, or prior arrests" for the crime of robbery.

addressed by use of the information thought to be problematic (i.e., variations in arrest probability) to develop estimates of offending rates.[7]

Using the above procedures in conjunction with population estimates from the 1980 census, I constructed race- and age-specific offending rates for robbery and homicide for each of the 171 largest cities in the United States for each of the years 1980–82. I am limited by FBI reporting rules, which do not permit calculation of age-race-sex rates, and only allow a race breakdown by juvenile (under eighteen years of age) and adult (eighteen and over) arrests.[8] Because of potential year-to-year variations in reporting and recording practices, a three-year average rate was computed to stabilize random fluctuations and reduce missing data, a practice followed in previous research (see, e.g., Sampson, 1986b; 1987).

A handful of communities had too few blacks to construct reliable offending rates and racially disaggregated family and economic characteristics (e.g., Livonia, Michigan, had seventeen black juveniles). Moreover, preliminary analysis identified these cities as disproportionately influencing parameter estimates.[9] Therefore, a selection criterion was imposed in that a city had to have at least a thousand blacks to qualify for analysis. After application of this criterion, the effective sample size for robbery is 156 cities, while for the homicide analysis, missing FBI data further reduced the number of cities to 153.

Finally, throughout the analysis I examined potential biases arising from multicollinearity among independent variables. For example, I examined variance inflation factors (see Fisher and Mason, 1981) that measure the amount that the variances in ordinary least squares (OLS) parameter estimates are inflated in the presence of multicollinearity. Commonly accepted practice regards variance inflation factors (VIF) above four as an indicator of possible inefficiency in estimates (Fisher and Mason, 1981). In the present data multicollin-

[7]The method of adjusting the raw arrest rates was selected because it is theoretically preferable (e.g., the transformation approximates an offending rate), and also because it is consistent with a body of prior research using arrest records to examine criminal-career offending patterns (see Cohen, 1986).

[8]If the proportion of the population known to be at low risk for serious offending (e.g., the elderly and young children) varies with city characteristics (e.g., racial composition), then estimates of the effects of these factors on offending may be biased. Therefore, each adult offending rate was constructed after eliminating those sixty-five and older from the denominator. Similarly, black and white juveniles under age five were removed from the denominator of the race-specific juvenile rates.

[9]All regressions were subjected to a case analysis to detect the possible importance of influential observations in estimating regression parameters. Specifically, Cook's D and Studentized residuals were inspected for each city in each model. A case is defined as influential if its deletion from the model results in a substantial change in the estimate of the parameter vector. After the elimination of cities with fewer than one thousand blacks where rates were unstable, no city exerted a disproportionate influence on the results. Natural logarithms of demographic-specific offending rates were also taken to reduce skewness and induce homogeneity of error variances.

earity does not appear to be a serious problem in the racially disaggregated analysis, as no VIFs were greater than four. In addition, bivariate correlations among exogenous predictors included in the same equations were usually less than .60.

Results

Before turning to the multivariate model, it is useful to note the variation across cities in sex ratios and employment rates. I suspect that one reason sex ratios have been largely ignored in past macro-level research on crime is the assumption that sex ratios are fairly constant across cities. This is simply not true, especially when one considers race differences. Indeed, although the mean level of males per females is .90 for both blacks and whites, the standard deviations and coefficients of variation are much higher for blacks. Specifically, the standard deviation of sex ratios is .19 for blacks and .06 for whites—a differential of over three. The ratio of black males per females ranges from lows of around .75 (e.g., Birmingham, Macon, Yonkers) to highs of 1.5 or more (Eugene, Salt Lake City, El Paso). Employment rates also vary considerably, ranging from .38 to .88 for blacks (mean = .59) and from .40 to .88 for whites (mean = .70). The question, then, is how these relative variations in components of the male marriage pool are linked to variations in family structure.

Table 8.1 presents the results of race-specific equations predicting variations in the percentage of total households headed by females. To compare causal effects across black and white equations, it is necessary to examine unstandardized coefficients to determine the change in the dependent variable associated with a unit change in exogenous factors. On the other hand, to compare the relative effects *within* race groups, we must look to the standardized coefficients (betas) which give us the change in family structure associated with a standard deviation change in the independent variable.

Looking first at within-race results, the strongest predictor by far of black family disruption is the black sex ratio. Net of all other factors, an increase in the number of black men relative to the number of black women tends to substantially reduce rates of female headship (beta = $-.65$). The next largest effect stems from the black male employment rate, which also has a negative effect (beta = $-.24$) on black female-headed families as expected. Thus, although *both* elements of the MMPI have independent effects on black family structure as implied by Wilson (1987), the more salient of the two appears to be sex ratios.[10]

---

[10]Although space limitations preclude discussion, note that the other results are largely consistent with past research—rates of family disruption are higher in cities characterized by economic deprivation (i.e., low per capita income), a low median age, and northern location.

TABLE 8.1

Race-Specific Effects of Sex Ratios, Male Employment Rates, and Control Variables on Female-headed Families: United States Cities, 1980

	Black Households with Female Head (%)		White Households with Female Head (%)	
	b	Beta	*b*	Beta
Sex ratio				
Black	22.86**	−.65	a	
White		a	−4.44**	−.17
Employment rate				
Black	−17.05**	−.24	a	
White		a	.71	.03
Per capita income				
Black	−6.55**	−.22	a	
White		a	−7.55**	−.47
Public assistance				
Black	2.57	.03	a	
White		a	5.87**	.35
Median age				
Black	−.88**	−.24	a	
White		a	−.00	−.00
Population size	.76	.08	.10	.04
Density	−.59	−.01	−1.97**	−.14
North	2.06**	.15	−.13	−.04
West	.46	.03	−.39	−.11
		$R^2 = .78$		$R^2 = .50$

[a]Not included in model specification.

**$p < .05$.

The third and fourth columns show the equivalent model for white female-headed families. The results support Wilson's race-specific hypothesis—both sex ratios and male employment are comparatively unimportant for white family disruption. For instance, the effect of the sex ratio, while significantly negative, is less than half the magnitude of the effects of welfare and income. More to the point, the unstandardized effect of white sex ratios is much smaller than the corresponding effect of black sex ratios—for example, the black sex ratio effect is some 3.8 times higher than the effect of white sex ratios. Furthermore, not only does white male employment have an insignificant effect on white female-headed families, the unstandardized effect of black employment is 24 times greater! The race-specific interaction predicted by Wilson is thus clearly supported with female-headed families as the criterion.

Table 8.2 repeats the analyses performed in Table 8.1 but with two alternative measures of family structure.[11] First, the upper half of the table displays the results for the percentage of married-couple families among those families with children aged six to seventeen. Consistent with expectations, we see a strong positive effect of the black sex ratio on the prevalence of married-couple families. Black male employment also exhibits a significant positive effect on family stability, although the magnitude of effect is less than half that of the sex ratio. For whites, we see a modest sex ratio effect and a small effect of employment. In addition, the unstandardized effect estimates of sex ratio and employment are two to three times higher for blacks than for whites.

The lower half of the table paints a similar picture with regard to the percentage of females aged fifteen to fifty-nine not living with a mate. In fact, for whites there is no effect of either sex ratio *or* employment on the proxy for females in a nonmarriage household. On the other hand, we again find strong effects of both sex ratio and employment on the family situation of black females. Moreover, the causal effect of black sex ratio is over five times greater than the white sex ratio effect, while the employment effect is twenty times greater for blacks than for whites.

To complete the family structure analysis the original MMPI variable was added to all the models presented in Tables 8.1 and 8.2. In general the interaction of employment and sex ratios (i.e., the MMPI) did not significantly add to the explanatory power of the equations. For example, the MMPI added less than 1 percent explained variance to the explanation of black female-headed families. Also, the MMPI is so highly correlated with constituent terms (e.g., .77 with sex ratio) that regression estimates were inefficient. The message then is that the MMPI does not add anything substantial beyond the effects of the separate dimensions of sex ratio and employment.[12]

The results thus far are strikingly consistent and lead to a general conclusion. Both the numbers of black men *and* their employment prospects have independent effects on the structure of black families in cities in the United

[11]To simplify presentation, the coefficients in Table 8.2 refer only to the major variables of interest—sex ratios and employment. However, all equations have the same control variables as Table 8.1.

[12]The MMPI is still an important summary measure for it captures the overall effect of the shortage of marriageable black males. One purpose of this study, however, is to determine the relative effects of the separate components that are reflected in this summary measure. Besides substantive reasons for disaggregation, it should also be noted that sex ratios and employment rates are weakly related. For example, the black sex ratio is correlated only .12 with black male employment, while the corresponding correlation for whites is .00.

TABLE 8.2

Race-Specific Effects of Sex Ratios and Male Employment Rates on Alternative Measures of Family Structure: United States Cities, 1980

	Black		White	
	b	Beta	*b*	Beta
Married-couple families with children (%)				
Sex ratio				
Black	31.17**	.58	a	
White	a		10.84**	.17
Employment rate				
Black	22.92**	.21	a	
White	a		8.74*	.15
		$R^2 = .68$		$R^2 = .61$
Women aged 15 to 59 not living with a mate (%)				
Sex ratio				
Black	− 15.16**	− .54	a	
White	a		− 2.66	− .12
Employment rate				
Black	− 14.01**	.25	a	
White	a		.71	.04
		$R^2 = .64$		$R^2 = .48$

Note: All equations control for per capita income, public assistance, median age, population size, density, North, and West.

a Not included in model specification.

$*p < .10.$ $**p < .05.$

States. By contrast, neither white male employment rates nor white sex ratios appear to have much influence on white family structure. In fact, the unstandardized effects of sex ratios and employment rates for blacks were substantially higher than for whites. This race-specific interaction supports Wilson's (1987) hypothesis regarding the structural sources of black family disruption in cities in the United States.

Concentration Effects

Before turning to the analysis of crime rates we can also examine the structural determinants of family disruption among those in poverty. Specifically, one of the main dimensions of the underclass according to Wilson is the prevalence of female-headed households with children *that are also in poverty* (see Wilson, 1987, pp. 8; 28–29; 58–61). Although the census does not provide race-specific city-level data on families in poverty that are female headed, it is possible to examine an *aggregate* measure and control for percent black. Therefore, Table 8.3 displays the total effects of sex ratios and male employment rates on a proxy measure of the urban underclass—the percentage of families that are female-headed, in poverty, *and* with children.

The results demonstrate the strong independent influence of the components of the MMPI—except for the large effect of percent black, the major determinants of the concentration of family disruption and poverty are sex ratios and employment. Since the present definition of the underclass has an economic component, it is not surprising that the negative effect of employment rates is higher than sex ratios. In fact, Wilson's (1987) general theory clearly suggests that the employment prospects of black males will have their greatest effects among the most disadvantaged families.

Urban Violence

Table 8.4 explains robbery and murder rates disaggregated by race and age. On substantive grounds, the percentage of married-couple households with children aged six to seventeen is used as the main family structure indicator for the prediction of juvenile crime, whereas the proxy for female nonmarriage rates is used in the adult crime models. The upper half of Table 8.4 indicates that the prevalence of intact black families with children has relatively strong negative effects on both robbery and murder by black juveniles. In fact, family stability has the largest effect on black juvenile homicide and the second largest effect on robbery. The direct effect of family disruption on black adult crime (lower half of table) is also significant, although its relative magnitude is somewhat less compared to juveniles (cf. Sampson, 1987). In any event, independent of nine other urban structural characteristics, the data clearly reveal that black family disruption has large effects on black robbery and murder.

Interestingly, Table 8.4 also reveals that the direct effects of black sex ratios and black male employment on violent crime are weak and inconsistent. For example, the black sex ratio is significant in only one of four equations (black adult murder), while employment has a small positive effect in two equations. The positive effect of employment seems counterintuitive, although it may simply reflect increased opportunities for crimes such as robbery (Cantor and Land, 1985; Sampson, 1987). That is, once factors that contribute to the supply of motivated offenders are controlled, it is reasonable to suggest that cities with high employment have increased opportunities for crime.

Overall, however, the data are fairly consistent in showing that the effects of black sex ratio and employment on crime are mediated in large part by family

TABLE 8.3

Total Effects of Sex Ratios, Male Employment Rates,
and Control Variables on the Urban Underclass:
Female-Headed Families with Children and in Poverty:
United States Cities, 1980

	Female-Headed Families in Poverty, with Children (%)	
	b	Beta
Sex ratio	−.057**	−.26
Male employment rate	−.086**	−.37
Percent black	.039**	.46
Median age	.001**	.09
Population size	.002**	.09
Density	−.001	−.01
North	.004**	.12
West	.002	.08
		$R^2 = .77$

**$p < .05$.

disruption. For example, of the total effect of sex ratios on black robbery, fully 100 percent is mediated by family structure for juveniles and 58 percent for adults. Failure to examine the indirect effects of the salient components of the MMPI would thus lead to an underestimate of their causal significance in explaining black violence. As to the interaction of sex ratios and employment, in no case was the MMPI significant when added to the crime models in Table 8.4.

Table 8.5 examines the equivalent age-specific model for the explanation of white violence. As was the case for blacks, family structure has important effects on both robbery and violence. For example, the proportion of females in nonmarriage households is the strongest predictor of white adult murder and the second largest predictor of white adult robbery (lower half). Similarly, the prevalence of white intact families with children has a substantial negative effect on white juvenile robbery (upper half). The corresponding effect on white juvenile murder is negative as well but it is insignificant.[13]

The pattern of effects for sex ratios and employment rates on white violence

---

[13]The number of murders committed by white juveniles is relatively low, leading to considerable instability in the measurement of rates across cities. The overall level of explanatory power and significance is thus reduced.

TABLE 8.4

Effects of Black Family Structure and Control Variables
on Black Homicide and Robbery Rates, by Age: United States Cities, 1980

	Murder		Robbery	
	b	Beta	b	Beta
Juvenile				
Black married-couple families with children (%)	−.04**	−.25	−.04**	−.35
Black sex ratio	−1.48	−.17	.02	.00
Black male employment	.43	.02	1.50**	.13
Black per capita income	−2.31	−.11	−3.48**	−.24
Black public assistance	−2.28	−.12	2.66**	.20
Black median age	.09	.11	.02	.04
Population size	.48**	.24	.08	.06
Density	.08	.01	3.28**	.35
North	−.15	−.05	.55**	.25
West	.40	.12	1.07**	.45
		$R^2 = .27$		$R^2 = .62$
Adult				
Black females 15 to 59 without a mate (%)	.03**	.25	.03**	.21
Black sex ratio	.82**	.22	.31	.08
Black male employment	1.05*	.15	.70	.09
Black per capita income	−2.85**	−.31	−2.76**	−.28
Black public assistance	−.02**	−.26	1.28*	.14
Black median age	.04	.11	.02	.06
Population size	.18**	.21	.08	.09
Density	−.11	−.02	2.26**	.36
North	.22	.16	.34**	.23
West	.79**	.54	.78**	.49
		$R^2 = .28$		$R^2 = .52$

$*p < .10. **p < .05.$

is similar to blacks. Namely, the direct effects of the availability and employment prospects of white men on violence are weak and inconsistent. Employment is significant only once, and that pertains to a small positive effect ($p < .10$) on white juvenile robbery. White sex ratios are significant at the .10 level and then only for white adult murder and white juvenile robbery. And again similar to blacks, the interaction of sex ratios and employment in the form of the MMPI had no effects above and beyond its component terms when added to the crime models in Table 8.5.

In brief, because sex ratios and employment rates have virtually no effect on white family disruption and hence negligible indirect effects on crime, their

TABLE 8.5

Effects of White Family Structure and Control Variables
on White Homicide and Robbery Rates, by Age: United States Cities, 1980

	Murder		Robbery	
	b	Beta	*b*	Beta
Juvenile				
White married-couple families with children (%)	−.05	−.17	−.07**	−.28
White sex ratio	2.74	.16	2.32*	.15
White male employment	2.77	.18	2.46*	.17
White per capita income	2.40*	−.22	−2.99**	−.29
White public assistance	.16	.00	−.38	−.01
White median age	.03	.09	.08**	.27
Population size	.63**	.43	.26**	.19
Density	−.29	−.03	2.21**	.24
North	−.31	−.13	.42**	.19
West	.40	.15	.64**	.27
		$R^2 = .32$		$R^2 = .51$
Adult				
White females 15 to 59 without a mate (%)	.21**	.40	.19**	.35
White sex ratio	1.65*	.16	1.54	.14
White male employment	1.01	.10	.93	.09
White per capita income	−1.04	−.15	−1.55**	−.22
White public assistance	−.23	−.01	−.43	−.02
White median age	.04**	.21	.07**	.36
Population size	.34**	.38	.24**	.25
Density	−.68	−.11	.79*	.12
North	−.54**	−.37	−.22*	−.15
West	.04	.02	.43**	.26
		$R^2 = .45$		$R^2 = .49$

$*p < .10.$ $**p < .05.$

substantive import seems quite limited. Specifically, white sex ratios and employment rates are relatively unimportant in understanding both white family disruption and white violence rates.

As a final test Table 8.6 presents the total effects of underclass family disruption on aggregate rates of homicide and robbery. This model allows us to examine how the concentration of poverty and family disruption among families with children influences rates of violence, independent of race per se. Also, given the results in Table 8.3 on the determinants of underclass family disruption, Table 8.6 permits the identification of the direct and indirect effects of aggregate sex ratios and male employment rates on robbery and homicide.

TABLE 8.6

*Total Effects of "Underclass" Family Disruption and Control Variables
on Aggregate Homicide and Robbery Offense Rates:
United States Cities, 1980*

	Homicide (Beta)	Robbery (Beta)
Families that are female-headed,		
in poverty, and with children (%)	.34**	.62**
Sex ratio	.03	.02
Male employment	.25**	.28**
Percent black	.50**	.37**
Population size	.33**	.18**
Density	− .12**	.17**
Median age	− .10	− .03
North	− .15**	.14**
West	.13**	.37**
	$R^2 = .61$	$R^2 = .63$

**$p < .05$.

The results are consistent and rather striking. First, underclass family disruption has powerful independent effects on both robbery and homicide. In fact, it has the second largest effect on homicide (beta = .34) and the largest effect by far on robbery (.62). Thus, despite controlling for key factors such as size, density, age composition, and region *in addition* to race, sex ratios, and employment, we see that underclass family disruption is one of the major predictors of robbery and homicide in cities in the United States.

Second, the results again suggest that sex ratios are important only insofar as they affect variations in family structure. For example, note that the direct effect of sex ratios on robbery and homicide is almost zero (.02 and .03, respectively). On the other hand, the strong negative effect of sex ratios on underclass family disruption (see Table 8.3) combined with the latter's strong positive effect on violence leads to a substantial indirect causal role for sex ratios. Specifically, 88 percent of the total effect of sex ratios on robbery is mediated by underclass family disruption, while the corresponding figure is 74 percent for homicide. Thus, similar to the case for race-specific violence (see Tables 8.4 and 8.5), virtually all of the explanatory power of sex ratios on total crime is mediated by family structure.

Third, the results indicate that the effects of employment rates on violence are even more complex than sex ratios. In Table 8.6 we see significant *positive* effects of employment on both homicide and robbery. As suggested above, controlling for other factors that presumably affect the supply of motivated offenders, the direct effect of employment may arise from city-level variations in opportunity structures (see Cantor and Land, 1985; Sampson, 1987).[14] On the other hand, in conjunction with the substantial *negative* effects of employment on underclass family disruption (Table 8.3) and the latter's positive effect on violence, the indirect effect of employment rates on violence is negative. In particular, the indirect effect of employment on robbery is −.23 compared to a direct positive effect of .28. The countervailing direct and indirect effects of employment on crime lead to possible suppression effects in misspecified models. The results thus suggest that it is necessary to control for family structure in order to identify the true causal role played by employment rates.

Conclusions

One finding from the present study seems beyond doubt. Family structure is one of the strongest, if not the strongest, predictor of variations in urban violence across cities in the United States. Substantively, the results indicate that, all else equal, in cities where family disruption is high the rate of violence is also high. The robustness of this finding was demonstrated in several ways: (*a*) three separate definitions of family structure were examined; (*b*) nine key dimensions of urban social structure were controlled; (*c*) both offense and offender rates were examined; and (*d*) the significant effect of family disruption emerged for both black *and* white violence. Therefore, the strong positive effect of family disruption on violence cannot simply be attributed to race-specific subcultures or other common third causes, or to specific operational definitions of crime and/or family structure. Rather, it appears that there is something generic about the structural effects of family disruption on crime. Although beyond the scope of this chapter, I believe that the significance of family structure for crime is linked to patterns of community social ties and informal networks of social control (see Sampson and Groves, 1989).

A second major finding pertains to Wilson's (1987) thesis of a race-specific interaction in the explanation of family disruption. Namely, both the numbers of black men *and* their employment prospects have independent effects on the structure of black families in cities in the United States. By contrast, neither rates of white male employment nor white sex ratios appear to have much influence on white family structure. This race-specific interaction clearly supports Wilson's (1987) hypothesis regarding the structural sources of black family disruption. However, the findings also underscore the need to disaggregate the global MMPI measure into its constituent parts. After all, the MMPI is composed of both a demographic *and* a socioeconomic dimension, and both

---

[14]However, the opportunity perspective would seem to have trouble explaining the positive effects of employment rates on homicide.

have independent effects on the black family. For blacks the sex ratio appears to be the more important of the two dimensions (cf. Schoen and Kluegel, 1988).

Third, the data showed that the effects of black sex ratio and employment on crime are mediated in large part by family structure. Indeed, well over 50 percent of the total effect of sex ratios on black robbery was mediated by family disruption. Therefore, failure to examine the indirect effects of sex ratios and employment leads to an underestimate of their causal significance in explaining black violence. On the other hand, since sex ratios and employment had weak effects on white family disruption, they in turn had negligible indirect effects on violence by whites.

Finally, the results demonstrated the strong independent influence of total sex ratios and employment on family disruption *among those families in poverty*. The lower the sex ratio and the lower the male employment rate the higher the rate of female-headed families with children and in poverty. In turn, this proxy measure of "underclass" family disruption had positive independent effects on both robbery and homicide. Hence, the results again suggested that sex ratios are important only insofar as they affect variations in family structure. The indirect negative effect of male employment on crime was also apparent, although it had countervailing direct effects on crime, perhaps because of opportunity effects.

Despite the general consistency of results, the present study suffers major limitations in its ability to render definitive conclusions. A major reason stems from the complex nature of the interplay between urban social structure and crime. In particular, because of data limitations I was unable to estimate reciprocal models that take account of feedback effects. For example, Figure 8.1 displays a conceptual model that introduces further but probably realistic complexity into the ideas developed in this chapter.

It is reasonable to assume that as the rate of violence goes up, the rate of incapacitation in the form of imprisonment, serious injury, and death by homicide goes up. This incapacitation effect may have *three* reciprocal effects as shown in the figure. First, it may reduce further violence through deterrence and/or removal of offenders from the community. Second, it may actually *increase* violence via a feedback loop by further decreasing the sex ratio, which in turn indirectly increases violence through its effect on family disruption. Third, imprisonment can also have negative feedback effects on male employment, which again serves to indirectly increase future crime rates. Before definitive conclusions can be drawn, models of this sort need to be examined.[15]

---

[15]There are other limitations as well that I cannot discuss because of space limitations. These include inadequate measures of the underclass, a one-sided focus on male employment and hence a gender-bias, reliance on official measures of criminal activity, a focus on cities rather than local communities as units of analysis, and the inability to study cultural values directly.

FIGURE 8.1

Complex model of association between male employment, sex ratio, and urban crime.

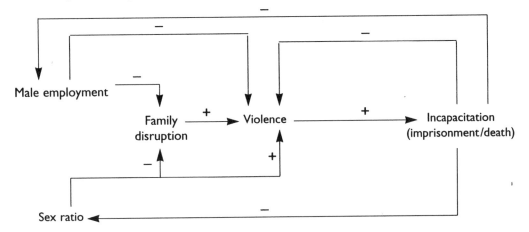

Therefore, I believe that whatever significance the present study may have, it lies not in methodological precision but in suggestions for future considerations by theory and especially public policy. As to the latter, the current mood of policy toward crime is severely punitive and shortsighted. Incarceration may be the preferred solution of both the public and leaders in Washington, but the long-term effects of such policies could well be disastrous. Simply put, by locking up an ever-increasing proportion of blacks we risk further disruption of black families via imbalanced sex ratios. Moreover, imprisonment has well-known negative effects on the prospects of future employment. Given that most offenders will in fact be released from incarceration, current policies will exacerbate black family disruption by contributing to the further marginalization of black men from the labor market (see Figure 8.1).

Although they are currently unpopular, we thus need to take a renewed look at social policies such as rehabilitation (e.g., job placement and training; educational services) that reintegrate offenders back into society. I am not suggesting that imprisonment is unnecessary nor undeserved in all cases, nor even that it has no deterrent effect on crime (in fact, I happen to believe that deterrence works, albeit to a small degree). Rather, I am suggesting that it is time to question received wisdom on crime-control policy based on a more complex and long-term perspective regarding the links among crime policies, employment, family structure, and the social organization of inner-city communities. Just as the demographers' prediction that crime would fall in the 1980s as the baby boom aged turned out to be erroneous, so too will be the crime-control advocates' prediction that by simply locking up more of the population, the crime problem can finally be solved.

AUTHOR NOTES

The research was supported in part by a grant funded by the National Institute of Justice (#86-IJ-CX-0060). Points of view expressed herein are those of the author and do not necessarily represent the position of the Justice Department.

REFERENCES

BISHOP, J.J. 1980. Jobs, cash transfers and marital instability: A review and synthesis of the evidence. *Journal of Human Resources,* 15:301–334.

BLUMSTEIN, A. 1982. On the racial disproportionality of United States' prison populations. *Journal of Criminal Law and Criminology,* 73:1259–1281.

BLUMSTEIN, A., COHEN J., AND VISHER, C. 1986. Linking the crime and arrest process to measure individual crime rates. Paper presented at the National Institute of Justice Annual Conference on Prediction, Denver, CO.

BUREAU OF JUSTICE STATISTICS. 1985a. The risk of violent crime. U.S. Department of Justice Special Report. Washington, DC: U.S. Government Printing Office.

BUREAU OF JUSTICE STATISTICS. 1985b. Capital punishment, 1984 U.S. Department of Justice Special Report. Washington, DC: U.S. Government Printing Office.

BUREAU OF JUSTICE STATISTICS. 1985c. The prevalence of imprisonment. U.S. Department of Justice Special Report. Washington, DC: U.S. Government Printing Office.

BYRNE, J., AND SAMPSON, R.J. 1986. Key issues in the social ecology of crime. In J. Byrne and R.J. Sampson, eds., *The social ecology of crime.* New York: Springer-Verlag.

CANTOR, D., AND LAND, K. 1985. Unemployment and crime rates in the post–World War II United States. *American Sociological Review,* 50:317–332.

COHEN, J. 1986. Research on criminal careers. In A. Blumstein, J. Cohen, J. Roth, and C. Visher, eds., *Criminal careers and "career criminals."* Washington, DC: National Academy.

CURTIS, L. 1975. *Violence, race, and culture.* Lexington, MA: Heath.

DEFRONZO, J. 1983. Economic assistance to impoverished Americans: Relationship to incidence of crime. *Criminology,* 21:119–136.

ELLWOOD, D., AND BANE, M.J. 1984. *The impact of AFDC on family structure and living arrangements.* Cambridge, MA: Harvard University Press. (Prepared for the U.S. Department of Health and Human Services under grant no. 92A-82.)

FELSON, M. 1986. Linking criminal choices, routine activities, informal social control, and criminal outcomes. In R. Clarke and D. Cornish, eds., *The reasoning criminal.* New York: Springer-Verlag.

FELSON, M., AND COHEN, L. 1980. Human ecology and crime: A routine activity approach. *Human Ecology,* 8:389–406.

FISHER, J., AND MASON, R. 1981. The analysis of multicollinear data in criminology. In J.A. Fox, ed., *Methods in quantitative criminology*. New York: Academic Press.

FLANAGAN, T., AND MCLEOD, M., eds. 1983. *Sourcebook of criminal justice statistics, 1982*. Washington, DC: U.S. Government Printing Office.

FREEMAN, R.B. 1983. Crime and unemployment. In J.Q. Wilson, ed., *Crime and public policy*. San Francisco: ICS Press.

GOTTFREDSON, M., AND GOTTFREDSON, D. 1980. *Decision making in criminal justice*. Cambridge, MA: Ballinger.

GOVE, W., HUGHES, M., AND GEERKEN, M. 1985. Are *Uniform Crime Reports* a valid indicator of the index crimes? An affirmative answer with minor qualifications. *Criminology,* 23:451–502.

GREENBERG, S., ROHE, W., AND WILLIAMS, J. 1985. *Informal citizen action and crime prevention at the neighborhood level: Synthesis and assessment of the research*. National Institute of Justice. Washington, DC: U.S. Government Printing Office.

GUTTENTAG, M., AND SECORD, P. 1983. *Too many women? The sex ratio question.* Beverly Hills: Sage Publications.

HINDELANG, M. 1978. Race and involvement in common-law personal crimes. *American Sociological Review,* 43:93–109.

HINDELANG, M. 1979. Sex-differences in criminal activity. *Social Problems,* 27:143–156.

HINDELANG, M., HIRSCHI, T., AND WEIS, J. 1981. *Measuring delinquency*. Beverly Hills: Sage Publications.

HOGAN, D., AND KITAGAWA, E. 1985. The impact of social status, family structure, and neighborhood on the fertility of black adolescents. *American Journal of Sociology,* 90:825–855.

HONIG, M. 1974. AFDC income, recipient rates, and family dissolution. *Journal of Human Resources,* 9:303–322.

KORNHAUSER, R. 1978. *Social sources of delinquency*. Chicago: University of Chicago Press.

LIEBOW, E. 1967. *Tally's corner*. Boston: Little, Brown.

LISKA, A., CHAMLIN, M., AND REED, M. 1985. Testing the economic production and conflict models of crime control. *Social Forces,* 64:119–138.

MAYHEW, B., AND LEVINGER, R. 1976. Size and the density of interaction in human aggregates. *American Journal of Sociology,* 82:86–110.

MESSNER, S. 1983. Regional and racial effects on the urban homicide rate: The subculture of violence revisited. *American Journal of Sociology,* 88:997–1007.

MESSNER, S., AND SOUTH, S. 1986. Estimating race-specific offending rates: An intercity comparison of arrest data and victim reports. Unpublished manuscript, Department of Sociology, State University of New York at Albany.

MOYNIHAN, D.P. 1965. *The Negro family: The case for national action*. Washington, DC: U.S. Department of Labor, Office of Policy Planning and Research.

MURRAY, C. 1984. *Losing ground: American social policy, 1950–1980*. New York: Basic Books.

RAINWATER, L. 1966. Crucible of identity: The Negro lower-class family. *Daedalus,* 95:172–216.

RAINWATER, L. 1970. *Behind ghetto walls: Black families in a federal slum*. Chicago: Aldine.

Ross, H., AND Sawhill, I. 1975. *Time of transition: The growth of families headed by women*. Washington, DC: Urban Institute.

Sampson, R.J. 1986a. Neighborhood family structure and the risk of criminal victimization. In J. Byrne and R.J. Sampson, eds., *The social ecology of crime*. New York: Springer-Verlag.

Sampson, R.J. 1986b. Crime in cities: The effects of formal and informal social control. In A.J. Reiss, Jr., and M. Toury, eds., *Communities and crime*. Chicago: University of Chicago Press.

Sampson, R.J. 1986c. Effects of socioeconomic context on official reaction to juvenile delinquency. *American Sociological Review,* 51:876–885.

Sampson, R.J. 1987. Urban black violence: The effect of male joblessness and family disruption. *American Journal of Sociology,* 93:348–382.

Sampson, R.J., AND Groves, W.B. 1989. Community structure and crime: Testing social-disorganization theory. *American Journal of Sociology,* 94:774–802.

Schoen, R., AND Kluegel, J.R. 1988. The widening gap in black and white marriage rates: The impact of population composition and differential marriage propensities. *American Sociological Review,* 53:895–907.

Skogan, W. 1986. Fear of crime and neighborhood change. In A.J. Reiss, Jr., and M. Toury, eds., *Communities and crime*. Chicago: University of Chicago Press.

South, S., AND Trent, K. 1988. Sex ratios and women's roles: A cross-national analysis. *American Journal of Sociology,* 93:1096–1115.

U.S. Bureau of the Census. 1982. *U.S. census of the population: 1980. General social and economic characteristics*. Washington, DC: U.S. Government Printing Office.

Wilkinson, K. 1980. The broken home and delinquency. In T. Hirschi and M. Gottfredson, eds., *Understanding crime*. Beverly Hills: Sage Publications.

Wilson, J.Q., AND Hernstein, R. 1985. *Crime and human nature*. New York: Simon & Schuster.

Wilson, W.J. 1984. The urban underclass. In L. Dunbar, ed., *Minority Report*. New York: Pantheon.

Wilson, W.J. 1987. *The truly disadvantaged: The inner city, the underclass, and public policy*. Chicago: University of Chicago Press.

Wilson, W.J., AND Neckerman, K. 1985. Poverty and family structure: The widening gap between evidence and public policy issues. Paper presented at the Conference on Poverty and Policy: Retrospect and Prospects, Williamsburg, Virginia.

Wolfgang, M., AND Ferracuti, F. 1967. *The subculture of violence*. London: Tavistock.

COMMENTARY

Melvin L. Oliver

O NE OF THE MOST pressing problems facing the black community is crime. Black residents of central-city communities feel overwhelmed with increased levels of street crime as expressed in acts of interpersonal violence, burglary, and homicide. Not only is there a perception of an increase in the rates of these criminal acts but also a grave concern with the extremities of violence that accompany these acts: the drive-by shootings in South Central Los Angeles; the use of automatic weapons; and the senseless violence that accompanies drug selling and drug abuse. These are important issues facing the black community that demand the attention of the social scientific community. But if anything, the scholarly community has inflicted upon the black community an onerous analysis of this condition. The dominant forms of analyses of crime in the black community shed little light on the causal factors responsible for these conditions. Instead, they provide convenient explanations that buttress a hostile judicial system and an avaricious economic system whose very functioning contributes much to the steadily deteriorating underlying conditions leading to crime.

It is within this context that Robert Sampson's corpus of work, including the chapter appearing in this volume, should be considered (e.g., Sampson, 1987; Sampson and Groves, 1989). Sampson's work has been in the forefront of providing a systematic treatment of black violence that vigorously situates black crime in a set of structural forces as opposed to the dominant themes expressed in subcultural theories of black crime or analyses based on individual-level explanations. We should not forget that various forms of subcultural theories continue to hold the attention of scholars and policymakers when the issue of crime in the black community is confronted. For example, Roger Lane in *Roots of Violence in Urban Black Philadelphia, 1860–1900* (1986) writes:

> Among Afro-Americans . . . current rates of criminality are relatively simple projections out of the past, products of a subculture of violence nurtured by

exclusion and denial. . . . The effect of [which] has been an atmosphere in which violent behavior is not only accepted but often expected or even celebrated. (p. 173)

This analysis received the Bancroft Award, which celebrates the best scholarly book of the year in American history

In a controversial book entitled *Seductions of Crime* (1988), sociologist Jack Katz argues that black criminality is rooted in an existential confrontation which blacks, particularly black men, have with their degraded status in American society. In an almost Fanon-like analysis, Katz argues that the traditional forms of black crime—burglary and armed robbery—are merely expressions of the "bad nigger" impulse rooted in a black culture whose sole purpose was to create avenues of self-affirmation denied in the wider society. Such analyses unwittingly create explanations of black crime which conform to conventional ideas held by the lay public and the political leadership. They see crime as rooted in the constitution of blacks, whether on the conservative side by way of innate factors (Wilson and Hernstein, 1985) or on the liberal side by way of a subculture generated initially by exclusion but sustained by a self-generating subculture of violence (Wolfgang and Ferracuti, 1967; Curtis, 1975). In either case the solutions offered and the policies pursued are geared to deterrence and punishment. Equally important is that these conceptions of black crime form a convenient rationalization of the general public's unwillingness to share social space with blacks. Racial segregation is legitimized by the perception that blacks are violent and prone to criminality, thus prompting whites to rationally evade the dangerous environs that blacks occupy not on the basis of race, but on the perception of their degree of safety (Massey, 1987).

Sampson's analysis provides a welcome respite from such explanations. Focusing on a structural analysis based on empirical tests, Sampson provides a way of looking at variations in black criminality and violence that allows the development of important interventions that can aid the black community in decreasing the deleterious impact of crime and violence. Put simply, Sampson argues that family structure has an important impact on crime in the black community. However, family structure is impacted by structural forces such as increasing rates of black male joblessness and the declining sex ratio. His empirical analysis in both the brilliant article, "Urban Black Violence" (1987), and in this chapter demonstrates that the black sex ratio and black male employment have a direct impact on black family structure. In an ensuing analysis he deftly illustrates how family structure is intimately related to both black and white criminality, with the effects of the sex ratio impacting indirectly on family structure in such models. Moreover, he argues rather convincingly that among poverty populations, particularly in those cities with large black populations, the effects of family structure and male unemployment are greatest on rates of crime. His empirical work supports Wilson's contention that black male joblessness and the sex ratio are important determinants of black criminality (Wilson, 1987).

It is clear to me that Sampson's structural approach and empirical strategy have a more productive payoff in terms of explanatory power and policy implications than the traditional approaches represented in subcultural theories. However, I think Sampson's approach raises a flurry of questions about the processes involved in his systemic analysis—particularly the processes involved in why family structure is implicated with crime. I approach this issue in terms of the relationship between structure and process.

Why Is Family Structure Important?

Sampson argues that family structure is important because married families are more likely to be able to provide the "guardian" behavior necessary to oversee and direct youth behavior. In particular, married families, Sampson argues, are more likely to be involved in local networks that allow for friends and neighbors to be involved in a wide range of guardian activity. His analysis of English data supports this notion (Sampson and Groves, 1989). However, it is clear that the data presented here cannot really test this notion nor even really support it. The issue is one of limited data. In Sampson's paper we have only city-based data. The notion of guardian behavior or integration in local social networks is, at most, a community-level attribute. Here problems of structure, process, and methodology come together. In order to understand the processes at work in the relationship of family structure and crime, we need community-based data that allow us to examine hypotheses about process. It is my contention that there is greater variation within cities, that is, between communities, than there is between cities.

This has an important implication for black communities and especially for Wilson's argument as well as Sampson's on the structural basis of black violence. With limited data, Sampson is not able to address the issue of variations between black communities. The nature of community has much to do with this as well. Communities have spatial boundaries that are quite problematic. Wilson recognizes this when he talks about extreme-poverty areas so as to differentiate them from areas that may have high poverty rates, but are nevertheless more heterogeneous. However, examining any black area in an inner city uncovers a multitude of communities. From block to block communities change; crime on one block is different from crime on another block. Guardian behavior may not necessarily be a function of family structure as much as it is a function of what my colleague James Johnson and I (1990) call "social resources." Not only do these social resources involve access to important local networks of friends, neighbors, and relatives, but they also include access to organizational entities such as churches and associations. These social groupings and institutions are not only important in establishing and sanctioning a set of controls that can enable guardian behavior to take place, but they also help people obtain resources. In Sampson's analysis I believe the nature and content of social resources is relatively overlooked. It is important to note that the key difference between single-parent and two-parent families is resources; in particular, women make 59 percent of what men make. I would suggest that a more community-specific analysis would uncover areas in which resources differ among single-parent households. For example, on Chicago's West Side where crime is certainly an important problem, there are still streets where crime is negligible; nevertheless, single-parent families may be present or even abundant in these areas. However, the nature of community organization in these blocks may be based on a strong set of social resources: block clubs, extended family houses (not an extended family in one house, but houses in close proximity which contain related families), common church membership, and access to job opportunities and social services. Another important social resource which we often overlook that is related to Sampson's notion of guardian behavior is a multigenerational population. Guardian behavior can be no more effective when two parents are working full time as when a single parent is working. What creates the conditions for a more thorough guardianship of the young is older adults in the community who occupy positions of respect. Older adults have the time to sit on porches and observe strangers and the respect to tell both youths and parents about unwanted behaviors. Such resources, however, are very unevenly distributed. They give poor black neighborhoods the quality of "street-to-street" differences. One street may have significant social resources that deter crime and the development of behaviors leading to crime among its youth, while another street, geographically in the same area, does not.

I am suggesting that we need to look more closely at the social organization of local black communities if we are to understand the processes that relate family structure to crime. Sampson runs the risk at his present level of analysis of reifying family structure into a determinant of crime without analyzing the constituents of family structure that are, in fact, the moving force related to crime. In this sense, social resources become a way in which interventions can be made at the family and community levels. With an emphasis parallel to Wilson's, which overly stresses black male joblessness, the policy implications of Sampson's analysis have a sex bias that directs attention to black men as the total answer to the problem. Free and inexpensive day care can be an example of the important kinds of intervention that Sampson's analysis would support, as well as increased job opportunities for black men, were he to consider a wider concept than just networks and guardianship. Likewise, decreasing the gender pay gap would provide resources enabling single-parent families to be in the position to provide more guidance over their young.

Also missing from Sampson's account are the important ways that the school system is implicated in crime. The recent increase in black pushout rates has created more opportunities for black juvenile criminal activities. While Sampson's measure of joblessness captures a substantial portion of the impact of deindustrialization, economic reorganization, and job discrimination, there is no concomitant emphasis on the creation of new supply-side opportunities for money-making in the drug economy. Furthermore, no mention is made of the impact of low-cost and rapid-firing instruments of destruction. The availability of cheap handguns and automatic weapons has rapidly escalated the nature of violent crime in the black community. And, finally, the black-white differences that Sampson uncovers are never explained in terms of the degree of racial segregation that characterizes the life of all Americans. While these are not fatal flaws, they appear to be necessary ingredients toward a full systematic theory of black crime.

Specific Comments on Sampson's Paper

There are some specific points in Sampson's paper that I believe need to be supplemented or amended. First, while Sampson is more careful than most analysts in using official crime reports, I do believe he overlooks the racial biases inherent in the early labeling of black youth by official social-control agencies. He uses the most serious crimes in his construction of crime rates for his units of analysis. Nevertheless, the case that the early biased labeling of black youth for common juvenile delinquency offenses, such as vandalism and theft, has an important impact on the probabilities that they show up in his statistics on serious crimes. This is the juvenile justice system's most deleterious impact on black criminal activity: the early labeling and resocialization of black youth for criminal careers. While Sampson is unable to include this in his analysis, I would hope that he would be aware of its contribution to high official crime rates.

Second, Sampson is not clear as to why the sex ratio and unemployment rates are not important for the white family structure. The most cogent answer seems to be statistical; that the variation for whites is much less and thus not able to explain much. Sampson needs to clarify both Wilson's analysis on this point and his own.

Third, while Sampson does not discuss the impact of variables other than the sex ratio, employment, and per capita income on black and white family structure in Table 8.1, the finding that public assistance had a strong positive effect on the percentage of white female-headed households but not on the percentage of black female-headed households deserves some notice.

Conclusion

Sampson has provided an intriguing and useful structural analysis of the effects of the sex ratio and family structure on black violence. He has demonstrated an important consequence of the impact of the decline of marriage upon black women. His analysis, however, needs to be broadened to take into account the social processes that underlie his model. In order to avoid slipping into notions about the pathology of black female-headed households, a stress on a broad range of social resources available to black households and the black community should be considered. This is a prime area in which the growing literature on the social organization of black communities can be used to flesh out and make whole the structure and processes related to black crime.

REFERENCES

CURTIS, L. 1975. *Violence, race, and culture.* Lexington, MA: Heath.

JOHNSON, J.H., AND OLIVER, M.L. 1990. *Modeling urban underclass behaviors: Some theoretical considerations.* Occasional working paper no. 2. Los Angeles: Center for the Study of Urban Poverty, UCLA.

KATZ, J. 1988. *Seductions of crime.* New York: Basic Books.

LANE, R. 1986. *Roots of violence in urban black Philadelphia, 1860–1900.* Cambridge, MA: Harvard University Press.

MASSEY, D.S. 1987. Trends in residential segregation for blacks, Hispanics, and Asians: 1970–1980. *American Sociological Review,* 52:802–825.

SAMPSON, R.J. 1987. Urban black violence: The effects of male joblessness and family disruption. *American Journal of Sociology,* 93:348–382.

SAMPSON, R.J., AND GROVES, W.B. 1989. Community structure and crime: Testing social disorganization theory. *American Journal of Sociology,* 94:774–802.

WILSON, J.Q., AND HERNSTEIN, R. 1985. *Crime and human nature.* New York: Simon & Schuster.

WILSON, W.J. 1987. *The truly disadvantaged: The inner city, the underclass, and public policy.* Chicago: University of Chicago Press.

WOLFGANG, M., AND FERRACUTI, F. 1967. *The subculture of violence.* London: Tavistock.

SECTION **FOUR**

Public Policy
and African American
Family Formation

9 FAMILY STRUCTURE AND THE MARGINALIZATION OF BLACK MEN: POLICY IMPLICATIONS

William A. Darity, Jr.
and
Samuel L. Myers, Jr.

WHAT ARE the causes and consequences of the decline in marriageable men in black communities? What are the implications for the future? In this chapter we argue that one of the statistical driving forces behind the recent rise in female family headship among African Americans is the reduction in the supply of marriageable mates. As fewer and fewer young black males make the transition from adolescence to adulthood—as a consequence of drugs, violent crime, incarceration, and eventual death—there will continue to be shortages of marriageable males. At least one of the central causes for the decline in two-parent families in black communities appears to be the reduction in the supply of economically able men suitable for the roles of husband and father.

There are many ways to conceptualize and measure this reduction in supply. One economically intuitive measure is the ratio of unmarried men to unmarried women in the labor force or in school. This measure, better than other indices of male availability, captures the attractiveness of potential marriage partners to women. The sex ratio problem, or the problem of decreasing numbers of men relative to women, is not a mere demographic phenomenon in our estimation. We contend that black men have become less useful in the emerging economic order; they are socially unwanted, superfluous, and marginal. Policies designed to contain or eradicate the unwanted or marginalized segments of the black male population invariably lead to reductions in the supply of marriageable mates. We recognize, however, that a dynamic economic process must be at work in order for such policies to reduce the supply of *desirable* mates.

In marshaling evidence in support of these contentions we recognize a competing set of explanations for the rise of female family headship among blacks. Some policy analysts will argue that sex ratios are immaterial in determining family structure. The cause of the rise in black female family headship, in this view, is the attractiveness of welfare. There is weak support for this popular view. We demonstrate that across jurisdictions and across individuals in a given year, higher welfare incomes are negligibly associated with higher percentages of families headed by women. Yet, these small impacts pale in comparison to the measurably larger effects of reduced supplies of marriageable mates. And, in a longitudinal sense, the welfare attractiveness argument appears unpersuasive: real welfare benefits have fallen precisely when the proportion of families headed by women has surged most dramatically.

The evidence we present, based on estimates of a model of sex ratios, expected welfare incomes, and female headship probabilities for blacks and whites in 1976 and 1985, provides the foundation for several policy simulations. We confirm the relative unresponsiveness of changes in family structure to changes in welfare and demonstrate the significant impacts of sex ratios on probabilities of female family headship. Most important, we are able to ask under a variety of assumptions of continuing demographic and economic patterns in African American communities, "What does the future hold?"

Changes in Black Family Structure

The black family has experienced a drastic decline in the presence of the traditional family structure. The fraction of black families headed by women has grown from its customary percentage of approximately one-quarter in the 1950s to the startling proportion of close to 50 percent in recent years. It is among this growing wave of black families headed by mothers that poverty strikes hardest (see Darity and Myers, 1984b).

Single-parent status also appears to be correlated with a variety of disadvantages for children that extend beyond the direct limitations imposed on their lives by poverty status. For example, even allowing for the effects of low-income status, a child from a single-parent family has a greater probability of dropping out of school (Shaw, 1983, McLanahan, 1985). Although less documented, others have attributed juvenile delinquency and early pregnancies, in part, to the experience of growing up in single-parent families (Loury, 1985).

Increasingly, we are persuaded that the changing structure of black families is rooted in a sex ratio problem. A declining supply of marriageable males means that fewer families will be headed by males. This idea has been expressed by Wilson and Neckerman (1986) and by Darity and Myers (1983, 1984b), following the seminal work of Oliver Cromwell Cox (1940). And yet, the sheer simplicity of the notion that marriage opportunities are constrained by the demographic mix of the population and sex ratios has doomed this insight to obscurity or dismissal among many economists and policy analysts.

Insightful discussions offered by Sampson (1987) and Tucker and Mitchell-Kernan (in press) persuasively argue that the marginalized are increasingly young black men who are being withdrawn from the productive labor market through institutionalization (jails, mental hospitals, and prisons). These black men are institutionalized because of dependence on potent dangerous drugs (such as PCP and crack, a highly addictive form of cocaine) and because of criminal violence often the result of black-on-black attacks related to drugs and thefts. The absolute number of young black men is shrinking because of diseases and injuries that normally are not life-threatening to healthy young men and because of excessive rates of mortality—often as a result of homicides. We have also been influenced by scholars like Guttentag and Secord (1983), Cox (1940), Wilson and Neckerman (1986), and others who contend that reductions in marriageable mates, or the economic marginalization of potential mates, have severe consequences for family formation.

In our early work we found sex ratios to be a key determinant of the rise in black female-headed families (Darity and Myers, 1983, 1984a). We sought to understand the interrelationship between declining pools of marriageable black men, welfare, family structure, and widening inequality in black and white family incomes. We sought to test the hypothesis that the "marginalization" of black men was at the core of the dual problem of rising female headship and declining labor-force participation.

Our finding, with respect to blacks in the United States, mirrors the conclusion of the sociologist Oliver Cox who, as early as 1940, determined that it was the fragile economic position of the black man, compounded by the inability of black women to find marriage partners in sufficient numbers, that lurked behind data revealing the high proportion of black families headed by women.

Circumstances are far worse today with respect to female headship, but the essential mechanism causing the situation is much the same. The social status of the black man, however, is even more tenuous. There is a numerical excess of women over men in every age group over fifteen. This excess remains even after adjustments for the notorious census undercount of black men. Because small increases in the sex ratio are added to an already overflowing surplus of black women, especially in the childbearing ages of fifteen to thirty, the effects cumulate sharply. The probability of marriage is declining for black women, and this can be traced to the growing excess of women over men at every age group in the marriageable years. When the sex ratio increases even by a small numerical amount, the cumulative probability of remaining unmarried goes up by more than the increase in the sex ratio.

While new female-headed black families are being formed, increasingly by younger, never-married heads, the outlook for these family heads becoming married is bleak. The average age at first marriage has been rising steadily among blacks, and the fraction of black women who have married by the age of forty-four has been declining. Historically more than 90 percent of black women were married by the age of forty-four; in the 1970s this proportion fell to 75 percent. By 1980, fully one-third of black women never had been married by the age of forty-four (Rodgers and Thornton, 1985, Strobino and Sirageldin, 1981).

For whites—as of now—the excess of females over males does not rise until the age of forty-four, well beyond the major childbearing years. Moreover, teenage marriages are much more prevalent among whites, even if these marriages eventually end in divorce. Thus, the proportion of female-headed white families (never-married, single, teenaged mothers) is much smaller than it is among blacks.

Correcting for the undercount only alters the magnitude of the excess of females over males among blacks. Additional research, of course, is needed to determine more precisely the size of the deficit. This can be accomplished by detailing exactly how black men are disappearing. Examining the Bureau of the Census estimate of the undercount and their corrections for the numbers of black males and females in various age groups, reveals that the pattern of sex ratio change remains unaltered. The percentage increase in the ratio of females over males using data corrected for the undercount turns out to be approximately the same as that found using uncorrected data (Darity and Myers, 1984a).

Economists and sociologists have differed in their recognition of significant imbalances in sex ratios among blacks. Until recently, economic models often began with the presumption that there were excesses of males over females in the marriage market. This is an essential element of the Becker model that seems to represent an adequate characterization of white "marriage markets." The assumption, however, is not valid for black "marriage markets."

Unlike economists, sociologists and other social scientists as far back as Cox in his pioneering research on black family structure have recognized the excess of black women over black men in the marriageable years and have sought to develop explanations—often economic ones—for how that excess translates into greater likelihood of female headship among black families. Social psychologists Guttentag and Secord (1983) give prominent attention to the role the surplus of women has had in influencing the structures of black families. They contend that the excess of women over men among the black population and the consequential adaptation among blacks to a female-headed family norm is not unique. Whenever there are too many women, they argue, such adaptation is bound to occur.

Yet, economists seem to have missed this insight. The whole range of economic choice models has been reviewed recently by Pollak (1985). Recent improvements upon the household production function approach—where marriage, childrearing, and wife's labor-force participation behavior are synchronized—extend to models of divorce, remarriage, and the impacts of nonearned income, like AFDC, on remarriage. For example, Becker, Landes, and Michael (1977) found that increases in a husband's income, the number of children, and the age at marriage lower divorce probabilities, while increases in the wife's income increase divorce. These findings are consistent with the predictions of a rational choice model under the assumption that there is an excess of males over females. In the presence of an excess of females over males, these predictions are not unambiguous. Thus, for example, while several models (e.g., Hutchens, 1979; Bishop, 1980) predict that welfare or AFDC ought to reduce remarriage probabilities and increase childbearing out of wedlock, these effects are strongest where there are no numerical constraints on the number of available mates. Much empirical work among economists has focused narrowly on the effects of transfers on marriage or family structure while relating market differences between blacks and whites to a dummy variable for race with no real theory for why such a dummy variable ought to be included.

Some sociologists, of course, recognized the difference between the marriage prospects of blacks and whites, and approached the analysis of family formation with a greater appreciation for the role of sex ratios. While Cox and later Jackson (1978) focused on cross-sectional differences, others have mapped out the dynamic effects. Tucker and Mitchell-Kernan (in press), moreover, have expanded the focus of male shortage to specific markets, and Sampson (1987) has investigated the impacts of the antecedents to male shortages on family disruption.

Guttentag and Secord (1983) explore various populations of the world that have experienced sex ratio imbalances. Prominent among those populations is the Orthodox Jewish population. Guttentag and Secord point out, for example, that Russian censuses for the period from 1867 to 1884 uncovered an excess of males over females in the range of 127 to 146, while the sex ratio excesses of males for other religious groups in Imperial Russia ranged from lows of less than 100 for Armenians in 1870 to averages of 105 for Russian Orthodox and Roman Catholics. Apparently this is a consistent phenomenon reported by numerous observers of the Orthodox Jewish population over the centuries. According to Guttentag and Secord, Orthodox Jews make exceptional investments in their children, assuring higher than average survival rates for male babies, thereby increasing the sex ratio:

> . . . (P)arental commitment to offspring, which results in better care of infants
> and older offspring, including adequate feeding. Although males are less robust

than females, both prenatally and during infancy, with especially adequate care these males survive, thus raising the sex ratio above what it otherwise would have been. Thus, prenatal care in a broad sense, including prenatal care, medical care, and adequate diet apparently accounts for the substantial differences in the sex ratios at birth. (1983, pp. 90–91)

Evidence on the significantly lower Jewish infant mortality rates as compared to other ethnic groups is offered to buttress this remarkable conclusion (pp. 93–95). Although Guttentag and Secord also point to aspects of sexual practices among Orthodox Jews, the most persuasive evidence they offer for the high sex ratios among Jews relates to the firm attachment to family life, deep religious commitment, and the significant positive role of women as childbearers and childrearers in Jewish society. And these factors, in our view, may be as much a consequence of high sex ratios as a cause.

The list of factors that contribute to sex ratio imbalances among blacks, according to Tucker and Mitchell-Kernan (in press) includes: differential migration patterns, inadequate prenatal care, high infant and childhood mortality rates among males, and particularly the high mortality rate among young adult black males. Here, the sex ratio concept refers specifically to the numbers of males and females in the general population. Wilson and Neckerman (1986), in contrast, have employed the use of a labor-market-based measure of sex ratios (a "male marriage pool index") that relates the numbers of employed males to the number of females. The low values of this measure are caused in part by the absence of jobs for many black men. We (Darity and Myers, 1983, 1984a) explicitly tested the notion that sex ratios drive changes in black family structures using time-series data for the United States for the period from 1955 to 1980. We found consistent evidence for the Cox hypothesis and, using a Granger-Simms methodology, found virtually no support for a transfers effect on female-headed family formation, mirroring the recent reanalysis of data from the Seattle-Denver Income Maintenance Experiment (SIME-DIME) by Cain and Wissoker (1987–1988).

Economists Greg Duncan and Saul Hoffman (1986a) contested our findings, along with the overall thrust of Wilson and Neckerman (1986), dismissing the first because aggregate data are used and rejecting the second because no "quantitative micro-level evidence" is marshaled. They virtually dismiss the importance of sex ratios and emphasize the weaknesses in the works of Ellwood and Bane (1985) and Danziger et al. (1982), who provide mixed evidence in favor of a transfer effect on family structure. Their own empirical work using the PSID (Panel Study of Income Dynamics) uncovers no impact of sex ratios on family structures. In a similar vein, Robert Lerman (1989), writing in the *American Economic Review*, contends that the sex ratio impacts alluded to by Wilson and Neckerman and uncovered by Darity and Myers are not consistent with other data on marriage and divorces. Thus, there is a growing unease among economists about what, if any, impact sex ratios have on marriage probabilities and family formation. Our response, based on the notion that declining sex ratios are a manifestation of marginalization of black men, is that the widely accepted evidence of declining black male labor-force participation is fully consistent with declines in the marriageability of these men. Mounting evidence supports the view that reductions in the supply of marriageable men contribute to the growth of female-headed families.

The Marginalization of Black Men

That a portion of the population is marginalized, is inextricably linked to recent discussions of the problems of the underclass. There are varying definitions of this class, but one of the most influential views is found in the works of William Wilson. In his *Declining Significance of Race* (1982), Wilson conceives of underclass in a broad Weberian concept of class. He emphasizes social relations of exchange as opposed to a Marxist notion of the social relations of production. Class is a socioeconomic identity. The underclass is a portion of the lower class of society. Wilson describes the underclass as:

> . . . the population which represents the bottom of the economic hierarchy and not only includes those with incomes below the poverty level but also the permanent welfare recipients, the long-term unemployed and those who officially dropped out of the labor market. (p. 156)

If such persons became full-time workers or reentered the labor market they would, in an overwhelming majority of cases, go onto the lowest rung of the job ladder. This implies that movement in and out of the underclass takes place mainly within the ranks of the lower class. For Wilson, underclass represents the more impoverished segment of the lower class.

Wilson retains this concept of the underclass in his more recent book, *The Truly Disadvantaged* (1987). He argues that there is a segment of the population of the United States disproportionately black, located in ghetto neighborhoods, and with characteristics which lead them to be isolated and divorced from the mainstream life-style of the American population. According to Wilson, this heterogeneous grouping of individuals and families is bound together in their apartness or outsideness from "the mainstream American occupational system." Included in this group are individuals who: (*a*) lack training and skills, or experience long-term unemployment; (*b*) are not seeking employment at all; (*c*) engage in street crime and other forms of aberrant behavior; and (*d*) have families who experience spells of long-term poverty and/or welfare dependency.

Wilson, in a sense, adopts the view that there are certain groups left behind as American society progresses along a particular evolutionary trend. These groups are left behind not only in a metaphorical sense but also in a literal sense. The segment of the black population that is middle class in characteristics—using the Weberian version of the nature of class structure—has presumably moved out of the ghetto and left the poverty population behind. Wilson explicitly refers to this poverty population as not only low in income but characterized by a set of particular social pathologies. The social pathologies reinforce their underclass status.

It appears in Wilson's analysis of the nature of underclass that the causal mechanism for pathological behaviors stems from other types of structural considerations that are taking place in the society at large. In contrast, we found Charles Murray, in his book *Losing Ground* (1984), describing the causes of these pathological behaviors as the responsibility of the poor themselves, albeit indirectly through the alleged perverse incentive effects of welfare programs. Again, what appears is a permanent or persistent poverty population in the particular sense that poverty seems to be passed from one generation to the next among the same set of families. Class and race harden into caste.

These families and their offspring are characterized by high crime rates, high rates of illiteracy, high incidence of female headship among the families, lower labor-force participation rates, low rates of graduation from high school, low test scores, and certain forms of cultural isolation. In much of Murray's discussion, this pattern of behavior identifies the underclass and simultaneously seems to be the cause of their poverty status.

Why particular individuals or members of a racial group are more predisposed than others to certain behaviors is the critical question that researchers have yet to resolve. In Wilson's analysis, there is a tendency for the previously described behavior to arise in communities that are spatially and culturally isolated from the norms that produce middle-class life-styles. In Murray's argument, it seems that the very nature of American social policy—the kinds of incentives and disincentives created by American social policy—has tended to reinforce antisocial behavior and compelled individuals to reproduce their own poverty status.

Another conceptualization of the underclass is offered by Douglas Glasgow (1980) in *The Black Underclass: Poverty, Unemployment and Entrapment of Ghetto Youth*. Glasgow espouses the notion that the underclass is a population locked into poverty over a long historical period, with the transmission of poverty status occurring from generation to generation, and the same families continuing to experience poverty status. Another feature of Glasgow's discussion has not been emphasized but is germane for our analysis of what we call the *marginalization of black males*. Glasgow reasons that it is useful to envision the underclass as a permanently entrapped population of poor persons, unused and unwanted, and accumulated in various parts of the country. We emphasize his phrase "unused and unwanted." The "unwantedness" notion corresponds to some extent to Wilson's suggestion that it is a population left behind; but it is a stronger statement. According to Glasgow, not only is this population left behind, it appears to be a population that will be subjected to public neglect or repudiation.

It is in this light that we approach the problem of the marginalization of black men. Black men are withdrawing from the productive spheres of American life. They are literally disappearing, as we described in our popular article, "Where Have All the Black Men Gone?" (1989). Again, the effect is a declining pool of marriageable black men.

Two important dimensions of the declining pool of black men especially concern us. One is the differential mortality rates. While mortality rates have been falling for both black men and black women, they have been falling faster for black women, resulting in a shortage of men in black communities. The other important dimension is the increased institutionalization of black men and their withdrawal from the civilian labor force.

In 1950, the age-adjusted mortality rate for black females of all ages was 1,107 per 100,000; in 1960, it was 917; and, in 1970, it was 814 (U.S. Bureau of the Census, 1971). By 1992, the number of black female deaths per 100,000 resident population had fallen to 575 (U.S. Department of Health and Human Services, 1992). Black women have been experiencing lower death rates and the downward trend seems to be continuing. Mortality rates have been falling for black men as well, but not as rapidly as for black women. In 1950, the age-adjusted number of deaths per 100,000 resident population for black men was 1,373. In 1960, this rate was 1,246 but in 1970, at the height of the Vietnam War, it rose again to 1,317 (U.S. Bureau of the Census, 1971). Today, while the black male death rate is lower in absolute numbers—795 per 100,000 (U.S. Department of Health and Human Services, 1992)—the net effect, because of the more steadily declining mortality rate for black females over the same period, is another decrease in the relative supply of men.

Family Structure

The transition from youth to young adulthood is a very uncertain time for many black men. They have the highest death rate among black males after infants and men over fifty-five. Death in this age period is overwhelmingly due to accidents and violence (i.e., motor vehicle accidents, suicide, homicide, etc.). In 1989, 188 out of every 100,000 black males aged fifteen to twenty-four died as a consequence of an accident or violence (U.S. Bureau of the Census, 1992a). The comparable death rates for black females was 34 per 100,000 and for white males, 107 per 100,000. The death rate for young black men aged fifteen to twenty-four has remained more than four times that of the five- to fourteen-year-olds since 1970. Thus, even though the death rates have fallen, the odds that a young black male will make it to adulthood have not improved.

Among black males in general, the greatest cause of deaths due to accidents and violence is homicide—although the rate has actually declined somewhat in recent decades. In 1970, there were 67.6 homicides per 100,000 black males;

in 1989, that figure was 61.1 (U.S. Bureau of the Census, 1992a). Homicide as a contributor to death among the young has steadily increased. In 1950, one percent of deaths in the fifteen- to twenty-four-year-old group of black males was due to homicides. In 1960, there were 36.7 homicide victimizations per 100,000 young black males; among comparable whites the homicide rate was 3.6 per 100,000. By 1980, the rate among black males rose to 66.6 per 100,000 while for white males it increased to 10.4 per 100,000 (U.S. Bureau of the Census, 1988). Violent death, unfortunately, has increasingly become the fate of these young men, and most of these murders are black men killing other black men (Hidenlang and Langan, 1985).

Marginalization leads to self-destruction. Furthermore, young black males are being drawn out of the labor market and into the criminal market. Labor Department estimates speculate that fully three-quarters of all black males can expect to be arrested at some point during their lives. Myers and Sabol (1988), in their NRC (National Research Council) study on the impact of crime in the black community, argued that imprisoned blacks are not visibly different from blacks free in the community.

In 1970, black inmates made up 41 percent of the federal and state prison populations (U.S. Department of Justice, 1970). By 1990, blacks accounted for 47 percent of the national prison population (U.S. Department of Justice, 1992). Just as black males are many more times likely to be found in the prisons than white males, so too are they overrepresented in the state and county mental hospitals. In 1990, black males comprised 28.8 percent of all males in mental (psychiatric) hospitals. Since blacks represent only 12 percent of the general American population, the overrepresentation is clearly evident.

In addition, alcohol and drug abuse take their toll. Precise numbers on the use of alcohol and illicit substances are difficult to come by. Household surveys indicate lower alcohol use among black males, as compared to white males, but higher use of marijuana, and higher recent use (past year, past month) of cocaine (National Institute on Drug Abuse, 1991). Overall use of PCP is lower among blacks in general, but heroin use is more than double that of whites (National Institute on Drug Abuse, 1991). Still, overall self-reported substance use does not differ greatly by race: 47 percent of black males admitted to ever using an illicit drug, compared to 42 percent of white males. However, figures on hospital and treatment admissions for substance use present another perspective. In 1990, blacks made up 22.4 percent of all males hospitalized for drug or alcohol abuse (U.S. Bureau of the Census, 1992b). Likewise, black males comprised 30 percent of the residents of group homes or halfway houses for drug or alcohol abuse. According to a review by Tucker (1985), there is a disproportionate use of "hard drugs" among blacks and Latinos, and male use is still considerably greater than female use.

A final dimension of the marginalization of black men is seen in the process by which black males have withdrawn from the civilian labor force and entered the armed forces. Blacks make up a large proportion of the military troop population. In the army alone, where blacks traditionally have been concentrated, black representation rose from 15.6 percent in 1972 to 28.7 percent by 1991 (U.S. Bureau of the Census, 1992a). Once in the army, blacks are more likely than whites to reenlist. The reenlistment rate in 1972 after the first term was 20.4 percent for blacks but only 12.6 percent for whites. By 1980, the reenlistment rates rose to 64.6 percent for blacks while white reenlistment rates rose to 43.1 percent.

What is objectionable about this trend? Blacks are crowded into the least desirable jobs the army has to offer. Blacks remain overrepresented in the infantry and gun crews, service and supply occupations, and clerical jobs. They are decidedly underrepresented in the touted "technical specialist" occupations. In 1981, blacks, who accounted for almost one-third of the army's noncivilian personnel, held 42 percent of the clerical jobs. By contrast, blacks were found in less than 25 percent of the technical specialist occupations (Schneider, 1983). In sum, the historical presence of female-headed families in America arguably is linked to the existence and persistence of the marginalized status of black males. A major quantitative index of this marginalization is the size of the pool of unwanted men. This translates into a surplus of unmarried women over marriageable men.

Evidence on Female-Headed Families

Of the over 66 million families in America in 1991, 17 percent or 11.2 million were headed by females (U.S. Bureau of the Census, 1992c). This number is up from 8.7 million in 1980 and 5.5 million in 1970 when there were totals of 59.5 and 51.5 million family units, respectively. Thus, female family headship has grown steadily in the United States in both absolute and relative terms. These trends have accompanied long-term declines in fertility, upward movements in divorce, and increases in the proportion of women who have never married by age twenty-four. Among blacks, the trends are particularly disturbing because fewer and fewer young children are growing up in two-parent homes. The rise in female-headed families among blacks has been swift. While an estimated 28 percent of black families were headed by females in 1970, 46 percent were female headed in 1990. This compares to percentages among white families of 8.9 and 13.2 in 1970 and 1990, respectively (U.S. Bureau of the Census, 1992c).

We hypothesize that an important demographic influence drives changes in black family structures: the reduction in the supply of marriageable mates. This decline in sex ratios creates a "marriage squeeze" and results in the formation of larger numbers of black families headed by females.

The cause of the depletion of the supply of marriageable males rests in increased mortality and institutionalization among black males, which in turn results in a reduction in two-parent families. To test this hypothesis, we must first compute estimates of male supply. We describe this computation below and then turn to results of estimating female-headed family probabilities incorporating these estimates.

Estimates of Sex Ratios

From microdata on individuals it is possible to estimate sex ratios that can be used in our subsequent analysis on families. The scheme is simple: estimate separate equations for the numerator and the denominator of the ratio as functions of independent characteristics. The resulting coefficient estimates can then be applied to the characteristics of family heads in order to compute the sex ratios relevant to the marriage markets apropos to these persons. The details of these estimations are presented in the Technical Appendix at the end of this chapter. Tables 9.1 to 9.4 show the averages of four different sex ratio measures by region. These averages conform to the actual sex ratios for persons over fourteen in 1976 and 1985 and the estimated sex ratios for family heads in those years. The four sex ratios computed are the ratio of males to females; the ratio of unmarried males to unmarried females; the ratio of employed males to females, the Wilson-Neckerman (1986) Male Marriage Pool Index (MMPI); and the ratio of unmarried males in the labor force or in school to unmarried females, a measure of the supply of marriageable males discussed elsewhere by Darity and Myers (1989).

Table 9.1 shows that from 1976 to 1985, for all blacks aged fourteen and over there were small declines in the ratio of males to females, employed males to employed females, and unmarried males in the labor force to unmarried females. Whereas there were about 83.3 black males per 100 black females in 1976, this ratio dropped to 82.9 in 1985; similar small reductions are observed for all but the ratio of unmarried males to unmarried females, which drifted upward imperceptibly. Wide regional variations are evident in each of these measures. Across all measures of sex ratio there are larger deficits of black men in northeastern and north central states relative to the western and southern states.

Considerably larger than the black sex ratios, however measured, are the white sex ratios computed for 1976 and 1985 for individuals fourteen and over, displayed in Table 9.2. For example, while the Wilson-Neckerman measure of the male marriage pool shows sixty to sixty-four employed white males per one hundred white females, among blacks the ratio is only about forty-three per one hundred in both years. And, while there were slight declines in most measures of the sex ratios among blacks from 1976 to 1985, all but the ratio of unmarried males in the labor force or in school to unmarried females rose from 1976 to 1985 among whites. For example, the ratio of white males to white females increased from .8982 to .9356 during those years and much of that

TABLE 9.1

Sex Ratios, Regional Breakdowns, Blacks, 1976 and 1985 (actual)

Actual[a] Sex Ratios	U.S.	Northeast	North Central	South	West
1976					
Males/females	0.8328	0.7884	0.7865	0.8457	0.9677
Unmarried males/unmarried females	0.7266	0.6461	0.6633	0.7592	0.8776
Wilson-Neckerman MMPI	0.4357	0.3386	0.4055	0.4573	0.4782
Darity-Myers marriageable males	0.5228	0.4647	0.4738	0.5440	0.6568
1985					
Males/females	0.8288	0.7853	0.8500	0.8191	0.9555
Unmarried males/unmarried females	0.7383	0.6899	0.7812	0.7198	0.8783
Wilson-Neckerman MMPI	0.4344	0.3858	0.3836	0.4561	0.5408
Darity-Myers marriageable males	0.5163	0.4837	0.5206	0.4997	0.7048

Source: From CPS March Supplement 1976, 1985.

[a] Refers to all individuals fourteen and older.

TABLE 9.2

Sex Ratios, Regional Breakdowns, Whites, 1976 and 1985 (actual)

Actual[a] Sex Ratios	U.S.	Northeast	North Central	South	West
1976					
Males/females	0.8982	0.9514	0.9873	0.8025	0.8728
Unmarried males/unmarried females	0.8238	0.9277	0.8197	0.7580	0.8076
Wilson-Neckerman MMPI	0.6039	0.6067	0.6871	0.5338	0.6044
Darity-Myers marriageable males	0.6490	0.7263	0.6486	0.6019	0.6303
1985					
Males/females	0.9356	0.8933	0.9221	0.9337	1.0021
Unmarried males/unmarried females	0.8759	0.7600	0.8692	0.8294	1.0952
Wilson-Neckerman MMPI	0.6388	0.6341	0.6226	0.6285	0.6815
Darity-Myers marriageable males	0.6374	0.5688	0.6319	0.5492	0.8588

Source: From CPS March Supplement 1976, 1985.

[a] Refers to a 5 percent sample of all individuals fourteen and older.

increase can be attributed to sharp increases in the white sex ratios in the South and West accompanied by declines in the Northeast and north central states.

Tables 9.3 and 9.4 report the estimated sex ratios for black and white family heads in 1976 and 1985. For blacks there are sharp drops in all four measures, with the largest occurring in the ratio of unmarried males to unmarried females followed by the major relative decline in the ratio of unmarried males in the labor force or in school to unmarried females. The Wilson-Neckerman measure only dips a few percentage points during this ten-year period. Indeed, the estimated ratio of employed males to females dropped more among white family heads than it did among black family heads.

In sum, there were small declines in most measures of black sex ratios from 1976 to 1985 using data on individuals. When focus is placed on family heads, the declines are magnified, particularly when marital status is considered. The odds are overwhelmingly against an unmarried black female head of family finding an unmarried male who is in the labor force or in school. According to our estimates, for every one hundred such women there were only thirty-two "marriageable men" in 1985, down from forty-six in 1976.

Female Family Headship

Why is it that among blacks families headed by females have been increasing? Charles Murray and others have said the answer is the inducements generated by the attractiveness of welfare. This is a puzzling line of thought since real welfare benefits have fallen in recent years. The alternative answer is sex ratios. We can examine the impact of depleting supplies of marriageable men on family formation among black and white families in 1976 and 1985.[1] We have estimated female-headship equations as a function of welfare, sex ratios, and several other independent variables. Tables 9.5 to 9.8 show that the Wilson-Neckerman MMPI and the Darity-Myers measure both influence black family structure. For blacks in 1985, neither the ratio of males to females nor the ratio of unmarried males to unmarried females exhibits any significant impact on the probability of female headship. In 1976, all four measures of male supply showed significantly reduced female-headed families among blacks and whites. Among white families in 1985, in contrast, the only measure not influencing female headship is the Wilson-Neckerman measure.[2]

The sex ratio equations include age-interaction terms. Thus, it is not suffi-

---

[1] Intermediate results used in estimating the model and details of the specifications are discussed in the Technical Appendix.

[2] The Wilson measure is the only one that does not diminish for blacks in every region between 1976 and 1985. It shows the smallest decline among the various measures of sex ratios, only falling from .49 in 1976 to .44 in 1985, when the Darity-Myers measure plunged from .46 to .32 in the same period.

TABLE 9.3

Sex Ratios, Regional Breakdowns, Blacks, 1976 and 1985 (estimated)

Estimated[a] Sex Ratios	U.S.	Northeast	North Central	South	West
1976					
Males/females	0.8689	0.8020	0.7718	0.9179	0.9724
Unmarried males/unmarried females	0.6728	0.6772	0.5787	0.6978	0.7495
Wilson-Neckerman MMPI	0.4935	0.3921	0.4410	0.5489	0.5297
Darity-Myers marriageable males	0.4594	0.4692	0.3763	0.4747	0.5513
1985					
Males/females	0.7325	0.7082	0.8024	0.7055	0.7973
Unmarried males/unmarried females	0.4751	0.4469	0.5757	0.4390	0.5319
Wilson-Neckerman MMPI	0.4407	0.4127	0.4014	0.4561	0.5088
Darity-Myers marriageable males	0.3210	0.3016	0.3417	0.3116	0.3800

[a] Refers to all family heads of primary and secondary families.

TABLE 9.4

Sex Ratios, Regional Breakdowns, Whites, 1976 and 1985 (estimated)

Estimated[a] Sex Ratios	U.S.	Northeast	North Central	South	West
1976					
Males/females	0.8873	0.9234	0.9700	0.8070	0.8488
Unmarried males/unmarried females	0.5953	0.6503	0.5725	0.5794	0.5840
Wilson-Neckerman MMPI	0.6480	0.6304	0.7474	0.5771	0.6397
Darity-Myers marriageable males	0.4638	0.4810	0.4492	0.4647	0.4615
1985					
Males/females	0.9645	0.8863	0.9609	0.9817	1.0278
Unmarried males/unmarried females	0.6890	0.5234	0.7193	0.6714	0.8653
Wilson-Neckerman MMPI	0.6809	0.6596	0.6679	0.6798	0.7239
Darity-Myers marriageable males	0.4925	0.3997	0.5146	0.4352	0.6646

[a] Refers to a 10 percent sample of all family heads of primary and secondary families.

TABLE 9.5

Maximum Likelihood Estimates of Logistic Model of Female Family Headship, Blacks, 1985

		Measure of Sex Ratio		
	Male/Female	Unmarried Male/ Unmarried Female	Wilson	Darity-Myers
Constant	2.6924	3.0812	5.0863	3.7984
	(2.77)	(4.309)	(4.99)	(4.954)
Abortion rate	0.0002	0.0002	0.0002	0.0003
	(0.897)	(0.865)	(0.971)	(1.074)
Estimated sex ratio	0.2224	−0.2574	−3.7251	−2.2035
	(0.327)	(−0.567)	(−3.574)	(−2.929)
Expected welfare	0.0003	0.0003	0.0002	0.0003
	(3.584)	(3.476)	(2.613)	(3.106)
Children under age 6	−0.2654	−0.3210	−0.2351	−0.1402
	(−1.771)	(−2.410)	(−2.543)	(−1.110)
Children 6 to 18	0.1065	0.0998	0.1892	0.2002
	(1.55)	(1.458)	(3.242)	(3.232)
Age squared	0.0007	0.0008	0.0014	0.0015
	(2.873)	(3.612)	(3.774)	(5.015)
Age	−0.0818	−0.1055	−0.1873	−0.1734
	(−3.082)	(−4.503)	(−4.660)	(−5.796)
Grade	0.0060	0.0414	0.0058	0.0694
	(0.077)	(0.610)	(0.896)	(1.088)
Grade squared	−0.0053	−0.0066	−0.0063	−0.0065
	(−1.632)	(−2.135)	(−2.057)	(−2.11)
Age × sex ratio	−0.0184	−0.0056	0.0765	0.0649
	(−1.306)	(−0.456)	(3.057)	(2.651)
Chi squared	172.0500	171.8100	182.4400	175.3900

Note: Figures in parentheses are the *t* statistics.

cient to look at the coefficients on sex ratios alone to gauge the extent of the impact of this variable on family structure. In Table 9.9, elasticities are calculated for various age groups. We also compute elasticities for the impacts of expected welfare incomes on family structure. The impact of increased welfare is extremely inelastic for both blacks and whites. A one percent increase in expected AFDC and public assistance income annually will increase the probability that a family head is female by two one-hundredths to ten one-hundredths of one percent.

In 1976, the responsiveness of black family structure to increases in welfare was smaller than that of whites. For whites, the elasticity was almost the size of the black elasticity in 1985, at about .08 percent; for blacks in 1976, the elasticity was not much higher than .02 percent. In 1985, the responsiveness

TABLE 9.6

Maximum Likelihood Estimates of Logistic Model of Female-Headed Families, Whites, 1985

		Measure of Sex Ratio		
	Male/Female	Unmarried Male/ Unmarried Female	Wilson	Darity-Myers
Constant	3.3112	1.7110	−0.1904	1.4921
	(2.014)	(1.402)	(−0.150)	(1.202)
Abortion rate	0.0003	0.0005	0.0006	0.0001
	(.696)	(1.300)	(1.685)	(1.611)
Estimated sex ratio	−2.4338	−2.1141	−1.7814	−3.0811
	(−2.349)	(−2.850)	(−1.492)	(−3.201)
Expected welfare	0.0002	0.0003	0.0002	0.0003
	(1.630)	(1.925)	(1.6)	(1.957)
Children under age 6	−0.3779	−0.5291	−0.2169	−0.4002
	(−3.328)	(−3.609)	(−2.123)	(−2.661)
Children 6 to 18	0.2547	0.1515	0.2368	0.2001
	(4.406)	(2.531)	(4.066)	(3.554)
Age squared	0.0004	0.0007	0.0005	0.0012
	(1.945)	(2.621)	(1.027)	(3.410)
Age	−0.0736	−0.1046	−0.6833	−0.1488
	(−2.274)	(−3.252)	(−1.382)	(−3.691)
Grade	−0.1877	0.0939	0.1335	0.1810
	(−1.264)	(0.856)	(1.399)	(2.061)
Grade squared	0.0048	−0.0082	−0.0086	−0.0112
	(0.761)	(−1.904)	(−1.920)	(−3.016)
Age × sex ratio	0.0143	0.0331	0.0310	0.0769
	(0.673)	(1.797)	(1.028)	(3.606)
Chi squared	83.2450	83.5790	74.2010	82.4890

Note: Figures in parentheses are the *t* statistics.

of blacks to increases in welfare was greater than it was among whites. For whites in 1985, it was about a .025 percent increase for a one percent increase in welfare; for blacks, it was almost .10 percent, or an elasticity nearly five times greater. Does this mean that black families are more likely to become female headed in recent years because of the attractiveness of welfare? Only if welfare incomes are rising. Our computations suggest just the opposite. Welfare incomes fell in real terms between 1976 and 1985; AFDC cutbacks should have resulted in *marginal declines* in fractions of black families headed by females. That this did not happen, even when the elasticities were rising, suggests that factors other than welfare were playing more fundamental roles in influencing the growth in female-headed black families.

TABLE 9.7

Maximum Likelihood Estimates of Logistic Model of Female Family Headship, Blacks, 1976

		Measure of Sex Ratio		
	Male/Female	Unmarried Male/ Unmarried Female	Wilson	Darity-Myers
Constant	5.0516	2.4019	1.1850	1.4702
	(4.923)	(3.310)	(1.530)	(1.944)
Estimated sex ratio	−2.5889	−1.0319	−2.3822	−1.0374
	(−4.550)	(−2.818)	(−2.785)	(−1.915)
Expected welfare	0.0000	0.0001	0.0000	0.0000
	(0.895)	(0.957)	(−0.079)	(0.657)
Children under age 6	−0.3097	−0.3384	−0.0004	−0.2160
	(−3.084)	(−3.133)	(−0.005)	(−2.027)
Children 6 to 18	0.0398	0.0519	0.1230	0.1079
	(0.876)	(1.148)	(2.831)	(2.5)
Age squared	0.0007	0.0008	0.0006	0.0008
	(3.070)	(3.450)	(1.590)	(2.925)
Age	−0.1124	−0.1028	0.2975	−0.1104
	(−4.677)	(−4.540)	(−2.356)	(−3.842)
Grade	0.0192	0.2305	0.2975	0.3395
	(0.172)	(2.928)	(3.868)	(4.733)
Grade squared	−0.0074	−0.0158	−0.0165	−0.0193
	(−1.531)	(−4.148)	(−4.357)	(−5.244)
Age × sex ratio	0.0189	0.0013	0.0303	0.0044
	(1.655)	(0.148)	(1.456)	(0.2850)
Chi squared	162.3100	156.0200	141.7300	140.8400

Note: Figures in parentheses are the *t* statistics.

Except for blacks in 1976, the underlying coefficients on the welfare elastici-ties are generally significant across many specifications. The small elasticity in that year is not significantly different from zero.[3] Expected welfare income dropped sharply for blacks and fell moderately for whites as well between 1976 and 1985. And yet, black and white families experienced growth in the number of female-headed families over that decade. While black expected welfare income dropped in real terms from $760 to $567, the proportion of black families headed by females soared from 36 percent in 1976 to 45 percent in 1985. And, while white expected welfare income dipped from $127 to $105, the proportion

[3] When public housing is accounted for in the female-headed family equations, the effects of AFDC are no longer significant even in 1985. It is unclear whether these estimations are biased since public housing may be endogenous. In any event, this variable is not measured in the 1976 version of the tape we used and thus was dropped in subsequent analysis.

TABLE 9.8

Maximum Likelihood Estimates of Logistic Model of Female Family Headship, Whites, 1976

	Measure of Sex Ratio			
	Male/Female	Unmarried Male/ Unmarried Female	Wilson	Darity-Myers
Constant	−3.0161	1.0549	−1.5822	2.0907
	(−1.988)	(0.560)	(−1.382)	(1.244)
Estimated sex ratio	0.3748	−3.4721	0.1308	−4.2214
	(0.426)	(−3.293)	(0.148)	(−3.658)
Expected welfare	0.0007	0.0007	0.0007	0.0007
	(3.202)	(3.088)	(3.309)	(3.112)
Children under age 6	−0.3234	−0.3114	−0.3608	−0.2166
	(−2.735)	(−1.289)	(−3.101)	(−1.092)
Children 6 to 18	0.0078	0.0886	0.0064	0.0646
	(0.124)	(1.071)	(0.100)	(0.932)
Age squared	0.0005	0.0019	0.0009	0.0023
	(1.944)	(4.672)	(2.211)	(5.094)
Age	−0.0490	−0.2254	−0.0888	−0.2397
	(−1.703)	(−4.266)	(−2.062)	(−4.543)
Grade	0.3958	0.4227	0.3202	0.2488
	(2.184)	(3.476)	(2.524)	(2.502)
Grade squared	−0.0215	−0.0214	−0.0192	−0.0154
	(−2.515)	(−3.927)	(−2.984)	(−3.381)
Age × sex ratio	0.0063	0.1150	0.0151	0.1500
	(0.389)	(4.565)	(0.747)	(5.116)
Chi squared	60.4140	81.5520	61.3140	89.8920

Note: Figures in parentheses are the *t* statistics.

of white families headed by females grew from 11 percent to 13 percent in that decade.

Clearly, then, while white AFDC income changed little, for blacks there was a sharp drop. Welfare cannot be the explanation for the rise in black female-headed families in the intervening years. Since the elasticity is so small, moreover, welfare cannot explain the rise in white female-headed families either.

Since our specification calls for an age-sex ratio interaction, the values of the elasticity of the probability that a family head is female with respect to the sex ratio depends on the age level. For computation we have used ages twenty, thirty, and the average for family heads (with ages ranging from forty-two to forty-eight). As can be seen in the last column of Table 9.9, by the average age, Darity-Myers sex ratio effects tend to become positive while the raw sex ratio generally remains negative. In the instance of white married females in 1976,

TABLE 9.9

Computed Elasticities[a]:
Impacts of Sex Ratios versus Welfare on Family Structure

	Measure of Sex Ratio			
	Male/Female	Unmarried Male/ Unmarried Female	Wilson	Darity-Myers
Blacks, 1985				
Expected welfare	0.1059	0.1056	0.0778	0.0924
Sex ratio				
20 years old	−0.0587	−0.0974	−0.5530	−0.1610
30 years old	−0.1330	−0.1121	−0.3604	−0.0455
Average age	−0.2337	−0.1321	−0.0993	0.1112
Whites, 1985				
Expected welfare	0.0205	0.0243	0.0197	0.0238
Sex ratio				
20 years old	−1.5511	−0.6544	−0.5341	−0.5673
30 years old	−1.4482	−0.5055	−0.3916	−0.2849
Average age	−1.2755	−0.2554	−0.1523	0.1893
Blacks, 1976				
Expected welfare	0.0228	0.0287	−0.0021	0.0196
Sex ratio				
20 years old	−1.2281	−0.4327	−0.5606	−0.2787
30 years old	−1.1234	−0.4271	−0.4651	−0.2657
Average age	−0.9890	−0.4199	−0.3425	−0.2489
Whites, 1976				
Expected welfare	0.0712	0.0708	0.0737	0.0685
Sex ratio				
20 years old	0.3979	−0.0622	0.2504	−0.5048
30 years old	0.4482	−0.0011	0.3377	0.1149
Average age	0.5294	0.0977	0.4789	1.1172

[a]Elasticities measure percentage change in probability of female head for one percent increase in expected welfare income or sex ratio; computed at means of independent variables unless otherwise noted.

the sex ratio is not significant. The Wilson-Neckerman measure is insignificant for whites in both years, although its size for blacks is greater than the size of the Darity-Myers measure. Indeed, the only measure to be statistically significant across all the years and for both races is the ratio of unmarried males in the labor force or in school to unmarried females—that is, the Darity-Myers measure.

This finding suggests to us that a simple demographic measure of sex ratio does not capture the dynamics of changing marriage markets for blacks or whites. The two economically determined measures of marriage markets—the ratio of employed males to females and the ratio of unmarried males in the labor force or in school to unmarried females—show remarkable consistency in determining black family structure in the youngest age groups.

Policy Considerations

In the preceding section we concluded that the impacts of welfare were relatively inelastic in affecting family structure. While we argued that the impacts of sex ratios were larger than those of welfare, these too were found to be inelastic. The critical question, then, is: How much does welfare matter relative to changing marriage opportunities among blacks and whites? We address this question in two ways.

First, we examine the simple impacts of welfare and sex ratio changes on black and white family structures from 1976 to 1985. Rather than asking what would probabilities of female headship be if there were a one percent increase in welfare and/or sex ratios, we simulate what these probabilities would have been had welfare and sex ratios remained at their 1976 levels. We also compute the 1976 and the 1985 black probabilities for black female headship assuming that blacks had the same sex ratios and expected welfare benefits as whites.

Second, we examine the more complicated simulations wherein characteristics of blacks and whites are allowed to vary as well as the inclusion of their sex ratios and expected welfare incomes. We then forecast female-headship probabilities for the year 2000, under various assumptions about the changes in sex ratios, welfare incomes, and other characteristics.

We conclude that even under the most optimistic assessments of slowing in the growth of the surplus of women, the black-white gap in family structure is likely to persist for some time to come. The impacts of welfare, it appears, largely have played themselves out. Further reductions in welfare are unrealistic and in any event would curb the growth of female-headed families by less than what can be expected through reduced depletion of the supply of marriageable mates.

Changes in Welfare and Sex Ratios: 1976 and 1985

Table 9.10 displays results from simulations of changes in sex ratios and expected welfare on the probability of female family headship. Four experiments are performed. First, we assume that expected welfare benefits remained unchanged between 1976 and 1985. The effect is to increase the proportion of black families headed by females by a little more than one percentage point. In other words, had the nearly $200 drop in real expected welfare income not materialized in 1985, there would have been an approximate 1.3 percentage

TABLE 9.10

Policy Simulations: Probability of Female-Headed Family, 1976 and 1985

	1976		1985	
	Blacks	Whites	Blacks	Whites
Estimated probability of female head	0.352894	0.096275	0.447566	0.123891
Expected welfare unchanged, 1976–85	0.352894	0.096275	0.461004	0.124121
Darity-Myers sex ratio unchanged, 1976–85	0.352894	0.096275	0.374857	0.111393
Blacks with white Darity-Myers sex ratios	0.352248	0.096275	0.393822	0.123891
Blacks with white expected welfare	0.346967	0.096275	0.414527	0.123891

Note: Simulations ignore age changes and age/sex ratio interactions.

points increase in the proportion of black families headed by females than did indeed occur. The proportion of white families headed by females would have been virtually the same with or without the change in welfare.

Next, we assume that sex ratios, measured by the ratio of unmarried men in the labor force or in school to unmarried women, remained unchanged between 1976 and 1985. For blacks and whites, this would mean an increase over the actual 1985 supply of men. Thus, the third row of Table 9.10 shows that for blacks and whites the 1985 proportion of families headed by females would have been lower—considerably lower for blacks—had sex ratios not dropped between 1976 and 1985. Instead of 45 percent of black families being headed by females, 37 percent of black families would have been female headed had the sex ratio remained stable.

In our third and fourth simulations, we consider the impacts of racially different sex ratios and expected welfare incomes. We ask whether the proportion of black families headed by females would have been much different in 1976 or 1985 had blacks faced the same expected welfare incomes or sex ratios as whites. The next to last row of Table 9.10 shows the impacts of racially identical sex ratios. There is virtually no impact in 1976 on the black proportion of families headed by females. In 1985, in contrast, black sex ratios fell dramatically from their 1976 levels. When white sex ratios were nearer to the 1976 black sex ratios, the effect was to reduce sharply the proportion of black families headed by females. Noticeably smaller impacts are registered for the simulated racially equated expected welfare incomes: black proportions of families headed by females drop from one to three percentage points when blacks receive white (and therefore lower) expected welfare incomes.

These simple simulations confirm what is already evident from the computed elasticities. While increases in expected welfare benefits tend to increase female headship, the magnitude of this welfare effect is small and is not as large as the impacts of reduced supplies of marriageable men.

Forecasts to Year 2000

As we have seen in the previous simulations, welfare changes will not fundamentally alter the pattern of family structures between blacks and whites in the short run. But what about the long run? What about the next generation, in the next several decades when the children of today's unwed mothers reach childbearing age? To answer this question, we must make often heroic assumptions about how the underlying factors influencing not only female headship but also sex ratios and welfare, age distributions, and educational attainment will change.

The dramatic changes in black family structures in the past generation may foreshadow even more alarming transformations in the future. There are essentially two major scenarios with vastly different implications for the black two-parent family over the next decades. One possible scenario is that the current pattern of reduced supplies of marriageable males will result in future generations of even greater numbers of black families headed by females and eventually virtually all black children will be raised in single-parent families. The other major scenario is one in which welfare continues to erode (according to our cross-sectional estimates, female headedness should diminish slightly), families will become older, and the sex ratio impacts will be less severe. In the latter case, the current crisis of female headedness must be viewed as an anomaly and the aging of the black family as a catalyst for the return to more normal patterns of two-parent family structures. In the former case, one speculates that the children of this generation's female-headed families will be struck as hard by the male shortage in the years to come as were their mothers. The effect, then, will be the formation of even younger female-headed families than we now observe in the 1980s.

We use the estimated model to forecast the proportion of black and white families headed by females to year 2000 to capture these two scenarios. We employ different methods to derive the forecasts, adopting a variety of assumptions about what changes and why. But the demarcation between the two scenarios lies in whether family heads are younger or older in the next generation and the conclusions are not critically dependent upon which other set of assumptions or forecasting method is employed. If the next generation's heads of families are younger, with average ages of twenty-five or thirty for example, then a substantial number of them will be females. In contrast, if the heads of families are older, then perhaps fewer new families will form and a greater proportion of families will be formed via marriage. The impact will be to increase the proportion of two-parent families.

Table 9.11 shows the results of our forecasts. There are three methods represented. In the first method, we use the averages of the coefficient estimates from the female-headed equations in 1976 and 1985 and the forecasts of the independent variables to year 2000. This method asks, what would female headship be in year 2000 if the determinants of female headship were all exogenous and they grew at the current rates through 2000? In the second method, the 1985 values of all independent variables in the female-headed family equation, except sex ratios and expected welfare, are held at their 1985 levels. Sex ratios and expected welfare are forecasted to year 2000 and then are inserted into the female-headship equation in order to derive this method's forecast. In the third method, we use the full simultaneous equation estimates of coefficients for 1985 and permit the forecasts of all the model's independent variables to drive the model's endogenous variables. Thus, age and education, which directly affect female headship, also indirectly affect our forecasts because of their impacts on welfare and on sex ratios.

Another important trend germane to the incidence of female headship is the growth of single-person households. While our simulations do not address this issue directly, they do point to the likelihood that even if younger, childless women choose not to marry and to instead form single-person households, reducing the numbers of new family formations, there still could be a growth of female-headed families in the years to come as fewer and fewer of these new family formations are the results of marriage or remarriage.

Conclusion

The decline in the supply of marriageable mates has dire consequences for the future of black families. If the effects of violent crime, homicide, incarceration, and other aspects of the marginalization of black men rob the next generation of fathers and husbands and the next generation's mothers form families at earlier and earlier ages, then our best estimates suggest that the vast majority of all black families will be female headed by year 2000. These families will be poor and increasingly isolated from the mainstream of American society. Curbing welfare will have no effect in halting this trend. And, unfortunately, not much hope seems to exist for slowing the withdrawal of young black men from productive spheres of the economy.

It is also not enough, according to our estimates, to speak of making blacks more like whites. If, of course, blacks had higher sex ratios, as a result of having had equal access to the labor market and education opportunities, then there would be far fewer female-headed families in the black community. Despite this evidence, when some contemporary writers speak of reducing the social isolation of the black underclass, they speak as if the values and the morals of low-income persons would be elevated via proximity to the middle class. In

TABLE 9.11

Forecast of Female-Headed Families to the Year 2000 (FHH 2000)

| | \multicolumn{6}{c}{Average Age of Head} | | Trend Average[d] | |
| | 25 | | 30 | | 35 | | | |
	Black	White	Black	White	Black	White	Black	White
Method 1[a]								
Wilson-Neckerman FHH 2000	0.555698	0.160078	0.480906	0.138954	0.419312	0.123883	0.339447	0.105390
Darity-Myers FHH 2000	0.601733	0.183330	0.510072	0.143350	0.431973	0.119697	0.327715	0.105885
Method 2[b]								
Wilson-Neckerman FHH 2000	0.564473	0.137536	0.489801	0.118966	0.428008	0.105796	0.412289	0.105519
Darity-Myers FHH 2000	0.606959	0.159800	0.515532	0.124171	0.437344	0.103301	0.407365	0.133288
Method 3[c]								
Wilson-Neckerman FHH 2000	0.324400	0.041367	0.300041	0.048012	0.291455	0.096117	0.309587	0.079161
Darity-Myers FHH 2000	0.556014	0.277099	0.491129	0.225031	0.444853	0.189257	0.360354	0.137898

[a]From female-headed family equation using forecasted value of independent variables and mean of 1976 and 1985 coefficients.
[b]From female-headed family equation using 1985 means of independent variables, forecasted values for expected welfare and sex ratio, and mean of 1976 and 1985 coefficients.
[c]From full model with forecasted values of independent variables for all equations and 1985 coefficients.
[d]Forecasted age in year 2000: blacks 44.75 years; whites 47.82 years.

this reasoning, the black underclass would be more mainstream, more white, by having middle-class neighbors.

This policy option of eliminating social isolation by attempting to narrow the gap between the characteristics of the black underclass and the middle class, in our estimation, will not assure that black family structures will stabilize, in much the same way that eliminating welfare will not assure black family stabilization. Changing the characteristics of underclass persons without affecting the adverse conditions that they face and the probable lack of opportunities that they confront, will in all likelihood leave them as far behind the mainstream in the future as they are in the present.

Implicit in our pessimistic assessment of contemporary policies to eradicate the blight affecting the black family is the view that the broader patterns of socioeconomic change dominate the current crisis. We are not so pessimistic, however, as to ignore temporary, even stopgap, measures that may be effective in reducing the deleterious impacts of these forces on black families.

Three types of policies are of direct short-term benefit to black families and may even have long-term impacts to halt the decline in marriageable mates. Transfer payments and policies designed to elevate the incomes of the poor present the most immediate choice. Since our estimates show that the decline in real welfare benefits has failed to curb the growth in female-headed families, the focus of transfer policies should revert back to the goal of lifting the poor out of poverty. Concerns about the detrimental disincentives of such policies seem moot in light of the long-term evidence that black families will sink deeper into a crisis of female headship with or without welfare. Better a world of welfare-dependent, near-poor families than one of welfare-free but desolate and permanently poor families.

A second strategy should be directed toward improving the health care of poor women and their children. In the most pessimistic scenario, this will amount to admitting our failure to curb the growth of female-headed families but acknowledging our social obligation to provide adequate prenatal, infant, and child care. A more optimistic tone arises if one accepts the contention of Guttentag and Secord (1983) that the quality of prenatal and child health care is one of the determinants of sex ratios. By assuring quality health care now, we may help stem the tide toward further depletion of young black males in the future.

A third policy calls for an improvement in the education of the underclass. An overhaul of the entire educational system may be needed to achieve this goal, but even simple initiatives like stay-in-school programs and college incentive awards to elementary school students promise to yield benefits for the next generation.

In sum, there is a major unresolved policy dilemma facing the African American community. The factors most closely associated with the destruction of the family and the marginalization of its young men may be factors that are global and a part of broader socioeconomic changes which are not under the control of black people and their community leaders. Widely heralded public policies, like those of curbing welfare growth or removing the social isolation of the underclass from the middle class, will be ineffective. While short-term ameliorative policies do exist—increased transfer payments, improved health care, better schools—in the long term, the future of the black community hinges upon the future of an economy that seems to have less and less need for the lowest-earning workers that the black community has provided for three hundred years.

AUTHOR NOTES

This chapter is condensed from sections of "The Problem of Family Structure, Earnings Inequality and the Marginalization of Black Men," presented at the Western Economic Association Meetings, Lake Tahoe, Nevada, June 1989, a revised version of "Measuring Inequality and Illusions of Black Economic Progress," presented at the Association for Public Policy and Management annual research conference, Seattle, Washington, October 27–30, 1988. An earlier version with the title, "Is There a Crisis in the Black Community? The Problem of Family Structure, Earnings Inequality and the Marginalization of Black Men," was presented at the American Economic Association Meetings, Chicago, Illinois, December 1987. Research presented here is supported by the Institute for Research on Poverty, University of Wisconsin and uses a data set compiled with the assistance of Dr. Tsze Chan. Programming assistance was provided by Dr. Chan with support from the University of Maryland, College of Behavioral and Social Sciences. Additional research assistance was rendered by Stacey Jordon and Kevin Hart.

REFERENCES

BECKER, G.S., LANDES, E.M., AND MICHAEL, R.T. December 1977. An economic analysis of marital instability. *Journal of Political Economy,* 85:1141–1187.

BISHOP, J.J. 1980. Jobs, cash transfers and marital instability: A review and synthesis of evidence. *Journal of Human Resources,* 15:301–334.

CAIN, G.G., AND WISSOKER, D.A. Winter 1987–1988. Do income maintenance programs break up marriages? A reevaluation of SIME-DIME. *Focus,* 10(4). University of Wisconsin-Madison, Institute for Research on Policy.

CHERLIN, A.J. 1981. *Marriage, divorce, remarriage,* pp. 6–31. Cambridge, MA: Harvard University Press.

COX, O. 1940. Sex ratio and marital status among negroes. *American Sociological Review,* 5:937–947.

DANZIGER, S., JACOBSON, G., SCHWARTZ, S., AND SMOLENSKY, E. 1982. Work and welfare as determinants of female proverty and household headship. *The Quarterly Journal of Economics,* 97:519–534.

DARITY, W., JR., AND MYERS, S., JR. May 1983. Changes in black family structure: Implication for welfare dependency. *American Economic Review,* 73:59–64.

DARITY, W., JR., AND MYERS, S., JR. November 1984a. Does welfare dependency cause female headship? The case of the black family. *Journal of Marriage and the Family,* 46:765–780.

DARITY, W., JR., AND MYERS, S., JR. 1984b. Public policy and the conditions of the black family life. *Review of the Black Political Economy,* 1 & 2:165–187.

DARITY, W., JR., AND MYERS, S., JR. 1989. Where have all the black men gone? *Black Excellence,* 1(2):29–31.

DARITY, W., JR., AND MYERS, S., JR. June 1989. *The problem of family structure, earnings inequality and the marginalization of black men.* Paper presented at the Western Economic Association Meetings, Lake Tahoe, Nevada.

DARITY, W. A., AND MYERS, S.L. 1990. Impacts of violent crime on black family structure. *Contemporary Policy Issues,* 8:15–19.

DUNCAN, G.J., AND HOFFMAN, S.D. December 1986a. *Race and family structure: Assessing the role of labor markets, marriage markets, AFDC benefits and individual preferences.* Presented at the American Economic Association Meeting, New Orleans, LA.

DUNCAN, G.J., AND HOFFMAN, S.D. August 7, 1986b. *Remarriage and welfare choices of divorced women.* Unpublished paper. University of Michigan/University of Delaware, sponsored by NICHD.

ELLWOOD, D.T., AND BANE, M.J. 1985. The impact of AFDC on family structure and living arrangements. *JAI Press, Research in Labor Economics,* 7.

GLASGOW, D.G. 1980. *The black underclass: Poverty, unemployment and entrapment of ghetto youth.* San Francisco: Jossey-Bass.

GUTTENTAG, M., AND SECORD, P.F. 1983. *Too many women? The sex ratio question.* Beverly Hills: Sage Publications.

HINDELANG, M., AND LANGAN, P. 1985. *Prisoners in 1983.* Washington, DC: U.S. Department of Justice.

HUTCHENS, R.W. June 1979. Welfare, remarriage and marital search. *American Economic Review,* 69(3):369–379.

JACKSON, J. 1978. But where are the black men? In Robert Staples, ed., *The Black Family: Essays and Studies.* Belmont, CA: Wadsworth.

LERMAN, R.I. 1989. Employment opportunities of young men and family formations. *American Economic Review,* 79(2):62–74.

LOURY, G.C. November 1985. *The family as context for delinquency prevention: Demographic trends and political realities.* Unpublished manuscript. Kennedy School of Government, Harvard University, Cambridge, MA.

MCLANAHAN, S. 1985. Family structure and reproduction of poverty. *American Journal of Sociology,* 9:873–901.

MURRAY, C.A. 1984. *Losing ground: American social policy, 1950–1980.* New York: Basic Books.

MYERS, S.L., JR., AND SABOL, W.J. January 1988. *Crime and the black community: Issues in the understanding of race and crime in America.* Report for the National Research Council's Political Participation Sub-Committee of the Committee on the Status of Black Americans.

NATIONAL INSTITUTE ON DRUG ABUSE. 1991. *National household survey on drug abuse: Highlights 1990*. DHHS Publication No. (ADM) 91–1732. Washington, DC: U.S. Government Printing Office.

POLLAK, R.A. April 1985. *The two-sex problem with persistent unions: A generalization of the birth matrix-mating rule model*. Preliminary Draft, University of Pennsylvania, Philadelphia.

RODGERS, W.L., AND THORNTON, A. 1985. Changing patterns of first marriage in the United States. *Demography,* 22:265–279.

SAMPSON, R.J. September 1987. Urban black violence: The effect of male joblessness and family disruption. *American Journal of Sociology,* 93:348–382.

SCHNEIDER, A. 1983. Black in the military. *The state of black America*. New York: National Urban League.

SHAW, L.B. 1983. High school completions for young women: Impacts of low-income and living with a single parent. *Journal of Family Issues,* 3:147–163.

STROBINO, D.M., AND SIRAGELDIN, I. December 1981. Racial differences in early marriage in the United States. *Social Science Quarterly,* 62:758–766.

TUCKER, M.B. 1985. U.S. ethnic minorities and drug abuse: An assessment of the science and practice. *The International Journal of the Addictions,* 20:1021–1047.

TUCKER, M.B., AND MITCHELL-KERNAN, C. In press. Mate availability among African Americans: Conceptual and methodological issues. In R. Jones, ed., *Advances in black psychology*. Hampton, VA: Cobb & Henry.

U.S. BUREAU OF THE CENSUS. 1971. *Statistical abstracts of the U.S.: 1971*. 92nd ed. Washington, DC: U.S. Government Printing Office.

U.S. BUREAU OF THE CENSUS. 1986. *Statistical abstracts of the U.S.: 1986*. 106th edition, Tables 202, 619. Washington, DC: U.S. Government Printing Office.

U.S. BUREAU OF THE CENSUS. April 1986. *The survey of income and program participation*. Washington, DC: U.S. Government Printing Office.

U.S. BUREAU OF THE CENSUS. 1987. *Statistical abstracts of the U.S.: 1987*. 107th edition, Tables 608, 609, and 611, pp. 357–359. Washington, DC: U.S. Government Printing Office.

U.S. BUREAU OF THE CENSUS. 1988. *Statistical abstracts of the U.S.: 1988*. 108th edition. Washington, DC: U.S. Government Printing Office.

U.S. BUREAU OF THE CENSUS. September 1988. Households, families, marital status and living arrangements: March 1988 (Advance Reports, series P-20). *Current Population Reports, 432*. Washington, DC: U.S. Government Printing Office.

U.S. BUREAU OF THE CENSUS. 1992a. *Statistical abstracts of the U.S.: 1992*. 112th edition, Tables 115 and 122. Washington, DC: U.S. Government Printing Office.

U.S. BUREAU OF THE CENSUS. 1992b. *1990 Census of the Population: General Populations Characteristics. United States*. (Publication no. 1990 CP-1-1). Washington, DC: U.S. Government Printing Office.

U.S. BUREAU OF THE CENSUS. 1992c. Household and family characteristics: March 1991 (Series P-20, No. 458). *Current Population Reports*. Washington, DC: U.S. Government Printing Office.

U.S. DEPARTMENT OF HEALTH AND HUMAN SERVICES. 1984. *United States 1982*. Washington, DC: U.S. Government Printing Office.

U.S. DEPARTMENT OF HEALTH AND HUMAN SERVICES. June 26, 1992. *Monthly Vital Statistics Report,* 41(2). Hyattsville, MD: Public Health Center for Health Statistics.

U.S. DEPARTMENT OF JUSTICE. 1992. Correctional populations in the United States, 1990. Publication no. NCJ-134946. Washington, DC: U.S. Government Printing Office.

WILSON, W.J. 1982. *The declining significance of race.* 2nd ed. Chicago: University of Chicago Press.

WILSON, W.J. 1987. *The truly disadvantaged: The inner city, the underclass, and public policy.* Chicago: University of Chicago Press.

WILSON, W.J., AND NECKERMAN, K.M. 1986. Poverty and family structure: The widening gap between evidence and public policy issues. In S.H. Danziger and D.H. Weinberg, eds., *Fighting poverty: What works and what doesn't.* Cambridge, MA: Harvard University Press.

Technical Appendix

Sex Ratio Derivation

Our measure of marriage supply is UMLF/UF, or the ratio of unmarried men in the labor force or in school to the number of unmarried women. Dividing both the numerator and the denominator by population and regarding the resulting fractions as probabilities, then:

$$MF = UMLF/UF = P(UMLF)/P(UF).$$

We assume that increases in mortality or institutionalization contribute to the decline in the availability of marriageable men. Since violent death and institutionalization are themselves functions of marginality, we must either specify and estimate simultaneously structural equations for both or derive reduced-form estimates of the sex ratios in question based on the underlying structural model. We primarily focus on the latter strategy.

We can specify, then, individual-specific measures of the ratio of unmarried males in the labor force to unmarried females from a reduced-form logistic model for the probability that a sample respondent was an unmarried male in the labor force ($\text{Pr}[(\text{UMLF}])$) and for the probability that a sample respondent was an unmarried female ($\text{Pr}[\text{UF}]$). These predictive equations, dependent on mortality ratios and institutionalization rates, can be used to compute in the sample of family heads the following sex ratio:

$$(UMLF/UF) = \text{Pr}[UMLF]/\text{Pr}[UF]$$

where

$$\text{Pr}[*] = 1/(1 + \exp(-Xb))$$

Similar procedures can be used to compute alternative measures of sex ratios. The alternatives we consider are:

Ratio of Males to Females:

$$Pr[M]/Pr[F]$$

Ratio of Unmarried Males to Unmarried Females:

$$Pr[UM]/Pr[UF]$$

Ratio of Employed Males to Females (Wilson-Neckerman):

$$Pr[EmpM]/Pr[F]$$

where in each case,

$$Pr[*] = 1/(1 + \exp(-Xb))$$

Factors in the X vector include age, education, region, central city location, state unemployment rates, and the presence of young children in the household. The impacts of these variables will vary depending upon the measure of sex ratio chosen. Our preferred measure, $Pr[UMLF]/Pr[UF]$, ought to fall as men and women age, when there are children present in the household, and when state unemployment rates rise. The effects of education are ambiguous because more educated men are more likely to be in the labor force—increasing the numerator—but less likely to be unmarried. And, more educated women are more likely to be unmarried—increasing the denominator. Whether the ratio rises or falls for more educated men and women is problematic. Among less educated persons, however, we can conjecture that the ratio rises for increases in education as the status of the male is elevated by increased labor force participation. This increased ratio also probably offsets the decline in marriage probability among women through similar increased education. We also expect lower supplies of marriageable men in the North and in central cities.

Tables A9.1 to A9.4 display the underlying equations used in estimating the sex ratios. The coefficient estimates come from Current Population Survey (CPS) March Supplement data on individuals aged fourteen and over. In these reduced-form results, we find that the unconditional probabilities of being unmarried and female or unmarried and male fall as one ages but that the probability of being employed and male rises as one ages. This is true for blacks and whites in 1976 and 1985. Such consistently strong effects are not found for education. For example, while more years of education increase the probability

TABLE A9.1

Maximum Likelihood Estimates of Logistic Models
of Underlying Equations Used to Estimate Sex Ratios, Blacks, 1985

	P(Male)	P(Female)	P(Unmarried Male)
Constant	−1.9266	−1.9266	−2.6144
	(−0.510)	(−0.510)	(−0.516)
Age	−0.0301	−0.0301	−0.1136
	(−.760)	(−.760)	(−2.190)
Age squared	−0.0002	−0.0002	0.0006
	(−1.880)	(−1.880)	(4.433)
Grade	−0.0791	−0.0791	−0.0921
	(−1.759)	(−1.759)	(−1.725)
Grade squared	0.0007	0.0007	−0.0021
	(0.342)	(0.342)	(−0.842)
Central city	−0.0865	−0.0865	0.1217
	(−1.144)	(−1.144)	(1.310)
Northeast	−0.1905	−0.1905	−0.2532
	(−1.255)	(−1.255)	(−1.355)
North Central	−0.0536	−0.0536	−0.0132
	(−0.357)	(−0.357)	(−0.072)
South	−0.1318	−0.1318	−0.1879
	(−0.913)	(−0.913)	(−1.0510)
State unemployment rate	0.0028	0.0028	0.0199
	(0.112)	(0.112)	(0.658)
Male institutionalization rate	0.1462	0.1462	0.6587
	(0.368)	(0.368)	(1.221)
Age × mortality ratio	0.0230	0.0230	0.0017
	(0.866)	(0.866)	(0.048)
Mortality ratio	3.8688	3.8688	6.6262
	(0.773)	(0.773)	(0.980)
Children 6 to 18	−0.1669	−0.1669	−0.3606
	(−3.835)	(−3.835)	(−8.743)
Children under 6	−0.4805	−0.4805	−1.8568
	(−6.803)	(−6.803)	(−12.504)
Mortality ratio squared	−1.2645	−1.2645	−1.7830
	(−0.751)	(−0.751)	(−0.779)
Institutionalization rate squared	−0.0241	−0.0241	−0.1479
	(−0.297)	(−0.297)	(−1.317)
Chi squared	109.1300	109.1300	679.1500

Note: Figures in parentheses are the *t* statistics.

P(Unmarried Female)	P(Employed Male)	P(Unmarried Male in Work Force or in School)	Mean
1.5709	−5.7492	−9.1348	
(0.397)	(−1.249)	(−1.490)	
−0.0729	0.0944	0.0713	38.4080
(−1.844)	(1.608)	(0.943)	
0.0009	−0.0021	−0.0002	1800.7000
(−7.863)	(−10.710)	(−0.902)	
0.0050	0.1392	0.5067	12.0100
(0.110)	(2.172)	(0.698)	
−0.0016	−0.0052	−0.0059	155.1600
(−0.079)	(−1.943)	(−1.846)	
0.1609	−0.2553	0.0223	0.5468
(2.092)	(−2.900)	(0.220)	
0.0179	−0.2015	−0.0738	0.1904
(0.117)	(−1.143)	(−0.364)	
−0.0163	−0.1783	−0.0236	0.2074
(−0.107)	(−1.018)	(−0.117)	
−0.1233	−0.0452	0.0406	0.5196
(−0.846)	(−0.274)	(0.209)	
−0.0276	−0.0485	0.0150	7.7035
(−1.107)	(−1.654)	(0.452)	
−0.2569	−0.4206	0.3607	2.3694
(−0.651)	(−0.906)	(0.635)	
−0.0055	0.0510	−0.0899	54.5490
(−0.207)	(1.268)	(−1.774)	
0.8568	4.6497	10.0410	1.4202
(0.161)	(0.752)	(1.249)	
0.0693	−0.1455	−0.0277	0.8514
(2.302)	(−3.886)	(−6.504)	
0.0570	−0.2235	−1.7192	0.2269
(0.888)	(−2.847)	(−10.655)	
−0.5949	−2.1336	−2.0779	1.4202
(−0.325)	(−0.991)	(−6.504)	
0.0276	0.0781	−0.0559	5.8280
(0.344)	(0.825)	(−0.481)	
93.2910	249.5200	640.0400	

TABLE A9.2

Maximum Likelihood Estimates of Logistic Models
of Underlying Equations Used to Estimate Sex Ratios, Whites, 1985

	P(Male)	P(Female)	P(Unmarried Male)
Constant	−2.3017	−2.3017	3.3434
	(−0.775)	(−0.775)	(0.778)
Age	−0.0130	−0.0130	−0.1419
	(−0.607)	(−0.607)	(−4.533)
Age squared	0.0001	0.0001	0.0015
	(0.696)	(0.696)	(12.654)
Grade	−0.2181	−0.2181	−0.3063
	(−5.115)	(−5.115)	(−5.899)
Grade squared	0.0096	0.0096	0.0098
	(5.724)	(5.724)	(4.582)
Central city	−0.1957	−0.1957	0.0176
	(−2.952)	(−2.952)	(0.193)
Northeast	−0.0828	−0.0828	−0.3102
	(−0.913)	(−0.913)	(−2.492)
North Central	−0.0680	−0.0680	−0.1683
	(−0.770)	(−0.770)	(−1.398)
South	−0.1643	−0.1643	−0.3178
	(−1.765)	(−1.765)	(−2.441)
State unemployment rate	−0.0011	−0.0011	−0.0296
	(−0.064)	(−0.064)	(−1.237)
Male institutionalization rate	0.1788	0.1788	0.0675
	(0.665)	(0.665)	(0.175)
Age × mortality ratio	−0.0006	−0.0006	−0.0362
	(−0.039)	(−0.039)	(−1.496)
Mortality ratio	5.1379	5.1379	3.0512
	(1.198)	(1.198)	(0.486)
Children 6 to 18	0.0273	0.0273	−0.2822
	(0.929)	(0.929)	(−6.366)
Children under 6	−0.1138	−0.1138	−1.4637
	(−2.279)	(−2.279)	(−11.914)
Mortality ratio squared	−1.6467	−1.6467	−0.7428
	(−1.055)	(−1.055)	(−0.323)
Institutionalization rate squared	−0.0196	−0.0196	−0.0103
	(−0.818)	(−0.818)	(−0.304)
Chi squared	81.6470	81.6470	1022.1000

Note: Figures in parentheses are the t statistics.

P(Unmarried Female)	P(Employed Male)	P(Unmarried Male in Work Force or in School)	Mean
9.0103	−7.0868	−0.9647	
(2.490)	(−2.136)	(−0.202)	
−0.1720	0.1698	−0.0603	41.6290
(−7.029)	(5.608)	(−1.254)	
0.0016	−0.0019	0.0004	2081.2000
(16.266)	(−14.466)	(2.297)	
0.0093	−0.0040	−0.1465	13.2110
(0.175)	(−0.075)	(−1.969)	
−0.0089	0.0034	0.0052	184.0200
(−0.420)	(1.651)	(1.796)	
0.5035	−0.2116	0.0758	0.2267
(6.391)	(−2.836)	(0.754)	
0.2522	−0.0264	−0.2839	0.2185
(2.233)	(−0.265)	(−2.101)	
0.0813	−0.1269	−0.2094	0.2566
(0.718)	(−1.305)	(−1.589)	
−0.2319	−0.0705	0.5228	0.3147
(1.938)	(−0.687)	(−3.640)	
0.0081	0.0008	−0.0660	7.5584
(0.385)	(0.043)	(−2.444)	
−0.3554	0.3398	−0.1035	1.0520
(−1.013)	(1.128)	(−0.244)	
0.0083	−0.0152	−0.0414	51.3830
(0.443)	(0.662)	(−1.115)	
−9.1964	4.3513	5.7435	1.2323
(−1.757)	(0.920)	(0.836)	
−0.1354	−0.0254	−0.2263	0.5727
(−3.344)	(−0.801)	(−4.840)	
−0.7921	−0.0264	−1.5988	0.2320
−8.4950	(−0.506)	(−10.925)	
2.9227	−1.3744	−1.6044	1.5265
(1.531)	(−.802)	(−0.641)	
0.0364	−0.0323	0.0054	2.1065
(1.186)	(−1.225)	(0.144)	
536.5300	604.3000	941.6300	

TABLE A9.3

Maximum Likelihood Estimates of Logistic Models
of Underlying Equations Used to Estimate Sex Ratios, Blacks, 1976

	P(Male)	P(Female)	P(Unmarried Male)
Constant	2.1023	2.1023	5.2363
	(1.995)	(1.995)	(4.144)
Age	−0.0196	−0.0196	−0.1725
	(−1.004)	(−1.004)	(−6.508)
Age squared	−0.0003	−0.0003	0.0008
	(−2.452)	(−2.452)	(5.167)
Grade	−0.2187	−0.2187	−0.1460
	(−4.237)	(−4.237)	(−2.426)
Grade squared	0.0070	0.0070	0.0007
	(2.968)	(2.968)	(0.235)
Central city	−0.0708	−0.0708	−0.0347
	(−0.857)	(−0.857)	(−0.338)
Northeast	−0.0017	−0.0017	0.0064
	(−0.010)	(−0.010)	(0.030)
North Central	−0.1374	−0.1374	−0.2561
	(−0.701)	(−0.701)	(−1.057)
South	0.0170	0.0170	−0.2840
	(0.086)	(0.086)	(−1.172)
State unemployment rate	0.0244	0.0244	−0.0673
	(0.345)	(0.345)	(−0.755)
Male institutionalization rate	0.1587	0.1587	0.2087
	(0.713)	(0.713)	(0.760)
Age × mortality ratio	0.0212	0.0212	0.0401
	(1.774)	(1.774)	(2.387)
Mortality ratio	−0.1461	−0.1461	0.3365
	(−0.106)	(−0.106)	(0.190)
Children 6 to 18	−0.0993	−0.0993	−0.1819
	(−4.310)	(−4.310)	(−6.115)
Children under 6	−0.2929	−0.2929	−1.4030
	(−4.562)	(−4.562)	(−10.695)
Mortality ratio squared	−0.2811	−0.2811	−0.8241
	(−0.483)	(−0.483)	(−1.057)
Institutionalization rate squared	−0.0068	−0.0068	−0.0209
	(−0.099)	(−0.099)	(−0.249)
Chi squared	92.5010	92.5010	473.2800

Note: Figures in parentheses are the *t* statistics.

P(Unmarried Female)	P(Employed Male)	P(Unmarried Male in Work Force or in School)	Mean
− 0.8708	− 2.7358	2.7138	
(− 0.744)	(− 2.184)	(1.844)	
− 0.0651	0.1750	− 0.0703	37.4050
(− 3.165)	(6.399)	(− 1.934)	
0.0014	− 0.0026	− 0.0005	1734.6000
(11.144)	(− 12.397)	(− 1.904)	
0.1049	− 0.0501	− 0.0030	11.3710
(1.846)	(− 0.846)	(− 0.039)	
− 0.0039	0.0032	− 0.0044	140.7200
(− 1.495)	(1.177)	(− 1.252)	
0.1943	− 0.1219	0.0256	0.5852
(2.153)	(− 1.236)	(0.222)	
− 0.1700	− 0.0574	− 0.0960	0.1887
(− 0.875)	(− 0.267)	(− 0.398)	
− 0.0072	0.0579	− 0.5086	0.1968
(− 0.034)	(0.241)	(− 1.856)	
− 0.2293	0.3665	− 0.3673	0.5145
(− 1.072)	1.5390	(− 1.354)	
− 0.0093	0.0494	− 0.1288	4.4677
(− 0.121)	(0.584)	(− 1.290)	
− 0.0365	0.2792	0.4144	1.9193
(− 0.153)	(1.017)	(1.340)	
− 0.0444	0.0279	0.0290	52.6530
(− 3.563)	(1.748)	(1.291)	
1.1015	− 2.5104	− 0.3289	1.4080
(0.718)	(− 1.570)	(− 0.164)	
0.1087	− 0.1629	− 0.1635	1.3536
(4.522)	(− 5.423)	(− 5.103)	
− 0.1650	− 0.0840	− 1.3170	0.2859
(− 2.410)	(− 1.133)	(− 9.371)	
0.2175	0.5973	− 0.2598	2.0158
(0.339)	(0.878)	(− 0.300)	
− 0.0399	− 0.0541	− 0.0917	4.3732
(− 0.539)	(− 0.638)	(− 0.957)	
222.7300	286.3200	429.1500	

Maximum Likelihood Estimates of Logistic Models
of Underlying Equations Used to Estimate Sex Ratios, Whites, 1976

	P(Male)	P(Female)	P(Unmarried Male)
Constant	−2.0535	−2.0535	−1.1292
	(−0.335)	(−0.335)	(−0.116)
Age	0.0172	0.0172	−0.2021
	(0.728)	(0.728)	(−5.532)
Age squared	−0.0000	−0.0000	0.0017
	(−0.531)	(−0.531)	(−5.532)
Grade	−0.2899	−0.2899	−0.2117
	(−5.832)	(−5.832)	(−2.945)
Grade squared	0.0138	0.0138	0.0079
	(6.940)	(6.940)	(2.740)
Central city	0.0893	0.0893	0.3885
	(1.272)	(1.272)	(3.780)
Northeast	0.1307	0.1307	0.0999
	(1.053)	(1.053)	(0.548)
North Central	0.1636	0.1636	−0.1556
	(1.278)	(1.278)	(−0.815)
South	−0.0454	−0.0454	−0.0947
	(−0.349)	(−0.349)	(−0.480)
State unemployment rate	−0.0012	−0.0012	0.0197
	(−0.023)	(−0.023)	(0.245)
Male institutionalization rate	0.7427	0.7427	−0.1640
	(1.771)	(1.771)	(−0.268)
Age × mortality ratio	−0.0136	−0.0136	−0.0061
	(−0.807)	(−0.807)	(−0.235)
Mortality ratio	2.9457	2.9457	8.6031
	(0.332)	(0.332)	(0.611)
Children 6 to 18	0.0207	0.0207	−0.1730
	(−0.824)	(−0.824)	(−4.486)
Children under 6	−0.0446	−0.0446	−1.3964
	(−0.807)	(−0.807)	(−9.991)
Mortality ratio squared	−0.6857	−0.6857	−3.1540
	(−0.213)	(−0.213)	(−0.616)
Institutionalization rate squared	−0.1307	−0.1307	0.0886
	−1.3630	−1.3630	(0.667)
Chi squared	101.2600	101.2600	930.7800

Note: Figures in parentheses are the *t* statistics.

P(Unmarried Female)	P(Employed Male)	P(Unmarried Male in Work Force or in School)	Mean
−0.0467	−11.3377	1.9916	
(−0.006)	−1.5870	(0.188)	
−0.2352	0.2143	−0.1619	40.5390
(−8.550)	(6.314)	(−3.127)	
0.0022	−0.0019	0.0010	2001.5000
(19.577)	(−13.697)	(4.665)	
0.0213	−0.1423	−0.0480	12.7680
(0.329)	(−2.476)	(−0.507)	
−0.0020	0.0101	0.0022	172.2000
(−0.744)	(4.515)	(0.592)	
0.3028	0.0940	0.5233	0.4319
(3.329)	(1.197)	(4.723)	
−0.1448	0.0174	0.2204	0.4229
(−0.888)	(0.125)	(1.115)	
−0.1890	0.2659	0.0891	0.4482
(−1.120)	1.8560	(0.430)	
−0.0891	0.0666	0.2017	0.4621
(−0.521)	(0.452)	(0.931)	
0.0128	0.0399	0.1360	0.8600
(0.182)	(0.663)	(1.571)	
−0.9028	0.5269	0.1856	0.2058
(−1.649)	(1.116)	(0.279)	
0.0170	−0.0454	0.0035	54.9880
(0.881)	(−1.924)	(0.095)	
6.4328	9.0355	−0.4436	1.3544
(0.531)	(0.881)	(−0.029)	
0.0038	−0.0173	−0.1405	0.8782
(0.113)	(−0.618)	(−3.451)	
−0.7176	0.0934	−1.3624	0.2377
(−6.923)	(1.597)	(−8.989)	
−2.8596	−2.6468	0.4265	1.8430
(−0.651)	(−0.715)	(0.008)	
0.1986	−0.0847	−0.0092	0.9894
(1.673)	(−0.781)	(−0.061)	
636.7900	519.0100	814.6000	

of being a male and employed among blacks in 1985, the same effect is not uncovered for whites in 1985 or blacks in 1976. Indeed, in 1976 increases in education lowered the probability of being employed and male among whites. Significant racial differences are also found between the effects of children on these underlying probabilities. While the number of children between the ages of six and eighteen in the household is inversely related to the probability of being unmarried and female among whites, it is positively related to that probability among blacks. Finally, the effects of incarceration and mortality are found to be statistically insignificant in these reduced-form equations.[4]

Derivation of Expected Welfare

We compute two reduced-form equations for the assignment of expected welfare values for each family head. The first is the probability that a family unit receives welfare. This probability depends on age, education, number of children, region, characteristics of the state—percentage of population that is black, population density—and state welfare parameters (for 1985 only). The second equation is the AFDC annual income for families receiving AFDC. It depends on similar variables except that population density is replaced by central city.

Tables A9.5 and A9.6 display the results for blacks and whites in 1976 and 1985. In 1976, age and education are only weakly related to the average AFDC benefits of welfare recipients; these variables, however, have statistically significant impacts on black welfare recipiency in 1976. Younger and better-educated black heads of families were more likely to receive welfare than older less-educated family heads, even though these impacts were quadratic. In other words, the impacts of age and education diminished for older family heads and those who were considerably educated. Similar quadratic impacts of education are found on white welfare recipiency, although no age effects are uncovered. By 1985, even these education effects among white family heads were diluted although strong impacts of education on welfare recipiency reemerge among black family heads. Again in 1985, probabilities of welfare recipiency increased for younger and better-educated black family heads. These findings, for both 1976 and 1985, may conceal cohort effects whereby more recent welfare recipients are members of a later generation of persons who are more likely to have completed some high school than earlier generations of welfare-eligible persons.

Not surprisingly, the most consistent predictor of both welfare recipiency and average welfare income is the number of children in the household. The number of children younger than six years and the number of children from

---

[4]We have also estimated structural equations for the underlying determinants of sex ratios. These equations, which include homicide rates instead of mortality ratios, are estimated using instrumental variables to account for the endogeneity of marginalization. See Darity & Myers, 1990.

TABLE A9.5

*Underlying Equations
for the Estimation of Expected Welfare Income, 1976*

	Blacks		Whites	
	P(AFDC > 0)	ln AFDC	P(AFDC > 0)	ln AFDC
Constant	−2.7157	6.9790	−3.0861	8.4672
	(−0.386)	(16.56)	(−2.216)	(6.889)
Age	−0.0743	−0.0072	−0.0218	−0.0086
	(−3.932)	(−0.548)	(−0.580)	(−.250)
Age squared	0.0005	0.0001	−0.0002	0.0001
	(2.505)	(−0.418)	(−0.532)	(0.295)
Grade	0.1222	−0.0324	0.3902	0.0400
	(1.637)	(0.731)	(2.018)	(.253)
Grade Squared	−0.0172	0.0006	−0.0352	−0.0023
	(−4.056)	(0.184)	(−3.472)	(−0.281)
Children under 6	0.6285	0.1926	0.4405	0.0197
	(9.197)	(5.341)	(4.019)	(0.2)
Children 6 to 18	0.3414	0.1418	0.3438	0.2286
	(9.932)	(6.877)	(4.868)	(3.734)
State AFDC work re-quirement	—	—	—	—
Northeast	0.1737	−0.3535	0.3412	0.1344
	(0.662)	(−2.077)	(0.820)	(0.446)
North Central	0.1838	0.1850	0.1460	−0.6455
	(0.830)	(−1.234)	(0.516)	(−2.645)
South	−0.5449	−0.2556	0.3763	−1.1280
	(−1.868)	(−1.285)	(0.685)	(−2.492)
State unemployed parent program	—	—	—	—
Percentage of population black	0.2621	0.0061	−0.0674	0.0261
	(−2.182)	(1.108)	(−2.377)	(1.040)
Guarantee/needs	—	—	—	—
Percentage of population on welfare	—	—	—	—
Mean AFDC in 1976	0.0036	0.0065	0.0073	−0.0047
	(1.718)	(5.128)	(1.815)	(−1.46)
Population density	−0.0002	—	−0.0011	—
	(−2.243)		(−1.577)	
Central city	—	0.1226	—	0.3834
		(1.480)		(2.116)
Sigma	—	0.7991	—	0.9313
		(32.588)		(16.971)

TABLE A9.6

Underlying Equations
for the Estimation of Expected Welfare Income, 1985

	Blacks		Whites	
	P(AFDC > 0)	ln AFDC	P(AFDC > 0)	ln AFDC
Constant	−1.1673	6.3436	−3.4531	5.1632
	(−1.287)	(9.188)	(−2.665)	(4.490)
Age	−0.0680	0.0343	−0.0057	0.0397
	(−2.940)	(1.902)	(−.141)	(1.098)
Age squared	0.0003	−0.0004	−0.0005	−0.0005
	(1.110)	(−2.116)	(−1.171)	(−1.28)
Grade	0.3411	0.0552	0.0526	−0.1481
	(3.295)	(0.731)	(.378)	(−1.494)
Grade Squared	−0.0278	−0.0030	−0.0178	0.0074
	(−5.307)	(−.0764)	(−2.53)	(1.454)
Children under 6	0.6717	0.1504	0.5742	0.3316
	(8.703)	(2.770)	(5.238)	(3.568)
Children 6 to 18	0.4769	0.1896	0.3993	0.2037
	(9.366)	(5.279)	(4.591)	(3.173)
State AFDC work requirement	−0.0215	−0.1097	−0.0228	−0.1378
	(−.117)	(−0.714)	(−.088)	(−.658)
Northeast	0.7982	0.0423	1.4415	0.4742
	(2.516)	(0.151)	(3.44)	(1.581)
North Central	1.1217	−0.2792	0.7110	0.2957
	(3.545)	(−1.031)	(1.896)	(1.030)
South	0.4100	−0.7081	0.2205	0.4628
	(0.953)	(−1.922)	(−.362)	(.978)
State unemployed parent program	0.0683	−0.0607	−0.0113	−0.0900
	(0.218)	(−0.233)	(−.026)	(−.255)
Percentage of population black	−0.0508	0.0231	−0.0491	−0.0249
	(−3.066)	(2.064)	(−1.766)	(−1.079)
Guarantee/needs	0.0011	−0.0010	−0.0046	0.0021
	(0.478)	(−0.578)	(−1.731)	(1.085)
Percentage of population on welfare	0.1513	−0.0641	0.0032	0.1765
	(2.571)	(−1.338)	(.035)	(2.398)
Mean AFDC in 1985	−0.0023	0.0106	0.0374	0.0026
	(−0.204)	(1.216)	(2.564)	(.256)
Population density	0.0001	—	−0.0010	—
	(1.410)		(−1.584)	
Central city	—	0.0962	—	0.0209
		(0.843)		(.146)
Sigma	—	0.9701	—	0.8312
		(29.967)		(18.000)

six to eighteen years increase the probability for receiving welfare as well as the annual welfare income of black and white family heads in 1976 and 1985.

There are also substantial regional differences in AFDC recipiency and welfare income. To get a good sense of the magnitude of these differences, we have computed the product of the probability of black welfare recipiency and the annual welfare income for those receiving welfare for all family heads using the coefficients from Tables A9.5 and A9.6. Broken down by region the "expected welfare benefits" are:

	West	North Central	Northeast	South
1976	$605	$1137	$1188	$459
1985	$717	$ 956	$ 939	$243

Clearly the implications of the differing signs of coefficients by region are confirmed for blacks. Expected welfare income is lower in the South in both years, principally because the probability for receiving welfare is either lower in the South or not significantly different from the rest of the nation. According to our calculations, a black family head residing in the South in 1985 could expect an annual welfare income of only about $243, down from $459 in real terms in 1976. This contrasts with expected welfare incomes of $700 to nearly $1200 in 1976 and 1985 in other regions of the nation.

Female Headship

As the supply of marriageable men falls, our model suggests that the proportion of families headed by females will rise. The microeconomic argument, however, would suggest that the inducements from welfare and public assistance ought to reduce the frequency of two-parent family formations as well. To support this argument, we must recognize that welfare recipiency and public assistance earnings are not strictly endogenous to the family formation decisions. Thus, a finding of a positive impact of AFDC on the probability that a family is female headed may be the consequence of the positive relationship between AFDC recipiency probabilities and female headship status. It will be necessary, then, to replace actual AFDC income with an instrument that is a function only of currently exogenous variables. One important set of variables determining both AFDC recipiency and welfare income includes a vector of state AFDC parameters.

Welfare, in this microeconomic interpretation, affects not only the odds that a family is headed by a female but also whether the head works or is looking for work. Moreover, in this reasoning, the status of the family head directly affects the decision to enter the labor market. As a result, any model that hopes to combine the sociological determinants of family structure with

TABLE A9.7

Forecast of Female-Headed Families to the Year 2000 (FHH 2000)

| | Average Age of Head | | | | | | Trend Average[d] | |
| | 25 | | 30 | | 35 | | | |
	Black	White	Black	White	Black	White	Black	White
Method 1[a]								
Wilson-Neckerman								
Estimated sex ratio	39.72%	33.34%	39.72%	33.34%	39.72%	33.34%	39.72%	33.34%
Expected welfare	$248.02	$91.42	$248.02	$91.42	$248.02	$91.42	$248.02	$91.42
FHH 2000	55.57%	16.01%	48.09%	13.90%	41.93%	12.39%	33.94%	10.54%
Darity-Myers								
Estimated sex ratio	9.56%	35.83%	9.56%	35.83%	9.56%	35.83%	9.56%	35.83%
Expected welfare	$255.06	$91.42	$255.06	$91.42	$255.06	$91.42	$255.06	$91.42
FHH 2000	60.17%	18.33%	51.01%	14.34%	43.20%	11.97%	32.77%	10.59%
Method 2[b]								
Wilson-Neckerman								
Estimated sex ratio	39.72%	33.34%	39.72%	33.34%	39.72%	33.34%	39.72%	33.34%
Expected welfare	$248.02	$91.42	$248.02	$91.42	$248.02	$91.42	$248.02	$91.42
FHH 2000	56.45%	13.75%	48.98%	11.90%	42.80%	10.58%	41.23%	10.55%
Darity-Myers								
Estimated sex ratio	9.56%	35.83%	9.56%	35.83%	9.56%	35.83%	9.56%	35.83%
Expected welfare	$255.06	$91.42	$255.06	$91.42	$255.06	$91.42	$255.06	$91.42
FHH 2000	60.70%	15.98%	51.55%	12.42%	43.73%	10.33%	40.74%	13.33%
Method 3[c]								
Wilson-Neckerman								
Estimated sex ratio	67.93%	116.34%	91.98%	175.65%	111.37%	237.99%	119.43%	307.32%
Expected welfare	$305.57	$68.19	$266.57	$60.95	$227.32	$51.69	$156.11	$28.07
FHH 2000	32.44%	4.14%	30.00%	4.80%	29.15%	9.61%	30.96%	7.92%
Darity-Myers								
Estimated sex ratio	86.28%	44.34%	74.43%	40.86%	60.70%	36.34%	34.66%	22.24%
Expected welfare	$305.57	$68.19	$266.57	$60.95	$227.32	$51.69	$156.11	$28.07
FHH 2000	55.60%	27.71%	49.11%	22.50%	44.49%	18.93%	36.04%	13.79%

[a] From female-headed family equation using forecasted value of independent variables and mean of 1976 and 1985 coefficients.
[b] From female-headed family equation using 1985 means of independent variables, forecasted values for expected welfare and sex ratio, and mean of 1976 and 1985 coefficients.
[c] From full model with forecasted values of independent variables for all equations and 1985 coefficients.
[d] Forecasted age in year 2000: blacks 44.75 years.

306

microeconomic antecedents of work and welfare must incorporate the effects of welfare on family structure and on labor-force participation.

The basic specification of the female-headed family equation included the variables age, education, presence of children, expected welfare income, the estimated sex ratio, and the abortion rate in the state. Four different sex ratios were obtained for family heads using micro equations estimated for individuals from the CPS March Supplement. For example, an estimate of the ratio of unmarried men to unmarried women was obtained for each family head—whether male or female, married or unmarried—first, estimating the unconditional probability that a sample observation from the CPS March Supplement was unmarried and male; then, estimating the unconditional probability that a person was unmarried and female; and then, using the estimated coefficients to form the ratio of the probability of an unmarried male to the probability of an unmarried female. This ratio could now be computed for each family head, given the estimated coefficients. The interpretation, for example, of a female head of family would be: given my characteristics, how many unmarried men can I expect to encounter in my marriage market for every unmarried woman. This expected number is a more appropriate estimate of the marriage prospects than the actual ratio in an area for such a woman since the actual number would involve a market that includes non-family heads with presumably more attractive characteristics and thus more expansive marriage prospects. Other ratios estimated include: ratio of men to women; ratio of employed men to women (the Wilson-Neckerman "Male Marriage Pool Index"), and our preferred measure of marriageability, the ratio of unmarried men in the labor force or in school to unmarried women. Full details of forecasts discussed in text and presented in Table 9.11 are provided in Table A9.7.

Data Sources

Sex ratios were computed from the 1976 and 1985 CPS March Supplement tapes. These estimates, derived from the person files of the tapes, are merged with the Institute for Research on Poverty's CPS Extract tapes, which merge person and household variables from the March Supplement tapes onto family records. Since the CPS March Supplement questions refer to the previous year's income and weeks worked or unemployed, we merge the previous year's measures on state AFDC parameters and other state variables such as unemployment rates. In some instances, where noted, we employ census year estimates for state aggregates.

Incarceration data came from the Census Bureau and the National Institute of Justice; mortality data came from the U.S. Vital Statistics; AFDC state parameters were compiled from SSA Annual Statistical Abstracts and state plans; abortion data came from the Allan Guttmacher Institute and the Centers for Disease Control; other state-level data are found in the U.S. Statistical Abstracts.

Exogenous variables include the following: the age of family head, age squared, and education; the number of children in the household under six years of age and the number between six and eighteen years of age; the type of residence (an apartment or house); the abortion ratio in the state in the previous census year; the fraction of abortions received by unmarried women in the state in the previous census year; the percentage of the population by race that is institutionalized in the state in the previous census year; the ratio of male to female mortality; the AFDC monthly guarantee for three children in 1975 and 1984; the ratio of the AFDC monthly guarantee to the state need-level; the percentage of the state's population on welfare in the previous census year; the percentage of the population that was black in the previous census year; population density in the previous census year; percentage change in welfare proportion in the previous censuses; the average AFDC monthly benefit per recipient in the previous census; and the work requirements or use of an unemployed parent program in the state's welfare system during the previous year.

The family structure is measured by a dichotomous variable equal to one if the family is female headed and zero if otherwise. The analysis includes all families except unrelated individuals (one-person families). Thus, the base for the computations includes primary families with no subfamilies, primary families with subfamilies, and secondary families.

COMMENTARY

Phillip J. Bowman

A S WE APPROACH the twenty-first century, the marginalization of African American men has become an increasingly controversial issue with widespread economic, social, and psychosocial implications (Bowman, 1993; Darity and Myers, 1989; Farley and Allen, 1987). The declining economic status of black men is not only statistically linked to their declining marriage rate, but may also be a pivotal factor in the raging debate about other problems related to family poverty in black communities (Bowman, 1988; Glasgow, 1980; Wilson, 1978). Indeed, in the last quarter of the twentieth century, a debate about the growth of concentrated poverty among blacks within urban communities—an underclass—has emerged as a major issue on the social science research agenda with profound public policy implications (Jencks, 1991; Jencks and Peterson, 1991; Lynn and McGeary, 1990; Wilson, 1987). Debate abounds over the underclass concept, pivotal causal variables, and viable policy initiatives. However, there is a growing consensus on the need to better understand a series of problems that are increasingly concentrated among the African American population—chronic male joblessness, crime involvement, father-absent families, and welfare dependence.

It is within this context that I focus my commentary on "Family Structure and the Marginalization of Black Men: Policy Implications" by William A. Darity and Samuel L. Myers. The marginalization of black men must be understood in terms of the paradoxical polarization in the status of black men which has occurred during the post–civil rights/postindustrial era. Since the mid-1960s, a small portion of black men have clearly profited from the eradication of legal segregation through unprecedented gains in higher education and earnings in highly skilled occupations (Bowman, 1991a; Jaynes and Williams, 1989; Wilson, 1978). However, during this same period, an even larger portion of black men find themselves with inadequate skills in a global postindustrial economy where they face unprecedented levels of chronic joblessness, crime, life-threatening psychosocial risks, and family estrangement (Bowman, 1989, 1991b; Farley and Allen, 1987; Wilson, 1987).

These trends toward increased black male marginality during the seventies and eighties are alarming, but social policy discourse continues to be restricted by ideological debates. Policy debates too often pit conservative against liberal ideologies rather than discussing empirical evidence on testable social science questions. To be sure, a balanced appraisal of social science evidence on competing theoretical models is seldom the primary basis for new policy initiatives (Dye, 1992; Hayes, 1992; Weiss, 1977). Two major problems contribute to this inadequate use of social science knowledge in effective policy formulation: first, a tendency for policymakers to advance ideology-driven proposals over evidence-driven proposals to address problems related to black poverty; and, second, a dearth of rigorous empirical studies that systematically evaluate competing theoretical models with policy relevance. To address these common pitfalls, the Darity-Myers chapter formulates and tests competing welfare incentive and male marginalization hypotheses to account for the growth in black female headship—a major issue in the underclass debate. Based on national data from the census and current population surveys, their descriptive and multivariate findings provide a systematic basis to evaluate these two competing hypotheses about the decline in marriage among black mothers. The Darity-Myers analysis goes beyond traditional economic choice models to estimate female headship as a function of welfare, sex ratio, and other independent variables.

Despite the systematic research methodology of Darity and Myers, their analysis raises some critical theoretical and social policy issues. First, their marginalization and welfare hypotheses are examined within the broader framework of four competing theoretical models that have been shaping research and policy agendas on the underclass debate recently. Next, the policy relevance of their analysis is examined in greater detail; the major empirical findings marshaled in support of the marginalization hypothesis are discussed in light of both the competing models and related social policy implications.

Competing Theoretical Models

A systematic review of the literature reveals several competing hypotheses which currently guide research on the growth in chronic joblessness among black men, the decline in marriage among black mothers, and related underclass issues. As illustrated in Table C9.1, four distinct research paradigms include the social pathology (e.g., Lemann, 1986; Murray, 1984), postindustrial dislocation (e.g., Bowman, 1988; Kasarda, 1989), mainstream coping (e.g., Farley, 1988; Jencks, 1989), and ethnic resource models (e.g., Bowman, 1990a; Greenstone, 1991). These four research models differ in two major ways: (1) an emphasis on maladaptive or adaptive behavioral patterns, and (2) an emphasis on internal

TABLE C9.1

Research Perspectives on the Underclass Debate

Causal Factors	Behavioral Patterns	
	Maladaptive	Adaptive
Internal	Social pathology	Ethnic resource
External	Postindustrial dislocation	Mainstream coping

Note: Adapted from Bowman (1989). Copyright 1989 by R.L. Jones. Reprinted by permission.

or external causal factors in the analysis of such behavioral patterns (Bowman, 1989).

Although some studies may incorporate more than one causal factor, researchers tend to emphasize hypotheses derived from one of these four models at the expense of the others. For example, the seminal work by Wilson (1987) acknowledges the importance of both social pathology and postindustrial economic dislocation, but emphasizes the pivotal impact of social isolation—the within-group economic segregation of the black poor caused by the movement of middle-class black professionals from areas of concentrated poverty. The social pathology model traditionally dominated research on black poverty, but Wilson's work has been especially instrumental in the recent shift in emphasis away from pathology to postindustrial economic and social dislocations. In the growing search for alternative explanations, the mainstream coping and ethnic resource models have emerged but have yet to generate much empirical research.

It is also important to note that these four competing theoretical models have distinct ideological underpinnings and systematic policy implications. Social pathology models support more conservative policy agendas to reduce deviance among the black poor through punitive or remedial action. In contrast, mainstream coping models are consistent with more liberal paternalistic or assimilationist agendas. Dislocation and resource models reflect more progressive agendas to reduce dislocation of the black poor while building on indigenous resources that facilitate individual mobility, self-reliance, and collective social change.

Social Pathology Model

The social pathology model views cultural and/or psychological deficits as the pivotal cause of both the growth in black male joblessness and the increase in female headship over the last two decades. Social pathology researchers choose to emphasize maladaptive behavioral patterns, and seek to support hypotheses that focus on internal deficits among blacks themselves as the primary causal factors. This model has been especially attractive to conservative scholars and policymakers; they share the popular belief that declining black socioeconomic conditions reflect a poverty of middle-class family values and/ or a lack of personal motivation to take advantage of privileges afforded by affirmative action (e.g., Dudley, 1988; Kluegel, 1990).

Social pathology views on black men and families not only dominated early studies, but continue to be well represented in mainstream attitudes, research, and policy arenas (Auletta, 1982; Bowman, 1989; Evans and Whitfield, 1988; Murray, 1987; Ryan, 1971; Taylor et al., 1990). The basic social pathology premise has guided studies of African Americans which emphasize a variety of concepts such as the culture of poverty, cultural deprivation, cultural deviance, psychological deficits, and the underclass. Lemann (1986) proposes a share-cropper culture hypothesis which suggests that deficient plantation-like values rooted in the southern background of most blacks have made many unable to profit from expanded opportunities. The Darity-Myers analysis critically evaluates a related welfare incentive hypothesis that was popularized in Charles Murray's book, *Losing Ground*. Murray (1984) argued that increased welfare benefits operated as the primary cause of black family instability by reinforcing deviant inclinations of both black women to have children out of wedlock and black men to escape family responsibilities.

Postindustrial Dislocation Model

Similar to social pathology research, postindustrial marginalization studies focus on maladaptive behavioral patterns among the black poor. However, rather than blame internal cultural or psychological deficits, external structural barriers are focused on as the root cause of the growth in black female family headship and related poverty. This perspective looks for causes of increased black joblessness and dislocation in the postindustrial displacement of manufacturing jobs by new labor-saving technology and related shifts in unskilled jobs from central cities to suburbs, from the rustbelt to the sunbelt, and from the domestic labor market to third-world countries (Bluestone and Harrison, 1982; Blumberg, 1980; Bowser, 1989).

In contrast to Wilson's social isolation hypothesis, other postindustrial marginalization researchers emphasize social dislocations such as spatial mismatch or intrafamily role strains as the primary mechanisms that mediate the adverse impact of macroeconomic transformations. The spatial mismatch hypothesis emphasizes the decline in demand for unskilled black labor in central-city neighborhoods combined with systematic barriers to expanding job opportunities in predominantly white suburbs (Jencks and Mayer, 1991; Kasarda, 1988, 1989). In addition to spatial distance, studies also suggest that class, racial, and cultural conflicts can operate as barriers between unskilled black males and suburban job opportunities (Bowman, 1991c; Farley et al., 1978; Kirschenman and Neckerman, 1991). Bowman formulated an hypothesis focused on the strain of family roles, which emphasizes the destabilizing impact of postindustrial job displacement within black families as provider role difficulties ripple from displaced fathers, to unmarried mothers, to children in poverty (Bowman, 1988).

In this vein, the Darity-Myers black male marginalization hypothesis states that sex ratio or the decline in the supply of marriageable black men is a pivotal factor in the growth of black female family headship. A particularly impressive feature of the Darity-Myers analysis involves the estimation of female headship as a function of four distinct measures of sex ratio. These included: (1) the ratio of males to females; (2) the ratio of unmarried males to unmarried females; (3) the Wilson and Neckerman (1986) Male Marriage Pool Index, which taps the ratio of employed males to females; and (4) the Darity-Myers marriageable males measure, which assesses the ratio of unmarried males in the labor force or school to unmarried females. The Darity-Myers marriageable male ratio is conceptualized to better reflect the economic marginalization of jobless, unskilled black males in a postindustrial labor market with increasing skill demands.

Mainstream Coping

Estimates showing that only about 20 percent of the changes in marriage rates for black men is attributable to decreasing employment raise some serious questions about alternative hypotheses (Jencks, 1991; Mare and Winship, 1991). As suggested in Table C9.1, the mainstream coping model focuses on external societal factors which support changing marriage and family patterns that are considered adaptive rather than maladaptive. Although still sparse, related literature on this model has focused on white-black convergences in both external societal opportunities and normative cultural response patterns. An expanded opportunity hypothesis states that growing economic independence among employed black and white women has provided both with the option to avoid undesirable marriages (e.g., Farley, 1988). Therefore, the general impact of improved female economic position on marriage declines among blacks may be exacerbated by growing black male marginalization, which further reduces the desirability of marriage. An alternative mainstream culture hypothesis suggests that a general shift toward liberal societal mores and expectations about relationships has culminated in decreasing marriage rates among both blacks and whites (Mare and Winship, 1991). For example, Jencks (1989) notes that the single-parent trend is the same in Beverly Hills as in Watts.

The Darity-Myers model did not explicitly test mainstream coping variables, but several related considerations further enhanced the meaningfulness of their analysis. All analyses were conducted separately for whites and blacks with more complicated simulations manipulating selected characteristics of both groups in 1976, 1985, and 2000.

Ethnic Resource Model: Beyond the Darity-Myers Analysis

Based on the discussion, the major strength of the Darity-Myers analysis is the systematic evaluation of hypotheses derived from the major models used in research on the underclass debate. To be sure, the Darity-Myers analysis provides an empirical basis to answer the critical policy-relevant question: "How much does welfare matter relative to changing marital opportunities among blacks and whites?" Despite its many virtues, the Darity-Myers analysis provides no basis to consider the role of ethnic resources in the growth or functioning of father-absent black families. Literature on such factors is still relatively sparse, but recent work has begun to expand the research agenda by examining the adaptive influence of cultural resources or strengths (e.g., Bowman, 1990a, 1993; Greenstone, 1991).

In general, the ethnic resource model emphasizes the pivotal influence of indigenous cultural strengths in: (1) protecting individual family members in the face of black male marginalization; (2) fostering adaptive marriage and family patterns which promote family functioning; and (3) empowering family members to share responsibilities for corrective actions (Berry and Blassingame, 1982; Gutman, 1976; Herskovits, 1941; Hill, 1971; McAdoo, 1988; Stack, 1974). Supportive research on this hypothesis has been restricted by an erroneous but persistent view that African Americans have not retained virtuous cultural traditions or values like other American ethnic groups (Bowman, 1989, 1991c; Fredrickson, 1971; Kinder and Sears, 1981). Therefore, rather than examine African American cultural strengths, research on race and culture has concentrated on racial or cultural deficits, cultural conflicts, or cultural assimilation. Despite the foregoing tendency, Greenstone (1991) proposes a multicultural hypothesis which suggests that corrective policy should seek to build on African American "subcultural" strengths, not try to replace them; the notion is that some unique patterns in father-absent black families reflect bicultural strengths and skills in the face of a growing shortage of marriageable black men. Moreover, Bowman (1990a) found support for an alternative cultural resource hypothesis which states that African American cultural strengths such as cohesive, extended-family bonds and strong religious beliefs buffer the deleterious impact of discouraging employment barriers on the family attachment of black husband-fathers. In their analysis, the erosive impact of both black male marginalization and welfare incentives on the growth of female family headship may have been mitigated by indigenous cultural resources at the individual, family, and community levels.

Policy-Relevant Findings

As suggested earlier, the policy relevance of the Darity-Myers analysis is based primarily on the evidence it provides regarding the relative efficacy of two competing hypotheses in the underclass debate. Ideology-driven policy initiatives continue to focus on incremental welfare reform (Dudley, 1988; Hayes, 1992). However, the Darity-Myers findings support a shift in emphasis to policy agendas that address the decline in supply of marriageable black men to resolve more effectively the growing poverty crisis in black female-headed families.

Among the most policy-relevant descriptive findings were the overwhelming odds against an unmarried black female head of family finding an unmarried male who is in the labor force or in school. For example, Darity-Myers estimate that for every hundred such women there were only thirty-two marriageable men in 1985, down from forty-six in 1976. However, the central finding is that welfare benefits are only weakly associated with increased female headship, while reduced supplies of marriageable black men contribute more substantially to the decline of two-parent black families. Thus, while these findings provide little support for the social pathology model, the postindustrial dislocation model is more firmly supported.

The postindustrial dislocation model also receives support from the pattern of findings across the various sex-ratio indicators of marriageable male supply. The only measure of sex ratio that was statistically significant across all the years and for both races is the ratio of unmarried males in the labor force or school to unmarried females—the Darity-Myers marriageable male ratio. Along with the Wilson-Neckerman Male Marriage Pool Index, this economically determined measure of marriage markets revealed striking consistency in accounting for black family structure in the youngest age groups. Each of the four sex ratios to some degree reflects the effects of homicide, violent crime, incarceration, and other noneconomic sources of marginalization on the reduced supply of black males in the marriage market. In addition, the Darity-Myers and Wilson-Neckerman ratios also consider the further erosive influence of growing postindustrial economic and educational marginality on the black male marriage market. Indeed, these findings suggest that the two more simple demographic measures of sex ratio do not fully capture the dynamics of the changing postindustrial marriage markets that face the present and future generations.

The mainstream coping model was not directly evaluated in the Darity-Myers analysis, but their white-black comparative data provide little basis to conclude that racial convergences are likely to mitigate the dire consequences of the decline of marriageable black men on the future of black families. Hence, there is little evidence that the disturbing racial gaps in either the supply of marriageable males or female family headship that emerged in the last two decades will narrow by the year 2000. In sum, the Darity-Myers analysis suggests that the potential to reduce black female family headship through welfare reductions is negligible. Moreover, there is little evidence for optimistic assessments that the supply of marriageable black men will naturally increase by the turn of the century—although such increases in supply could significantly reduce the decline in black husband-wife families.

Summary and Conclusions

The Darity-Myers analysis represents a significant contribution to a sparse social science literature which empirically evaluates competing theoretical models that have clear policy relevance. Their evaluation of competing welfare incentive and male marginalization hypotheses regarding the growth of black female family headship has some important theoretical implications. This study can inform the growing number of scholars who seek to broaden the scope, clarify the conceptual parameters, and improve the quality of empirical research on issues emerging from the underclass debate (e.g., Jencks and Peterson, 1991; Lynn and McGeary, 1990; Wilson, 1987). Going beyond the conventional focus on social pathology, findings reinforce a growing recognition that a broader range of variables must be considered to adequately account for increases in black female headship and other poverty-related problems over the past two decades. Despite these virtues, future studies need to address more directly the unanswered questions that emerge from the mainstream coping and ethnic resource models. In this regard, interdisciplinary research may be crucial for a better specification of how social, psychosocial, and cultural factors might buffer the marginalizing impact of economic dislocation documented in the Darity-Myers study.

Darity and Myers have also clearly demonstrated the importance of expanded conceptualizations of black male marginalization and marriageability. Future research should further extend this work by clarifying other social and psychosocial dimensions of marriageability among African American males. In an earlier paper, Darity and Myers (1989) emphasized the importance of considering how the surplus of black unmarried women over marriageable black men is exacerbated by psychosocial factors such as the high rates of black male homicidal violence, imprisonment, and mental hospital residency. We need to better understand the relationship between postindustrial job displacement and these psychosocial dimensions. One set of studies suggests that discouragement in job search may be a pivotal psychosocial risk factor as increasing numbers of jobless black males negotiate structural barriers to employment in postindustrial America (Bowman, 1980, 1984, 1988, 1990b; Bowman et al., 1982). This job search discouragement has been found to occur among both mature black men who are disproportionately displaced from unskilled industrial jobs and black youth who enter the postindustrial labor market during the transition from adolescent to adult. Such discouragement or hopelessness in job search may be a pivotal precursor of declining labor-force participation, declining marriage, and a range of other psychosocial problems among black males. Hence, a jobless black male who is optimistic about job search may be far more "marriageable" than one who has completely given up hope of finding a job, and who is ready to seek alternatives. The growing number of discouraged black males may be at greatest risk of psychosocial problems when they are restricted to neighborhoods where the opportunity structure makes drugs, crime, and violence much more accessible alternatives than legitimate employment. Hence, job search discouragement may not only be a proximal precursor to psychological distress, but also to the other psychosocial factors that erode marriageability—homicidal violence, imprisonment, and mental hospital residency (e.g., Bowman, 1989).

In terms of social policy, the Darity-Myers analysis provides clear evidence for policymakers interested in shifting the emphasis from ideology-driven to evidence-driven proposals to address the growth in poverty-related problems within black female-headed households. First of all, it is important to note that such problems have not been caused by any actual increase in either teen pregnancy or parenting rates (e.g., Farley and Allen, 1987; Jaynes and Williams, 1989). Instead, female family headship is empirically associated with a decline in marriage between black fathers and mothers; moreover, the related growth in black family poverty is associated with declines in family support provided by economically marginal black fathers. The Darity-Myers findings clearly suggest that effective policy to deal with such issues in the underclass debate may require a de-emphasis on incremental welfare reform and a greater willingness to incorporate the facts regarding the postindustrial marginalization of jobless black males into responsive policy agendas (Danziger and Weinberg, 1986).

Without such responsive policy initiatives, the North American Free Trade Agreement and related trends are likely to further exacerbate the marginalization of black males well into the twenty-first century; they will suffer disproportionately from dislocations resulting from the predicted relocation of unskilled manufacturing jobs from the domestic labor force, given their concentration in the most vulnerable jobs. Growing international economic competition, persistent racial antagonism, and an increasing tendency to blame black jobless victims of postindustrial dislocation for its marginalizing consequences all conspire to make such responsive policy agendas major challenges for America as we approach the next century. To be sure, future progress on this policy challenge will require governmental leadership to move beyond the traditional politics of blame to forge effective partnerships with both the private sector and high-risk communities such as African Americans. Without responsive policy that reflects such shared responsibility, reversal of the growing postindustrial marginalization of African American men seems unlikely.

Evidence presented by Darity-Myers makes some things clear but also raises other important questions. A major challenge is to better specify pivotal social dislocations that mediate the marginalizing impact of postindustrial economic transformations. For example, should policies focus primarily on macroeconomic trends? Or should responsive social policy also focus on issues of social isolation, spatial mismatch, family-provider-role difficulties, institutionalization, or schooling? Future research should seek to clarify the efficacy of related policy options such as industrial policy, urban development, family support, criminal justice, health promotion, employment/training, or school reform.

The Darity-Myers findings suggest that existing policy such as the Family Support Act would be more effective among African Americans if provisions addressed the economic marginalization of growing numbers of chronically jobless black fathers. Similarly, Bowman (1988) suggests that employment and training agendas need to be incorporated into a more comprehensive family work-sharing policy: (1) to increase employment among displaced black fathers in the postindustrial economy; (2) to provide pay sufficient for employed black fathers and mothers to share in adequate child support; and (3) to provide incentives for working fathers and mothers to also share in responsibilities for child care. Moreover, growing community-based demands for cultural diversity, multicultural sensitivity, or African-centered reforms may require more responsive policy formulation and implementation. Such policies should build on, rather than disregard, indigenous ethnic resources in efforts to reduce the marginalizing impact of postindustrial economic dislocations among African Americans. For example, employment-training activities among jobless black fathers should build on traditional family values among African Americans—male responsibility despite racial barriers, flexible provider roles, and adaptive family work sharing (e.g., Berry and Blassingame, 1982; Bowman, 1993; Gutman, 1976; Hill, 1971). Hamilton (1986) argues that such emphasis on jobs, earned entitlements, and self-reliance over welfare, government handouts, and dependence represents a potential convergence of conservative "workfare," liberal "supported work," and traditional black "self-reliance" policy agendas.

REFERENCES

AULETTA, K. 1982. *The underclass.* New York: Random House.

BERRY, M.F., AND BLASSINGAME, J.W. 1982. *Long memory: The black experience in America.* New York: Academic Press.

BLUESTONE, B., AND HARRISON, B. 1982. *The deindustrialization of America.* New York: Basic Books.

BLUMBERG, P. 1980. *Inequality in an age of decline.* New York: Oxford University Press.

BOWMAN, P.J. 1980. Toward a dual labor market approach to black-on-black homicide. *Public Health Reports,* 95:555–556.

BOWMAN, P.J. 1984. A discouragement-centered approach to studying unemployment among black youth: Hopelessness, attributions and psychological distress. *International Journal of Mental Health,* 13:68–91.

BOWMAN, P.J. 1988. Post-industrial displacement and family role strains: Challenges to the black family. In P. Voydanof and L.C. Majka, eds., *Families and economic distress.* Newbury Park, CA: Sage Publications.

BOWMAN, P.J. 1989. Research perspectives on black men: Role strain and adaptation across the life cycle. In R.L. Jones, ed., *Black adult development and aging,* pp. 117–150. Berkeley, CA: Cobb & Henry.

BOWMAN, P.J. 1990a. Coping with provider role strain: Adaptive cultural resources among black husband-fathers. *Journal of Black Psychology,* 16:1–21.

BOWMAN, P.J. 1990b. The adolescent to adult transition: Discouragement among jobless black youth. In V.C. McLoyd and C. Flanagan, eds., *New directions in child development,* pp. 87–105. San Francisco: Jossey-Bass.

BOWMAN, P.J. 1991a. Worklife. In J.S. Jackson, ed., *Life in black America,* pp. 124–155. Newbury Park, CA: Sage Publications.

BOWMAN, P.J. 1991b. Joblessness. In J.S. Jackson, ed., *Life in Black America,* pp. 156–178. Newbury Park, CA: Sage Publications.

BOWMAN, P.J. 1991c. Organizational Psychology: African American perspectives. In R.L. Jones, ed., *Black psychology,* 3rd. ed., pp. 509–531. Berkeley, CA: Cobb & Henry.

BOWMAN, P.J. 1993. The impact of economic marginality on African American husbands and fathers. In H. MacAdoo, ed., *Family ethnicity: Strength in diversity.* Newbury Park, CA: Sage Publications.

BOWMAN, P.J., JACKSON, J.S., HATCHETT, S., AND GURIN, G. 1982. Joblessness and discouragement among black Americans. *Economic Outlook U.S.A.,* 9:85–88.

BOWSER, B.P. 1989. Generational effects: The impact of culture, economy and community across the generations. In R.L. Jones, ed., *Black adult development and aging,* pp. 3–30. Berkeley, CA: Cobb & Henry.

DANZIGER, S.M., AND WEINBERG, D.H. 1986. *Fighting poverty: What works and what doesn't.* Cambridge, MA: Harvard University Press.

DARITY, W., JR., AND MYERS, S., JR. 1989. The problem of family structure, earnings inequality and the marginalization of black men. Paper presented at the Western Economic Association Meetings, Lake Tahoe, Nevada.

DUDLEY, W. 1988. *Poverty: Opposing viewpoints.* San Diego, CA: Greenhaven Press.

DYE, T.R. 1992. *Understanding public policy.* Englewood Cliffs, NJ: Prentice Hall.

EVANS, B.J., AND WHITFIELD, J.R. 1988. *Black males in the U.S.: An annotated bibliography from 1967 to 1987.* Washington, DC: American Psychological Association.

FARLEY, R. 1988. After the starting line: Blacks and women in an uphill race. *Demography,* 25 (November):477–495.

FARLEY, R., AND ALLEN, W.R. 1987. *The color line and the quality of life in America.* New York: Russell Sage Foundation.

FARLEY, R., SCHUMAN, H., BIANCHI, S., COLOSANTO, D., AND HATCHETT, S. 1978. Chocolate city, vanilla suburbs: Will the trend toward racially separated communities continue? *Social Science Research,* 7:319–344.

FREDRICKSON, G.M. 1971. *The black image in the white mind.* New York: Harper & Row.

GLASGOW, D.G. 1980. *The black underclass.* San Francisco: Jossey-Bass.

GREENSTONE, J.D. 1991. Culture, rationality and the underclass. In C. Jencks and P.E. Peterson, eds., *The urban underclass*. Washington, DC: Brookings Institution.

GUTMAN, H.G. 1976. *The black family in slavery and freedom, 1750–1925*. New York: Pantheon.

HAMILTON, C. 1986. Social policy and the welfare of black Americans: From rights to resources. *Political Science Quarterly,* 101:239–257.

HAYES, M.T. 1992. *Incrementalism and public policy*. New York: Longman.

HERSKOVITS, M.J. 1941. *The myth of the Negro past*. New York: Harper & Row.

HILL, R. 1971. *Strengths of black families*. New York: Emerson Hall.

JAYNES, G.D., AND WILLIAMS, R.M., eds. 1989. *A common destiny: Blacks and American society*. Washington, DC: National Academy Press.

JENCKS, C. 1989. Deadly neighborhoods. *The New Republic*. June 13:23–32.

JENCKS, C. 1991. Is the American underclass growing? In C. Jencks and P.E. Peterson, eds., *The urban underclass,* pp. 28–102. Washington, DC: Brookings Institution.

JENCKS, C., AND MAYER, S.E. 1991. Residential segregation, job proximity, and job opportunities. In L.E. Lynn and M.G. McGeary, eds., *Inner-city poverty in the United States,* pp. 187–222. Washington, DC: National Academy Press.

JENCKS, C., AND PETERSON, P.E. 1991. *The urban underclass*. Washington, DC: Brookings Institution.

KASARDA, J.D. 1988. Jobs, migration, and emerging mismatches. In M.G. McGeary and L.E. Lynn, Jr., eds., *Urban change and poverty,* pp. 148–198. Washington, DC: National Academy Press.

KASARDA, J.D. 1989. Urban industrial transition and the underclass. *Annals of the American Academy of Political and Social Science,* 501(Jan.):26–47.

KINDER, D.R., AND SEARS, D.O. 1981. Prejudice and politics: Symbolic racism versus racial threats to the good life. *Journal of Personality and Social Psychology,* XL:416.

KIRSCHENMAN, J., AND NECKERMAN, K.M. 1991. We'd love to hire them, but . . . . The meaning of race to employers. In C. Jencks and P.E. Peterson, eds., *The urban underclass,* pp. 203–232. Washington, DC: Brookings Institution.

KLUEGEL, J.R. 1990. Trends in whites' explanations of the black-white gap in socioeconomic status, 1977–1989. *American Sociological Review,* 55:512–525.

LEMANN, N. 1986. The origins of the underclass. *Atlantic Monthly,* June:31–61.

LYNN, L.E., AND MCGEARY, M.G. 1990. *Inner-city poverty in the United States*. Washington, DC: National Academy Press.

MARE, R.D., AND WINSHIP, C. 1991. Socioeconomic changes and the decline of marriage for blacks and whites. In C. Jencks and P.E. Peterson, eds., *The urban underclass,* pp. 175–202. Washington, DC: Brookings Institution.

MCADOO, H.P. 1988. *Black families*. Beverly Hills, CA: Sage Publications.

MURRAY, C.A. 1984. *Losing ground: American social policy, 1950–1980*. New York: Basic Books.

MURRAY, C.A. 1987. White popular wisdom. In R. Takaki, ed., *From different shores: Perspectives on race and ethnicity in America,* pp. 231–250. New York: Oxford University Press.

RYAN, W. 1971. *Blaming the victim*. New York: Pantheon.

STACK, C. 1974. *All our kin*. New York: Harper and Row.

TAYLOR, R.L., CHATTER, L.M., TUCKER, M.B., AND LEWIS, E. 1991. Developments in research on black families: A decade in review. *Journal of Marriage and the Family,* 52:993–1014.

WEISS, C.H. 1977. *Using social research in public policy making.* Lexington, MA: Lexington Books.

WILSON, W.J. 1978. *The declining significance of race.* Chicago: University of Chicago Press.

WILSON, W.J. 1987. *The truly disadvantaged.* Chicago: University of Chicago Press.

WILSON, W.J., AND NECKERMAN, K.M. 1986. Poverty and family structure: The widening gap between evidence and public policy issues. In S.H. Danziger and D.H. Weinberg, eds., *Fighting poverty: What works and what doesn't,* pp. 232–259. Cambridge, MA: Harvard University Press.

10 POLICY IMPLICATIONS OF A DECLINE IN MARRIAGE AMONG AFRICAN AMERICANS

Lynn C. Burbridge

MAKING PUBLIC policy is difficult. In the social policy arena, it often involves making assumptions about human behavior and trying to influence the behavior of people to achieve a given policy goal. But ill-conceived policies may be ineffective or even harmful, making extremely important the need for clarity about the problem being addressed and the repercussions of any excursion into the policy arena.

In modern times, the decision to marry is usually a personal decision involving two individuals. There is no inherent reason to be concerned about it. Underlying the policy debates about declines in marriage and increases in female-headed households, however, is the assumption that these phenomena cause a range of other social ills. Thus, it is issues such as welfare dependence, school dropout rates, crime, and violence—often associated with the rise in female-headed households in general and out-of-wedlock births among teenagers in particular—that become enmeshed in any discussion of a decline in marriage. Thus, any policy discussion of a decline in marriage must first recognize the assumptions—sometimes unstated—that underlie the debates that have occurred.

In inner-city communities where minorities are disproportionately represented, these assumptions seem particularly warranted since high percentages of female-headed households occur along with high crime rates, high teenage pregnancy rates, high welfare recipiency rates, and high high school dropout rates. In the minds of many, the decline in marriage among African Americans is seen as directly *contributing* to these other social problems. One must always be careful in making these kinds of associations, however, since all of these phenomena, including a decline in marriage, could be caused by another set of variables. Furthermore, the increase in female-headed households is occurring throughout the Western industrial countries, without similar increases in violence and other social problems, and the increase in female-headed households is occurring among all races and social classes in the United States, not simply in inner cities.

This is not to suggest that there is no cause for concern. While the same phenomenon is occurring in other places and with other groups, few groups have experienced high rates of single-parent households for as long as African Americans have. It could be argued that the problems experienced in some minority communities may reflect the cumulative effects of many generations of single-parent households. On the other hand, it could be argued that since African Americans have coped with single-parent households throughout their history without these negative social outcomes (or at least not to the extent as is found presently), something else must explain issues of crime and violence in inner-city communities.

An important variable to recognize is that families do not, and never have, existed in a vacuum, but in communities. Community ties and social structures, the health and vitality of communities, have a profound effect on the well-being of families. Thus, if communities change, families change. The problems of marriage and families ultimately are problems of community.

Thus, while marriage has always been a difficult proposition, community structures and expectations have historically bolstered that institution. Similarly, while single-parent families are under greater financial and psychological stress, a strong and supportive community can mitigate against the possible negative outcomes of those stresses. In examining public policy alternatives with respect to the decline in marriages, it is important to support those policies that will support communities and to provide communities with the resources needed to support the families contained within them.

Keeping these concerns in mind, the policy implications of the decline in marriage among African Americans are addressed by asking three questions. First, to what extent does the decline represent a "problem" to society: who is affected, how are they affected, and what are the implications for society as a whole? Second, what aspects of the "problem" fall within the purview of government policy? This is not an easy issue to address since, as the social policy debate over the past ten years indicates, there is no clear agreement in this country about social goals or the proper role of government in achieving them. The third question is more practical: what policy approaches will be most effective in attaining desired outcomes? Of course, political and financial concerns will often limit which, out of a range of possible policies, will be implemented. In this chapter each of these issues is discussed in turn.

Decline in Marriage as a Social Problem

Decline in Values

For many observers, high divorce rates, increases in out-of-wedlock births, and the overall decline in marriage as we have come to know it, all reflect and contribute to a perceived deterioration in values in post-industrial America. For them, it is primarily a moral issue. While this point of view has been associated with political conservatives, concerns have been expressed in many quarters about the self-involvement and lack of commitment that have become characteristics of modern life (e.g., Sidel, 1989; West, 1993; Wolfe, 1989).

It is within the family, after all, that social values and norms are transmitted from one generation to the next. There are many who wonder whether a breakdown in this mechanism, in the absence of another one to replace it, will do irreversible harm to society. Can any other institution carry and transmit values as effectively and with the same care as the family unit?

Many others will argue, however, that a female-headed family is still a family, capable of carrying out the functions of a two-parent family. In addition, such a family may be a decided improvement over one that has both father and mother present, but is dysfunctional. The strains on one-parent families can be significant, however. Access to the time and resources needed to supervise children and impart values to them is very limited.

Although a substantial amount of psychological and anthropological research has focused on values in society, an empirical measurement of a decline in values in the present context is difficult to document, since the values that people espouse may not always be reflected in actual behavior. Some have inferred a value shift from the work that has been undertaken on the intergenerational transmission of poverty and welfare dependence, and, particularly, the increase in out-of-wedlock births among teenagers. These observers have suggested that dysfunctional behavior is being passed on from one generation to the next and that much of this is taking place among poor, single-parent families (e.g., Murray, 1984).

This viewpoint was not substantiated in an analysis conducted using the University of Michigan's Panel Study of Income Dynamics (PSID), a longitudinal database that permits comparison of parents and their children. Martha Hill and her colleagues found that while young adults who had come from poor families were more likely to be poor, there was considerable intergenerational mobility; that coming from a single-parent household did not have a significant effect on young adult outcomes; and that coming from families that were heavily dependent on welfare did not predict a high degree of welfare dependence among the young adults in the sample, particularly among blacks (Hill et al., 1985).

Nevertheless, even though a high degree of welfare dependence may not be transmitted easily from one generation to the next as is often assumed, children of parents with some reliance on welfare are more likely to be on welfare than children of parents who have *never* received welfare (U.S. Congress, House Committee on Ways and Means, 1993). Nor is it possible to ignore the increase in out-of-wedlock births among teenagers. The most dramatic increase has been among whites—a 164 percent change for white fifteen to seventeen-year-olds between 1970 and 1990 compared to a 4.2 percent change for black fifteen to seventeen-year-olds between 1970 and 1990. But blacks still have significantly higher rates of out-of-wedlock teen births than whites: 81.2 per thousand births for black fifteen to seventeen-year-olds in 1990 compared to 19.8 per thousand births for white fifteen to seventeen-year-olds. Interestingly, the birthrates for all teenagers, married or unmarried, have actually declined by 20 percent for blacks and 14 percent for whites (U.S. Congress, House Committee on Ways and Means, 1993). The data suggest cause for concern, nevertheless, since teenagers are not generally prepared for parenthood emotionally, financially, or even physically in many cases. But if teen pregnancy rates represent a shift in values in recent decades, particularly among African Americans, the data do not provide strong support for this.

It is also important to note that scholars such as W.E.B. Du Bois and E. Franklin Frazier have commented on the issue of single-parent families among African Americans since the turn of the century, largely attributed to the difficulty black men have always encountered in finding jobs in urban areas (Du Bois, 1967; Frazier, 1940). An analysis of historical data by Hernandez (1993) shows that the majority of black children have not lived in a household consisting of a father working full time and year round, at least since 1940. In that year, only 25 percent of black children lived in a family with a father working full time, year round and with a mother who was a homemaker. Thus, more "traditional" conceptions of family have not pertained to African Americans for a long time. (It should be noted that white families did not correspond to the nuclear family model to the extent that is often assumed, either.)

In addition, Kamerman and Kahn (1988) document the growth of female-headed families in many other Western countries, with Sweden topping the list as a society in which 32 percent of all families with children are headed by a single parent. Thus, if there is a change in values regarding marriage, it is specific neither to the United States nor to the inner-city poor within this country.

As indicated earlier, the changes in values that are of concern to many observers go beyond marriage and childbearing. Rather, there is a constellation of social issues that increasingly has been associated with single-parent households: dropping out of school, crime, violence, and long-term welfare receipt. If out-of-wedlock births had increased without increases in these other social indicators, the attention focused on single-parent families might have been considerably less.[1] Even if there is a legitimate association between these social problems and high numbers of single-parent households, this does not mean that one causes the other. They may all be caused by another set of variables. Receiving considerable attention have been the economic changes that have occurred in recent decades, changes that have destabilized the family, undermined communities, and caused a range of other socially undesirable outcomes.

Economic Variables

Since the mid-1970s there have been many changes in the economy of the United States: declines in manufacturing and in male wages; globalization of the economy with growing competition from abroad; and increasing reliance on high-skilled workers (e.g., Harrison and Bluestone, 1988; Levy, 1988; Reich, 1991). Many scholars concerned about the decline in marriage have focused specifically on the economic causes of this decline, particularly in the case of African Americans who have a greater economic vulnerability in the first place. From a socioeconomic standpoint, a decline in marriage among blacks has been viewed both as a symptom of economic hardship on the part of those who would otherwise marry as well as a cause of economic hardship—especially for children but also for the mothers who must care for them. Each of these factors is discussed below.

A symptom of economic hardship.   There has been considerable scholarly interest in black male joblessness and its impact on the decline in marriage among blacks. This interest goes back as far as early work by Du Bois (1967) but has received heightened attention in recent decades. Black unemployment rates have consistently been twice as high as those of whites, and the wages of black men have declined in real terms in recent decades (Blank, 1994). These changes have largely been attributed to declines in relatively high-paying jobs in manufacturing. While these changes have affected both white and black men, the former have been more successful in making gains in other fields than have the latter (Burbridge, 1994). The impact of these changes has been so dramatic for black men that there are now more black women in the labor market than black men, as shown in Table 10.1. While some of the difference in this table can be explained by the relatively high proportions of black men in the military who would not be counted in the civilian labor force, the gap between black men and women is projected to grow (U.S. Department of Labor, 1992).

These changes will clearly affect marriage. Research by William Julius Wilson and others included in this volume suggests that inner-city men who are

---

[1] Nathan Glazer (1994) makes this point regarding the current wave of welfare reforms, suggesting that it is not welfare dependence per se that is causing so much concern as it is the association of welfare dependence with crime and violence in inner cities.

TABLE 10.1

*Black and White Wage and Salary Workers
as a Percentage of the Labor Force, 1950–1990*

| | Black | | White | |
	Women	Men	Women	Men
1950	3.4%	6.4%	24.2%	65.5%
1960	3.9	5.9	28.7	60.7
1970	4.4	5.3	32.6	54.6
1980	5.0	5.1	34.3	47.5
1990	5.4	5.0	35.3	42.7
Percent change				
1950–1970	29.4	−17.2	34.7	−16.6
1970–1990	22.7	−5.7	8.3	−21.8

Source: U.S. Census of Population Public Use Tapes, 1950, 1960, 1970, 1980, 1990.

Note: Figures for 1970, 1980, and 1990 are for non-Hispanic blacks and whites.

employed are two and a half times more likely to legitimate a birth than men who are not employed and nearly twice as likely to marry after the birth of a child (see Wilson, 1987, and Testa and Krogh, Chapter 3, this volume). Similarly, an extensive National Research Council study of the status of black Americans found that if black men had the same income distribution as whites, the percentage of never-married black men (aged thirty-five to forty-four) would drop from 14 to 9 percent—much closer to the 7 percent found for whites in that age range (Jaynes and Williams, 1987). Bennett, Bloom, and Craig (1989) found that the annual probability of marriage of black men employed full time and year round was twice that of black men experiencing some unemployment or time out of the labor force. Further, their research showed that the incidence of marriage among black men is more sensitive to their employment status than it is for whites.

Bennett, Bloom, and Craig (1989) also found that a woman's employment status was an important variable explaining subsequent marriage. This is not surprising when one considers that the most economically successful structure among blacks is the two-parent family in which both parents are working. Table 10.2 shows the median weekly earnings of families by race or Hispanic origin and by family type. Weekly earnings for African American two-parent, two-earner families are 85 percent of the median earnings for similar white families. However, black wives must work longer hours than white wives in order to

TABLE 10.2

Median Weekly Earnings of Families,
by Race or Hispanic Origin and Family Type, 1992

	Black	Hispanic	White	Black/White Ratio	Hispanic/White Ratio
Total families with earnings	$478	$496	$716	66.8	69.3
Married-couple families					
All	646	552	791	81.7	69.8
One earner	309	333	483	64.0	68.9
Husband	359	365	561	64.0	65.1
Wife	279	264	296	94.3	89.2
Two or more earners	806	743	954	84.5	77.9
Husband and wife only	783	721	923	84.8	78.1
Families maintained by women	328	341	409	80.2	83.4
Families maintained by men	412	476	545	75.6	87.3

Source: U.S. Bureau of the Census, *Statistical Abstract of the United States, 1993.*

bring black family incomes close to those of comparable whites, and black wives contribute more to family income than do white wives (Cancian, Danziger, and Gottschalk, 1993). The only other families to approach this parity are those in which women are the primary earners: in two-parent families where the sole earner is female and in female-maintained (headed) families. This is because the earnings of women are more similar across races. But these families have considerably lower earnings, since women of all races make less than their male counterparts. It is understandable, then, that the economic prospects of African American women, as well as those of men, will have a significant impact on marriage rates.

Among low-skilled African Americans, however, incentives to maximize joint income do not exist. Poor, unskilled women with children have access either to welfare or to low-paying jobs that offer few benefits, low wages, and, often, fewer or more erratic hours of work (Hartmann and Spalter-Roth, 1993). Moreover, wages in the kinds of jobs available to women on welfare have declined in real dollars over time (Burtless, 1994). While the value of welfare benefits has also declined in real terms, the welfare system still offers a consistent, monthly income. Thus for many low-skilled women, welfare has offered more stable income and benefits either to them or to the men in their lives than is available in the labor market. If an AFDC recipient chooses to marry and combine her income with her husband's earnings, she would lose the more stable AFDC benefits.[2] Both she and her spouse would have to subsist on unreliable work, without health benefits in most cases. Remaining a single parent on welfare becomes a "rational" decision. Thus, high welfare dependence among black families is a corollary to high joblessness among African American men and women, with the resulting decline in marriage. Of course, as noted earlier, it has been argued that the reverse holds true: the availability of welfare has caused the decline in marriage by reducing the incentive to marry (see Murray, 1984). However, as discussed by Darity and Myers in Chapter 9 of this volume, most of the empirical work on this question fails to provide support for this argument.[3]

The major exception to the lack of support for this view has been the results of the Seattle-Denver Income Maintenance Experiments, which attempted to estimate the impact of a guaranteed income, at varying levels, and which demonstrated a significant effect of cash transfers on marital stability for blacks and whites (SRI International, 1983). However, these results have been disputed by Cain and Wissoker (1990), who found no relationship when accounting for effects of time dependence on the rate of marital breakups and making other adjustments in their reanalysis of the data.[4]

In addition, as they have discussed in detail in Chapter 9, Darity and Myers found that while the attractiveness of welfare had no effect on female-headed families, there was an effect of nonwhite male mortality rate and sex ratio. Since mortality rates and sex ratios are themselves determined to a significant extent by economic factors, these findings also support the argument that the decline in marriage among African Americans is symptomatic of economic hardship.

A cause of economic hardship. While there is disagreement about the causes of the rise in female-headed households, there is considerably less disagreement about the consequences. The research indicates that increases in female headship have resulted in higher levels of child poverty among blacks and whites than would have existed if the composition of families had not changed—although decreases in family size and increases in mother's education

---

[2] Even though under the Unemployed Parents program (AFDC-UP) husbands who work less than one hundred hours a month could be in a family that is also receiving some welfare, eligibility rules are such that there are very few two-parent welfare families. (Until the Family Support Act of 1988, only half of the states provided any eligibility to two-parent families.) A discussion of the AFDC-UP program follows in another section.

[3] William Julius Wilson in *The Truly Disadvantaged* (1987) provides a fairly thorough review of the literature on this subject, concluding that "there is little evidence to provide a strong case for welfare as the primary cause of family breakups, female-headed households, and out-of-wedlock births" (pg. 90).

[4] Also included with the Cain and Wissoker (1990) article is a rebuttal by Michael T. Hannan and Nancy B. Tuma, who conducted the original analysis, with a response to this rebuttal by Cain and Wissoker.

have prevented child poverty rates from rising even higher (Gottschalk and Danziger, 1993). As indicated in Table 10.2, not only do families with one earner make considerably less than those with two earners, women make less than men. Families maintained by a single black woman have earnings that are 60 percent less than that found in black families with two earners.

Although child poverty rates have been influenced by increases in single-mother families, overall child poverty rates have increased by less than 10 percent for blacks between 1971 and 1991, while increasing sharply for whites (48 percent) over the same period (U.S. Congress, House Committee on Ways and Means, 1993). Nevertheless, child poverty rates are significantly higher for blacks than for whites (44 percent for the former, 16 percent for the latter) since they have historically been higher. Again, this suggests that the black family has been under stress for a relatively long time, the bigger recent changes being found among whites.

These figures are all the more discouraging in light of Marian Wright Edelman's trenchant statement that "poverty is the greatest child killer in the affluent United States . . . [M]ore American children die each year from poverty than from traffic fatalities and suicide combined" (Edelman, 1986, p. 29). To the extent that the decline of marriage contributes to child poverty among blacks, it exacerbates the already desperate condition of many black children.

There are few alternatives available to single black parents to alleviate this situation, particularly for those with few skills. The low wages and high unemployment rates they face have already been discussed. The segregation of low-skilled black women into low-wage occupations, even when they do find employment, also has been documented (e.g., Malveaux, 1986). Moreover, cost-of-living studies have found that a minimally sufficient family budget for a working single mother with two children and child care expenses would require at least nine dollars per hour (Bailis and Burbridge, 1991; Helburn and Morris, 1989). This is considerably more than many of the jobs available to inner-city black women will pay.

Furthermore, in no state are AFDC benefits sufficient to take a family out of poverty. In only five states are combined AFDC and food stamp benefits within 90 percent of the poverty level (U.S. Congress, House Committee on Ways and Means, 1993). Whether a black female head tries to make it on her own or attempts to rely on public assistance, she will have an extremely difficult time providing for her family.

It should be noted, however, that in recent years the largest growth in female-headed households has been among college-educated black women (Hill, 1993), who have better economic opportunities. Even among skilled black women, however, maintaining a family alone is a challenge. Although skilled women have higher wages, the average earnings of a professional black woman are only comparable to those of a skilled, male, blue-collar worker, approximately $26,000 (Burbridge, 1994). Further, skilled black women rely heavily on employment in the government and nonprofit sectors, which have faced frequent budget cuts in recent years (Burbridge, 1994). This is complicated by the fact that middle-class black families still have only one-third the wealth of middle-class white families (Jaynes and Williams, 1987), thus giving them fewer resources to fall back on in hard times. In the 1980s, 47 percent of children in families headed by a single, college-educated black woman were in poverty, compared to 23 percent of children in families headed by similar white women (U.S. Congress, House Committee on Ways and Means, 1993).

In addition, many studies of poverty of single-parent families do not factor in the "time poverty" experienced by female heads. Clair Vickery (1977) found that a family with two or more children must have two adults to carry out minimal work and household tasks. Without income to purchase additional services or without some form of social support, single parents will suffer from an impoverishment of time. It is no surprise, therefore, that Harriet McAdoo (1986) found high levels of stress among black single mothers and that those who lived with other family members, who could provide support, experienced stress at lower levels. While black single mothers do receive considerable in-kind support from extended family networks, they are less able to purchase support services than their more financially able white counterparts (Okongwu, 1993).

The Context of Community

Much has been written about the role of the extended family and community institutions, such as the church, as valuable sources of support to the African American family (Allen, 1978; Billingsley, 1968; Jackson, 1991). In spite of the important role played by these structures historically, they have not been able to grapple with all of the problems of the inner city. The movement of jobs and people out of the city, the reduced tax base resulting in diminished community services, as well as budget cuts on the federal and state levels have overwhelmed these community support systems. Jobs, schools, and social services are also a part of the social infrastructure within which families must live.

If, as indicated earlier, the primary policy concerns are behaviors that have been associated with female-headed households—dropping out of school, crime, and welfare dependence—rather than female headship itself, a focus on community structures becomes all the more relevant, as issues such as school attendance and crime have been the concern of communities as well as of families. Yet less research attention has focused on the breakdown of community mechanisms, particularly the extent to which they have been diminished over time. This is partly because community variables are much more difficult to quantify.

Nevertheless, a loss in community is not just a theme for the inner city. It has been a concern expressed by observers of the United States and Western countries overall (e.g., Etzioni, 1993; Wolfe, 1989). The greater mobility of people and a weakened attachment to institutions that lent cohesion to everyday life has been a theme expressed in several books. Wolfe argues that the values of the marketplace have come to determine the situation of the modern family, rather than the values of the families or of their communities. This will be no less true in the inner city and may, in fact, be heightened by the greater suscepti- bility of inner-city residents to the negative consequences of economic change. Thus, Cornell West (1993) sounds a similar theme, that "the recent market- driven shattering of black civil society . . . leaves more and more black people vulnerable to daily lives endured with little sense of self and fragile existential moorings" (pp. 24–25).

The Role of Government Policy

A second key question concerns what role, if any, government policy should play with respect to the decline in marriage among African Americans. Govern- ment cannot make people marry, without violating their rights. Attempts have been made to encourage people to marry, however, by reducing the "marriage penalty" in the federal tax system, for example. But it is not entirely clear whether these marginal changes will have a significant impact on the marriage decision of African Americans, particularly those whose incomes are quite low.

Because the decline in marriage among African Americans is both cause and effect of a variety of economic and social problems that traditionally have been the concern of policymakers, action can be taken in the social policy arena that may affect marriage rates. However, one must be cautious in pursuing these policies for purposes of increasing marriage since that is not what they are designed to do.

For example, increasing levels of education and more vigorous enforcement of antidiscrimination laws could raise the employment and earnings of blacks, resulting in higher marriage rates. But education and civil rights policies gener- ally focus on people as individuals: individual students and individual plaintiffs. Educators and legal experts cannot focus on the effect of their actions on mar- riage rates. Further, most people consider access to employment and education as individual rights, regardless of the impact of marriage.

Similarly, income support and safety net programs can mitigate against some of the effects of a decline in marriage, such as child poverty. But the goal of most of these programs is the overall health and well-being of economically disadvantaged groups. Most modern societies provide for the needs of the poor as a social responsibility, again, regardless of the effect on marriage.

It should be noted, however, that there are those who would eliminate social programs as harmful to the interest of families and, perhaps, suspend individual rights in the interest of "family values" (or, perhaps more accurately, "two-parent family values"). Charles Murray has proposed eliminating welfare since he feels that it encourages the formation of female-headed households and teenage pregnancy (Murray, 1993). He makes a direct link between single-parent households and inner-city crime and violence. In addition to cutting benefits, he proposes taking the children of nonmarried mothers and placing them in two-parent households or in orphanages—steps that could clearly violate individual rights as they are now understood.

Murray's proposals would also undermine community institutions that are trying to grapple with the problems of inner-city residents. Under the scenario proposed by Murray, community institutions would lose all legitimacy among those who face losing their very own children because of these proposals. The final result would not be reductions in crime and violence, but considerably more, as those in the inner city would undoubtedly do whatever they could— legally or illegally—to maintain their families.

Finally, policies designed to provide social support to families potentially have the best chance of having a direct impact on marriage. For example, teen parent programs, directed to young fathers, may encourage the eventual legitimation of an out-of-wedlock birth. Public policy can also play a role in funding community-based organizations that serve and counsel families under stress. These efforts would probably be most effective, however, in concert with policies to increase employment and reduce poverty. Otherwise, underlying economic conditions will undermine these other efforts.

Clearly, there is no silver bullet for the causes and consequences of a decline in marriage. Multiple approaches appear to be necessary. Reductions in racial inequality have the greatest potential for improving the lot of African American families. The data are fairly clear: people marry when they feel they can afford to marry. Some families will need social support, nevertheless, as the legacy of generations of poverty weighs heavily on many African American families. Creative approaches are needed to strengthen community support systems as well. While it may be difficult to prevent family crises, community institutions that are prepared to step in before a problem gets out of control can play a powerful role in assuring that families do not become overwhelmed by crisis.

Policy Approaches

There is a wide range of policy instruments that can be used to achieve the broad policy goals outlined above, many of which are already familiar to the knowledgeable reader. This section highlights some crosscutting issues that require consideration in setting policies, in light of the above discussion on the decline of marriage. The first issue, before all else, is the extent to which there is a national commitment to do anything about the problems involved. This is followed by a discussion of policies that affect men, women, children, and communities that are relevant to the functioning of families.

Political Priority

It may seem an obvious point, but without a political commitment to address the needs of families, it will be difficult to move ahead, particularly in a time of fiscal constraint. Further, the United States is already behind other Western countries in expenditures on programs benefiting families and children. Compared to other Western countries, for example, the United States has the least-developed social safety net for children. In his comparison of the United States with nine other OECD (Organization for Economic Cooperation and Development) countries, Michael O'Higgins (1988) found that the United States spent the least in tax and transfer expenditures for children as a percentage of gross earnings: 1.4 percent compared to an average of 7 percent in the other industrialized countries. Using the Luxembourg Income Study data file, Smeeding, Torrey, and Rein (1988) found that tax and transfer policies in the United States affecting families with children had a poverty reduction rate of 17 percent compared to 40 percent in the United Kingdom, 58 percent in Sweden, 47 percent in Norway, and 37 percent in Canada.

While welfare programs are politically unpopular, even Headstart, a program well regarded by most administrations, has never had enough funding to serve all eligible youngsters (although funding has increased in recent years). Education and employment programs generally have been underfunded, and civil rights enforcement programs received funding cuts in the 1980s (Burbridge, 1986). Funding for Title XX Social Services Block Grant, the federal program that funds many community-based organizations, declined almost 57 percent between 1977 and 1993 (U.S. Congress, House Committee on Ways and Means, 1993). There has been increased interest in urban economic development programs, however. Compounding the question of political priority, the current federal deficit has insured that opportunities to change priorities will be limited. There are some important directions to head toward, nevertheless.

Incorporating Men into the Policy Agenda

While children have been underserved in the social welfare system, adult black men have remained very much on the periphery. Many feel that welfare rules that have resulted in the exclusion of families with an able-bodied man present have contributed to the growth in female-headed households in the black community. It did not pay two-parent families in need of income support to remain together, since access to assistance was easier for one-parent families.

Thus, in spite of concerns about welfare dependence and female-headed households among African Americans, black men are conspicuously underrepresented in the welfare system which, in turn, may have resulted in more single-parent households. In 1991, the AFDC-UP (Unemployed Parents) programs that specifically included two-parent families constituted only about 5 percent of all AFDC cases. Of the AFDC-UP cases, 63 percent were white, 16 percent Asian, 10 percent Hispanic, 9 percent black, and the remainder were American Indian or race unknown (U.S. Congress, House Committee on Ways and Means, 1993). This is astonishing when one considers that black families constitute about 39 percent of the overall AFDC caseload. A study by Greg Duncan (1984) found that while black men made up 16 percent of the nonelderly, persistently poor (compared to white men who make up 4 percent), they were only 5 percent of nonelderly, long-term welfare dependents (compared to white men, who are 16 percent). Administration welfare reform proposals under consideration at this time incorporate plans to bring men further into the welfare system, although funding restraints will limit what will actually be accomplished.

Black men are also underrepresented in that part of the social welfare system which requires an obligation from them: the child support system. According to Table 10.3, while only 20 percent of all black women (and 17 percent of poor black women) who were eligible for child support in 1989 actually received any funds, 45 percent of all eligible white women (and 32 percent of poor white women) received some payment. The table indicates that the primary reason for low receipt of child support among black women was that they were less likely to receive an award of child support. Black women were about as likely as white women to receive a payment once they had an award. The greater poverty of black males probably makes both the courts and the women themselves less likely to pursue child support cases.

As Table 10.3 indicates, the mean payments made by black men who do pay child support are 72 percent of the mean payments made by white men, and represent a smaller proportion of black women's total income compared to their white counterparts. Nevertheless, child support contributions are a more significant proportion of the income of poor women, in spite of the lower amount received.

More importantly, Mercer Sullivan (1989)—in his study of young, low-income black, Hispanic, and white fathers—found that most of the young fathers felt a strong commitment to their children and often provided in-kind support (e.g., babysitting) when they were unable to provide financial support. He suggests policy initiatives that tap into these feelings, such as linking a commitment to child support with job training and employment programs or recognizing in-kind contributions for cash payments. The point is that these young men should not be written off because they cannot support their families in the short run or in traditional ways.

At the time of this writing, pending welfare reform legislation will strengthen child support enforcement. Since so many low-income black males are unemployed or underemployed, policy initiatives that would combine the provision of employment opportunities with a child support requirement would have the largest impact on families.

TABLE 10.3

Child Support Awarded and Received,
by Race and Hispanic Origin and by Poverty Status, 1989

	All Women			Women Below Poverty Level		
	Black	Hispanic	White	Black	Hispanic	White
Awarded						
Percentage eligible	34.5	40.6	67.5	29.2	33.0	54.6
Received support						
Percentage awarded	69.7	69.8	76.5	69.8	63.5	67.8
Percentage eligible	19.9	22.8	44.9	17.3	17.5	31.8
Mean child support received	$2263	$2965	$3132	$1674	$1824	$1972
Percentage of total income	16.3	20.1	18.8	32.4	36.8	39.4

Source: U.S. Congress, House Committee on Ways and Means (1993).

Employment Problems of Low-Skilled Women

Many of the policy concerns about single-parent families have focused on women, rather than on men, largely because women and children represent the bulk of the AFDC caseload. There has been a tremendous push on federal and state levels to put AFDC women to work, particularly since so many non-AFDC women with children also work. Pending welfare reform legislation proposes time-limited welfare, requiring women to work after two years on welfare and includes provisions to "make work pay," by providing child care and health benefits, and by making use of an expanded earned income tax credit (EITC) that will subsidize the incomes of low-income workers. Because of fiscal constraints, the legislation may focus on teenage parents who are at greatest risk of becoming long-term welfare recipients.

Nevertheless, while it is certainly true that there is a greater expectation that women with children can and should work, as discussed earlier, employment opportunities have not increased for low-skilled women as they have for skilled women (Blank, 1994). Policy prescriptions that do not take into account the difficulties low-skilled women encounter in obtaining stable employment to provide an adequate family income will not result in felicitous outcomes.

Previous studies of welfare-employment programs suggest, in fact, that although it is possible to reduce reliance on welfare, it is very difficult to end it completely. While studies have shown increased earnings as a result of these programs, they have not been sufficient to get recipients off welfare altogether. The most successful welfare-employment programs have increased earnings for welfare recipients by a thousand dollars a year at most. Since increased earnings result in reduced benefits, women in even the most successful programs have been unable to earn their way out of poverty (Gueron and Pauly, 1991).

Unfortunately, few studies have assessed the impact of long-term education and employment programs on welfare recipients, although interviews with women who have obtained four-year college degrees indicate that they have had the greatest success in leaving welfare (Gittell, 1990). But not all women can or wish to pursue a college education. High proportions of women on welfare have poor literacy skills and have limited job opportunities as a result (Burtless, 1994). Thus a two-year time limit would not provide sufficient time for many women to improve their skills so they could work. While the current proposals are considering possible exceptions for women who need extra schooling to improve basic skills or who want to finish college, the willingness to make exceptions will vary by states.

Another concern with pending legislation is whether women will be required to work full time or part time. Since most women with young children work only part time, there is little reason to make women on welfare more "time-poor" than other women. It is not clear that requiring women with family responsibilities to work full time fosters family values, if that is a concern.

There are demonstration programs under way that would guarantee women on welfare a minimum level of income if they worked a certain number of hours, in addition to providing subsidized child care and health care. These programs are promising in encouraging women to work without impoverishing their families. They tend to be expensive, however—their success depending on the priority given to antipoverty goals as well as to welfare reduction.

It is difficult to determine the effect that pending legislation will have on African Americans. While African Americans are disproportionately represented on the AFDC caseload overall, 95 percent of black AFDC recipients are in twenty-five states and the District of Columbia. States will have considerable discretion in determining the shape of welfare-employment programs. Their responsiveness to the Family Support Act of 1988 varied substantially, suggesting that the impact on African Americans will vary as well.

Although there is little high-quality data on welfare-employment programs, Table 10.4 summarizes those that are available. It presents data for the twenty-five states and the District of Columbia where most blacks are found (high black) and for the other states where there are few blacks (low black).[5] It also controls on average annual pay for the state, as this will have an impact on welfare caseloads and fiscal flexibility. Most African Americans are in high-pay (48.4 percent) and medium-pay (32.5 percent) states. High-black states tend to have somewhat higher AFDC recipiency rates, although among the high-pay

---

[5] Calculations were also made for states where blacks were high percentages of the total caseload (rather than states in which high percentages of the black caseload were concentrated) and the results were similar to those reported here.

TABLE 10.4

AFDC Programs in States with High and Low Proportions of the Black AFDC Caseload, by Average Annual Pay in the State, 1992

	High Pay	Medium Pay	Low Pay
Benefits and JOBS expenditures			
Average benefits/poverty rate	82	69	65
High black	79	61	52
Low black	91	77	70
Average JOBS and child care			
Expenditures	$243	$269	$325
High black	230	223	176
Low black	283	319	379
Child support			
Average child support			
Collections/AFDC unit	581	535	656
High black	531	476	447
Low black	750	600	732
Paternity establishment			
1,000 Births	34.2	34.5	34.3
High black	35.8	42.0	41.4
Low black	28.6	26.4	31.8

Source: U.S. Congress. House Committee on Ways and Means, 1993.

and low-pay states these recipiency rates have declined since 1975. (In low-black states and in medium-pay states, recipiency rates have increased, on average.) In high-black states average AFDC benefits tend to be lower and welfare-employment expenditures per AFDC unit (JOBS program and related child care expenditures) also are lower than in low-black states. Average child support collections per AFDC unit are lower in high-black states but paternity establishment rates are higher.

That the states in which most black AFDC recipients are found tend to have lower benefits and smaller expenditures for welfare-employment programs should not imply causality. Most black AFDC recipients are either in the older, industrial Northern states or in the Southern states which have had their share of financial problems. Nevertheless, it does suggest that within the states where most blacks have been concentrated, there have been fewer expenditures per unit for welfare programs. The only area in which high-black states do better than low-black states is with respect to paternity establishment.

Informing all welfare reform initiatives that affect men and women should be the recognition that having good, stable employment encourages marriage.

This is true for both black men and black women. Low-paying, intermittent work—which is the kind of work that is often available to low-skilled workers—will not encourage marriage, no matter how much people want it to be so.

Children

The gravest consequences of a decline in marriage have fallen on children. It is obvious that the well-being of children is linked to that of their parents, yet little research has focused on the impact of employment and welfare programs on the well-being of children. There is much that can be done in this area.

Nevertheless, even if the life chances of children can be improved by improving the economic opportunities of their parents, there is still the need to protect children in families in crisis. Hostility to the welfare system, resulting in reduced benefits in many states, will do the greatest harm to children. Thought needs to be given to providing a universal child allowance, to protect children, regardless of the situation of their parents.

Insofar as people are concerned about the transmission of "bad values" to children growing up in poor families, the institution outside of the family that has the greatest possible impact is, of course, the school system. It is unfortunate that so many poor, black children find themselves in schools that are significantly inferior to those available to middle-income white students (Kozol, 1991). Yet there have been important innovations in urban education that have focused on providing a mix of services to inner-city youngsters that can help them not only get an education but provide them with an experience that will enhance their own sense of possibilities (Comer, 1988).

It is also important to note that while poverty itself is an important risk factor leading to "rotten outcomes" for children and youth (Schorr, 1989), there appears to be a large number of young people from all backgrounds engaging in what is considered risky behavior (Dryfoos, 1990). Whether this represents a decline in family or community values is difficult to know. It highlights the importance of recognizing that the problems of youth extend far beyond inner-city youngsters from "broken homes." While these problems may be exacerbated in depressed areas, they are not exclusive to them.

Community Involvement

The final element needed to achieve the policy goals outlined earlier is the involvement of the local community in the development and implementation of many of these policies. Families operate in a community context and cannot be expected to thrive when community structures are weakening. Efforts to support communities to develop and strengthen economic and social infrastructures are extremely relevant to family functioning.

To the extent that public policy can encourage or expand existing social support networks, it will contribute to a reduction in the stress and sense of isolation many inner-city families experience. To the extent that policymakers want to encourage an increase in two-parent families or to encourage a greater involvement of men in their families through child support or other activities, the moral imperative has greater legitimacy coming from the community. Thus, these are not issues that can be addressed from the top down. They involve the concern and commitment of those at all levels of government and the active involvement of the affected communities.

Conclusions

This chapter has considered a broad set of issues surrounding the decline in marriage among African Americans. The focus has been on those aspects of the decline in marriage that are relevant to social policy goals in the United States. Only passing acknowledgment has been given to broader, contextual issues such as the structural transformation of the economy, overall changing attitudes toward marriage and single parenthood, and the redefinition of male and female roles at home and in the labor market. The meaning of the term "marriage" itself is being transformed as more and more adults move from one marriage to another, and as more couples cohabitate without legal sanction. In recent years, as writers, journalists, and social scientists have exposed the abuses that have occurred within the context of the family, the "traditional" vision of the family unit as a safe haven from the ills of society has also been shattered.

In the case of African Americans, however, the decline in marriage has represented much more than changing values or new opportunities. It is a compelling example of how fragile the institution is in the face of social and economic instability. The most profitable response in the long run would be to focus on the causes of the decline in marriage, while working to ameliorate the consequences of this trend as well. Such a response represents a real challenge to policymakers and the communities involved, with a long road ahead.

REFERENCES

ALLEN, W.R. 1978. The search for applicable theories of black family life. *Journal of Marriage and the Family,* 40:117–129.

BAILIS, L.N., AND BURBRIDGE, L.C. 1991. *Report on cost of living and AFDC need and payment standard options.* Prepared for The State of New Hampshire Committee for SB 153.

BENNETT, N.G., BLOOM, D.E., AND CRAIG, P.H. 1989. The divergence of black and white marriage patterns. *American Journal of Sociology,* 95:692–722.

BILLINGSLEY, A. 1968. *Black families in white America*. New York: Simon & Schuster.

BLANK, R. April 1994. Outlook for the U.S. labor market and prospects for low-wage entry jobs. Paper presented at the conference *Self-sufficiency and the low-wage labor market: A reality check for welfare reform*. Urban Institute, Washington, DC.

BURBRIDGE, L.C. 1986. Changes in equal employment enforcement: What enforcement statistics tell us. *Review of Black Political Economy*, 15(1):71–80.

BURBRIDGE, L.C. 1994. *Government for profit and third sector employment: Differences by race and sex, 1950–1990*. Special report no. CRW8. Wellesley, MA: Center for Research on Women, Wellesley College.

BURTLESS, G. April 1994. The employment prospects of welfare recipients. Paper presented at the conference *Self-sufficiency and the low-wage labor market: A reality check for welfare reform*. Urban Institute, Washington, DC.

CAIN, G.G., AND WISSOKER, D.A. 1990. A reanalysis of marital stability in the Seattle-Denver Income-Maintenance Experiment. *American Journal of Sociology*, 95: 1235–1269.

CANCIAN, M., DANZIGER, S., AND GOTTSCHALK, P. 1993. Working wives and family income inequality among married couples. In S. Danziger and P. Gottschalk, eds., *Uneven tides: Rising inequality in America*, pp. 195–221. New York: Russell Sage Foundation.

COMER, J.P. 1988. Effective schools: Why they rarely exist for at-risk elementary school and adolescent students. In Council of Chief State School Officers, *School success for students at risk: Analysis and recommendations of the council of chief state school officers*. Orlando: Harcourt Brace Jovanovich.

DARITY, W.A., JR., AND MYERS, S.L., JR. 1984. Does welfare dependency cause female headship? The case of the black family. *Journal of Marriage and the Family*, 46: 765–779.

DRYFOOS, J.G. 1990. *Adolescents at risk: Prevalence and prevention*. New York: Oxford University Press.

DU BOIS, W.E.B. 1967. *The Philadelphia Negro: A social study*. New York: Schocken Books.

DUNCAN, G.J. 1984. *Years of poverty, years of plenty: The changing economic fortunes of American workers and families*. Ann Arbor: University of Michigan, Institute for Social Research.

EDELMAN, M.W. 1986. *Families in peril: An agenda for social change*. Cambridge, MA: Harvard University Press.

ETZIONI, A. 1993. *The spirit of community: The reinvention of American society*. New York: Simon & Schuster.

FRAZIER, E.F. 1940. *The Negro family in the United States*. Chicago: University of Chicago Press.

GITTELL, M. 1990. *From welfare to independence: The college option*. New York: Howard Samuels State Management and Policy Center.

GLAZER, N. April 1994. Making work work: Or, welfare reform in the 1990s. Paper presented at the conference *Self-sufficiency and the low-wage labor market: A reality check for welfare reform*. Urban Institute, Washington, DC.

GOTTSCHALK, P., AND DANZIGER, S. 1993. Family structure, family size, and family income: Accounting for changes in the economic well-being of children, 1968–1986, pp. 167–193. In S. Danziger and P. Gottschalk, eds., *Uneven tides: Rising inequality in America*. New York: Russell Sage Foundation.

GUERON, J.M., AND PAULY, E. 1991. *From welfare to work.* New York: Russell Sage Foundation.

HARRISON, B., AND BLUESTONE, B. 1988. *The great U-turn: Corporate restructuring and the polarizing of America.* New York: Basic Books.

HARTMANN, H.I., AND SPALTER-ROTH, R. 1993. The real employment opportunities of women participating in AFDC: What the market can provide. Paper presented at the conference *Women and welfare reform: Women's poverty, women's opportunities, and women's welfare.* Institute for Women's Policy Research, Washington, DC.

HELBURN, S., AND MORRIS, J. 1989. Welfare reform and the adequacy of the poverty budget. In *Proceedings from the First Annual Women's Policy Research Conference.* Washington, DC: Institute for Women's Policy Research.

HERNANDEZ, D.J. 1993. *America's children: Resources from family, government, and the economy.* New York: Russell Sage Foundation.

HILL, R.B. 1993. *Research on the African American family: A holistic perspective.* Prepared under the auspices of the William Monroe Trotter Institute, University of Massachusetts, Boston. Westport, CT: Auburn House.

HILL, M.S., AUGUSTYNIAK, S., DUNCAN, G.J., GURIN, G., GURIN, P., LIKER, J.K., MORGAN, J.N., AND PONZA, M. 1985. *Motivation and economic mobility.* Research Report Series, Institute for Social Research, The University of Michigan.

JACKSON, J.S., ed. 1991. *Life in black America.* Newbury Park, CA: Sage Publications.

JAYNES, G.D., AND WILLIAMS, R.M. 1989. *A common destiny: Blacks and American society.* Washington, DC: National Academy Press.

KAMERMAN, S.B., AND KAHN, A.J. 1988. *Mothers alone: Strategies for a time of change.* Dover, MA: Auburn House.

KOZOL, J. 1991. *Savage inequalities: Children in America's schools.* New York: Crown.

LEVY, F. 1988. *Dollars and dreams.* New York: Norton.

MALVEAUX, J. 1986. Comparable worth and its impact on black women. In M.C. Simms and J.M. Malveaux, eds., *Slipping through the cracks: The status of black women,* pp. 47–62. New Brunswick, NJ: Transaction Books.

McADOO, H.P. 1986. Strategies used by single mothers against stress. In M.C. Simms and J.M. Malveaux, eds., *Slipping through the cracks: The status of black women,* pp. 153–166. New Brunswick, NJ: Transaction Books.

MURRAY, C. 1984. *Losing ground: American social policy 1950–1980.* New York: Basic Books.

MURRAY, C. October 29, 1993. The coming white underclass. *The Wall Street Journal,* p. A14 (E).

O'HIGGINS, M. 1988. The allocation of public resources to children and the elderly in OECD countries, pp. 201–228. In J.L. Palmer, T. Smeeding, and B.B. Torrey, eds., *The vulnerable.* Washington, DC: Urban Institute.

OKONGWU, A. 1993. Some conceptual issues: Female single-parent families in the United States. In J. Mencher and A. Okongwu, eds., *Where did the men go? Female-headed households in cross cultural perspective,* pp. 107–130. Boulder, CO: Westview Press.

REICH, R.B. 1991. *The work of nations: Preparing ourselves for 21st century capitalism.* New York: Knopf.

SCHORR, L.B. 1989. *Within our reach: Breaking the cycle of disadvantage.* New York: Anchor Books.

SIDEL, R. 1989. *Women and children last.* New York: Penguin Books.

SMEEDING, T., TORREY, B.B., AND REIN, M. 1988. Patterns of income and poverty: The economic status of children and the elderly in eight countries. In J.L. Palmer, T. Smeeding, and B.B. Torrey, eds., *The vulnerable,* pp. 89–120. Washington, DC: Urban Institute.

SRI INTERNATIONAL. 1983. *Final report of the Seattle Denver Income Maintenance Experiments: Design and results.* Menlo Park, CA: SRI International.

SULLIVAN, M.L. 1989. Absent fathers in the inner city. *Annals of the American Academy of Political and Social Science,* 501:48–58.

U.S. CONGRESS, HOUSE COMMITTEE ON WAYS AND MEANS. 1993. *Material and data on major programs within the jurisdiction of the Committee on Ways and Means: 1993.* Washington, DC: U.S. Government Printing Office.

U.S. DEPARTMENT OF LABOR, BUREAU OF LABOR STATISTICS. 1992. *Outlook: 1990– 2005.* Washington, DC: U.S. Government Printing Office.

VICKERY, C. 1977. Time poor: A new look at poverty. *Journal of Human Resources,* 12:27–48.

WEST, C. 1993. *Race matters.* Boston: Beacon Press.

WILSON, W.J. 1987. *The truly disadvantaged.* Chicago: University of Chicago Press.

WOLFE, A. 1989. *Whose keeper? Social science and moral obligation.* Berkeley: University of California Press.

11 AFRICAN AMERICAN MARITAL TRENDS IN CONTEXT: TOWARD A SYNTHESIS

M. Belinda Tucker
and
Claudia Mitchell-Kernan

A s STATED in our preface, the primary intent of this volume is to contribute substantively to the discussion of marital decline among African Americans by presenting empirical evidence from multiple perspectives. Readers of a volume such as this, however, are undoubtedly seeking a "bottom line." Does the sampling of research presented here on this provocative topic produce any clear answers? On the whole, do these studies tell us where our energies should be focused, if we are to address the critical social problems that are inextricably linked to family formation and structure? Has this discussion revealed whether our concern with family formation is appropriate—or would the efforts of researchers and policymakers be more usefully directed elsewhere? Responses to questions such as these are a legitimate expectation of a book such as this. In this chapter, we address these issues and place our efforts in larger context.

Are Clear Findings Evident?

The studies reported have employed a variety of methodologies and disciplinary approaches, and have been conducted at both individual and aggregate levels of analysis. We have therefore achieved, to some degree, a *triangulated* appraisal of the problem (i.e., the use of a combination of methods to study the same phenomenon). All four of the forms of triangulation offered by Patton (1990) are present in our analysis: data, investigator, theory, and methodological triangulation. However, since we have selected particular researchers and

345

studies for inclusion in this book, it is appropriate to question whether we have, in effect, stacked the deck with respect to the direction of findings presented. We can only assure the reader that our invitations to the conference that spawned this volume were based on a wide assessment of who was actively engaged in researching this topic. In most cases, the results of the participants' studies had not yet been realized. Neither of us knew at the time whether their research would confirm or reject particular theoretical perspectives. We therefore believe that our initial selection of conference participants was broadly representative of the scholars involved in empirical study of this issue. Given the breadth of our appraisal, then, conclusions that emerge in a consistent fashion across these studies should carry a special weight and be important statements about current understanding of recent changes in patterns of black family formation. Indeed, several findings have repeatedly emerged from the empirical reports included in this book.

Mate availability is a key determinant of African American marital behavior. There is fairly strong evidence, at both individual and aggregate levels, implicating sex ratios/mate availability as a factor in African American family formation. Kiecolt and Fossett (Chapter 5) show through their individual-level analysis of national data that the sex ratio affects the likelihood that black women will have ever been married, and that ever-married black women will be separated or divorced. Their aggregate-level analyses of Louisiana cities and counties demonstrate that the sex ratio had strong positive effects on the percentage of black women who were married with spouse present, the rate of marital births per thousand black women aged twenty to twenty-nine, the percentage of husband and wife families, and the percentage of children living in husband and wife families. Also, they find a very strong negative relationship between sex ratios and nonmarital births—that is, fewer men relative to women was associated with an increase in births outside of marriage. In Chapter 8, Robert Sampson, using aggregate data, reports that black sex ratios in cities in the United States were predictive of female headship, the percentage of married couples among families with school-age children, and the percentage of black women who are single.

Using other national aggregate data, Darity and Myers in Chapter 9 also report that the ratio of males to females, as well as the ratio of unmarried males to unmarried females, were significantly related to female headship in 1976. However, the relationship did not hold in 1985. When Darity and Myers used indicators of mate availability that also took into account economic marriage-ability—the Wilson-Neckerman (1986) Male Marriageability Pool Index (MMPI) and their own ratio of unmarried men in the labor force or in school to unmarried women—they found that both measures are predictive of female headship in 1976 as well as 1985, with one exception. The MMPI did not predict white female headship in 1985. The relationships are more complex when analyzed by age, however. Darity and Myers found that only their own measure of mate availability, which combined demographic and economic indicators, was consistently predictive of female headship across time, age, and race.

From a psychological perspective, Tucker and Mitchell-Kernan (Chapter 6) show that among blacks, Latinas, and whites, married persons believe that there is greater availability of the opposite sex, and more men relative to women, than do single persons. (The relationship did not hold for Latino men.) Furthermore, for all except black men, persons who perceive greater availability of the opposite sex also have higher expectations of marriage.

What is especially noteworthy about this set of findings is the powerful effect of sex ratio, a demographic indicator, on family formation. That is, we expected that an indicator of the availability of potential mates that would take into account demographic factors, as well as personal preferences and resources (e.g., economic), would influence marital behavior (as Darity and Myers have shown). However, these studies demonstrate that gender imbalance, regardless of the "qualities" of available mates, strongly affects marital behavior. It should be noted that although these findings are supported by very recent studies (e.g., Lichter et al., 1992; Rolison, 1992), these notions have been either dismissed or ignored in some sectors of academe. Darity and Myers described the hostile reception among economists to their research linking sex ratios and family structure. They note:

> Until recently, economic models often began with the presumption that there were excesses of males over females in the marriage market. This is an essential element of the Becker model that seems to represent an adequate characterization of white "marriage markets." The assumption, however, is not valid for black "marriage markets."

This is a very significant point—that a fundamental disciplinary assumption on which other influential conceptualizations are based is simply not valid in the case of African Americans.

Although we can hardly claim to have presented definitive evidence of the role of sex ratios in African American family formation behavior, these studies, in concert with mounting evidence by others, make it clear that the continuing high mortality and incarceration rates of black men are having a very profound impact on African American families.

Male employment is strongly related to African American family formation. Several studies found that economic factors are related to black family structure. Testa and Krogh, in Chapter 3, reporting individual-level data on black men in low-income communities in Chicago, show that black men in stable employment are twice as likely to marry as black men who are not in school, in the military, or at work. Furthermore, the relationship between male employment and first marriage becomes stronger as the age of the men declines. In contrast, the relationship between premarital fatherhood and marriage has weakened among younger men to the point where male employment has virtually no impact on marriage in the case of nonmarital pregnancy. In Chapter 8, Sampson demonstrates that the black male employment rates in cities in the United States are predictive of female headship, the percentage of married-couple families among those with school-age children, and the percentage of females who are single.

Conclusions from the psychological studies are also supportive of the salience of economic factors in marital behavior. In Chapter 6, Tucker and Mitchell-Kernan report that black men with higher household income have higher expectations of marriage than those with lower incomes. Also, black men and women who believe that an adequate income is an important factor in marital success believe that their likelihood of marriage is higher. Hatchett, Veroff, and Douvan, in Chapter 7, find that black husbands who have intense concerns about their role as provider are more likely to have marital difficulty than those without such concerns.

Conceptual refinement.   In addition to these findings concerning the direct effects of mate availability and economic factors on family formation, several other issues of both conceptual and methodological significance have been raised in these chapters. First, Sampson argues that because Wilson's Male Marriageability Pool Index (MMPI) and similar indicators confound demographic and economic factors, findings based on these measures are ambiguous. The effects of the two factors must be disentangled in order to understand the distinctive causes of changing patterns of family formation. When Sampson examined these contributions independently, he found that sex ratio was a much stronger predictor of family formation than the male employment rate. Although few of the other studies examined both mate availability and economic factors, others also attempted to disentangle their effects. The findings presented by Kiecolt and Fossett and by Testa and Krogh are evidence of the unique effects of sex ratio and male employment, respectively.

As noted above, when Darity and Myers directly compared relative predictiveness of female headship based on pure sex ratio indicators, and those that combine economic and demographic considerations, they found that the combined measure was a more stable and effective predictor. This finding is perfectly consistent with the major conclusions of this book. That is, the research reported here demonstrates that both demographic sex ratio and male employment are factors in family formation. Logically, we would expect that a measure that combines both would be even more powerfully related to family structure.

A second issue raised by this book concerns the relative significance of these effects as a function of ethnicity. Theorists differ in their views of whether the demographic and economic phenomena under discussion are race neutral or race specific. For example, Wilson (1987) argued that the effect of male economic viability on marriage rates would be observed among African Americans, but not among whites.

Nearly all the empirical studies presented here carried out racial comparisons. Sampson shows that the causal effect of sex ratios on family structure among blacks is over five times greater than the white sex ratio effect, and the employment effect is twenty times greater for blacks than whites. Tucker and Mitchell-Kernan report that although household income was a central factor in marital expectations among black men and women, it was unrelated to marital expectations for white and Latino men and *negatively* related to marital expectations among white women. Similarly, Darity and Myers find that the MMPI did not predict white female headship in 1985. These latter findings are supportive of Wilson's (1987) notion that white marriage rates were more affected by the increasing economic independence of white females. That is, higher income would be related to a lower likelihood of marriage among white women and increased marriage among black women. Also, with respect to marital disruption, Hatchett, Veroff, and Douvan demonstrate that white male provider concerns are *not* related to marital difficulties, as is the case for black husbands.

These studies together provide compelling evidence that economic factors play a distinctive and critical role in African American family formation. Even though the economic viability of young men generally in the United States has declined (e.g., Easterlin, 1980; Lichter, LeClere, and McLaughlin, 1991), employment plays a unique and powerful role in the development and maintenance of black families.

Related Findings

Other economic results. Although the direct impact of mate availability and male employment on marital behavior has been repeatedly substantiated in this volume, other findings presented enrich our conclusions and raise important corollary concerns. In particular, the pervasive impact of economics in family formation is evident along several dimensions. Schoen in Chapter 4 provides evidence that the underlying inclination to marry is lower among blacks than among whites at all educational levels and that black women marry up with respect to educational level less than white women. He argues that this likely reflects the recognition among black women that, for them, the economic payoff from marriage has traditionally been limited. It also seems clear that the potential for black women to marry up educationally is significantly lower than that available to white women.

Sampson presents another facet of the economic family structure link. He finds that the strongest independent effect of sex ratio and employment on family structure is observed among black families in poverty—that is, the lower the sex ratio and the lower the male employment rate, the higher the rate of female-headed families with children and in poverty. Apparently, the deleterious effects of low sex ratio and male unemployment on family structure are exacerbated among those who are most economically deprived.

Crime and family structure. Perhaps the most provocative, disturbing, yet compelling finding cited and discussed in this book emerged from the work on crime and family formation reported by Robert Sampson (Chapter 8). In his own words, "One finding from the present study seems beyond doubt. Family structure is one of the strongest, if not the strongest, predictor of variations in urban violence across cities in the United States." This effect was observed among both blacks and whites. He believes, and we would agree, that this relationship is linked to the role of community social patterns and the social control that results from such informal networks. Sampson also shows that the effects of sex ratio and employment on crime are mediated by family structure: for example, over 50 percent of the effect of sex ratios on black robbery was mediated by family disruption. He concludes that a focus entirely on the direct effects of sex ratios and employment, ignoring their indirect effects, could lead to an underestimate of their causal significance in explaining rising community violence and, in our view, a host of other possible outcomes.

Marital disruption. A number of studies presented here included indicators of marital disruption, but only one study examined the *process* of marital discord. As noted above, Hatchett, Veroff, and Douvan find evidence that provider-role anxiety is a major contributor to marital instability. However, their research also suggests that the historically unstable economic situation of black couples, within a culture that exalts male economic dominance, has placed special strains on black marriages. The negotiation of roles and tasks is quite complex and places unique demands on wives in terms of role flexibility. This dilemma has quite likely contributed to the very high divorce rate of African Americans described in Chapter 1. It also demonstrates the limitations of census data and one-time surveys in gaining an in-depth understanding of how aggregate phenomena are experienced at the individual level.

Contribution of public assistance/welfare payments to family structure. As discussed by a number of the authors in this book, a favorite political target in discussions of family formation behavior has been welfare payments to unmarried women with children (e.g., Murray, 1984). Although this issue was not a primary focus of this book, one study specifically examined the effects of public assistance on family structure. Darity and Myers's analyses show little relationship between increases in welfare payments and increased female headship: a 1 percent increase in expected AFDC and public assistance income annually will increase the probability that a family head is female by only .02 to .10 of 1 percent. They argue further that since welfare increases have essentially become a thing of the past, such financing is an unlikely source of support for single motherhood. Despite the fact that expected welfare income dropped sharply for blacks between 1976 and 1985, there was a substantial increase in the number of female-headed families over that decade. Suggestive data are also included in Sampson's chapter. Table 8.1 shows that mean public assistance payments were unrelated to black female headship, although significantly predictive of white female headship.

The Interrelatedness of Poverty, Marriage Patterns, and Gender

Throughout this book, the link between particular patterns of family formation and poverty has been repeatedly established. Sampson noted that the impact of sex ratio and economic factors on family structure was especially great among impoverished persons. Indeed, Wilson's theorizing about the linkage between male employment and marital behavior was specific to the black underclass—those who represent the lowest socioeconomic stratum in this society. As a number of the studies presented have demonstrated, economic factors (in particular male economic prospects and experiences) have contributed to marital decline. But, as Lynn Burbridge in Chapter 10 also notes, there is evidence for the reverse as well—that these changes in family structure have in turn caused further economic erosion. Sheldon Danziger, in his commentary on Chapter 3 (Testa and Krogh) asserts that recent family formation trends have contributed to increasing poverty and are associated in particular with rising child poverty:

> Children in two-parent families have much lower poverty rates than children in mother-only families; children living with never-married mothers have much higher poverty rates than those living with ever-married mothers. Living arrangements are now more important than race when it comes to child poverty—black children in two-parent families have a much lower poverty rate than white children living in mother-only families.

It seems, then, that we have entered a seemingly endless cycle of poverty-induced behaviors that further erode a family's economic capabilities. But Darity and Myers in their chapter, and Danziger and Burbridge in their commentaries, raise another critical point. That is, the populations most adversely affected by these family formation changes are women who head families alone, and their children. There is evidence that the rise in child poverty that occurred during the late 1970s and the 1980s was due in part to the rise in female headship (e.g., Duncan and Rodgers, 1991; Eggebeen and Lichter, 1991). The reason for this seems clear. Women in general, and black women in particular, remain at the bottom of this society's economic ladder. Even the position of working black women has deteriorated: in 1979, 24.3 percent of year-round, full-time civilian black female workers had low earnings; by 1992 that figure had risen to 26.9 percent (U.S. Bureau of the Census, 1994). (Indeed, low earnings figures rose among all major ethnic-gender groupings, with corresponding increases of 14.0 percent to 19.4 percent for black men, and 19.8 percent to 21.1 percent for white women.) Women with children to support have greater demands on their financial resources and fewer options for increasing those resources. To the extent that the men who would normally be expected to contribute to such households (i.e., partners, husbands, fathers) are less able to do so, and may be less willing to do so, the women's positions are further compromised. Alice Rossi (1984) warned a full decade ago that women were shouldering a much greater (and increasing) share of the responsibility of childrearing and that men's connection to families was becoming more tenuous. Due in large part to the continued lower economic prospects for women, these circumstances have led to a situation in which children are now more likely to be raised in poverty than at any time since the 1960s.

There are other alarming aspects to this problem. Research on nonresidential fathers shows that, regardless of race, their participation in childrearing leaves much to be desired. Over two decades of Census Bureau data on child support indicate that only a third of men make payments and that the amount contributed is rather small (Select Committee on Children, Youth, and Families, 1989). There is also mounting evidence from the divorce literature that when men no longer reside with their children, contact becomes and remains fairly minimal (Furstenberg and Harris, 1992; Teachman, 1992). Just as disturbing, recent studies suggest that a supportive extended kin network is simply not as available as previously presumed for single mothers. Jayakody, Chatters, and Taylor (1993) found that only a quarter of never-married black mothers in a national sample received financial help from relatives and less than a fifth received assistance with child care. It seems clear that although single parenthood has become much more prevalent, the traditional sources of support for such households are simply not available.

The social meaning of many of the trends we have discussed is a growing estrangement of men, especially black men, from family life. If we wish to encourage, rather than discourage, men's involvement with families, we must begin to think more creatively about mechanisms for doing so. Since the ability of young men in general to provide economic support to families has declined, we must identify other forms of male support and facilitate familial participation in those areas.

Although discussions of poverty and family structure invariably focus on the deteriorating situation of single mothers and children, other household types have been affected by recent family formation trends. Tucker, Taylor, and Mitchell-Kernan (1993) have discussed how the lives of older black women might change socially and psychologically as the numbers without partners, and possibly without children, increase. Increased numbers of single-person households and homes made up of unrelated individuals suggest a need for other kinds of support networks. We see more discussion of the growing "wider" family phenomenon in the United States, in which non-kin relationships take on characteristics of family (Bogan, 1991; Marciano, 1991). There are undoubtedly both positive and negative aspects to these changes, but they do represent a reconfiguration of social relationships that may require new adaptive strategies.

The Global Context of Changing Patterns of Family Formation

In our introduction, we noted that recent changes in African American family formation, including marital decline, are, to a great extent, more exaggerated versions of trends evident in the population of the United States more generally. In fact, in a number of critical respects, white patterns of the early 1990s mirror black family formation patterns of the 1960s. Currently, one of every six white children lives in mother-only families, which is nearly identical to the proportion of black children in such families in the 1960s. Today, 25 percent of white births occur outside of marriage, which was precisely the proportion among blacks when Moynihan (1967) wrote his treatise. Although divorce is expected to stabilize during the 1990s, current marriage patterns are expected to continue throughout the decade (U.S. Bureau of the Census, 1992), suggesting that single parenthood will become more prevalent in the general population.

These changes also parallel shifts in family formation patterns occurring in other societies around the world, especially Europe and North America. As Popenoe (1988) has observed, "[s]tarting in the early 1960s, in virtually every advanced, Western nation family changes that had been under way before the World War II not only resumed their force and character, but began to accelerate at breakneck speed" (p. 31). Lesthaeghe (1983) traced changes in European family formation patterns over the last century. Although the transformations he identified are not strictly parallel to African American patterns, some similarities are evident, including a steep decline in marital fertility, cohabitation outside of marriage, increased childbearing outside of wedlock, higher divorce rates, and lower remarriage rates. Although Lesthaeghe cited changing philosophical doctrines (e.g., the development of secular individualism, the weakening of social controls) and political movements as key factors in the European changes, he also noted economic determinants. Notably, the mode of production was no longer based in the family.

Clearly, the mere detection of similar trends does not denote similarity of causation. However, comparative analysis of these trends may allow us to discern what are indeed global trends, and what changes might be culture or population specific. Clues from one societal analysis may help us to better understand phenomena in other contexts. For example, Lesthaeghe's (1983) theory about the shifting base of family economies may offer some additional insight into the African American situation. That is, changing black family formation patterns may be related in part to the rapid and extensive urbanization of the African American population. In 1940, over half of the black population lived in rural areas, while most whites (nearly 60 percent) lived in cities (U.S. Bureau of the Census, 1979). In 1980, nearly one-quarter of black Americans lived in nonmetropolitan areas; and by 1992 that figure had dropped to 15 percent (compared to 22 percent of the general population) (U.S. Bureau of the Census, 1993). Recent change among blacks in the South has been even more dramatic, declining from 40 percent in 1980 to 26 percent in 1992. In a complete reversal of the pre-1960s pattern, African Americans are now more likely to live in cities than any other major ethnic sector of the population of the United States. Blacks are no longer significantly engaged in farming, and are also less likely than other ethnic groups in this country to own small businesses—both family-intensive pursuits. Brewer (1988) goes further and argues that after World War II, black urbanization was also accompanied by high unemployment rates in certain sectors, leading to an increased dependence on public assistance. In her view, this "generated a tension between work and family life" (p. 338) that was not characteristic of the white population, where nucleation had been sustained and protected. Whites' greater involvement in the private sphere maintained the connection between the generation of capital and family life.

It should be noted that theorists who have taken a much longer and broader view of the evolution of family systems, examining cultures in all parts of the world over centuries, emphasize the contextual features of such shifts. Popenoe (1988) asserts that "family nucleation" has generally been resisted worldwide and that most societies currently exhibit kin-based systems. As van den Berghe (1979) has observed, nucleation has a curvilinear relationship with development, with nuclear households being characteristic of both the smallest, simplest societies and advanced, industrial societies. Shifts between nuclear households and kinship domination are a strong feature of family evolution.

Limitations and Needs: A Research Agenda

Limitations. This book has not addressed all of the issues that emerge from closer examination of changing family formation patterns. We have deliberately focused on economic and demographic factors as central features of the problem, primarily because that has been the thrust of past and ongoing research. Nevertheless, other factors have contributed to recent transformations—if not directly, then in an indirect fashion. These would include global value shifts (including concepts of gender roles), the changing economic prospects of women, and changes in the availability and reliability of contraception. None of these factors, however, has been shown to be as prominent as mate availability and male economic prospects as factors in recent African American family formation trends. Although Rolison's (1992) examination of 1980 census data from one hundred cities across the United States shows a positive association between opportunities for black female employment and the proportion of black families with children headed by a woman, he found a much stronger negative association with male employment. Stevenson's historical analysis in Chapter 2 suggests that, in many ways, the stage for these recent changes was set much earlier. In her words, ". . . the diversity of slave marriage and family norms, as a measure of the slave family's enormous adaptive potential, allowed the slave and the slave family to survive." The assaults on families that occurred during slavery and in the post-slavery period may have fostered an adaptive fragility that would make African American families more sensitive to recent economic and demographic upheavals.

The conference that inspired this book included the participation of a number of noted scholars who commented on aspects of these issues that have not been raised elsewhere in this volume. Although their papers could not be included here, the points they raised are of considerable consequence. Clinical psychologist Gail Elizabeth Wyatt noted that these changes have very significant implications for sexual behavior. That is, if individuals are going to spend a much greater proportion of their adult lives outside of marriage, they will undoubtedly have more sexual partners. Extended singlehood results in both an increased likelihood of pregnancies outside of wedlock, as well as an increased risk of sexually transmitted diseases, including AIDS. In view of the fact that the incidence of AIDS is increasing faster among African American females than in any other group in this country, the association between these facts may be more than coincidental.

Legal scholar Kimberle Crenshaw noted that law and social policy on these matters must begin to address the ways in which black women are uniquely affected on both racial and gender grounds. As she has discussed extensively in previous writings (Crenshaw, 1989), the concerns of black women have been viewed in "unidirectional" terms, as either race or gender based, but rarely in terms of the intersection of the two. Using a traffic analogy, she notes that a person standing in an intersection can be affected by movement from any of the four directions, individually or simultaneously. Crenshaw asserted that criticisms of the Moynihan report (1967) and the similarly toned 1986 PBS telecast of "The Vanishing Black Family," hosted by Bill Moyers, have generally failed to note the patriarchal assumptions in both. Even Wilson's (1987) attempt to reframe the discussion of black family structure as a consequence of male underemployment, in Crenshaw's view, assumes the dysfunctionality of female-headed households without a proper analysis of how the structure of the economy subordinates the interests of black women. Crenshaw argues that societal reform must not only focus on improvement of the financial viability of African

American men, but must confront the sexism inherent in our economic system that deprives single mothers of the resources to support their families.

Research needs. Despite the fact that the studies included here have evidenced coherent and consistent conclusions, there is a need for work that both replicates these studies and expands the bounds of understanding. For example, Sampson's study demonstrates that when sex ratio and male employment are examined for their independent contributions to family structure, sex ratio emerges as the more important predictor of the two. However, using a different methodology and a different data set (i.e., the National Longitudinal Surveys of Labor Market Experiences of Youth), Lichter et al. (1992) found exactly the opposite—that is, that male employment was more predictive than the sex ratio. We need studies that can tease out the sources of such differences.

Macro-focused studies dominated early discussion on this issue, as sociologists attempted to understand the impact of social phenomena on family structure. Sociologists also examined individual behavior as related to social-structural features of the environment. It would seem that anthropologists could make a significant contribution to these analyses, with in-depth investigations of the communities that seem most affected by these changes. Indeed, Carol Stack's (1974) intensive study of survival strategies used in a low-income black community has provided an analytical base for some of the findings reported here. In particular, her observations of the role of economics in male-female relationships give "texture" to statistical associations:

> . . . couples rarely chance marriage unless a man has a job; often the job is temporary, low paying, insecure, and the worker gets laid off whenever he is not needed. Women come to realize that welfare benefits and ties within kin networks provide greater security for them and their children. (p. 113)

This study was done over twenty years ago. Although some aspects of these communities may have remained stable, other remarkable phenomena have come into play, including increased violence, substance abuse (increasingly involving women), and the lure of urban gangs. We need clearer descriptions of how the daily lives of people are affected by these challenges, and how family formation decisions are now being made.

There has also been a disturbing absence of psychological study in this area. Yet several theories offer the possibility of increasing our understanding of changing individual behavior. Social exchange theory (Thibaut and Kelley, 1959) has long been used to understand the mate-selection process (e.g., Berscheid and Walster, 1969; Murstein, 1973). The theory assumes that individuals attempt to maximize rewards and minimize costs when seeking an attractive outcome. Guttentag and Secord (1983) used the theory to explain the role of sex imbalance in romantic involvements. They argued that when imbalance exists, the sex in greater supply has more difficulty finding a partner and may find relationships less satisfying, since the other partner has more potentially satisfactory alternatives. The partner in greater supply is therefore more dependent and more committed to the relationship than the partner in less supply. At least one study has provided support for this hypothesis (Jemmott, Ashby, and Lindenfeld, 1989). This theory may help us to understand one oft-made criticism of the male employment theories of marital decline—i.e., higher-income African American males are also less likely to marry today.

Psychological analysis may also help us to understand the gap between African American marital attitudes (which remain supportive of marriage) and marital behavior. The gap between attitudes and actions is addressed by the social psychological theory of reasoned action (Ajzen and Fishbein, 1980; Fishbein and Ajzen, 1975) in which the intention to act is viewed as a function of one's attitude toward the behavior as well as perceived social pressure to perform the behavior. In Thornton's (1989) comprehensive assessment of how family attitudes in the United States had changed from the late 1950s to the middle 1980s, he found that although the desire to marry eventually had remained strong, the "normative imperative" to marry had weakened substantially. If there has been a decline in the social pressure on people to marry, left unexplained is the reason why such a change has occurred.

If we are to achieve a fuller understanding of changing family formation patterns, there is a need for research that connects and integrates these multiple levels and types of analysis. There have been remarkably few attempts to integrate aggregate- and individual-level theorizing. To our knowledge, no studies have combined psychological perspectives with the sociological, largely aggregate, conceptualizations. In 1988, Rose Brewer commented on our limited understanding of the concentration of black poverty in female-headed households with children—despite the existence of substantial data on the question. She noted the necessity of analyzing both the "microlevel cultural/familial" sphere and the "macrolevel political economic" sphere:

> If the family is understood to be an institution influenced by the confluence of economic, state, racial, gender, and external cultural forces, on the one hand, and as a cultural meaning system and social structure, on the other hand, the black family becomes a strategic unit for understanding the convergence of macro and micro social forces. (p. 335)

In our view, this kind of contextual analysis, combined with the integration of multiple perspectives, is the greatest empirical need in this area.

Policy Implications and Directions

We would have preferred a more optimistic ending to this volume. However, the economic factors that are implicated in African American marital decline and related poverty increases are characteristic of fundamental change in this postindustrial era. As described by Bowman (Commentary on Chapter 9), the root causes are located in "the postindustrial displacement of manufacturing jobs by new labor-saving technology and related shifts in unskilled jobs from central cities to suburbs, from the rustbelt to the sunbelt, and from the domestic labor market to third-world countries." [See Johnson and Oliver, 1991, for a more detailed analysis of the impact on black male joblessness of the restructuring of the economy of the United States.] Bowman (1988) has written previously of the impact of these displacements on families through the creation of "provider-role strain." Although recent upturns in the economy suggest that the recession of the early 1990s is over, the time when a person—woman or man—without postsecondary school training could secure wages sufficient to support a family is (in all likelihood) gone forever. How will this society deal with the growing ranks of persons qualified only for low-level service jobs, and the consequent impact on families?

It is also clear that we must view family change as one in a series of interrelated risks—all causes as well as consequences: joblessness, crime, substance abuse, declining schools, the diminishing supply of low-income housing, homelessness, and so forth. The fact that these challenges have reached crisis proportions at a time when public funding is less available makes our task even more daunting. Nevertheless, the studies presented here, and their discussants, have pointed with great consistency to several key directions for policy formation. The two papers specifically focused on public policy offer clear recommendations. Darity and Myers assert that short-term policies should include: (*a*) designing transfer payments and policies to lift the poor out of poverty; (*b*) improving the health care of poor women and their children; and (*c*) improving the education of the underclass. We would also add that improving the health of black men is central, since high male mortality is the primary factor in imbalanced sex ratios. This would necessarily include confronting the enormous problem of community violence.

As many of the authors presented here have pointed out, long-term resolution means confronting problems that have been exacerbated by global economic shifts, and doing so in a period of fiscal constraint. Lynn Burbridge notes current reforms being considered by the federal administration. There are plans to bring men further into the welfare system and to strengthen child-support enforcement. She emphasizes, however, that because of high unemployment and underemployment among black men, child-support initiatives must include employment provisions. Many states are adopting welfare reform initiatives with employment requirements for AFDC recipients. Burbridge's expectations of such programs are guarded, since evaluations of long-term education and employment programs for welfare recipients are rare. The few existing studies indicate that these programs are most successful with participants who receive college degrees. This level of educational attainment may be an unrealistic expectation for many participants. She also argues in support of a "universal child allowance" that would protect children regardless of their parents' financial situation. Finally, she sees the improvement of public education, particularly in inner cities, as key to employment gains.

The results of the 1994 congressional elections, giving Republicans control of both houses, place the earlier administrative proposals in jeopardy. Winning support for the measures suggested by Darity and Myers and by Burbridge will require greater awareness of the complexity and systemic character of these problems and more effective strategies of political mobilization.

Even if marital decline among African Americans stabilizes or reverses, it seems clear that marriage alone will not significantly improve the economic prospects of poor families. Some years back, an article in an issue of *Mother Jones* magazine (Ehrenreich, 1986) asserted that because of the economic situation of poor black men, impoverished black women would have to be married to three such men—simultaneously—to achieve an average family income! Although obviously written tongue-in-cheek, the message was startling. Unless and until employment opportunities are greatly expanded for those on the bottom rungs of our economic ladder, their families, whether nuclear, extended, single-parent, or some other configuration, will require societal support.

Finally, in Western societies and increasingly in others as well, the institution of marriage is undergoing redefinition. As Thornton's (1989) analysis of surveys of family attitudes has demonstrated, Americans are much more tolerant of a range of family types and family roles. A number of authors in this volume have pointed out that many "stable" marriages of the past and present have not been healthy environments for their members. An "intact" family is not necessarily better than a range of alternatives. That divorce is an option for abused women and children is an advantage that was denied to many in the past. We know that there are aspects of marriage, as currently conceived by many, that are in need of reconsideration. The fact that "marital rape" is a crime in some states and not in others is indicative of our societal conflict about roles and rights in marriage. We therefore are not arguing that simply increasing the prevalence of marriage will solve the problems of either African Americans or Americans more generally. This book has helped to demonstrate, however, that there are constraints on the pursuit and maintenance of marriage among blacks. We believe that these constraints are modifiable and can be addressed through great societal will and societal clarity about our desired goals. To the extent that this volume facilitates and encourages that process, our contribution will have been substantial.

REFERENCES

AJZEN, I., AND FISHBEIN, M. 1980. *Understanding attitudes and predicting social behavior.* Englewood Cliffs, NJ: Prentice-Hall.

BERSCHEID, E., AND WALSTER, E. 1969. *Interpersonal attraction.* Reading, MA: Addison-Wesley.

BOGAN, E.C. 1991. Economics of the wider family. *Marriage and Family Review,* 17:9–27.

BOWMAN, P.J. 1988. Post-industrial displacement and family role strains: Challenges to the black family. In P. Voydanof and L.C. Majka, eds., *Families and economic distress,* pp. 75–96. Newbury Park, CA: Sage Publications.

BREWER, R.M. 1988. Black women in poverty: Some comments on female-headed families. *Signs: Journal of Women in Culture and Society,* 13:331–339.

CRENSHAW, K. 1989. Demarginalizing the intersection of race and sex: A black feminist critique of antidiscrimination doctrine, feminist theory and antiracist politics. *The University of Chicago Legal Forum 1989.* Feminism in the law: Theory, practice and criticism, pp. 139–167.

DUNCAN, G.J., AND RODGERS, W.L. 1991. Has children's poverty become more persistent? *American Sociological Review,* 56:538–550.

EASTERLIN, R.A. 1980. *Birth and fortune: The impact of numbers on personal welfare.* New York: Basic Books.

EGGEBEEN, D.J., AND LICHTER, D.T. 1991. Race, family structure, and changing poverty among American children. *American Sociological Review,* 56:801–817.

EHRENREICH, B. July/August 1986. Two, three, many husbands. *Mother Jones,* pp. 8–9.

FISHBEIN, M., AND AJZEN, I. 1975. *Belief, attitude, intention and behavior.* Reading, MA: Addison-Wesley.

FURSTENBERG, F.F., AND HARRIS, K.M. 1992. The disappearing American father: Divorce and the waning significance of biological parenthood. In S.J. South and S.E. Tolnay, eds., *The changing American family: Sociological and demographic perspectives,* pp. 197–223. Boulder, CO: Westview Press.

GUTTENTAG, M., AND SECORD, P. 1983. *Too many women: The sex ratio question.* Beverly Hills: Sage Publications.

JAYAKODY, R., CHATTERS, L.M., AND TAYLOR, R.J. 1993. Family support to single and married African American mothers: The provision of financial, emotional, and child care assistance. *Journal of Marriage and the Family,* 55:261–276.

JEMMOTT, J.B., ASHBY, K.L., AND LINDENFELD, K. 1989. Romantic commitment and the perceived availability of opposite sex persons: On loving the one you're with. *Journal of Applied Social Psychology,* 19:1198–1211.

JOHNSON, J.H., AND OLIVER, M.L. 1991. Economic restructuring and black male joblessness in U.S. metropolitan areas. *Urban Geography,* 12:542–562.

LESTHAEGHE, R. 1983. A century of demographic and cultural change in Western Europe: An exploration of underlying dimensions. *Population and Development Review,* 9:411–434.

LICHTER, D.T., LeCLERE, F.B., AND McLAUGHLIN, D.K. 1991. Local marriage markets and the marital behavior of black and white women. *American Journal of Sociology,* 96:843–867.

LICHTER, D.T., McLAUGHLIN, D.K., KEPHART, G., AND LANDRY, D.J. 1992. Race and the retreat from marriage: A shortage of marriageable men? *American Sociological Review,* 57:781–799.

MARCIANO, T. 1991. A postscript on wider families: Traditional family assumptions and cautionary notes. *Marriage and Family Review,* 17:159–171.

MOYNIHAN, D.P. 1967. The Negro family: The case for national action. In L. Rainwater and W.L. Rainwater, eds., *The Moynihan report and the politics of controversy*, pp. 39–124. Cambridge, MA: MIT Press.

MURRAY, C.A. 1984. *Losing ground: American social policy, 1950–1980*. New York: Basic Books.

MURSTEIN, B. 1973. A theory of marital choice applying to interracial marriage. In I. Stuart and L. Abt, eds., *Interracial marriage*, pp. 17–35. New York: Grossman.

PATTON, M.Q. 1990. *Qualitative evaluation and research methods*. 2nd ed. Newbury Park, CA.: Sage Publications.

POPENOE, D. 1988. *Disturbing the nest*. New York: Aldine de Gruyter.

ROLISON, G.L. 1992. Black, single female-headed family formation in large U.S. cities. *The Sociological Quarterly*, 33:473–481.

ROSSI, A.S. 1984. Gender and parenthood. *American Sociological Review*, 49:1–19.

SELECT COMMITTEE ON CHILDREN, YOUTH, AND FAMILIES. 1989. *U.S. children and their families: Current conditions and recent trends, 1989*. Washington, DC: U.S Government Printing Office.

STACK, C. 1974. *All our kin: Strategies for survival in a black community*. New York: Harper & Row.

TEACHMAN, J.D. 1992. Intergenerational resource transfers across disrupted households: Absent fathers' contributions to the well-being of their children. In S.J. South and S.E. Tolnay, eds., *The changing American family: Sociological and demographic perspectives*, pp. 224–226. Boulder, CO: Westview Press.

THIBAUT, J.W., AND KELLEY, H.H. 1959. *The social psychology of groups*. New York: Wiley.

THORTON, A. 1989. Changing attitudes toward family issues in the United States. *Journal of Marriage and the Family*, 51:873–893.

TUCKER, M.B., TAYLOR, R.J., AND MITCHELL-KERNAN, C. 1993. Marriage and romantic involvement among aged African Americans. *Journal of Gerontology: Social Sciences*, 48:S123–S132.

U.S. BUREAU OF THE CENSUS. 1979. The social and economic status of the black population in the United States: An historical overview. *Current Population Reports*, series P-23, no. 80. Washington, DC: U.S. Government Printing Office.

U.S. BUREAU OF THE CENSUS. 1992. Marriage, divorce and remarriage in the 1990's. *Current Population Reports*, series P-23, no. 180. Washington, DC: U.S. Government Printing Office.

U.S. BUREAU OF THE CENSUS. 1993. The black population in the United States: March 1992. *Current Population Reports*, series P-20, no. 471. Washington, DC: U.S. Government Printing Office.

U.S. BUREAU OF THE CENSUS. 1994. The earnings ladder: Who's at the bottom? Who's at the top? *Statistical Brief*, SB/94-3. Washington, DC: U.S. Government Printing Office.

VAN DEN BERGHE, P. 1979. *Human family systems: An evolutionary view*. New York: Elsevier.

WILSON, W.J. 1987. *The truly disadvantaged*. Chicago: University of Chicago Press.

INDEX

church attendance—*Continued*
204–205, 214; as predictor of marital
instability, **190–191, 192**; relationship between marital stability and,
206
churches, white, 31*n*
Churchill, J.C., 123*n*, 134
cities with population greater than
100,000, 235, 237, 249, 355; effects
of family structure on homicide and
robbery rates in, **246, 247**; effects of
sex ratios and male employment rates
on urban underclass in, **245**; effects of
underclass family disruption on aggregate homicide and robbery offense
rates in, **248**, 248; race-specific effects
of sex ratios and male employment
rates on family structure in, 242, **243**;
race-specific effects of sex ratios and
male employment rates on female-
headed families in, **241**; sex ratios in,
240, 346; variation within, 257
Civil Rights Act of 1964, 5
Clark, K.B., 4, 22
Clark, M.H., 8, 22
Clark, M.P., 4, 22
Clarke, R., 252
Clinton, C., 30*n*, 53
Cody, C.A., 34, 53
cohabitation, 19, 353; acceptance of,
148; among black and whites couples,
186, **188**; premarital, **180, 182**, 212
Cohen, J., 238*n*, 239*n*, 252
Cohen, L., 231, 252
college education, 66, 338; of brides and
grooms, 107, **109, 110–111, 112**. *See
also* women, black
Colonialists, 34
Colosanto, D., 319
Comer, J.P., 340, 342
commitment, **159**, 161; marital, 195,
219, 226, **227**
communication, **180, 183**, 214; dysfunctional spousal, 219; styles of, 179
communities, 356; crime in black, 255,
256, 257–259; inner-city, 323

community: institutions, 174, 334;
involvement, 340–341; structures,
324, 332–333; support system, 332,
334, 350
comparison of slave families and European Americans, 28–29, 52–53. *See
also* black-white comparisons
compatibility, 226, **227**
competence, **181**, 184; marital, **204,
205**
Computer Assisted Telephone Interviewing (CATI), 151
conception: estimates of effects on age-
specific rates of premarital, **90**; marriage before, 60, 88; premarital, 61,
90, 93, 98; relationship between employment and premarital, 60, 89–90
Coner-Edwards, A.R., 211
conflict, 221, 222, 313; destructive, **197,
198, 200**, 201, **204–205**, 214; destructive, as predictor of marital instability, **190–191, 192**, 206; management, **180, 183**, 219, **227**; styles, 199,
209, 223
contraception, 354
control: informal social, 230, 230*n*, 231;
in marital relationship, **181**, 184; personal, 226
conventional marriages, 60, 71, 82, 123;
declines in, 66; likelihood of, 83; models for, 88. *See also* pre-conception marriages; traditional marriages
coping, 225; resources and style, **227**;
styles, **180, 182**, 203, 206. *See also*
mainstream coping model
co-residential parenting, 28
Cornish, D., 252
couples: annual incomes of black and
white, 223; economic concern of, 221;
expectations of, 183, **189**; in first years
of marriage panel, 186, 186–187;
first-year socioeconomic and demographic characteristics of black and
white, 186, **188–189**; marital instability among black and white, 177; marital status across three years for black

post-conception marriage(s), 61, 80, 83; decline in rates of, 64; effects of employment on, 60; estimates for factors affecting, **85, 87**; to mother of first child, **89**; reasons for, 65; relationship between male employment and, 66, 68

postindustrial dislocation model, 310, **311**, 312–313, 315

poverty, 101, 243–244, 257; among African American families, 334; among families with children, 14, 338, 357; among female-headed families, 264, 312, 315, 317; child, 97, 330–331, 332, 351–352; correlation of crime and, 234, 247; growth of, 99; intergenerational transmission of, 325; interrelatedness of marriage patterns, gender, and, 351–353; reduction rate, 335; status, 270; time, 332, 338. *See also* Chicago poverty tracts

power, 221, 225

power balance, **180, 193, 197, 198, 200**, 208; husband-wife, 183, **190**, 199, 214

pre-conception marriages, 80, 83, 84; estimates for factors affecting, **84, 87**

precursors, 225, 226, **227**

pregnancy: causes of early, 264; intended, 81, 82, 84, 85; effects of premarital, 178; effects of unintended, 80, 81, **81**, 82, **83**, 84, **85**, 85, 348; legitimation of premarital, 64; premarital, 61, 81, **180**, 182, 355; prevention of unwanted, 92, 93; rates for teenagers, 323, 326

premarital social context, **180**, 196, **197–198, 200, 204–205**, 212; related to marital instability, 182, **190, 192**, 193–194, 206

prenatal care, 268, 288

Prentice, R., 70, 94

Preston, S.H., 123, 135

prison, 90, 272. *See also* incarceration

programs, 335; social, 333; welfare-employment, 337, 338, 339, 340, 358

propensity to marry. *See* marriage propensities

proposals, 333–334

provider role, 215, 350; black male, 194, 195, 199, 207, 208, 220, 348; white male, 349

PSID (Panel Study of Income Dynamics), 268

psychological analysis, 356–357

public assistance, **241**, 305, 350–351, 352. *See also* welfare; specific programs

Public Use Microdata tapes, 107

Puerto Ricans, 69, 69*n*, 70*n*, 147

race, 27, 104, 223, 230, 256, 349; importance of similarity of, **159**, 161; marriage propensities by, 107, 109, 111, **112**, 112, **113**, 114; median weekly earnings of families by, 328, **329**; numbers of marriages by, **108**, 110–111; robbery and murder rates disaggregated by, 244

racial-caste hypogamy, 118

racial differences, 6–7, 223, 302; in criminal behavior, 259; in intraracial marriage behavior, 104, 112, 114; in marital behavior, 147, 150. *See also* ethnic differences

racism, 5, 229

Rainwater, L., 23, 170, 229, 253, 361

Rainwater, W.L., 23, 170, 361

Ransford, H.E., 105, 115, 195, 211

Rasinski, K., 72*n*

Raush, H., 178, 179, 211

Ravensworth estate, 44–45

Rawick, G.P., 39*n*, 52*n*, 55

reality, 155–156

Reed, M., 238, 253

reenlistment rates, 273

region, 293: expected welfare by, 302, 305; sex ratios by, 276, **277**

Reich, R.B., 327, 343

Rein, M., 335, 344

Reiss, A.J., Jr., 254